1998

PROBLEMS IN THE HISTORY OF MODERN AFRICA

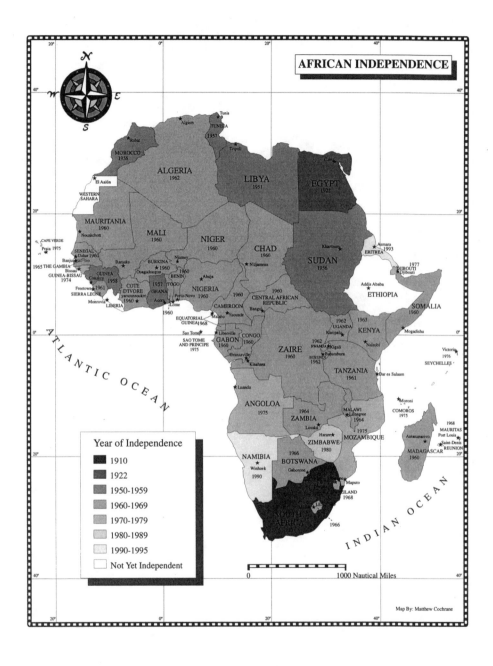

AFRICAN INDEPENDENCE

Year of Independence
- 1910
- 1922
- 1950-1959
- 1960-1969
- 1970-1979
- 1980-1989
- 1990-1995
- Not Yet Independent

0   1000 Nautical Miles

Map By: Matthew Cochrane

TUNISIA 1957
Tunis
Algiers
Tripoli
Rabat
MOROCCO 1956
ALGERIA 1962
LIBYA 1951
EGYPT 1922
El Aaíon
WESTERN SAHARA
MAURITANIA 1960
Nouakchott
CAPE VERDE
Praia 1975
MALI 1960
NIGER 1960
CHAD 1960
Khartoum
SUDAN 1956
Asmara 1993
ERITREA
1977
DJIBOUTI
Djibouti
SENEGAL
Dakar 1960
Banjul
1965 THE GAMBIA
Bissau
GUINEA-BISSAU 1974
GUINEA
Conakry 1958
Bamako
BURKINA 1960
Ouagadougou
Niamey
1960
BENIN
Abuja
N'djamena
Addis Ababa
ETHIOPIA
SOMALIA 1960
COTE D'IVORE 1960
1952
GHANA
yamoussoukro
TOGO
Porto-Novo 1960
NIGERIA 1960
CENTRAL AFRICAN REPUBLIC 1960
Mogadishu
Freetown 1961
SIERRA LEONE
Monrovia
LIBERIA
Accra
Lome
1960
CAMEROON
Malabo
Yaounde
Bangui
EQUATORIAL GUINEA 1968
1962
UGANDA
KENYA
1963
Sao Tome
SAO TOME AND PRINCIPE 1975
Libreville
GABON 1960
CONGO 1960
ZAIRE 1960
Kampala
1962
RWANDA Kigali
BURUNDI 1962
Bujumbura
Nairobi
Victoria
1976
SEYCHELLES
Brazzaville
Kinshasa
TANZANIA 1961
Dar es Salaam
Luanda
ANGOLOA 1975
1964
ZAMBIA
Lusaka
MALAWI
Lilongwe 1964
1975
Moroni
COMOROS 1975
1968
MAURITAS
Port Louis
Saint-Denis
REUNION
Antananarivo
MADAGASCAR 1960
Harare
ZIMBABWE 1980
MOZAMBIQUE
NAMIBIA 1990
Winhoek
1966
BOTSWANA
Gaborone
Maputo
ZILAND 1968
SOUTH AFRICA
1966

Problems in the History of Modern Africa

Edited by
ROBERT O. COLLINS
JAMES McDONALD BURNS
ERIK KRISTOFER CHING
KATHLEEN S. HASSELBLAD

Department of History
University of California, Santa Barbara

 **Markus Wiener Publishers**
Princeton

For information write to:
Markus Wiener Publishers
114 Jefferson Road, Princeton, NJ 08540

Library of Congress Cataloging-in-Publication Data

Collins, Robert O., 1933–
    Problems in the history of modern Africa/edited by
Robert O. Collins . . . [et al.].
    (Topics in world history. Problems in African history series; v. 3)
    Includes bibliographical references.
    ISBN 1-55876-124-1
    1. Africa—History—1884-1960.   2. Africa—History—1960.
I. Title   II. Series.
DT30.C567   1996
960.3'2—dc20   96-28368
                                                     CIP

Printed in the United States of America on acid-free paper.

Dedication

To Damazo Dut Majak

A scholar, teacher, and a man for all seasons
who will be missed by all who knew him.

Contents

Preface

This collection of excerpts from books, journals, and papers on the history of Modern Africa follows the same methodology of the previous volumes published by Markus Wiener, *Problems in African History: The Precolonial Centuries* and *Historical Problems of Imperial Africa*. I was first introduced to this teaching technique as a very junior lecturer at Williams College many more years ago than I wish to remember. Then, as now, it has aroused and stimulated students to confront and think about the major themes in history, whether they be those of Western Civilization or African History, and demanding the students to make decisions on these central issues and to take responsibility for their opinions. This is not easy, but the writing of history has never been a simple matter. This volume, like its predecessors, is the product of discourse and debate with my graduate students at the University of California, Santa Barbara. There, in Ellison Hall on Wednesday afternoons over many years, the "Problems" were thrashed out, digested, and determined. It was an exhilarating experience for me, and I would like to think a learning exercise for the participants. We argued longer than I would like to think about what were the principal and significant issues confronting independent Africa. There is nothing more instructive than informed discourse, as Socrates made clear in the 5th Century B.C., and through the years of devoted digging and discourse my students and I have collectively compiled a guidebook for the student interested in the History of Modern Africa. The purpose of this enterprise on the part of myself, my students, and the publisher is to pass on to others the distillation of our discourse and discoveries.

The pedagogical rationale of "Problems" is through inquiry to select major themes, in this volume those of the history of contemporary Africa, and then to present the conclusions of learned scholars who have devoted their research to the subject. The students, whatever their educational or intellectual baggage with which they might be afflicted, are then free, liberated, to read the material and make a choice, take a stand, be intellectually responsible to defend their decisions before themselves and their peers and instructors who may have very different views. In the rough and tumble of the discourse, which inevitably follows, much is learned, opposing opinions are more respected, and students are made to think and defend, often with vehemence without violence, about what they have thought. In my humble opinion, this is what education is all about, and I have found myself, more often than not, as a referee keeping the peace amongst the protagonists than as the dispenser of wisdom. These debates and discussions in the sterile confines of the seminar room take on a reality from the material and are all the more exciting since this volume is more contemporary, historically, dealing with issues of controversy of the present day, but it is also a continuation of the African past into the present.

This volume could not have evolved without the veterans of the two previous volumes, James McDonald Burns and Erik Kristofer Ching who have been joined by a most knowledgeable addition to the seminar, Kathleen S. Hasselblad, whose enthusiasm for the African past has grown from the discourse of those students who have come before them and who have provided ideas, criticism, and discriminating commentary. Their knowledge, skills, and determination, not to mention discipline, to change the rhetoric into a manuscript has brought this volume to a meaningful conclusion. Their efforts and contributions have been in the best tradition of fine scholarhsip and are gratefully appreciated and deserve special acknowledgment. I am also indebted to Rebecca Ivy Riggs, who has helped to sort out those of us who remain mystified by modern technology.

As in the previous two volumes the Digital Computer Cartographic Laboratory of the University of California, Santa Barbara, has done the maps. The graphic design and cartography for the map of indpendent Africa was prepared by Matthew C. Cochrane under the supervision of Violet Gray of the UCSB Geography Department.

Our thanks also go to the following authors and publishers for permission to reprint their works or portions thereof: Kofi Ermeleh Agovi, David Anderson, Charles Anyinam, Randall Baker, Robert Browne, Kevin Cleaver, Michael Crowder (deceased), Basil Davidson, Francis Deng, David Fieldhouse, Ibrahim Gambari, David Goldsworthy, Edward Green, Jeffrey Gritzner, John Hargreaves, John Holm, Robert Jackson, Douglas Johnson, Andrew Kamarck, Michael Lofchie, William Roger Louis, D. A. Low, Una Maclean, Ali A. Mazrui, Patrick Molutsi, Molara Ogundipe-Leslie, William Pfaff, Ronald Robinson, Dianne Rocheleau, Carl Rosberg, Brooke Schoepf, Gotz Schreiber, Timothy Sisk, Elliot Skinner, Wole Soyinka, Kathleen Staudt, Robert Stock, Jean Suret-Canale, Lloyd Timberlake, Barbara Thomas-Slater, Jack Woddis (deceased), Godfrey Woelk, Crawford Young, Aristide Zolberg.

Special mention should also go to Roger Egan, the indomitable editor from Mystic Island and to Betty Reeves who has seen the previous volumes and this one through the tides and surf of publication.

All but the most necessay footnotes have been eliminated from the selections that follow with the permission of the publishers.

ROC
Santa Barbara, California, 1996.

Introduction

The study of any people cannot be complete without their past. Who were they? When did they come? What is their culture history? These may seem mundane questions, not particularly relevant to independent Africa and its history, but this would be an egregious error. One cannot divorce the present from the past. First, the facts must be determined, often controversial to be sure, as most facts of recent vintage have a habit of being in the unravelling of history. Second, the past must be interpreted, placed in the context of culture and of time. This obligation, indeed duty for the historian, becomes more difficult as one moves in time to the present. Yet, devoid of commentary, judgment, and interpretation, the historian is reduced to a teller of tales, the Celtic minstrel, the bard, or the African *griot*—hagiography in the pay of those who bought his/her skills to sing praise-songs. This task has become more difficult when attempting to make some sense out of the history of Modern Africa.

The information for Modern Africa does not come from dusty archives but the more flamboyant media, which one should approach with caution. This does not mean that the more thoughtful and reflective observers of Africa are not aware of the issues that have confronted independent Africa that were not there in the past. The themes of the past have changed as anyone who has read *Problems in African History: The Precolonial Centuries* or *Historical Problems of Imperial Africa* would conclude, but the "Problems" of contemporary Africa remain in history.

Independent Africa began with the end of empire and today there is a voluminous literature, not without controversy, as to this hasty abandonment of the continent. Unlike the long struggle in Asia, the Europeans left Africa in a hurry. Why? That is for the reader to determine in the extraordinary experience of decolonization. Was Africa not that important in the economic international world? Were the nationalists strong enough to push the Europeans out of Africa? Were the great powers, at that time the United States and the Soviet Union, who were ideologically opposed to colonialism, dominate factors in accelerating the departure of the Europeans? These are the questions that one must answer.

Upon the departure of the imperialists, there were few who were concerned about the African environment. The excitement was the winning independence, the political kingdom. Elephants were still plentiful. Africans, particularly the rural people, were aware of ecological decay, but in independent Africa the rural folk have had little to say in the policies of the central government that affect them. This was partly motivated by ideology and the conviction that the future lay with industry or mechanized agriculture, not with the African farmer who had a deep understanding and instinct with his relationship to the environment yet often abused it. Mother Nature, as is her wont, changed all that with the failure of the traditional rains in the

1

1980s, resulting in the acceleration of the desertification of the Sahel, the failure of crops further south, famine, and human tragedy. Drought and famine are not new to Africa, but in the twentieth century, the last decades of which coincided with independence and drought, they were magnified across the world by the technology of the international media and brought to the attention of those concerned with the environment. The difficulty is to understand what happened to the African environment and why. The literature and the interpretations are as numerous as they are controversial. Neverthless, all the authorities appear to agree that the African environment is rapidly deteriorating to the detriment of an expanding and hopeful population. Why?

One of the more positive results of imperial rule was the research and implementation against tropical disease. The devastating sleeping sickness epidemic at the turn of the century was contained; efforts to control malaria and a variety of other tropical diseases were made in the first half of this century. The imperial medical services were frequently ruthless in stamping out tropical disease, but they had some remarkable success. Through the failure of the public health organizations in independent Africa, many of these diseases have revived and are now complicated by disease that the imperial doctors did not have to experience. What are the human and financial costs? What is to be the health policy of the independent African states? This is a fundamental question of much controversy for Africans as well as for Americans. Primary health care is critical and lacking in funds, but the major issue is AIDS and other sexuallly transmitted diseases. These are not unique to Africa, but what is not fully realized is that these diseases occur mostly frequently in the urban areas among civil servants, and these are precisely the people who make the state function. Their loss can be devastating to the administration of government, producing instability in an already fragile social and political environment.

There has also been much anguish about the future of democracy in Africa. When the imperialists departed, they thought, with some illusion, that they had bequeathed democratic forms of government behind them. To the dismay of those of liberal and democratic persuasion in the West, democratic government has not fared well in Africa. Everyone asks why? What went wrong with the legacy that was passed on by the imperialists who ironically were not very democratic themselves? One after another, democratic governments in Africa have been dissolved by military autocracies. Some will argue that it was the failure of the intellectual elite who inherited the political structures of the departing Europeans. Others are convinced that the attempt to build nations in Africa was bound to fail with their bizarre boundaries and ethnic anomalies. The controversy is fueled by the role of African women in the democratic process or lack thereof, where hitherto the influence of women was always pervasive, it remained invisible.

Upon independence there was much excitement and money to develop what that old rogue, King Leopold II of Belgium, called that "Magnificent African Cake." Well, development in independent Africa has produced more controversy than results. There is little agreement on how financial aid from the West can stimulate development throughout the continent. There are those who maintain that the improvement of the quality of life of the African by the infusion of funds for development projects only benefits the beneficiaries. Others are angry that development schemes, presumably to assist Africans, have been sabotaged by corrupt elites. Then there are those who would describe the "Magnificent African Cake" as a myth. The resources of Africa are either insufficient or too expensive to develop. The issues of development are contentious, but they cannot be ignored.

To the distress of those who were present at the birth of independent Africa, many have now witnessed the collapse of African states, resulting in anarchy and horror. They are shocked by the violation of human rights and those hundreds of thousands who have perished in the violence frequently referred to as genocide. This spectre of the breakdown of society and cultures has resulted in some advocating the return to Africa of Europe, not just the brief military intervention to secure the safety of European nationals, but a "recolonization" that would mean European readministration of former territories in dissolution. There are others who argue that the collapse of African states is the result of foreign intervention, direct or indirect, usually called "neo-colonialism." Realizing that the Europeans have no interest in reinventing colonialism, not to mention "recolonizing" Africa, a policy that the Africans would fervently oppose, the restoration of security and order must be the responsibility of the international community, the United Nations and its neutral intervention in collapsed states.

All of these Problems in the History of Modern Africa are challenging and controversial, but they need to be addressed. Africa is not going to disappear from this world nor will its current difficulties. One should place them in the context of history and seek for the amelioration of the suffering and difficulties of a continent thrust onto the international stage.

PROBLEM I

DECOLONIZATION AND THE END OF EMPIRE

The transfer of power from the colonial rulers to the Africans, commonly known as decolonization, is not without different interpretations and controversy. Colonization and its continuation depended upon three variables. First, that the colonial subjects would acquiesce in the future to the colonial presence and its authority. Second, that the politicians and the electorates in Europe would continue to accept responsibility for the administration and development of their colonies. Third, that empire would receive international approval and acceptance.[1] The subsequent controversy about the nature of decolonization invariably has emphasized one or all of these factors as the reason for the end of formal empire. The problem arises as to which one is to give the most significance or to all.

John Hargreaves argues that decolonization was the product of Europeans deciding, for various reasons, that they no longer desired to administer and control their colonies. This decision lay in Europe, not in Africa, and its rationale is to be found more in the contemporary history of modern Europe than in the history of Africa, and in the wrangling and bargaining in which European politicians engaged with one another over the dismantling of empire. Consequently, the decision to abandon their colonies was a long time in coming and dependent upon the agreement to do so by a sufficient consensus among the number of those who made policy in the metropole. For instance, it was only when the conservatives agreed to support decolonization that it became a reality.

D.A. Low does not necessarily disagree with Hargreaves, but he points out that

---

1. See William Roger Louis and Ronald Robinson, The United States and the Liquidation of British Empire in Tropical Africa, 1941-1951, in Gifford and Louis (eds.), *The Transfer of Power in Africa: Decolonization,* 1940-1960, (New Haven: Yale University Press, 1982), p. 53.

decolonization in Asia preceded the end of empire in Africa. In fact, Low suggests that decolonization in Africa was dependent upon the termination of the European colonies in Asia. There is, however, a noticeable difference between decolonization in Asia and Africa in that the former encompassed a long, drawn-out conflict against the colonial powers, often involving revolutionary war by Asian peoples. In contrast, decolonization in Africa occurred in a sweeping, rather hasty and relatively peaceful fashion. Moreover, decolonization in Asia appeared to loosen the ties that bound Europe to Africa and taught the Europeans to search for a less painful and, in the long run, a less violent route to divest themselves of their African colonies.

William Roger Louis and Ronald Robinson argue that the end of empire in Africa was brought about, not so much by the Europeans realizing that their colonies were no longer important to their well-being, but by the United States, which had risen to global supremacy after the Second World War. The ideological belief of the right of self-determination for colonial peoples was deeply ingrained in the minds of Americans, for after all they had once been colonists themselves, and the appeal of liberating those under imperial rule had great popular sympathy in the United States, which mobilized the power and influence of America to oppose the continuation of the subjection of Africa to Europe. The aspirations for independence on the part of the Africans and the potential of their armed resistance were perceived by the United States as creating conditions that would lead to the intervention of the Soviet Union and the proliferation of Communist ideology throughout the continent, to which the United States was adamantly opposed. The Europeans found it to be in their best interests to tolerate and even encourage the ambitions of the Africans for independence rather than risk alienating the United States, upon which they had become dependent for aid, trade, defense, and diplomacy.

Jean Suret-Canale strongly disagrees with all the above arguments. He considers them all too deeply rooted in the politics of capitalist society to the exclusion of the very structural origins that made decolonization inevitable. Writing from an unabashed Marxist perspective, Suret-Canale argues that decolonization was the product of the dialect inherent in history. The colonial powers were historically neither prepared for nor interested in independence for their colonies; it just occurred. Imperialism, as Lenin has proclaimed, is the highest stage of capitalism, a system that operates under its own logic and rules. In the case of Africa, the necessities of capitalist imperialism led to the decolonization of Africa, just as they had, some six decades ago, led to the colonization of Africa in the first place. For the reader interested in pursuing this line of reasoning to decolonization, the editors direct you to the work of Daniel Fogel, listed in the Suggestions for Further Reading at the end of this Problem.

Jack Woddis makes an entirely different and popular argument for the decolonization of Africa than those previously cited. To him decolonization was brought about by the African liberation movements. In blunt terms, it was not the Europeans, the Asians, the Americans, or the historical dialectic that produced decolonization, but the fact that the Africans simply forced the Europeans to leave. Burdened with the disgrace, if not the guilt of colonialism, and the arrogant exploitation they had suffered at the hands of their European masters, the Africans mobilized, united, and kicked the Europeans out of Africa. Woddis defines the end of empire as the dynamics of the national liberation movements. He argues that they were totally national in composition, transcending regional, ethnic, and class divisions. Workers, the bourgeoisie, the intelligentsia, the peasants, and even African chiefs all came to regard colonialism as a baneful influence upon their collective existence. When these groups set aside their differences and demanded the departure of the Europeans, decolonization became an inevitable consequence of the mass mobilization of the African peoples.

Unlike some of the Problems of the African past, about which there has been a growing consensus on the part of scholars and even the debate over the Imperial interlude of this century, the controversies rage with vigor and not a little vitriol over the end of empire.

Decolonization in Africa

JOHN D. HARGREAVES[2]

Certainly the end of the colonial empires can only be understood within the total context of contemporary history. Reductionists might explain it as a simple consequence of the declining power of the colonial rulers in an international system dominated, during the critical period, by two anti-imperialist superpowers. But to understand the nature of the change, and its varying effects on different countries, it is necessary to ask, not only Why?, but such questions as How? When? By whom?—in short, to study history. . . . [T]his book attempts to show how the historical conjuncture of the mid-twentieth century eventually led colonial rulers to perceive that their interest lay in such policies. In this more restricted usage, "decolonization" implies intent: the intention to terminate formal political control over specific colonial territories, and to replace it by some new relationship. This did not necessarily mean independence; neither France nor Britain, at the end of the Second World War, envisaged a general lowering of flags. But both, it will be argued, (though not, until later, Belgium, Spain, or Portugal) did set out to change political relationships—to substitute collaboration for force or, in the words of Sidney Caine, counsel for control. . . . [W]hen the assumed stability of colonial rule became more questionable during the 1930s, a certain number of persons in both countries conceived programmes of reform and renewal which would eventually lead towards the independence of their African colonies.

Eventually, if not intentionally. The irony of political history lies in the processes through which the results of human statesmanship come to diverge form the intended purpose. The original reform plans were formulated by disillusioned practitioners concerned to discharge their imperial trusteeship more effectively. "Development" and "welfare" were the initial keynotes of the British Colonial Office, with "self-government" added as a means towards these ends. French reformers gave even greater priority to economic and social improvement, and their political horizons remained obscure. . . . [W]hile the world crisis developed from depression into war, reform plans were progressively amended, accelerated, and ultimately transformed, as pressures from their more powerful allies, and from with-

2. Hargreaves, John D., *Decolonization in Africa*, (London: Longman, 1988). Excerpts taken from pages 2, 3, 32, 34, 52, 53, 61, 62, 113, 180, 187, 191, and 192.

John D. Hargreaves has served as Lecturer at the University of Manchester, Senior Lecturer in History at Fourah Bay College, Sierra Leone, and as Professor of African History at the University of Aberdeen since 1962. He is author of *The End of Colonial Rule in West Africa: Essays in Contemporary History*, (London: MacMillan, 1979).

in Africa, obliged Britain and France to formulate their political objectives more clearly.

After the war contradictions developed between the forces working for decolonization and the need experienced by both Britain and France to mobilize colonial resources to support the restoration of their international power. . . . British Ministers redesignated their development policies as "nation-building": designs for self-governing democracies within the Commonwealth, some based on institutionalized racial partnership, within an ever-shortening future. The French, still less precisely, envisaged decolonization within the framework of the new French Union, through the full assimilation of some communities and the autonomy of others. Some of the objectives proclaimed in this period now seem to resemble mythological beasts, incapable of existence in twentieth-century Africa; what realistic plans for political evolution were made were aborted by the rapid acceleration of timescale demanded by economic and political realities. By about 1960, those controlling policy in Britain, France and Belgium had come to regard the possession of colonies (with a few strategic exceptions) as a positive hindrance to their new national objectives. . . . [T]hey now hastened to liquidate the remains of their formal empires with the greatest speed compatible with an appearance of responsible trusteeship, sometimes without much concern about future relationships.

It may be thought that this interpretation devalues the importance of those African initiatives which at one time occupied the centre stage of contemporary historiography. Yet the most effective critics of racial injustice were always Africans who drew from their reading of European history a Mazzinian faith in the capacity of the independent nation-state to promote material progress and cultural renewal; in the euphoric 1950s, the political parties they founded seemed the natural heirs to colonial authority. In the 1980s, some of their hopes appear incredibly naive. Those who followed Nkrumah's advice to seek first the political kingdom did not find all else added to them. That "Third World" which idealists once hailed as a new source of creative energy has become a heavy burden on western consciences; while in many African nations continuing immiseration and poverty is made all the more conspicuous by the prosperity of a favoured few. . . .

The first great shocks to colonial tranquillity originated in the economic depression which began to affect the international economy from about 1929. The financial crisis, which led to cuts in investment, large-scale unemployment and impoverishment in industrial countries, drastically reduced demand for the minerals and agricultural produce on which the export trade of every colony depended. If African farmers tried to maintain their incomes by increasing production, this only accelerated the fall in the prices they received; and although the cost of manufactured imports also fell it rarely did so proportionately. There were of course variations in the effects of world price movements on different colonies and in different years, and detailed econometric research is still proceeding, notably on the French empire; but for the 1930s, the general picture is one of deterioration in Africa's net barter terms of trade (the quantity of imports obtainable for a given quantity of exports). . . . For colonial governments were in their own way as badly hit as any of their subjects. The political representatives of metropolitan taxpayers almost invariably insisted that the costs of administration and development in the colonies (and to some extent those of their defence) should be met out of local revenues, derived in varying proportions form the taxes or unpaid labour services of their subjects, and from indirect duties on trade. In order to finance the construction of ports, railways and other forms of social overhead capital necessary for commercial growth, colonial governments had borrowed substantial sums, at rates which, even if relatively favourable at the date of the loan, constituted fixed prior charges on colonial budgets. Colonial governments also had heavy commitments, difficult to reduce, for the salaries and pensions of their own officials, the highest of course being payable to expatriates. When falling prices slashed the value of customs revenue (the Sierra Leone Government's income, for example, fell by almost a third between 1928 and 1934), governors had little choice but to penalize African subjects: by reducing expenditure on schools, roads, and medical services, by cutting the public payroll at the expense chiefly of junior African staff, or by increasing direct taxation. None of these courses was adopted willingly, for each was liable to undermine such legitimacy as the colonial state had been able to achieve in the eyes of its subjects; and some provoked ominous new forms of African resistance. . . .

It was wartime economic necessities which had the most drastic effects on African life. Dislocation of prewar trade patterns, shipping shortages, and maritime blockades weakened whole sectors of the commercial economy, while others were strained by increased demands—for strategic minerals, for example. Restrictions on imports—including some essential foods, as well as consumer goods—created inflationary pressures, in the colonies of neutral Portugal and Spain as well as in the belligerent empires. Governments were obliged to adopt interventionist policies which existing machinery was ill-prepared to execute. Command economies were improvised on the basis of forced (or heavily constrained) labour, compulsory cultivations, hastily-created marketing controls; undermanned colonial states began to make heavier demands on their subjects than ever before. Prices paid to producers of essential commodities were held down, and the ensuing profits temporarily appropriated by the British Treasury in the overriding cause of imperial survival. And from 1942, the extension of the war and the loss of Allied empires in Southeast Asia meant that all these pressures were greatly intensified. . . .

For some Africans these demands entailed sufferings comparable to those of the battle-fronts. Conscious cruelties by labour contractors were often less serious than the totally inadequate arrangements made for the health and diet of men displaced from their home environment, or the devastating effects on many areas of drought and famine in 1942-43. Sanitary conditions in Nigerian tin mines were particularly scandalous, and many hundreds of workers died. But even where minimal standards were maintained and wages regularly paid, shortages of imported goods and local food supplies inflated prices, depressing living standards for the prewar labour force as well as for the new recruits. . . . Pressures from all directions—international,

African, and domestic—were now working towards political reforms. When the Labour Party entered Churchill's coalition government in May 1940, one effect was to speed up the appointment of Labour Officers to oversee conditions and encourage trade unionism in the larger colonies. George Hall, a Welsh miner who spent two years as Under-Secretary at the Colonial Office, encouraged "experimental appointments" of British trade unionists to these posts. Many of these men, who saw a responsibility to go beyond the encouragement of peaceful collective bargaining and educate African workers in the principles of social democracy, made new and distinctive contributions to African political life. Outside the government a few socialists with African interests or experience formed the Fabian Colonial Bureau in 1940; this became an influential pressure group, less through its political weight than because of overlaps in outlook and membership with the liberal imperialists inside the Colonial Office. Fabians emphasized progressive social engineering—welfare provision, education, economic planning—as necessary preparations for self-government; but they also cautiously endorsed calls from their African friends for greater freedom and early constitutional reform. A colonial version of the coalition government's consensus on the need for postwar reform gradually emerged, influenced less by theoretical critiques of colonialism than by the experience of disillusioned practitioners. Even those who dismissed Roosevelt's anti-imperialism as ill-informed, self-interested or mischievous acknowledged that discontents fomenting in Africa would require at least homeopathic doses of political freedom....

During the postwar years both British and French governments were faced with growing contradictions between their intention to substitute counsel for control in relationships with their African dependencies and more urgent incentives to use the economic and military resources of those dependencies to strengthen their international influence. Their need provided Africans who could establish credentials as spokesmen in the colonial dialogue with opportunities to insist that the political independence of their countries provided the only acceptable basis for collaboration. Events in Asia, where independence was relatively successfully conceded to India, Pakistan, Burma and Ceylon but bitterly contested in Indo-China and Indonesia, seemed posthumously to justify Roosevelt's insistence on the importance of that word. In face of insistence from African leaders and of international pressures colonial reformers in London, if not yet in Paris, had to suppress their persistent doubts as to whether international sovereignty and universal suffrage represented viable or desirable objectives for every colony. A crucial struggle to secure control over the process of decolonization took place in the Gold Coast, where British colonial reformers at times lost the initiative to a new type of political party which mobilized African discontents on a platform of populist nationalism. Because Nkrumah's success had wide repercussions, this confrontation will be examined at some length. After 1951, careful distinctions between different stages of local autonomy, and between self-government and independence, became increasingly irrelevant, at least in colonies where there were no powerful immigrant minorities. But much constitutional ingenuity was still applied in vain searches for alternative goals in colonies where expatriate interests could exert influence in the metropolis.

Even before [a crisis in] the Congo...focused international attention on tropical Africa, Harold Macmillan [the British Prime Minister] was realizing that his attempt to maintain a privileged relationship with the United States at the head of the Atlantic alliance could be jeopardized if Britain remained too closely identified with the residues of her colonial empire in eastern and southern Africa. Besides damaging British relations with new Commonwealth members and with the UN, colonial commitments might also prejudice any application for membership of the EEC, within which de Gaulle was clearly planning to redefine Euro-African relationships for the post-colonial age. As the pressure on Britain's financial and military resources continued to tighten, Africa seemed a region where many commitments could safely be contracted.

For a Conservative leader, imperial contraction was a delicate political operation. Since the Suez debacle, the old imperialist elements in the party had begun to regroup. One of the eight MPs who had then resigned the Whip was Julian Amery, son of the former Colonial Secretary and also Macmillan's son-in-law; on returning to the party he served as Lennox-Boyd's Under Secretary at the Colonial Office, among other Ministerial appointments. The Joint East and Central African Board which represented business and settler interests in that region had links with the Conservative Party, and some MPs were closely involved with such companies as Tanganyika Concessions, strong supporters of Tshombe's secession in Katanga. Others placed high value on loyalties to "kith and kin" in Central Africa, but still more so in Kenya, where, the Prime Minister noted, "settlement has been aristocratic and upper middle-class (much more than Rhodesia) and has strong links with the City and the Clubs." Lord Salisbury remained a prestigious and powerful patron of all these groups.

In the General Election of October 1959, African policy for the first time became a party issue, if a minor one. While Party manifestoes naturally placed overwhelming emphasis on domestic issues, the Labour Party declared that "the future of Africa is poised as perilously as that of India in 1945"; attacking Macmillan's rejection of the Devlin Report, it reiterated the Party's commitment, since 1956, to self-determination on the basis of "one man, one vote." The Conservatives spoke only of ending racial discrimination in multi-racial countries and of protecting rights of minorities—which were hardly those at issue in Central Africa. Sixty per cent of Labour candidates, but only four per cent of Conservatives, mentioned Central Africa in their personal manifestoes; almost a third of Labour candidates but no Conservatives referred to the Hola Camp atrocity. Both parties referred to African issues in television broadcasts. In Scotland many churchmen, alerted by persons whom the Prime Minister regarded as "dangerous and subtle agitators," criticized the government's discharge of its trusteeship for African rights in the Federation; this possibly played a minor part in its loss of four Scottish seats, with a contrary swing to Labour of 1.4 per cent.

Though generally reassuring, these results may have reinforced Macmillan's belief that a change of course was needed. Lennox-Boyd, whose strong commitment to Federation was reassuring to imperialists, had already decided to retire from politics to business; to replace him at the Colonial Office Macmillan appointed his former Minister of Labour, Iain Macleod. Macleod's dedication to politics, allied to a capacity for coolly ruthless calculation which appealed to all sections of the Conservative Party, had already marked him, at 46, as a likely future leader. But not all had yet perceived the moral passion which this Yorkshire-born Highlander could bring to issues affecting the liberty of nations and individuals; Macleod had been deeply shocked to discover that the government in which he served had tried, however unwittingly, to dissemble its responsibility for the brutal atrocities of Hola Camp. Sensitive both to the moral challenge of African nationalism and to the political perils of resisting it, Macleod concluded, as he later put it, that the dangers of over-rapid decolonization were less than those of moving too slowly. "Terrible bloodshed in Africa" would also bring terrible problems, domestic and international, for the government. His sense of urgency increased when in early 1960, de Gaulle finally agreed to independence for his Black African colonies, and the Belgians announced their intention to follow. . . .

In a world where so much public discussion focused on the ethics of race relations, Macmillan's hopes of plastering over the contradictions in the Commonwealth were frustrated. On 5 October 1960, white South Africans voted for a Republic; precedent required her re-application for Commonwealth membership, which Macmillan ruled must be considered by a new conference in March. Opposition began to grow. The Canadian Prime Minister, Diefenbaker, became convinced that "to give unqualified consent to South Africa's application would be to condone the policies of apartheid." Abubakr Tafawa Balewa, at his first conference, was aware of deep feelings in all Nigerian parties. On the eve of the meeting Julius Nyerere declared that Tanganyika, now scheduled for early independence, could not join any association including a racialist South Africa. Such lectures on racial morality merely stiffened Verwoerd in rejecting Macmillan's attempts at compromise; he refused to remain in the Commonwealth on terms which would expose him to further attack at later meetings or to accept the full accreditation of African ambassadors. On 15 March 1961, he announced the withdrawal of South Africa's application for continued membership.

These dramatic events, coupled with the unfolding of Macleod's policies for eastern Africa, suggested that the Anglo-African Commonwealth might be about to become a central plank of Britain's world policy. But appearances proved deceptive. Britain's close economic, military and intelligence relations with South Africa continued. Still more significant was the announcement three months later that the British government was applying for full membership of the EEC. For those political leaders who now believed that Britain's future lay in closer relations with Europe were coming to regard many of her colonial links as economic and political liabilities.

The Asian Mirror to Tropical Africa's Independence

D.A. LOW[3]

There are two central themes in the history of the attainment of independence by the countries of tropical Africa which warrant closer attention than they have received. In the late 1950s and early 1960s, independence came to many of these countries a great deal faster than anyone, most nationalists included, had ever anticipated. And in almost every case it came without a war of independence. . . .

[African independence] had been preceded by the attainment of political independence by the former European dominated countries in Asia. In seeking to elucidate the characteristics of the tropical African story, a good deal more than has usually been understood is to be gleaned from considering the Asian cases. . . .

When one turns to consider British attitudes to the transfers of power in Africa, the influence of the British encounter with nationalism in Asia is difficult to gainsay. It is in no way fanciful to assert that many of the critical battles for British colonial Africa were fought, not on the banks of the Volta, the Niger, or the Zambezi, but on the Ganges. Britain, after all, was the most powerful of the Western imperial powers. Had it held onto its empire in Asia, the demise of other Western empires would not have occurred so readily. Thus the epic struggle of the Indian National Congress, particularly during the 1920s and 1930s is central to the whole story of the transfer of power in the Third World and set the scene for this as did no other anti-imperialist struggle. In particular, it showed what the combination of "tactical action" and "positive action" (to use Kwame Nkrumah's subsequent formulations) could effect. It indicated that widely based nationalist parties were worth creating. It revealed, too, that, however slow British constitutional reforms might seem in coming, they had their own ultimate logic. Above all, it indicated that there could

3. Low, D.A., "The Asian Mirror to Tropical Africa's Independence," in Prosser Gifford and William Roger Louis (eds.), *The Transfer of Power in Africa: Decolonization, 1940-1960*. (New Haven: Yale University Press, 1982). Excerpts taken from pages 1-5, 18, and 28-29.

D.A. Low was born in Naimi Tal, India and having received his D.Phil. from Oxford University has written extensively on African and Indian History. Having served in professorial positions at numerous universities, including the University College of East Africa, Makerere, Uganda, and the University of Sussex, Brighton, England, where he was the founder and dean of the School of African and Asian Studies. He is currently Professor of History and also the Vice Chancellor at the Australian National University. Included among his many publications are *Uganda and British Overrule, Political Parties in Uganda, 1900-1955* (with Cranford Pratt), (London, Oxford University Press, 1960.) and *Lion Rampant: Essays in the Study of British Imperialism.* (London, Cass, 1973).

be circumstances where violent colonial rebellion against a reluctant colonial power was not necessarily the only way to move forward.

To attempt to separate the African from the Asian half of the story of the demise of the British Empire—as, indeed, to separate the two of them from the story of the ending of Britain's imperial relationship with its "white" colonies—is to tear at long-continuing historical threads. Four comments here will suffice. In Britain no great debate about the end of empire occurred between the great debate over India in the early 1930s and the great debate over Central Africa in the late 1950s. There was an all-but-smooth progression in the public realm in Britain from independence for South Asia in the late 1940s and the beginning at that time, by those who read the signs, of preparations for Britain's later withdrawal from Africa. The significance of their previous experiences in Southeast and South Asia for, respectively, Sir Charles Arden-Clarke and his chief secretary, Reginald Saloway, in the Gold Coast in the years before independence provides a footnote to the larger point. It should always be remembered, too, that the prime minister who presided over Britain's transfer of power in South Asia, and over the Cabinet in which Arthur Creech Jones, the reforming British colonial secretary, sat, was one and the same man, Clement Attlee—a member of the much-abused Simon Commission in India in the late 1920s, but also the man who secured reconsideration of Britain's policy there when it took its final conservative turn in the middle of the Second World War.

The French revision of the end of empire in Asia was much more traumatic for them than for the British, and as a consequence its impact upon their African policy turned out to be much more sharply delineated. In the late 1940s, the French strove more mightily than any other colonial power to maintain their Asian empire. Their bitter denouement came with the defeat of French arms at Dien Bien Phu in 1954. In the years that followed, France's reaction in Africa to its Asian experience trifurcated. In *Afrique Noire* those inclined to disown their French connections, as in Guinea, were quickly isolated. But where "Bao Daist" regimes (Senghor, Houphouët-Biogny) could be created, there was little argument about an early transfer of power. Where, however, there seemed to be no case for a transfer of power— as in Algeria—then the honor both of French arms and of French colonialism was to be upheld at well nigh any cost. The shadows—and they were sharply varying shadows—of Dien Bien Phu seem, from an Asian perspective, to lie right across the last decade of France's empire in Africa.

The Belgian experience was rather different. They had no empire in Asia as they did in Central Africa. But in Europe they were neighbors to the Dutch, and the Dutch had had their fill of disappointment, abandonment, defeat, and protracted recriminations over the ending of their empire in Asia. It may perhaps be suggested, therefore, that the Belgians' precipitate actions in the Congo in 1959-60 owed more than has been generally appreciated to their conclusion that once their anti-nationalist stance—which was as strong in the Congo as it had been among the Dutch in Indonesia—had cracked, there was no point in any way prolonging the agony, as their Netherlands neighbors had, at so much commercial and diplomatic cost to themselves. Belgium's proximity to France in Europe reinforced this thought, particularly following the Algerian crisis....

Thus far, the Asian mirror to independence in tropical Africa can therefore be said to have contained the following reflections. Even though the circumstances in various Asian countries differed considerably, there were enough broad similarities in their varying colonial experiences to suggest that where the general circumstances did not differ so greatly, as over so much of tropical Africa, even closer similarities were likely. The Asian experience indicated, too, that armed conflict in the ending of empire was a distinct possibility. Wherever such conflict occurred, the effect was traumatic—and it could be quite appallingly prolonged. But it was now also evident that there could be an alternative to violence. If certain terms were accepted by both sides (which in the last analysis turned on the acceptance by the departing imperialists of the assurances of their likely successors), a transfer of power without armed conflict could be achieved. In view of the clear tendency for there to be a concurrence in the patterning of events, it is perhaps especially significant here that peaceful transfers had occurred in Asia where America—now the greatest of the world's powers—and Britain—still the largest of the imperial ones—had held sway. The potentialities for peaceful transfers were thus rising....

We may say therefore . . . that by contrast with events in Asia, independence came to tropical Africa after the Second World War with remarkable rapidity. Quite obviously the imperial grips in tropical Africa were loosened by the immediately preceding upheavals in Asia. It may seem at first sight that in their day the various Asian histories ran independently of each other. But upon closer inspection this does not seem to have been quite the case. Despite significant differences in the outlooks of the various imperial powers, and substantial differences in national cultures, parallel developments abounded in Asia. Where there was a greater congruence of outlook among the colonial powers (not least as a consequence of their experiences in Asia), as in tropical Africa; where (as in tropical Africa) there was a lesser degree of cultural diversity between different countries; and where, in the post-Second World War era, boom and recession propelled and then frustrated a great continent-wide burgeoning. There the parallelism in the steps toward independence turned out to be even greater than in Asia. There was as a consequence little holding the immediacy of the repercussions of events occurring in one part of Africa upon those in another. The ebullience which characterized tropical Africa in the two decades after the Second World War (of which there had been no real counterpart in Asia) soon broke the tenuous authoritarian and territorial barriers which the imperial powers had imposed upon her. For this reason there was little need in Africa for nationalist forces to develop the degree of dedication and organization that leftist forces in particular had established in Asia. (Socially radical movements were thus rarely in vogue in Africa.) In short, nationalist movements in Africa were less dependent upon systematic political organization, and to a greater extent were the political embodiment of continent-wide social impulses than they were in Asia;

being more diffuse, they were, moreover, more difficult for the imperial powers to curb, but easier for them to accommodate, than they had been in Asia. Herein lay the central elements, it may be suggested, which made for the relatively non-violent precipitancy which in retrospect still seems to characterize the story of tropical Africa's attainment of political independence.

The United States and the Liquidation of British Empire in Tropical Africa: 1941–1951

WILLIAM ROGER LOUIS and RONALD ROBINSON[4]

The fall of Europe's colonial empires in Africa has usually been attributed to a magpie's choice of African nationalism, shifts in national ideology, and changes in the international balance of power. Clearly a catalogue of such forces is not enough. The difficulty in assessing the collapse of the European regimes lies in relating the international, metropolitan, and colonial factors in a comprehensive framework that reveals both the chronology and the interacting forces. This chapter attempts to move the subject forward toward such an explanation by examining the problem through one particular but cardinally important aspect. It begins with the emergence of the United States as a global power—a global power that during the Second World War suddenly developed an intense interest in the British Empire, including its African components. When the center of world power shifted from London to Washington (and eventually to Moscow as well), the British felt the blow to their economy and their colonial position throughout the world. Did this shock trigger the changes of mind on the part of the British that eventually accelerated the transfer of power and the nationalization, or Africanization, of colonial administration?

A brief historical comment may help to explain the background of these remarks. After the partition of Africa at the turn of the century, the colonial powers of Europe supported each other against Africans. They only rarely interfered in each others

---

4. William Roger Louis and Ronald Robinson, "The United States and the Liquidation of British Empire in Tropical Africa, 1941-1951," in Prosser Gifford and William Roger Louis (eds.), *The Transfer of Power in Africa: Decolonization, 1940-1960.* (New Haven: Yale University Press, 1982). Excerpts taken from pages 31, 32, 44, 45, 48, 49, 54, and 55.

William Roger Louis is the Kerr Professor of English History and Culture in the University of Texas at Austin and a Fellow of St. Antonys College, Oxford. He is Editor-in-Chief of the forthcoming *Oxford History of the British Empire.* He is also the author of numerous books and articles including *The British Empire in the Middle East* (New York: Oxford University Press, 1984) and *Imperialism at Bay: The United States and the Decolonization of the British Empire, 1941-45.* (New York: Oxford University Press, 1978).

Ronald Robinson is the Emeritus Beit Professor of the History of the British Commonwealth and former Reader in Commonwealth Studies at Cambridge University. He is a Fellow of Balliol College, Oxford and the co-author of *Africa and the Victorians: The Official Mind of Imperialism.* (New York: St. Martin's Press).

affairs. There was, in fact, what could be called an international colonial system (interrupted, of course, by the First World War). Through international treaties the African powers of Europe accepted each others colonies as exclusive spheres of influence—spheres recognized by international law. Though there were important protests against this system, notably on the part of Woodrow Wilson in 1919, the European powers administered their territories without fear of external intervention. So long as Europeans dominated the balance of power, colonial administrators could enjoy freedom of action without fear of international subversion. One way of looking at the beginning of the end of the colonial system is to analyze the impact which the emergence of the United States from isolation had on colonial affairs.

The momentous shifts in the bedrock of world politics during the Second World War raised one set of problems in Washington and another set in London. Should the Americans collaborate with British imperialism for purposes of winning the war and securing the peace? Or would their anticolonial tradition and expansive economic strategy bring them to insist on the liquidation of the empire? . . .

From the time of the Atlantic Charter in August 1941, the United States officially espoused the principle of self-determination. Self-determination for whom? Churchill thought that the pledge referred exclusively to the conquered peoples of Europe under the Nazi yoke. Roosevelt believed that it should apply to colonial peoples as well. With that mixture of disarming idealism and intuitive realism that characterized him, the president held that the European colonial empires should be placed under some sort of international administration. The colonies would eventually become independent on the model of the Philippines. . . . And was not the scheme for international administration perhaps camouflage for the beginning of a gigantic, even if informal, American empire? . . .

In the immediate postwar era, American involvement in European colonial affairs can be summed up in the names Cyrenaica, Indochina, and Indonesia. Each of these carried a chilling message to the British. In the dispute over the future of the Italian colonies, Ernest Bevin, the foreign secretary in the Attlee government, hoped that Britain would be able to acquire trusteeship status over Cyrenaica and create a strategic base there in order to lessen British dependence on Egypt. When the negotiations for the renewal of an Anglo-Egyptian alliance broke down in 1946-47, and when it became clear that the Palestine problem could not be resolved to British advantage, the question of Britain's security in the Middle East became acute. To Bevins dismay the Americans could not be counted on to back British trusteeship claims to Cyrenaica. American policy fluctuated in reaction to possible Russian expansion into the eastern Mediterranean and in relation to the strength of the Communist movement in Italy (for European reasons, the Americans were willing to consider an Italian trusteeship if it would strengthen an anti-Communist government in Italy). In 1945-48 the British were forced to turn to Iraq as the linchpin of British defense in the Middle East. What the British learned from the episode of the Italian colonies was that American policy toward colonial areas in North Africa and the Middle East would change according to the fortunes of the Cold War and would not necessarily accommodate the strategic requirements of the British Empire. . . .

The international situation that necessitated the planning and actual beginning of the transfer of power from 1947 to 1951 looked very different from that of the wartime era. It was no longer simply a question of Anglo-American relations, of keeping the colonies without risking loss of the American alliance. With the beginning of the Cold War, colonies and ex-colonies became potential or actual pawns of great power rivalry on a scale not seen since the comprehensive partitions of the late nineteenth century. Now once again there were competing centers of expansion in world politics. A major domestic crisis in a colony might attract the intervention of one of the great powers. Immediately after the war, the Cold War mainly affected the colonial area of Southeast Asia; but the possibility of Africa becoming involved could not be ignored. The international factor was impinging upon colonial affairs more and more intensely.

The onset of the Cold War helped the British in their colonial problem with the Americans in one way but made it more difficult in another. While the United States gave priority under the Marshall Plan to the reconstruction of Europe and the containment of communism, it tended to act more often than not as a guarantor of Europe's remaining colonies. But there were two implicit conditions. Colonial policies had to be adopted that would provide internal tranquility and future political stability; and the colonies had to serve American strategic requirements as buffers against Russian expansion. The difference that these two conditions could make in a colonial emergency was shown when the Americans gave their blessing to the French in Indochina and withdrew it from the Dutch in Indonesia. The difficulty the British found in fulfilling the American conditions was twofold. First, the United States continued to identify colonial stability with liberal advances toward independence. Though the Americans were not as outspoken on this issue as during the wartime era, the British could not rely on the relaxation of American pressure. Second, the British found it difficult to forecast where the State Department or the Pentagon would discover a strategic interest. It often proved to be far from where the British Foreign or Colonial Offices thought it should be. London regarded American support of the British Empire as too sporadic and unpredictable to be relied upon. British anxiety not to provoke American anticolonialism continued. In the shadow of their powerful American ally, the British followed certain golden rules more warily than ever: handle the colonies with kid gloves; concede to subjects rather than risk confrontations with them; and above all avoid all dangers of possible uprisings, armed repression, and colonial wars. Only thus could the possibility of American intervention in the African empire be averted. Colonial imbroglios that might drag the area into the international arena could be forestalled. . . .

The interdependence of terms for the toleration of colonial empires became sharply apparent in the mid-twentieth century. For example, the decline of the European powers in world politics tempted not only the Soviet Union but also the

United States to stiffen the conditions for acquiescing in the continued existence of the overseas colonial regimes; the international balance of power, in turn, encouraged nationalists in the colonies to organize support and demand more concessions. Increasing international pressure together with growing resistance from colonial subjects thus tended to test the willingness of the metropolitan peoples to tolerate the burden of colonial empires. The extent of that toleration varied with the financial and military cost of colonial upkeep, the supposed economic benefit, and the prevailing ethic or ideology. In the British case (and perhaps in that of some of the other European powers also), so few politicians knew enough about colonial economics that most were forced to rely on ethical yardsticks of trusteeship to measure the value of empire and hence their own willingness to tolerate the burden. As the humane values of democracy, pacifism, and social welfare increasingly pervaded a war-weary Europe, the limits of metropolitan toleration tended to shrink from coercion to concession; in other words, where once the colonial power coerced its subjects, it now made concessions to them. The increased reluctance of the metropole to pay the cost of retaining colonies in turn diminished the imperial administrators power to bargain for the acquiescence of their colonial subjects.

Just as international and metropolitan conditions reflected in part the tensions in the colonies, so the circumstances in the colonies themselves were profoundly affected by the changing balance of forces at the international and metropolitan levels. Colonial governments have always stood or fallen as the rulers and the ruled have accommodated or resisted each others major interests. The rulers usually came to the negotiating table with the idea of retaining imperial authority up to the brink of a crisis in which they would have to shoot or get out; subjects, on the other hand, came with the intention of enlarging their share of governing power up to the point of getting shot or backing down. For the proconsul the colonial problem was how much power to share with subjects in exchange for their cooperation; for the subject the question was how much noncooperation would elicit the maximum share of power. Between the two extremes the terms for obtaining acquiescence in colonial rule depended on several variables: for example, the expenditure of finance and use of force which the peoples of the metropolitan country would tolerate for purposes of keeping a colony; the extent of a colonial governments demands on it subjects for land, labor, and produce and of the resistance thus provoked; the volume of metropolitan investment offering partnerships to subjects in the profits of the international economy; and the extent of power-sharing with indigenous elites.

In short, the existence of the Western overseas empires depended on conditions which made them acceptable to the politics of the metropolitan countries, and these terms also had to be practicable both in international relations and in the local politics of colonial or quasi-colonial societies. Empires eventually fall when the conditions necessary for their survival at one of these levels become impossible to translate acceptably at the other two levels. If this thesis holds good, it would be futile to debate the question whether the main cause of the fall of empires is to be found either in shifts in the international balance, or in the vicissitudes of metropolitan politics, or in the rise of colonial nationalism. No simple, single-cause explanation can be found. Change at any level caused changes in the others. In the British case, Colonial Office planners ultimately concluded that there could be no resolution of the tensions—international, metropolitan, and colonial—other than by swift transfers of power. The transfers of power were intended to sustain British influence through African agents.

From Colonization to Independence in French Tropical Africa: The Economic Background

JEAN SURET-CANALE[5]

When one considers the economic evolution of French-influenced tropical Africa between 1946 and 1960 along with its contemporary, postindependence extensions, and not neglecting the social, political, and ideological components of this evolution, it seems impossible to explain either in terms of decolonization or of the transfer of power.

The word *decolonization,* at least in France, is loaded with ambiguity. One may certainly construe it in the "neutral" sense of transition from colonial status to that of juridical independence. In practice, however, the use of the term connotes a certain idea of the way in which this process took place. The imperialist powers, it is thought, once having colonized, suddenly changed their policy and deliberately "decolonized." Some consider this a generous and disinterested program (the approach of a certain de Gaullist mythology which credits the General with such clear-sightedness); whereas to others it was proof of a diabolical perfidy, since the purpose of decolonization was better to exploit the dominated peoples.

I believe I have shown that imperialism deserves neither this excessive honor nor this insult. The empires did not deliberately decide upon decolonization, did not desire it, and did not really prepare for it. It simply happened, and measures that today appear to constitute preparatory steps toward independence in fact never intended to lead to it, as Jean Stengers has rightly demonstrated, but on the contrary,

5. Suret-Canale, Jean, "From Colonialism to Independence in French Tropical Africa: The Economic Background," in Prosser Gifford and William. Roger Louis (eds.), *The Transfer of Power in Africa: Decolonization, 1940-1960,* (New Haven: Yale University Press, 1982). Excerpts taken from pages 476, 477, 481, and 481.

Jean Suret-Canale served in the French Resistance between 1940 and 1944. He received his Docteur 3 cycle en Geographie from the University of Paris-Sorbonne in 1966. Earlier, in 1963, he received his Docteur es sciences historique from the African Institute at the USSR Academy of Sciences, Moscow. His current affiliation is with the University of Paris VII. He is the former Director of the Center for Marxist Studies, Paris. Suret-Canale's other best known work in English is *French Colonialism in Tropical Africa, 1900-1945.* (New York, Pica Press, 1971).

meant to raise an obstacle to it by granting partial concessions calculated to preserve the essence of imperialism.

What we are in fact witnessing on the global scale (for in this domain one cannot consider Africa in isolation) is a bitter, complex, and continuing struggle between imperialism (that is, high international monopolistic capital and the states that serve it), on the one hand, and on the other, all those forces that are objectively in contradiction to imperialism: the socialist countries, the laboring classes (and more generally the working masses), and the national liberation movements of those peoples subjected to imperialist exploitation. In French tropical Africa this struggle reached a first culmination around the year 1960, with the collapse of a traditional colonial system badly shaken since 1945, partly because of external factors (essentially, the Algerian War). The result, in most cases and in forms that varied according to the forces emerging in the respective countries, has been that imperialism has fallen back upon indirect methods of domination which do little to alter economic realities. But this neocolonialism was called into question from its birth by avantgarde groups, including, in some cases, those at the state level (Guinea, Mali until the military coup d'etat, Congo in 1963, and more recently Benin and Madagascar). Today it is increasingly challenged and finds itself considering more and more often the socialist alternative as the only guarantee of authentic independence.

The common characteristic of the experiments we are concerned with here has been to embark simultaneously upon changes in political structure—more or less extensive nationalizations aimed at eliminating the direct presence of foreign imperialism, and measures intended to inhibit or prevent the formation of a local bourgeoisie—and upon a struggle within the system on which they are still dependent, in order to thwart broader economic and political pressures by relying on the socialist countries and playing rival empires off against one another. Such a policy is often laden with ambiguities, even leaving aside "socialist" countries in name only, of which Senghor doubtless offers the most typical example. These ambiguities, which are attributable to the effects of internal social and political struggles, to setbacks, and sometimes to outright failures (as in the case of Mali), can exist as long as the question, "Which will win, capitalism or socialism?" continues to be raised within the country itself. None of these states is in fact "socialist" in the strictly objective sense of the term, which assumes the preponderance in the country's economy of collective ownership of the essential means of production. . . .

The choice is not between access to the international market and an isolationist policy, nor between advanced technology and primitive technology; the choice is between an economic and technological policy that meets the requirements of the imperialist firms and one that meets the requirements of independent, self-centered development. Orthodox liberalism and one form of neo-Marxism both, in fact, fall victim to a sort of "economism," a unilateral determinism, forgetting that, while society's economic base (which is different from "economics" in general) plays a determining role in the course of history in the *final instance* (which excludes any unilateral determinism), the class struggle at the international level (which must be conceived in terms of polarization, not social stratification), states, politics, and ideology—all are involved as constituent elements of economic realities. That was Marx's point of view, and it is absolutely alien to any "economic fatalism"; otherwise, it would be difficult to understand how he could have ended up appealing for revolutionary action and concluding that "men make their own history" (though not in just any way whatever, or in whatever circumstances).

However summarily these considerations have had to be presented within the limits set for this chapter, they lead back to the question raised at the beginning of this study: what role did economic factors play in the historical process that led the former colonies of French tropical Africa to political independence?

If one insisted upon a unilateral economic determinism, this process would remain strictly incomprehensible, for what took place in the economic field, until 1960 and beyond for most of the countries concerned, was an accentuation of "colonialist" features: increasing and continuously perfected integration and subordination to the great imperialist powers' economies—namely, their large companies—to their profit objectives, and thus to their aim of exploitation. Unilateral determinism would have to conclude that political dependence had to be reaffirmed and intensified, and that independence would therefore be incongruous (an argument often used between 1946 and 1960 under the euphemism "interdependence").

But this determinism is not unilateral; the "development of underdevelopment," to use A.G. Frank's phrase, produces contradictory effects. On the social and political plane it produces social, political, and ideological forces which are self-destructive:—in Marx's words, "their own gravediggers."

Independence entered into the logic neither of economic development, narrowly conceived, nor of the colonialist tutors' intentions. It asserted itself as a consequence of the dialectic of history—that is, of history's contradictory development; it was (and still is) the stake in a rearguard action on the part of imperialism in which phases of resistance alternate with phases of concession and retrieval. From this point of view, history has not ended: it is just beginning.

Africa: The Roots of Revolt

BY JACK WODDIS[6]

Although it is only since the Second World War that the national liberation movements in Africa south of the Sahara have become strong enough to roll back the tyranny of colonialism, it should not be assumed that these movements are entirely a post-1945 phenomenon. The African people were never reconciled to foreign conquest and oppression but fought continually, first to defend themselves against the invaders, and then, after defeat, in protest against the consequences of conquest. In the twentieth century these strivings took on a new importance and scope, and began to acquire quite new characteristics. Strikes and political demonstrations took place; there were revolts and notion-wide upheavals; and political parties began to appear. All these struggles in the period prior to the Second World War undoubtedly helped to pave the way for later developments; although, generally speaking, there were as yet no cohesive, permanent, nation-wide African political organisations with clearly defined aims and programmes directed towards gaining complete national independence. The most common demands were for reforms, not for the abolition of colonial rule. The epoch of national political parties, with a broad mass basis and the unequivocal demand for national independence "in our time"—and established in every single African territory—only really opened after 1945. . . .

The speed with which the national movements in Africa have surged forward—and this is a phenomenon which daily becomes more apparent—is partly due to the very rapidity with which African society itself has been changed in this period. The destruction of African traditional agriculture, the drawing of millions into migrant wage labour, the growth of an African capitalist class—all constituting a process which is by no means complete—have undergone acceleration, particularly since the end of the Second World War. Old forms of society are collapsing and new class forces are being thrown up, forcibly and ruthlessly. And as they emerge from the crucible of colonialism they press ever more persistently against the barriers which

6. Woddis, Jack, *Africa: The Roots of Revolt,* (New York: The Citadel Press, 1960). Excerpts taken from pages 246, 251, 255, 256, 260, 261, 263, 264, 265, 266, 267, 269, 273, 274, 275, 276.

Jack Woddis, a British political activist and author, has been affiliated with the Communist Party of Great Britain since 1942. In 1965, Woddis was appointed head of the organization's international department. He has also worked with the World Federation of Trade Unions as head of its Press and Publicity Department. Among his publications are *Africa; The Way Ahead.* (London, Lawrence and Wishart, 1963.) and *New Theories of Revolution; A Commentary on the Views of Frantz Fanon, Regis Debray and Herbert Marcuse.* (New York, International Publishers, 1972).

would hold them back.

The interests of colonialism have hindered and delayed the economic development of the African territories, prevented their industrialisation, ruined their agriculture, and left them with a distorted economy. Thus all national development has been throttled and the whole people, including often the chiefs, have been hurled into the struggle for national liberation as the essential pre-condition for the advancement of their own class and sectional interests.

The working class . . . is still a relatively small minority of the African population. Moreover, it is a young class, most workers being of the first generation. But it is a growing force—it has grown particularly during the last two decades—and already numbers some ten millions. Most of it, it is true, is migrant labour, but labour migration has a two-fold effect. While, on the one hand, it has prevented the emergence of a permanent, stabilised, modern proletariat—and this has meant a weakening of the working-class movement—on the other hand it has resulted in the majority of African males, in large parts of Africa, having experience of wage labour at some stage or other in their lives. In the mines, on plantations, in railways, in factories and on construction sites, they have met migrants from other African territories. They have exchanged experiences, found that they suffer the same common exploitation at the hands of the same masters, and that they have the same aspirations. This has helped to develop a feeling of all-African solidarity which is a powerful force in present-day African politics. . . .

The struggles that have shaken Africa in the past decade—and that will shake her even more in the next ten years—are not purely proletarian struggles, important as may be the participation of the workers in them. They are, as we have noted, *national* movements, movements in which whole peoples are involved and in which the aim is not the particular interests of one class or section but the common aspiration of all to end imperialist rule, destroy the colonial system, and open up the way to the national development of each territory.

An important role in these movements is being played by the African bourgeoisie. It is, of course, true that the national bourgeoisie is still numerically weak in most African territories south of the Sahara, and that economically it is still not a powerful force. Its main spheres are agriculture, trading and commerce, and to some extent transport; but as an industrial and manufacturing bourgeoisie it is naturally in an embryonic stage, for, as we have already seen, industrial development in Africa is everywhere held back by imperialism, and even where it does take place, it is almost completely in the hands of European monopolies.

The small, yet growing, African capitalist class cannot but find itself constantly at loggerheads with the colonial system. As a capitalist class it is naturally concerned with profits. To make profits, it needs control of its own domestic market, and it needs, too, a considerable expansion of that market. No less, it requires to build up its own industry in order to make the goods to supply to that market. But everywhere the African bourgeoisie turns it finds the imperialists holding the controls in their hands, dominating the market, owning the raw materials of which they rob the country and shipping in the manufactured goods with which they flood and monopolise the local market. Even where Africans own the raw materials, such as cash crops (only rarely do they own minerals), they find themselves at a great disadvantage, for the imperialist monopolies, which control the world markets, compel the African growers to sell their crops at a low price but to pay highly for the manufactured goods which they need to purchase. . . .

The postwar period has also seen an increase in the number of African intellectuals. The African people have made heroic efforts to secure education for themselves, even on occasions setting up their own schools to make up for the appalling deficiencies in official education for Africans. Many an African mother has slaved from morn to night doing domestic work, taking in laundry, making some native brew on the side, all to earn money to give her son an education. Something of the heartbreaking sacrifices which this entails have been described with great vividness and poignancy by Ezekiel Mphalele in his *Down Second Avenue*. Kwame Nkrumah worked as a dish-washer in the United States in order to complete his education. Dr. Hastings Banda walked hundreds of miles, as a young man, from his native Nyasaland, to seek education in the Union of South Africa and later to complete it overseas. Many a national leader in Africa can tell similar stories. . . .

The humiliations, insults and indignities suffered daily by African intellectuals cannot but play their part in impelling them towards involvement in the struggles of the whole people. When white doctors from Southern Rhodesia came to work in Nyasaland, following on Federation, they insisted on African doctors no longer being permitted to wear white medical coats, as they had done previously. Frequently the trained African, with many years' experience behind him, sees a raw, white recruit step ahead of him—at several times the rate of pay. The struggle for the Africanisation of government departments in Ghana, Nigeria, Sudan—and soon to open out in other territories—is one long story of stubborn resistance by entrenched interests against ending a situation of white privilege based on no other considerations than those of racial discrimination. . . .

Thus the African intellectual is subject to two opposing influences. On the one hand the imperialists try to suborn and seduce him by offering him small privileges and by smothering his national pride and loyalty through a subtle and deliberate process of de-Africanisation and of Westernisation. On the other hand, because imperialism is anxious to retain all the key plums of office and profession, the African intellectual finds his ambitions, both for himself and for his people as a whole, constantly thwarted and frustrated. Thus he comes to realise that neither his own personal or sectional interests nor the total culture of his people can be advanced while colonialism and imperialist rule continues. It is the two-fold nature of the pressures on African intellectuals—to have privileges over the rest of his people, yet be subordinated to the European rulers—that explains the hesitations, indecisions, or sudden shifts of position from one extreme to another which so often characterise their role in the national movement. Yet their influence is a very important one, and there is not a single national political party of the African people, in any of the territories, in which intellectuals will not be found playing a significant and often leading role. . . .

What of the rural African, the destitute land-hungry peasant, and the cash-cropping farmer? For these constitute the majority of the African people. As we have seen, sixty years of imperialism has dealt them devastating blows. Much of the African countryside lies in ruins. The villages and Reserves are largely populated by women, children, and old people. Soil erosion spreads like a foul disease, and on his dwindling lands the African peasant sinks deeper and deeper into poverty. His very poverty becomes an additional barrier to economic development, preventing him the possibilities of fertilisers or irrigation projects, and periodically compelling him to abandon his poor fields to seek wage labour in European mines, plantations or urban enterprises.

The widespread agrarian crisis in Africa, which is a natural consequence of colonial rule, has been to some extent concealed by the migrant labour system, just as emigration over the years has successfully masked the agrarian crisis in Eire.

One result of this is that the African peasantry has not yet taken part in the national movement as a separate, conscious and organized political force. No large-scale, sustained peasant revolts have taken place in Africa as they did, for instance, between the two world wars, in China, Burma, the Philippines, Indo-China and Indonesia, although there have been, in the last thirty years, a number of local sporadic outbursts in Africa, often against taxation or land seizures by European settlers.

The African peasant has in the main, done his fighting against imperialism in the towns, as a migrant worker. . . .

There is an assumption among many people that all African chiefs are on the side of reaction, that they represent the forces of feudalism and tribalism and are therefore hostile to the struggle for African independence. Many chiefs do, of course, play such a role, not only relatively powerful ones in West African territories, but even lesser chiefs who are often mere government appointees. But to dismiss all African chiefs as reactionaries would be a distortion of fact.

From the very start of Africa's resistance to European imperialism there have been kings and chiefs who led their people in opposition to foreign rule. Yet it was not merely in the first stage of resistance to imperial conquest that many chiefs played a progressive role. Throughout the twentieth century there have been examples of chiefs siding with their people against particular exactions or acts of repression by the authorities, especially in defences of land or in opposition to taxes. . . .

[I]t can be said, broadly speaking, that for the first half of this century imperialism was able to make use of the institution of chiefs for its own ends. The introduction of indirect rule, combined with the deposition of unwilling chiefs, and backed by imperialist arms, proved sufficient in this period to preserve the colonial system.

In the last decade, however, as the movement for national independence has grown stronger, and as the issues around which this struggle is being fought have pressed sharper and sharper, so have the chiefs found themselves, in a number of cases, placed in an acute dilemma.

In many territories the use of chiefs, converted into paid Civil Servants to act as imperial puppets who would hold the African people in check, is no longer possible to the extent that it was in the past. . . .

In many other territories the same trend is to be noticed of chiefs turning away from the imperialist governments; while those who remain "loyal" to their white rulers become so discredited that their utility and effectiveness is extremely limited. . . .

Thus Africans, as a whole, have reached the point of no return. The old life has been destroyed—and there can be no going back. Africa has been drawn inexorably into the money economy by the forcible actions of imperialism. The destruction of old classes and the formation of new ones is going ahead.

The system of imperialist exploitation and colonialism has brought the African people to the edge of the abyss. It has produced a discontented proletariat, a ruined peasantry, a cramped bourgeoisie and a thwarted intelligentsia.

It has become impossible for the majority of Africans to find a haven and security on the land. Nor can they find security in wage labour in the mines, plantations and urban areas. Like Ishmael, they wander from countryside to town and back. But nowhere is there any hope.

The African intelligentsia and the emergent capitalists, too, find at every turn that their aspirations and advancement are checked. For them, too, colonialism offers little hope.

This shared conviction of all progressive classes in African society, the recognition that only through their joint struggle can they succeed in defeating their common enemy, engenders national feeling and speeds up the national consolidation of the peoples. Tribal loyalties, though still not without influence and utilised very often by imperialism for reactionary ends, are melting in the crucible of the anti-colonial struggle. The concentration of large masses of African people in towns and mining centres, the development of capitalist relations right in the heart of African society, the creation of national and class organisations which group people together independently of any parochial or tribal affiliations—all this is breaking down tribal barriers. National and class interests have now come to the fore, and nations are being formed. Class interests and aspirations have become merged with national interests, and the cry for national independence has been taken up by the whole people.

The people of African can no longer bear to go on living in the same old way. Colonialism has squeezed them dry and life has become impossible. The daily humiliations to individual and nation alike can no longer be tolerated. Held back economically, culturally, socially and politically, each class and section is driven to the inescapable conclusion that if they are to live and grow, then colonialism must go.

But equally, the imperialist rulers can no longer rule in the old way. They twist and turn to seek a solution, the rifle in one hand and the restricted ballot paper in the other. They offer a political post under white domination or tutelage, coupled with the threat of prison. While they talk of advancing the people to independence, they lock up the people's independence fighters and strive to uncover a handful of African puppets who will help them to adorn themselves with the fig leaf of democratic respectability.

But all this cannot stop colonialism hurtling down the road to ruin and disaster. Each fresh attack on the African people, each new wave of repression, only serves to increase the anger, the bitterness, the determination and resolve of the African people to win their freedom, now, "in our time," in 1960. As it feels the ground slip beneath its feet, imperialism attempts to keep its grip by making a concession here and a concession there. But each paltry concession is taken by the African people and used as a platform for further demands, as a stepping-stone to further concessions. The imperialists hesitatingly open the door an inch, hoping to keep it that way. But once ajar, the door can no longer be shut. The African stands with his powerful, calloused foot firmly planted in the doorway, and at his back stands all the misery and horror of the hundred million who died or were taken in slavery, the centuries of massacres and robbery, the whip-lash, the death camps, the finger-printed passes, the ruthless exploitation in field and mine, the starvation, disease and illiteracy, the cultural degradation and national humiliation, the attempt to crush the African personality and maintain Africa in perpetual helotage.

But twentieth-century barbarism, with all its Western refinements, cannot determine the course of history. Africa is not going back. It is going relentlessly forward. Africa, in fact, has reached the stage of revolution—of the overthrow of colonialism.

It is now clear, on looking back, that Accra was the beginning of the end. What had been burgeoning slowly and increasingly beneath the hot soil of Africa suddenly burst forth in all its strength and majesty. *Afrika! Mayiube! Africa! Come back!*—comes the cry from the Union. *Kwacha! The Dawn!*—echo the voices in Rhodesia. *Uhuru! Freedom!*—shout Kenya, Tanganyika and Uganda. *Ablode! Liberty!*—cries Togo.

And the Welenskys and Verwoerds, the Kenya settlers and Algerian *colons*, the Belgian Baudouins and Portuguese slave-owners, the Macmillans and Macleods, turn and twist as they may in their desperate panic to hold on to their African Eldorado, cannot succeed.

They, and their would-be successors in Washington, are too late. The sands are running out. The African people are standing up. And the colonial system in Africa is doomed.

Suggested Readings

Bangura, Yasuf, *Britain and Commonwealth Africa: The Politics of Economic Relations, 1951–1975* (Manchester: Manchester University Press, 1983).

Chinweizu, *Decolonising the African Mind* (Lagos, Nigeria: SUNDOOR, 1987).

Emerson, Rupert, *From Empire to Nation: The Rise to Self-Assertion of Asian and African Peoples* (Cambridge, MA: Harvard University Press, 1960).

Fieldhouse, D.K., *Black Africa, 1945–1980: Economic Decolonization and Arrested Development* (London: Allen and Unwin, 1986).

Fogel, Daniel, *Africa in Struggle: National Liberation and Proletarian Revolution* (Seattle: Ism Press, 1982).

Gallagher, John, *The Decline, Rise, and Fall of the British Empire: The Ford Lectures and Other Essays* (New York: Cambridge University Press, 1982).

Gifford, Prosser, and Louis, William. Roger, *Decolonization and African Independence: The Transfer of Power, 1960–1980* (New Haven: Yale University Press, 1988).

Louis, William. Roger, and Robinson, Ronald, "Empire Preserv'd: How the U.S. Helped Prevent the Collapse of the U.K.," *Times Literary Supplement*, no. 4805 (May 5, 1995).

Louis, William. Roger, *Imperialism at Bay, 1941 - 1945: The United States and the Decoloni- zation of the British Empire* (Oxford: Clarendon Press, 1977).

Mazrui, Ali, *Nationalism and New States in Africa from about 1935 to the Present* (Nairobi: Heinemann, 1984).

McHenry, Donald, "The United Nations: Its Role in Decolonization," in Carter, Gwendolen, and O'Meara, Patrick, *African Independence: The First Twenty-Five Years* (Bloomington: University of Indiana Press, 1985), 31–44.

Murphy, Philip, *Party Politics and Decolonization: The Conservative Party and British Colonial Policy in Tropical Africa, 1951–1964* (Oxford: Clarendon Press, 1995).

Noer, Thomas, *Cold War and Black Liberation: The United States and White Rule in Africa, 1948–1968* (Columbia, MO: University of Missouri Press, 1985).

Weinstein, Warren, *The Pattern of African Decolonization: A New Interpretation* (Syracuse, NY: Syracuse University, 1973).

Wilson, Henry, *African Decolonization* (London: E. Arnold, 1994).

Yansane, Aguibou, *Decolonization in West African States, with French Colonial Legacy: Comparison and Contrast: Development in Guinea, the Ivory Coast, and Senegal, 1945–1980* (Cambridge, MA: Schenkman Publishing Co., 1984).

PROBLEM II

THE AFRICAN ENVIRONMENT: ORIGINS OF A CRISIS

The environment in that we live is a concern and a controversy, but in Africa its deterioration has been dramatic and destructive. Africa is a continent on the periphery of subsistence which has neither the resilience nor the resources to withstand the ravages to its traditional environment by nature or man. Drought, brought about by the failure of the rains in the 1980s, has resulted in famine. But the desiccation of the land cannot be solely blamed on Mother Nature. The Africans have exploited the land as did the imperialists, many of whom had little interest in what Prime Minister, Lord Salisbury in the 1870s dismissed as "light soil." Drought destroys the environment, but even in the 1990s when the rains have returned, the Africans, who traditionally have been very conscious of land use, have lost their herds, and cultivations and in search of survival have migrated in the millions to the cities where they have become the urban poor, dependent upon the assistance from the plethora of Western relief agencies. Famine creates the destabilization of states that frequently results in social disorder and even violent civil conflict. The dissolution of authority, whether it be local or that of the central government, has had an impact on the African environment resulting in the desperation of Africans to survive by destroying forest lands for fuel, exhausting cultivable soils, and diminishing the scarce water supplies. Who is to blame for the environmental crisis that has overwhelmed Africa? The vagaries of nature, the global change of the earth's atmosphere, commonly known as Greenhouse, the misuse of the African land mass by the incomers and the inhabitants have all produced the "Problem of the African Environment," but whatever conclusion the investigators may reach as to the cause, they all agree that the African environment is in crisis.

This perspective is perhaps made most dramatic by Lloyd Timberlake who writes that Africa is on the brink of an environmental disaster. Africans are starving on an unprecedented scale, and the continent is subjected to a continuing and debilitating underdevelopment because of a deteriorating environment. He argues, as have others, that the principal cause of the plight, is not so much the lack of water—the drought—but the magnetism of the cities that have drawn Africans off the arid countryside, to the real and imagined opportunities of urban Africa. Who is to blame? The burden of guilt cannot be laid at the doorstep of Mother Nature. To be sure, drought in the countryside will drive the displaced to seek relief in the towns and cities, but the exodus was apparent even before the drought decade of the 1980s and was encouraged by African governments determined to "modernize" with the enthusiastic assistance of the international lending agencies and the international aid organizations, both governmental and private. Collectively, they emphasized the importance of producing cash crops for the world markets to the exclusion of the African producer who grows the bulk of Africa's food. Modernization, often described as mechanization, overtaxed the soil, deforested the countryside, and diminished Africa's ability to provide for its inhabitants accustomed to managing limited resources. The Faustian bargain is becoming more evident with every passing day.

David Anderson and Douglas Johnson disagree. They argue that interpretations, such as published by Timberlake, belong to the "Africa in Crisis" literature that portrays Africa and its inhabitants as being in a constant state of environmental decay. Instead, they propose that one should approach environmental change from an historical perspective. Anderson and Johnson argue that droughts and other massive environmental changes have been recurrent in the African past. In response to the vagaries of nature, the Africans have always adapted to weather these environmental storms. The strategies they employed were many. They moved to more verdant regions; they altered the pattern of pastoral pursuits; they changed the crops and methods of agricultural production to accommodate changing climatic conditions. A "crisis" only existed in the Africans' frustration to contain its impact. Thus, in discussing the origin of the environmental crisis it is inappropriate to apply Western models but to regard the environment from an African perspective and their communities where one must see the environment in a more natural setting and not necessarily in "crisis."

Kevin Cleaver and Gotz Schreiber could not disagree more with Anderson and Johnson. They argue, like Lloyd Timberlake, that Africa is on the verge of an environmental catastrophe, which has been created by an overpopulation of unproductive inhabitants throughout the continent. They are simply reproducing too many human beings to survive on the limited available resources. Obviously, the solution to this "crisis" is to lower the birthrate. The Reverend Thomas R. Malthus (1766-1834) advocated the same remedy for Britain early in the nineteenth century when, like Cleaver and Schreiber, he argued that sex should be restrained to inhibit overpopulation (the environmental consequences of proliferating procreation had yet to be discovered) and that prosperity could only be attained by controlling the birthrate and having smaller families. They argue that this objective can best be achieved when African women are given economic opportunities that will result in their choice to reduce the number of their children. The strategy to accomplish this goal is not strictly economic, as Malthus thought, but is embedded in culture and gender. The economic deprivations of women is not simply the result of an underdeveloped economy but the demands placed on women because of their gender. In Africa women cultivate the fields, perform mundane domestic chores, and bear and rear children. The demands of indigenous agriculture combined with the cultural and traditional roles expected of a woman result in ever larger families and an increasing pressure on a fragile environment.

If Cleaver and Schreiber link the decline of the African environment to gender, Thomas-Slater and Rocheleau embrace it. They argue that one cannot understand the environmental crisis in African unless it is viewed through the sharp focus of gender. Government policies on land and the environment are formulated in the capital where women have no formal or legal voice. Particularly important has been the recent trend toward the privatization of communal lands, a phenomenon that has been prejudicial toward women. Moreover, when governments, dominated by males, make environmental policy, women are relegated to their role as child-bearing and labor whether in the house or the field, and to be placed to whatever policies that the men have decided.

Michael Lofchie and Randall Baker introduce two different and opposing arguments into the environmental problem in Africa. Michael Lofchie maintains that famine, the principal result of environmental degradation, has been the result of policies perpetrated by the independent African governments whose decisions have undermined the viability of the rural population to produce crops for their subsistence. They have manipulated African agriculturalists and pastoralists by currency overvaluations, price regulations, and import preferences that have collectively encouraged the critics who cynically point out the difference in life styles of the policy makers from that of the rural producer.

Randall Baker has the same objective as Professor Lofchie but argues that the environmental crisis has been caused, not by internal African politics, but rather by the effects of external exploitation, be they direct as was European imperialism or indirect in the precolonial era by the vicissitudes of the control of the terms of international trade. The foreigners who have come to Africa since independence, whether as self-proclaimed entrepreneurs or beneficent patrons, have consistently imposed their perceptions onto the reality of Africa and consequently misunderstood the continent and its people and what they wish to have or produce to improve the quality of life.

Finally, it is important to place the environmental "crisis" in historical perspective. Jeffrey Gritzner argues for a much longer historical reckoning than David Anderson and Douglas Johnson. Environmental history must be measured in centuries if not millennia. His interpretation is that the current environmental problems in Africa are, in fact, the result of degradation that began over 500 years ago with the arrival of the Muslims and the Christians to Africa. Prior to their arrival, African societies lived in harmony with the environment, or as Gritzner writes, "indigenous . . . social systems . . . were linked to their associated ecosystems." But, first the Muslims and later the Christians introduced new agriculture, new weapons, and new markets that encouraged, even forced Africans to degrade their environmental livelihood.

This is a provocative proposition with which many scholars of Africa disagree. Space does not permit the comments of Graham Conah, S.C. Munro-Hay, and D.N. Beach who have all studied and written extensively on African societies that presumably disappeared because of a changing environment. These scholars, unlike Gritzner, argue that the Africans did not need to learn of environmental destruction from the incomers whether they be Muslims or Christians. For the reader who seeks to explore this subject simply consult the "Suggested Readings" at the end of this Problem.

Africa in Crisis: The Causes, the Cures of Environmental Bankruptcy

LLOYD TIMBERLAKE[1]

[In mid-1985] . . . it was said that at least 30 million Africans in 20 nations did not have enough food to live on; that 10 million had abandoned their homes and farms in search of food and water; many had abandoned their countries. But these figures were mere guesses. No one knew the numbers of dead and dying, least of all the governments responsible for their welfare.

The African droughts and famines are not sudden natural disasters, nor are they simply caused by a lack of rainfall. They are the end results of a long deterioration in the ability of Africans to feed themselves, a decline caused largely by mistakes and mismanagement—both inside and outside the continent.

Fifteen years ago the Sahel, that strip of nations just south of the Sahara desert, was ravaged by a similar tragedy, and its causes were largely identified by international experts. But the same mistakes have continued almost without change: that catastrophe taught the world little. Now, radical changes must be made, or "disaster" will become a permanent way of life for many Africans.

Unless policies are altered, "development in Africa will continue to be frustrated, leading to what the Economic Commission for Africa has called a political, social and economic 'nightmare' by the turn of the century," the normally cautious and conservative World Bank said in a 1984 report. The Bank was not talking about the famine, it was talking about the steady decline in living standards and agricultural production which preceded and caused it.

"Many institutions are deteriorating, both in physical capacity and in their technical and financial ability to perform efficiently," said the report. "Although the picture varies from country to country, even those with good records in the 1970s now face serious difficulties. In short, the economic and social transformation of Africa,

1. Timberlake, Lloyd, Africa in Crisis: *The Causes, the Cures of Environmental Bankruptcy,* (London: International Institute for the Environment, 1985). Excerpts taken from pages 7, 9, 10, and 12.

Lloyd Timberlake is the author of numerous works on the environment in Africa. They include *Environment and Conflict: Links between Ecological Decay, Environmental Bankruptcy and Political and Military Instability,* (London: Earthscan, 1984), and *Only One Earth: Living for the Future,* (London: British Broadcasting Corporation, 1987).

begun so eagerly and effectively in the early years of independence, could be halted or even reversed."

Africa's plight is unique. The rest of the world is moving "forward" by most of the normally accepted indicators of progress. Africa is moving backwards. "Features of modern society to which many Africans have been exposed are withering: trucks no longer run because there are no spare parts and roads have become impassable; aeroplanes no longer land at night in some places because there is no electricity to light the runway," according to the World Bank. The continent's living standards have been declining steadily since the 1970s. Its ability to feed itself has been deteriorating since the late 1960s.

The scramble to get emergency food aid into Africa is necessary and may save lives, but it offers no long-term hope for the continent.

The tragedy has had one positive effect: it has started a painful reappraisal among those responsible for Africa's "development," and brought a new willingness to admit mistakes. . . .

Africa is dying because in its ill-planned, ill-advised attempt to "modernise" itself it has cut itself in pieces. The cities where the governments live have been torn from the countryside, and development budgets have gone to filling those cities with hotels, factories, universities, and cars. This has been paid for by milking the seven out of every ten Africans who live on the land, by taking much from them in labour and produce and giving back little in money or support. In these policies, Africa has been advised, financed and assisted by Northern governments and aid agencies.

The result? Cities surrounded by shanties, hotels full of Northern development experts, factories either idle or producing goods few can buy, universities producing graduates who can find no work, expensive cars full of civil servants, businessmen, soldiers and policemen. East Africa has a Swahili word for them: the *Wabenzi*—the Mercedes-Benz tribe.

"It's the town that's done for the peasants," said one elderly Senegalese farmer. "Twenty years on we've come to realise what Independence really meant. It was just for the towns. One of these days we'll be asking Dakar for a reckoning, you'll see."

But in taking too much from its farmers, Africa has taken too much from its land as well. It has overdrawn its environmental accounts, and the result for much of Africa has been environmental bankruptcy. The big farm schemes of the Northern experts, and the small efforts to stay alive of the rapidly growing rural populations, have overcultivated, overgrazed and deforested the soil.

As the soil erodes, so do Africa's living standards. Bankrupt environments lead to bankrupt nations—and may ultimately lead to a bankrupt continent.

To describe Africa's crisis as "environmental" may sound odd. In Europe and North America the environment is often a luxury issue. Is the air more or less hazy? Are there as many birds as there were a decade ago? Are the cities clean? What have environmental concerns to do with the fact that in 1985 the entire Hadendawa people of northeastern Sudan faced extinction due to starvation and dispersal?

The Sudanese government, with the help of Northern aid, World Bank loans and Arab investment, has put vast sugar and cotton plantations on its best land along the Nile. It has ignored rapidly falling yields from smallholder farming in the 1970s. It seems not to have noticed that the land—the "environment"—upon which eight out of every ten Sudanese depend for their livelihoods is slowly perishing due to over-use and misuse. It invested little in dryland regions where people like the Hadendawa live. So when drought came, these pastoralists and peasants had no irrigated settlements in which to take temporary refuge, no government agencies to buy their livestock, no sources of drought-resistant sorghum seeds ready for planting when the rains resumed. But neither have the government's investments in cash crops produced money to pay the nation's way through the drought. The result is starvation and debt: Sudan's external debt in 1985 was estimated at $9 billion. President Nimeiri, overthrown in April 1985, has paid a personal price for leading Sudan to environmental bankruptcy.

Soil erosion matches the erosion in farmers' political power, as they are more and more squeezed out of their nations' political and economic life. In democracies where large proportions of the population live off the land, the farming lobby forces governments to put money and attention into the soil. In the 1890s and 1910s, US farming families starved to death in droughts on the Great Plains. But today soil and water conservation programmes, crop insurance, rural credit, agricultural education and advice, forestry services, fish and wildlife services—all these make it possible for rural people in the industrialised world to survive natural disasters such as drought and flood. . . .

The answers to environmental bankruptcy are not technical ones. The colonial solution was for the rulers to impose on the ruled a series of regulations and edicts, ignoring the socio-economic factors which forced the people to degrade their environment. This view blamed the victim, saw the African as lazy, ignorant, backward and irrational. The same essentially colonial attitude dominates much environmental thinking today: the stupid peasant must be educated not to cut down trees.

And the purely technical solution also ignores the depressing political and economic realities of modern Africa. Just as the rural peasant exists on a day-to-day, hand-to-mouth basis, so too does his government—beset by low commodity prices, by high oil prices, by high interest rates, by a high-value dollar and by debts which are huge in proportion to foreign exchange earnings.

In the short to medium term, the threats to these fragile governments come not from the countryside but from the *Wabenzi*—the disaffected urban elites: the entrepreneurs, civil servants, police and armed forces. Zaire is ruled by a former army sergeant, Burkina Faso (formerly Upper Volta) by a former captain, Liberia by a former master sergeant, Ghana by a former flight lieutenant, Nigeria by a former major general, Libya by a colonel—all of whom seized power in coups. Such leaders see little short-term political gain in paying attention to a rural majority which has no political power—this despite the lesson of the 1968-73 Sahel crisis, during which every government fell, largely because the rural crisis became so severe that it *did* reach the capitals.

The policies of nearly all African governments favour the urban elite, by keeping food prices low, or by seeing to it that profits from major cash-cropping schemes go to urban-based companies and individuals. Governments see little economic motive for investing in the rural hinterland. One of Africa's many vicious cycles is at work here: government policies degrade the rural resource base; degraded farmland produces little of economic value. . . .

Ecology and Society in Northeast African History

DAVID ANDERSON and DOUGLAS JOHNSON[2]

This book examines the historical continuities of ecological change and ecological stress in northeast Africa. Since it is intended to take a longer view of ecological problems than is usual in "disaster" or "crisis management" literature, it is not primarily concerned with the region's most recent environmental crisis, which has been the subject of wide journalistic coverage. The media focus on northeast Africa has been direct and to the point. It has served to make a large segment of the Western world more conscious of the immediate problems of the region, but it has often done so by building on some very old stereotypes. The images we have been presented—the conservative cultivator overfarming his exhausted land, the reckless stock keeper increasing his herd unmindful of the consequences to the environment, the fatalism of traditional societies when confronted with unexpected natural disasters, the deplorable lack of understanding of true economic forces by indigenous governments and their callous indifference to the sufferings of their own peoples— all of these have a long pedigree in expatriate descriptions of African societies in the past. The famines of the early 1980s have left a legacy of concern and alarm in much of the developed world. Coming so soon after the Sahelian drought of the 1970s, they have reinforced a popular perception of Africa in decline. Journalists, scholars, politicians, bankers, development experts and the general public alike now describe the continent's present condition almost exclusively in terms of "crisis": environmental crisis, economic crisis, debt crisis, development crisis, political crisis.

The urgency implied may be counterproductive. The preoccupation with identifying all manner of "crises" makes it more difficult to distinguish between major crises and more common occurrences of stress; therefore, more difficult to decide

---

2. David Anderson and Douglas Johnson, "Introduction: Ecology and Society in Northeast African History," in Douglas Johnson and David Anderson (eds.), *The Ecology of Survival: Case Studies from Northeast African History* (London: Lester Crook Publishing, 1988). Excerpts taken from pages 1, 2, 4, 12-14, 17-19, and 23-24.

David Anderson is currently a Lecturer in History at Birbeck College, University of London. He is co-editor for the *Journal of African History*. Among many publications, he is the co-editor of *Conservation in Africa: People, Policies and Practices,* (New York: Cambridge University Press, 1987).

Douglas Johnson is the author of numerous articles on Sudanese history and a Lecturer at St. Antony's College, Oxford.

the most efficient allocation of energy and resources. There is the risk that governments, planners and the public at large will be rapidly exhausted to the point of inaction or indifference by repeated rallying calls. They may even become cynical if catastrophes leave more survivors than predicted; thus becoming immune to future dire warnings. But it is precisely survivors and survival which concern us here. We do not wish to understate the severity of the suffering of the recent famines, but in examining the nature of the crisis we must also look beyond it. To look beyond it we feel we must look backwards, into the past.

The study of Africa has too often suffered from an assumption of "timelessness." Africans are seen either as having been locked into unproductive activity "from time immemorial," or as having existed "in equilibrium" with their environment until the forces of colonialism and capitalism combined to disrupt the natural balance which African societies have since been struggling to restore. The former has been explicit in much of the journalistic writing on the 1980s famine, which, though sometimes acknowledging that serious famines have a long history in northeast Africa, has assumed an unchanging and static pattern of rural life from one generation to the next. The latter notion, of the African environment "in equilibrium," is a more romantic view of man's ideal relationship with nature which has been invoked both as an explanation for the continent's predicament and as a justification for implementing policies aimed at the conservation of rural Africa. Here the assumption of timelessness is expressed in the image of a mythical pre-colonial "Merrie Africa," where man existed in harmony with nature. Such assumptions, muddled and misleading as they are, have been reinforced rather than reassessed as international attention came to focus upon northeast Africa in the 1980s, and as the bureaucratic reflex action of "crisis management" began to dominate development and aid responses.

. . . [This volume] . . . seeks to challenge the bundle of stereotypes and assumptions that have come to shape the popular image of environmental crisis in northeast Africa. By viewing ecological change and environmental adversity in an historical perspective, and by examining the social dynamics that have operated as communities have responded to changing ecological conditions in both the past and the present, we hope that we can move towards a better understanding of the nature and degree of crisis, and of its short- and long-term impact upon the societies it has affected. Disasters...may "expose, at a particular point in time, the inner workings of a society," but we must understand equally how societies adjust to small changes as well as cope with crisis. We must be aware of, and be able to plot, the progressive nature of ecological change, but we must also recognize continuities of response to environmental adversity through time and across societies. It is precisely these aspects of social context and historical perspective which are ignored by much of the "Africa in crisis" school of literature; for the urgency of the crisis allows no time for detailed historical reflection. Yet these factors must be understood if we hope to arrive at a fuller explanation of northeast Africa's present situation. . . .

It is possible to reconstruct a chronology of ecological stress for our case studies, and for the region as a whole throughout the last two centuries, that illustrates the regularity of adversity. There have been recorded widespread failures of rain in northeast Africa in the 1830s, 1880s and 1890s, in 1913, the late 1920s and early 1930s, and again during the 1970s and 1980s. There have also been occasions of heavy East African rains producing high Nile floods in many areas within the region, as in 1878, 1916-18, and most recently in the early 1960s. Some of these sharp fluctuations in rainfall and flood levels also coincided with extensive and severe epidemics: cholera in the 1830s, rinderpest, smallpox and cholera in the 1880s and 1890s, influenza and cerebrospinal meningitis in 1918-19. If purely localised droughts, floods and epidemics are added to these more universal catastrophes, then one can appreciate how a given society's memory of past stresses is continually reinforced by recent experience. The generation which reached maturity in 1916, for instance, will still be the oldest generation surviving today in many parts of northeast Africa. Its members have direct knowledge of many of the worst environmental disasters of this century, but they can also draw on their parents' memories of the drought and rinderpest of the 1880s and 1890s, and perhaps even their grandparents' memories of earlier epidemics and famines. Throughout the severe drought and hunger of the early 1980s, then, there were members within each society who could recall its experiences at points over the past hundred years.

Of course, during an individual's lifetime, local environmental conditions will fluctuate between relatively dry and relatively wet phases. While memory of past adversity informs and reinforces the social networks of survival, many communities are also prepared to exploit opportunities that may emerge during periods of more favoured ecological conditions. In this respect the relationship between wet and dry phases is significant. John Gowlett highlights the importance of this over the longer-term, but in more recent times we can see how short term fluctuations between wet and dry phases have influenced changes in settlement and land use patterns. During the wetter phases, for example from 1900 to 1914 and through the 1950s, cultivators have frequently taken advantage of favourable conditions to expand the farming frontier into lowland areas, only to encounter serious difficulties in producing adequate harvests during subsequent drier phases. James McCann provides us with the recent example of the resettlement of farmers in northern Ethiopia, in this case politically inspired, during an initial few years of good rainfall. The aspirations of these settlers altered sharply as a series of drier years set in. In the western Sudan, as both Leif Manger and Mustafa Babiker Ahmed describe, the expansion of mechanised cash-cropping in the 1960s and 1970s was undertaken on the assumption that the favourable rainfall patterns of the 1950s were the norm. Expanding areas of cultivation and enlarged or shifting patterns of grazing are, of course, not solely determined by favourable environmental conditions: demographic pressures and changing political circumstances can dictate such movements, as Manger illustrates with the Nuba. However, it is important to realise that short-term "crises" emerging with the onset of prolonged drought can sometimes be the product of very recent changes in settlement and land use patterns, and that short-term fluctuations in rainfall patterns can help to explain shifts in relationships between neighboring groups.

This leads us to make two simple, but important, points. Firstly, the impact of any period of ecological stress in northeast Africa is inevitably uneven, affecting certain societies more directly than others. Thus, ecological stress experienced by one community can present an opportunity to another. Drought and famine in the Kamba regions of eastern Kenya during the early 1940s allowed neighboring Kikuyu, themselves affected by drought less severely, to sell grain at vastly inflated prices to the beleaguered Kamba. Here the Kikuyu were subjecting long-established networks of exchange with the Kamba to powerful market forces. Secondly, and as a consequence of this unevenness of experience, each community provides an internal definition of what constitutes ecological stress, and when conditions have deteriorated to the proportions of a "crisis." These internal definitions are crucial to an understanding of how any society copes with ecological stress, and are therefore more valuable in analysing the causes and consequences of such stress than external definitions of crisis—those employed by the State to determine when relief measures are required, or indeed those marked by the consciousness of the Western media. . . .

The definition of ecological stress must include a political dimension, whether colonial or precolonial, as political decisions do affect the way societies utilise or perceive both their economies and their natural environment. Husbandry practices and survival strategies have, at times, been influenced by a history of belonging to a state or, more generally, sharing an ethnic identity. Indeed, as Ethiopia's experiences in the 1970s and 1980s serve to indicate, the impact of environmental adversity can be intensified and deepened by the political decisions and actions of the state. Similarly, in the western Sudan cases here described by Holy, Manger and Mustafa, while successive years of low rainfall from 1969 through the 1970s generated the gradual emergence of ecological stress in the region, it is evident that the decisions taken by the government of the Sudan over this period failed to cope with the manifestations of the situation, and, in certain respects, accentuated the problems brought about by poor rainfall.

The creation of colonial states in northeast Africa, defined by new boundaries which often arbitrarily dissected ecological zones and cut across the links between neighboring peoples, had the ultimate effect of creating new sets of identity. The colonial experience "created" Kenyans, Ugandans and Sudanese, and finally defined who were to be recognised as Ethiopians. But it can also be argued that periods of ecological stress have had an equally profound impact upon the definition of the more particular identities based on ethnicity and community. As each of the following chapters on the experience of the Maasai in the late nineteenth century, the Il Chamus since the 1840s, and the Mursi since 1900 illustrate in differing ways, periods of ecological stress have been closely linked to the process of formation, fracture and reformation of political units in the region. The weakening or breaking up of rural networks brought about at such times as the 1890s disasters resulted in the transformation of identities, with some communities being broken up and reformed and new identities emerging. The same process can be seen to operate in parts of Ethiopia and the Sudan in the wake of the 1980s famine. But the reformation of communities happens not only as a result of a major catastrophe. As Johnson describes in his chapter, Nuer and Dinka groups have merged or differentiated from each other to a very large degree because of the pattern of sustained flooding in their region over the last century and a half. Turton, in his chapter, suggests that Mursi identity is also changing as a result of their progressive occupation of new territories during the last ninety years. Identity in northeast Africa has much to do with understanding periods of expansion and contraction of groups, of states, and this in turn is closely related to the patterns of ecological change. With this in mind, we can move on to consider the ways in which awareness of the relationship of ecology and society in northeast Africa can be used to reinterpret the history of the region. ...

Ecological stresses are nothing new in northeast Africa, and the rural communities of the region have long experience of coping with the consequences. The case studies that make up the chapters of this book cannot provide an exhaustive picture of the evolving relationship of ecology and society, but the sample that is offered does present a coherent, and linked, picture of the response of societies to ecological change over time.

Relatively few studies have previously explored the relationship between society, ecology and history in northeast Africa, or over the continent more widely. ... . In many earlier studies the construction of extended chronologies of ecological stress have taken precedence over the historical analysis of processes of adaptation, and responses to ecological change have been studied primarily through documentary sources. Here both the data and the perspective of field observations intrude more forcibly, making an important departure from earlier work. A more comprehensive picture of ecological change in northeast Africa can emerge only if there is a sustained interest in both field work and historical reconstruction. All of the contributors to this volume have been forced, by the very nature of their field experiences, to recognize the importance of ecological change in their own areas of study. Working anywhere in the field in northeast Africa from the 1960s to the 1980s, whether as an anthropologist, archaeologist, or historian, has been a sobering experience. Yet, reconstructing the responses to past ecological stress has also been enlightening, revealing as it frequently has a sustained endurance and resilience among societies classified as engaged in "subsistence economies."

We began this introduction with an explicit rejection of the limitations which "crisis management" imposes upon understanding the recent experiences of rural northeast Africa. The thrust of the chapters which follow, therefore, is explanatory rather than prescriptive. We need informed and well-researched explanations, based on a good knowledge of the social and economic dynamics of the societies of the region, before we can arrive at useful and lastingly effective prescriptions. In the wake of the 1980s famine "crisis management" has encouraged the quest for "Quick Fixes"—immediate remedies to alleviate the ills of rural life. Based upon a superficial analysis of the present "crisis," and in ignorance of the complex set of responses societies have been able to invoke in past periods of ecological stress, we think it unlikely that such prescriptions will be effective. But the greater danger is that "crisis management" will itself further erode the capacity of the societies of northeast Africa to rebuild their own strategies of survival.

Indigenous survival strategies are the cement of rural life. Their failure or collapse in the 1980s does not imply that they are inappropriate, or that something better can be speedily thrown up in the name of aid or development, but rather tells us something about the extent and degree of the mounting crisis in the region over the past two decades. The historical experience of the more distant past illustrates the ways in which disasters of similar magnitude have resulted in the subsequent reconstitution of rural life, new networks being gradually constructed to replace those shattered by drought, famine or epidemic. Events of this scale are rare; the links which bind rural communities together remain an essential element in survival during frequent, but less acute, periods of ecological stress. The means of survival are the concern of the following chapters. It is our hope that their example may stimulate more systematic studies of the ecology of survival in northeast Africa.

Reversing the Spiral: The Population, Agriculture and Environment Nexus in Sub-Saharan Africa

KEVIN CLEAVER and GOTZ SCHREIBER[3]

Shifting or long-fallow cultivation and transhumant pastoralism have been appropriate under conditions of slow population growth, abundant land, limited capital, and limited technical know-how. The ecological and economic systems were in equilibrium. The key to maintaining this equilibrium was mobility. People shifted to a different location when soil fertility declined or forage was depleted. This allowed the fertility of the land to be reconstituted through natural vegetative growth and decay. For field cropping, this typically involved farming a piece of land for two to four years, then leaving it fallow for as long as fifteen to twenty-five years. Herders' mobility generally involved a greater geographic range, but a far shorter temporal cycle, dictated by the seasonal availability of water and forage.

As long as land was abundant, more land could be gradually brought into the farming cycle to accommodate the slowly growing populations. Where population density increased slowly, the traditional extensive agricultural production systems gradually evolved into more intensive, and eventually permanent, systems which included soil conservation, fertility management, various forms of agroforestry, and the integration of livestock into farming systems. This has happened, for instance, in the Eastern African highlands, in Rwanda, and in the more densely settled areas of northern Nigeria.

But in most of Sub-Saharan Africa the scope for further expansion of cropland has drastically narrowed. Large areas of forests, wetlands, river valley bottoms, and grassland savanna have already been converted to farmland. This can be seen particularly in most of West Africa and in traditional grazing areas of eastern and

3. Cleaver, Kevin and Schreiber, Gotz, *Reversing the Spiral: The Population, Agriculture and Environment Nexus in Sub-Saharan Africa.* (Washington, D.C.: The World Bank, 1994). Excerpts taken from pages 4-8 and 10-11.

Kevin Cleaver is Director of the World Bank's Technical Department. Among his many publications are *A Strategy to Develop Agriculture in Sub-Saharan Africa, A Focus for the World Bank,* and *Conservation of West and Central African Rainforests,* (Washington, D.C.: The World Bank, 1992.)

Gotz Schreiber is the Principal Economist in the World Bank's West Central Africa Department.

southern Africa. On average, per capita arable land actually cultivated declined from 0.5 ha per person in 1965 to slightly less than 0.3 ha per person in 1990. In many areas, rural people are increasingly compelled to remain on the same parcel of land, yet they continue to use their traditional production techniques. Soil fertility and structure deteriorate rapidly where fallow periods are too short and traditional cultivation methods continue to be used. As a result, crop yields decline and soils erode. In most areas, population growth has been so rapid that the reduction of arable land per farmer and the associated soil degradation have greatly outpaced the countervailing innovation and adjustment by farmers. When farming is no longer viable, people migrate to establish new farms on land previously not used for farming—in semiarid areas and in tropical forests where soil and climatic conditions are poorly suited to annual cropping. Migrants bring with them the knowledge of only those farming techniques they practiced in areas they left, and these are often detrimental to their new environment.

In some countries, land continues to be more abundant in relation to current population. But in some of these land-abundant countries, much of the land is under tropical forests which need to be preserved. In most of Africa, rapid population growth is pushing settlers to extend farming and grazing into areas that are agroecologically unsuited to these forms of land use.

One of the conditions that stimulated Asian farmers to adopt "green revolution" technology—the abundance of labor relative to cultivable land—is increasingly emerging in parts of [Sub-Saharan Africa]. . . . But institutions and individuals have not been able to adapt quickly enough in the face of very rapid population growth. Slow technological innovation because of ineffective agricultural research and extension systems is only part of the reason. The poor transport infrastructure throughout most of SSA severely blunts farmers' incentives to switch from subsistence to market production and from extensive to intensive farming. Inappropriate agricultural marketing and pricing as well as fiscal and exchange rate policies have reduced the profitability of market-oriented agriculture, prevented significant gains in agricultural productivity, and contributed to the persistence of rural poverty. Poorly conceived and implemented agricultural projects have not helped. The lack of agricultural intensification in most of Africa has meant that expanding rural populations must depend on increasing the cropped area, to the detriment in many cases of natural resource sustainability.

The widespread prevalence of gender-specific (gender-sequential and/or gender-segregated) roles and responsibilities in rural production systems may be a major factor contributing to agricultural stagnation and environmental degradation and even to the persistence of high fertility rates. In many areas, women have primary or sole responsibility for food crop production, and they usually manage separate fields for this purpose. Women also tend to have significant obligations concerning labor to be performed on men's fields and with postharvest processing activities.

Given women's triple roles—child bearing/rearing, family and household maintenance, and production/income-earning activities—the pressures on their time continue to intensify. With increasing deforestation, combined with growing populations requiring more fuelwood, fuelwood has become scarcer. Women must walk farther to fetch it—or reduce the number of hot meals prepared. Increasing populations put greater pressure on available water resources, while environmental degradation reduces the availability and accessibility of water. Women must walk farther to fetch water, and get their daughters to help them. Throughout much of rural Sub-Saharan Africa, women also are the primary means of porterage. In the absence of adequate rural transport infrastructure and of means of transport other than human porterage, women spend substantial time headloading not only water and fuelwood, but farm produce and other commodities to and from their homes.

As growing numbers of men leave the farms to work in towns and cities, women are increasingly taking on primary responsibility for farm operations—while their recourse to adult male labor is diminishing. About 70 percent of Congo's farms are today managed by women, for example, and in Ghana more farmers are women than men. Moreover, the expansion of higher-input cash cropping under male control tends to increase demands on female labor for traditional female activities such as weeding and harvesting. In Zambia, women in farm households headed by males contribute more hours daily than men to farm work (8.5 hours versus 7.4 hours) and nonagricultural tasks (5 hours versus 1.1 hours). At the same time, women are traditionally confronted with severe restrictions on access to land and capital. These restrictive attitudes persist and today are reflected in limited access to extension advice; to productive land; to institutional credit; and to improved production, processing, and transport technology. In Botswana, a 1984 study found women contributing almost 70 percent of the value of crop production, but receiving the benefit of less than 15 percent of national agricultural outlays. These constraints, combined with intensifying pressures on women's time, severely impede productivity improvements and intensification of women's farming operations. Most women farmers have little choice but to continue practicing traditional low-input, low-productivity farming which, with sharply shortened fallow periods, is neither environmentally sustainable nor viable in terms of longer-term agricultural productivity. The severe pressure on women's time also retards progress in cash crop production controlled by men that depends on significant female labor input at critical times.

The heavy pressure on women's time also has implications for infant and child welfare and, hence, infant and child mortality—with significant repercussions on fertility aspirations and attitudes toward family planning. More contentious is the hypothesis that the multiple work burdens and the heavy time pressure on women may be a contributing causal element behind the persistent high population fertility rates. Additional labor is often the only factor of production that women can easily add, or are able or even compelled to add, in order to meet their multiple and increasing production and household management responsibilities. The combination of traditional attitudes and constraints with greatly increasing workloads of women may thus be part of the explanation for the continuing extraordinarily high fertility rate in SSA, now about 6.5 children per woman on average (compared to less than 4 in other developing countries).

There are, of course, many other factors that contribute to these high fertility rates. Traditional attitudes that favor numerous offspring, particularly sons, play an important part. Polygamy and the widespread practice of women marrying considerably older men are both phenomena that tend to increase women's economic and social dependency on sons and, hence, their willingness to bear many children. High infant and child mortality rates, resulting, among other things, from poor nutrition and poor maternal and child health care, are potent inducements to maintaining high fertility rates. The relative importance of these and other factors has not been established, and may never be. Nevertheless, the severe and increasing pressure on women's time and the significant gender-based constraints faced by women in their pursuit of both traditional and nontraditional farming activities may be preventing the emergence of women's *demand* for fewer children and thereby contribute to the persistence of high fertility rates. . . .

Agricultural stagnation and environmental degradation probably inhibit the demographic transition because they retard economic development, which is the driving force behind this transition. The extraordinarily high fertility rates prevailing in Sub-Saharan Africa are the result of many factors. The fundamental problem is low *demand* for smaller families. In many societies, becoming a parent is a precondition for becoming a socially recognized adult. Fertility enhances female and male status, while infertility can result in severe anxiety and, particularly for women, can be socially and economically devastating. Such widespread phenomena as polygyny and women marrying considerably older men tend to increase women's eventual economic and social dependence on sons and hence their willingness to bear many children.

Infant and child nutrition and mortality are affected by the availability of safe potable water and by the number of nutritious and warm meals provided. Where environmental degradation reduces the availability and accessibility of water and fuelwood, there is a negative impact on infant and child mortality and hence a positive impact on parental demand for more children. Where girls are kept out of school to help with domestic tasks, including water and fuelwood fetching, there are strong negative repercussions for their fertility preferences and their ability to make knowledgeable decisions about family planning once they reach childbearing age.

The preference for many children is also linked to economic considerations. In many communal land tenure systems, the amount of land allotted for farming to a family by the community (through its head or its *chef de terre*) is a function of the family's ability to clear and cultivate land. With hired labor in most settings being rare (although labor pooling for certain tasks is not uncommon), it is family size or, more correctly, family labor that determines land allotment. This is also true in open-access systems where the size of holding equals land cleared and cultivated. This counteracts efforts to stimulate demand for fewer children. Moreover, as long as there is (or is perceived to be) as yet unfarmed and unclaimed land available, there is no incentive for individuals to manage their land more intensively or to limit their family size so they can bequeath a viable farm to their offspring.

Gender, Resources, Local Institutions: New Identities for Kenya's Rural Women

BARBARA THOMAS-SLATER and DIANNE ROCHELEAU[4]

Women's involvement in community organization and the changing relations of women to the state are central to this discussion, given the critical roles of women in agricultural processes, rural livelihood systems, and the management of natural resources. Research on gender in Africa has focused on a variety of issues, including the impact of colonialism on African women, women's roles in food production, changing land tenure patterns, the impact of colonial policies on women's rights to land, and the marginalizing impact of commercialization and commodity production on women. Scholars are also exploring the relationships between women and the new, independent African state, the institutional dimensions of male privilege, the impact of the state's extractive and distributive decisions on gender relations, and women's organizations.

The politics of community organization and state-society relations appear differently when viewed from a gender perspective. In general, women have a different relationship with and access to states than do men. Gender is important in state formation, political participation, and resource allocation. Parpart and Staudt suggest that "states are shaped by gender struggle; they carry distinctive gender ideologies through time which guide resource allocation decisions in ways that mold material realities."[5] Others suggest there is an emerging micro politics that relies on tempo-

4. Thomas-Slater, Barbara and Rocheleau, Dianne, "Gender, Resources, Local Institutions: New Identities for Kenya's Rural Women," in Barbara Thomas-Slater and Dianne Rocheleau (eds.), *Gender, Environment and Development in Kenya* (Boulder, CO: Lynne Rienner, 1995). Excerpts taken from pages 11-18.

Barbara Thomas-Slater is an Associate Professor in International Development at Clark University and the Director of the International Development Program. She is author of *Politics, Participation and Poverty: Development Through Self-Help in Kenya*. (Boulder, CO: Westview Press, 1985).

Dianne Rocheleau is an Assistant Professor of Geography in the Graduate School at Clark University. She is a member of the Board of the Land Tenure Center at the University of Wisconsin, Madison. She is the co-author of *Agroforestry in Dryland Kenya*. (Nairobi: International Council for Research in Agroforestry, 1988).

5. Parpart, Jane and Standt, Karen, *Women and State in Africa* (Boulder, CO: Lynne Rienner, 1989), p. 6.

rary and mobile coalitions to deal with specific struggles. Some explore the forms of everyday resistance, providing a gendered reinterpretation of Scott's "weapons of the weak."[6] One reinterpretation suggests that identities and interests are not "given and fixed" but are "forged through political struggle (in its extended sense) on multiple and intersecting sites." Furthermore, "gender is central to understanding the processes through which class identity is produced or undermined."[7]

Women in most African countries have virtually no formal power in state structures. In Kenya, there is no doubt that the state shapes and limits women's use of organizations and networks, even as it promotes and patronizes their formation. Women struggle to find ways to use this "space" to further their own objectives within or vis-a-vis state structures. They face numerous contradictions between what they need to survive and what is possible under current legal codes and traditional social structures. Given their primary and expanding responsibility for agricultural activities and resource management, Kenyan women are greatly—and often adversely—affected by these contradictions with limited (if any) legal control over resources.

Within the last several decades, enormous changes have taken place in many parts of Kenya primarily through the privatization of land. The results have been the transfer of virtually all common lands to state or private ownership; a widening rich-poor gap within communities; increasing male migration from many communities; and an increase in the numbers of women functioning as de facto heads of household. These phenomena have enormous implications for resource access, work loads, responsibilities, and levels of deprivation of the poorest households, particularly for the women in them. Such households have relied most heavily on access to common forests, rangelands, and water points for food, fuel, fodder, and water.

With the privatization and increasing subdivision of land, many women see the erosion of their resource base and face a challenge to their social networks, which historically have been tied to shared access to common property resources. Most have little knowledge of their legal rights to land and its use. Young women from poor households have little hope of obtaining land or of acquiring the skills that could give them good jobs. Many find their way to the plantation work force as a last resort.

For the last two decades, national and international environmental agencies addressing the problem of a diminishing natural resource base have sought to involve Kenyan women in a way that fits into their own agendas. The state has defined environmental priorities in rural areas in terms of protecting productive resources to serve urban and national interests. Soil and water conservation took precedence during the late 1970s and early 1980s, when the national government

---

6. Scott, James, *Weapons of the Weak: Everyday Forms of Peasant Resistance* (New Haven: Yale University Press, 1985).

7. Hart, Gillian, "Engendering Everyday Resistance: Gender, Patronage and Production Politics in Rural Malaysia," *Journal of Peasant Studies,* vol. 19, no. 1 (1991), p. 117.

was concerned about protecting hydroelectric dams from sedimentation and conserving soil and water for rural agricultural production. During the 1970s the energy crisis also loomed large in the eyes of national and international planners, and they identified fuelwood supply as a major national problem. Biodiversity and wildlife protection became increasingly important in the late 1980s and continue to command the attention of the state primarily because of the importance of tourism in the economy.

Government responses to each of these concerns relied heavily on the involvement of rural women, both individually and in groups. Women's groups throughout the country were mobilized to construct terraces, repair gullies, construct small dams, and rehabilitate denuded slopes and degraded grazing lands. In many areas soil conservation gave way to reforestation efforts, some geared toward fuelwood, fodder, and fruit on farms and others aimed at community woodlots and protected common areas. Women were also the targets of several energy conservation programs including alternative cookstove designs to reduce fuelwood consumption. Women's participation in reforestation and cookstove programs was mediated largely by national and international NGOs [Non-Government Organizations] linked to local and national women's groups on the one hand and to state agencies on the other.

Based on their own perception and prioritization of environmental issues in their home areas, rural women often placed clean water supply first and fuelwood access next, followed by substantial interest in tree planting for fruit, poles, fodder, and medicinal uses. Their efforts to construct terraces and water storage dams have contributed to soil conservation as well as to their own concerns about crop production and domestic water supply. In short, Kenyan women in agrarian landscapes have found common cause with some of the state's environmental priorities, although their own interpretations focus more directly on water and food supply, health, and access to fuelwood, fodder, and fiber at the household and community levels.

Evidence from the cases presented in this volume suggests that in the context of uneven power relations, men's and women's roles continue to be renegotiated, based on a logic of flexible complementarity with frequent instances of overlap and changing boundaries. Yet there is a growing disjuncture between the changing responsibilities and work load for women and their legal status. For example, in Mbusyani and Kathama (Machakos District), cultural, social, and economic practices are being adapted according to the reality of male out-migration and the exigencies that many households face, but the legal system, land tenure, and other regulations have not been modified accordingly. In particular, the woman's livelihood and that of her family depend on the land, yet insecure tenure and lack of rights and control characterize women's legal relationship to the land.

Although responsibilities for men and women are changing, it is evident that women continue to have primary responsibility for meeting the family's basic needs for food, water, and fuel. The husband's responsibility has been to generate sufficient income to pay for school fees and major capital expenditures. Increasingly, in the Machakos sublocations and in Gikarangu (Murang'a District), households are managed by women while their husbands are away working in other towns such as Nairobi or Machakos or perhaps seeking employment outside their communities. This puts and additional burden on the woman, who then has the entire responsibility of running a household on a daily basis.

Related to these changing land use patterns are resource issues linked to environmental problems of soil deterioration and deforestation. Women in many communities have to walk long distances in search of water during the dry season. In many part of Machakos, for example, the majority of households face water, vegetation, and fuelwood scarcity, while some households have water storage or delivery infrastructure and surplus fuelwood resources. Women and children may spend fifteen hours or more a week, depending on the season, on the two tasks of gathering fuel and obtaining water. No doubt it is because of such demands that poor women are increasingly aware of environmental issues and are willing to sacrifice time to protect their natural resources and, more broadly, the environment in which they live.

How do rural households and communities manage ecological change and, at times, crisis? What are their approaches for dealing with the breakdown of traditional systems or perhaps for transforming such systems? How can responses at the local level be made relevant to policymakers at district, national, and international levels? We can identify three basic household and community strategies.

The first involves redeployment of different members of the household. With increasing poverty, declining welfare, and inadequate productivity, many households respond by dividing up responsibilities in new ways. The objective is to diversify sources of income and, in particular, to seek nonfarm work. Usually, the husband leaves and the wife stays behind to manage the farm and the children. There has been an outpouring of men from the countryside seeking wage labor primarily in the cities. As Ngugi wa Thiong'o puts it, the able-bodied men have fled "in search of the golden fleece in cities of metallic promises and no hope."[8] In many parts of Kenya the number of woman-headed rural households is estimated at 27 percent; women-managed households (with migrant husbands) often account for another 47 percent. These figures are not uncommon for other parts of Africa as well. It is in fact commonplace for young men to be flooding into towns and cities seeking jobs. Older men may have spent a working life in the city, returning for visits several times a year; they retire back to the countryside when their days of employment are over. It is equally common for women to manage the farm and care for large families under difficult circumstances without a partner present.

A second strategy for coping with these challenges involves strengthening informal networks comprising kin, friends, and colleagues or patrons and clients. Informal networks are based on reciprocal exchange of goods, services, and information; there is no expectation of a direct return or other kinds of gifts. Rather, such recip-

---

8. Ngugwa, Thiong'o, *Devil on the Cross* (London: Heinemann, 1982), p. 49

rocal exchange is part of a relationship that maintains social ties and identity and provides security or support in times of need, as well as new opportunities and benefits. Households invest in the social relationships that provide them with access to resources—a form of investment as important as ones they might make in productive capacity. Thus, they put effort into maintaining certain entitlements by virtue of kinship, patron-client obligation, or communal loyalty. Economic incentives may be as important in strengthening these relationships as they are in increasing the productive capacity of resources. In fact, the reaction economic decline may be to diversity and build social networks as a form of safety net and flexible access to new resources. These resources may include fodder, fuelwood, food, water, building materials, and raw material for crafts, as well as economic resources such as informal credit.

Networks have become key elements in individual and household strategies for survival, accumulation, and mobility. For example, in many rural communities poor women are particularly dependent on access to the commons for fuelwood and other forest products. With a decline in common property resources and an increase in privatization, they have been among the first to suffer losses. In the face of this decline, networks and association are proving valuable instruments for providing poorer households with increased access to productive and exchange resources from private holdings of other members. In addition, networks may enable their constituents to address community problems on an ad hoc basis.

A third strategy involves membership in formal groups and organizations. This strategy differs in important ways from involvement in networks. Networks may solve individual problems, but organized solidarity—a group—is needed to bring about significant changes in any system. Associations may offer a means to deal formally with the political system because they have an explicit structure, sustained and visible membership for political leverage, and a clear purpose and mandate.

In many parts of Kenya, strong and viable women's associations have emerged from traditional group activity originally focused on sharing agricultural labor and helping one another meet critical domestic needs. Today, participation in these associations can be key household strategy for meeting the challenges of increased involvement in the market and a cash economy. The strategy can either diminish risk or create new opportunities for household members, especially women; it can help to meet goals for maintenance, accumulation, or mobility.

The specific purpose of such a strategy may be improved access to productive assets: land, labor, and capital. For example, women's groups often construct and repair cropland terraces, fences, and sometimes houses or storage structures. Such groups may also generate exchange opportunities (both market and nonmarket) involving cash, goods, services, information, and/or influence. Or, the strategy may be used to obtain access to common property, including resources such as water and communal grazing lands, or to institutions and services such as schools and health clinics. Households employ both informal networks and formal associations to enhance their access to productive resources and to exchange information, as well as to enjoy the benefits of common property or, alternatively, to share the use of private property.

Thus involvement in women's associations can be an important strategy to assist women and their households with access to land, water, cash, labor, and information, five resources on which most African farmers face critical constraints. Women may, in fact, use long-standing and time-honored ways of organizing the factors of production. Drawing on roots in traditional labor exchange mechanisms, both women and the state have formalized and expanded these relationships. For the Kenyan state, encouragement of rural women's groups has a twofold origin. The international women's movement, with its focus on development opportunities for poor rural women, has provided the rationale and impetus for various NGOs [Non-Government Organizations] and international aid agencies such as SIDA, the Swedish International Development Agency, to provide strong financial support for women's programs through women's groups since the mid-1970s. This effort has coincided very conveniently with both the Kenyatta and the Moi governments' wishes to conserve resources at the center, decentralize development efforts, and return to local communities the initiative for undertaking local development efforts in the spirit of *harambee*, or self-help. Furthermore, a patriarchal ideology has permitted a significant opportunity for administrative officers to control the collective labor of these groups for common purposes, such as building a school or repairing a road. Thus, in many corners of Kenya, the women's groups provide a pool of labor that can be called upon by local officials for public works.

Collective labor is undertaken by women's associations largely for two reasons: to generate income for the group members, both individually and collectively, and to provide needed labor inputs for their own farms at peak times in the agricultural cycle. They may cooperate as a work force seeking wage labor on neighboring farms and plantations. They may also contribute their labor to public works, such as feeder road construction or school repair upon request, as noted earlier.

In addition to provision of labor for each other and the community, women's associations may organize revolving credit schemes for generating cash income, rotating allocation of funds among members. They may establish mechanisms for providing and managing collective goods and services, such as water tanks and delivery systems, nursery schools, literacy lessons, maize mills, meeting halls, and shops. Some groups also provide a means for members to market agricultural produce and handicrafts under more favorable conditions than individual sales.

These groups are particularly useful to poor households and female-headed households. Akamba women, for example, whose husbands are often in Nairobi seeking work and whose forebears engaged in a complex and mobile system of survival under harsh ecological conditions, are organizing themselves to address different environmental problems and implement new resource management approaches. However, many women from the very poorest households, or those with very young children and no child care, may be unable to meet the attendance, contribution, and work requirements of groups and thus are excluded from their benefits.

Resources are at the heart of Africa's food production problems and ultimately need to be managed by local, small-scale, collaborative efforts linked to larger-scale planning and regulatory functions. For example, erosion control is labor intensive— planting trees, terracing hillsides, and damming gullies require a great deal of effort. Activities need to be organized not simply on one household's two or three hectares but across a hill or valley, perhaps throughout a catchment area. If the measures are to be effective, they cannot be done in isolation. There are economies of scale, and there must be a fit to the particular ecological setting.

These patterns of cooperation, reciprocity, and exchange include both informal networks and formal associations or organizations to which men and women belong to enhance access to resources, to public and private goods and services, and to centers of power and decisionmaking. Such patterns have implications not only for the access of individuals and households to resources but also for stratification patterns within communities. Formal and informal organizations may lead, in some instances, to increased equity or democratization and, in others, to increased social stratification. The consequences are significant for distinct groups of people based on differences in race, ethnicity, age, class, and, of course, gender.

Ultimately, resource issues must be considered in gender-based terms. Throughout most agrarian communities in Kenya, the women have primary responsibility for feeding the family, for carrying water, and for maintaining the homestead. In some areas they manage the farms whether men are present or not. The men are more free to move and to pursue other life options. They do not have the same stake in the viability of the rural community. Yet, women do not often perceive themselves as possessing an organizational capacity to demand accountability from political and administrative officials and from representatives, such as Members of Parliament, who should be responsive to local needs and priorities. They may have succeeded beyond expectation in managing soil or water on their farms as well as in gaining accountability within their groups. Rarely do they have formal institutional capacity to hold leaders at the sublocation, location, or district levels responsible for responding to sublocation needs. They do, however, engage in acts of resistance and mobilize their collective strength to exert influence on local and higher-level politicians through traditional and/or informal channels.

Thus, most women's organizations, strong though they may be in managing particular resources, are fledgling in terms of obtaining access to the national political system. The boundaries of traditional gender relations and public authority are blurred. Given male ascendance in state institutions, rarely do these groups see themselves as having a role in modifying the formal system of resource access and use to benefit the residents of the community. Rather, they focus on transforming daily practice and long-term process on the ground.

Nevertheless, activities that provide access to cash and to extra-household labor and that enable women to participate in collective labor and in decisions about support for community infrastructure inevitably affect a woman's position in terms of decisionmaking and resource allocation vis-a-vis other members of her household.

Over time, suggests Ghai, such activities lead to slow but profound changes in the social status and economic position of women. Such changes generated by involvement in women's associations, as well as the emergence of new roles for those associations, constitute part of a far-reaching reassertion and transformation of women's roles in rural Kenya and perhaps in other parts of Africa as well.

The Decline of African Agriculture: An Internalist Perspective

MICHAEL LOFCHIE[9]

The theoretical point of departure for an internally focused analysis of Africa's agricultural crisis is the proposition that African governments have intervened in rural markets in ways that pose fundamental disincentives to agricultural production. The most influential scholarship elaborating this position has been that of Robert Bates and Elliot Berg[10]. Bates presents a convincing argument that, since independence, African governments have adopted a set of economic policies that effectively reduce the economic incentives to agricultural producers by shifting the internal terms of trade against the countryside. The common denominator of these policies has been an attempt to use the agricultural sector as a source of economic resources to be dispensed elsewhere in the society. But the cumulative result of these policies has been a virtually pandemic pattern of agricultural stagnation as manifested in falling per capita food production and a steady loss in the continent's share of the world trade in exportable agricultural commodities.

The first question of importance in the internalist approach is precisely why such a large number of African governments have framed agricultural policies that have adverse effects on the most important sector of their national economies. The basic reasons are not difficult to identify. Agricultural policy in Africa is driven by three overriding imperatives: (a) the commitment to a radical expansion of public services; (b) the commitment to the promotion of an industrial sector; and (c) the need to respond to the political demands of powerful urban interest groups. With the advent of independence, African governments assumed a set of socioeconomic and political objectives that required vastly greater economic resources than had previ-

9. Lofchie, Michael, "The Decline of African Agriculture: An Internalist Perspective," in Glantz, Michael (ed.), *Drought and Hunger in Africa: Denying Famine a Future,* (Cambridge: Cambridge University Press, 1987). Excerpts taken from pages 90-93 and 95-100.

Michael Lofchie is a Professor of Political Science and former Director of the UCLA African Studies Center. He is the author of *Zanzibar: Background to Revolution.* (Princeton: Princeton University Press, 1965.); *The Policy Factor: Agricultural Performance in Kenya and Tanzania,* (Boulder, CO: Lynne Rienner, 1989), and the editor of *The State of the Nations: Constraints on Development in Independent Africa.* (Berkeley, University of California Press, 1971).

10. See "Suggested Readings" at the end of this Problem.

ously been available. All of these goals required a dramatic expansion of the financial resources of the state, and agriculture was clearly the only economic sector large enough to provide revenues for this expansion. During the generation that followed the end of colonial rule, agriculture came to be treated as an object of economic extraction, an almost infinitely elastic source of tax revenue for state expansion and finance capital for enormously expensive industrial projects.

Agricultural policy in independent Africa can be understood as an attempt to transfer economic resources from rural producers to the state, to be expended on such services as health, education and the expansion of rural infrastructure. Newly independent African governments have also considered themselves under a deep obligation to deal with urgent social problems such as urban unemployment. Though rarely articulating explicitly the principle of the state as employer of last resort, many African governments have in fact behaved as if this were an essential basis for ongoing political legitimacy. They have rapidly expanded their employment rolls to provide jobs in the public sector to persons who could not be absorbed elsewhere in the economic system. The result was a wholesale enlargement of the state bureaucracy and this expansion, like the proliferation of public services, required revenues that could only be provided by the agricultural sector.

A second broad imperative that underlay adverse governmental intervention in the agricultural sector had to do with the commitment to promote industrialization. Until the early 1970s, there was a strong consensus among development economists that the most expeditious means to achieve this goal was through the creation of industries based on the principle of import substitution. This strategy of industrial development seemed to offer a quick and efficient means not only of generating urban industrial employment but of conserving foreign exchange resources that were being spent to import light consumer goods. The only question for debate was where to obtain the capital with which to finance these new industries. The obvious answer was to obtain it from agriculture for, although some capital investment might be forthcoming from abroad, it was unlikely to be sufficient, and in any case many African political leaders harbored deep suspicions about multinational corporations and their investment activities in the Third World. Import substitution as an industrial strategy, then, required that agriculture be treated as a source of investment capital for the establishment of urban manufacturing, rather than as the object of policies designed to further its own development.

Of all the factors that have stimulated adverse governmental intervention in the agricultural sector, however, none is so important or powerful as the simple imperative of political survival. African governments are desperately concerned about the volatility of their urban constituencies. Keith Hart has stated this point bluntly with respect to western Africa:

> The short-term preoccupation of West Africa's rulers is with the immediate danger of an unsatisfied urban mob. Long-term planning for the countryside is entirely incompatible with the siege mentality of politi-

cians, soldiers and bureaucrats who are literally counting the days before they lose their power (and lives) in the face of growing anger . . . This anger means most in the major cities; it commands constant attention and the award of temporary palliatives, one after the other, all adding up to the relative impoverishment of farmers.[11]

Otherwise highly diversified and potentially antagonistic urban interest groups find common cause in the implementation of agricultural policies that reduce the incomes of rural producers. Wage earners, for example, benefit from cheap food but, since food is a wage good, industrialists as well have an interest in keeping the price of foodstuffs as low as possible. Governments also satisfy their own interests by cheapening the price of food, since they can stabilize the wage scales for lower-paid governmental officials. Political leaders, industrialists and workers alike benefit when the export sector of agriculture can be compelled to yield up abundant supplies of cheap capital for urban investment. Thus, suppression of the agricultural sector is a policy that unites the total ensemble of urban interests.

African governments have intervened in their agricultural sectors in a variety of ways. Of these, by far the most common is direct governmental regulation of producer prices. Bates (1981) presents a convincing argument that African governments, since independence, have employed their ability to establish monopolistic control of agricultural pricing to suppress the farmgate prices of agricultural commodities far below levels that would have prevailed if a free market in agricultural commodities had been allowed to operate. Surveying a range of producer prices for export crops, for example, Bates concluded that "in most instances, they (agricultural producers) received less than two-thirds of the potential sales realization, and in many cases they received less than one-half"[12]. . . .

The impact of currency overvaluation on agricultural exports has been disastrous, since the producer price of export crops is normally a direct function of the conversion rate between foreign and domestic currencies; the greater the overvaluation, the fewer units of local currency per unit sold realized by the agricultural producer. This problem may help explain the sever cash squeeze experience by many of Africa's export-oriented agricultural marketing boards. To the extent that their income in local currency is also a function of the conversion rate, they are penalized, as well, by a policy that overvalues that currency in relation to the foreign exchange their crops have generated. The general tendency, however, has been for the marketing parastatals [public enterprises formed to achieve economic goals of the state] to pass the systemic penalty on to the farmers by making either partial or late payments for their crops. African governments concerned about the political loyalties of parastatal personnel invariably make up for parastatal operating deficits

11. Hart, Keith, "The State in Agricultural Development," in *The Political Economy of West African Agriculture,* (Cambridge: Cambridge University Press, 1982).

12. Bates, Robert, Markets and States in *Tropical Africa: The Political Basis of Agricultural Policies,* (Los Angeles: University of California Press, 1981), p. 29.

through supplemental budgetary appropriations. The final result is that only the producers really suffer from the artificial exchange rate. Since their prices remain low and since governments rarely seem to feel that it would be as worthwhile to subsidize the growers as they do the parastatals, the net effect of overvaluation is an income transfer from rural farmers to the urban middle classes. . . .

The principal means that African governments have used for regulating and administering their agricultural sectors has been the creation of a system of official agricultural marketing boards. As parastatal corporations, these marketing boards are typically given a legalized monopoly over the acquisition, processing and vending of stipulated agricultural commodities. If a crop has been given over to the authority of an official marketing agency, it is generally illegal for a producer to sell more than a specified amount to any other agency or for a purchaser, whether individual or commercial, to obtain a supply from any other agency. In many cases, the agricultural marketing boards are also entrusted with the responsibility for carrying out a number of critically important service functions such as credit provision, the distribution of inputs and the conduct of research on improved methods of crop husbandry. The marketing board system was originated during the colonial era to conduct the international vending of export crops, but official marketing agencies are as common today in the field of domestic food production. Since it has become increasingly commonplace for African governments to establish an official marketing agency for any crop of economic significance, many African countries have as many as a dozen of these parastatal corporations operating in the rural sector.

Contemporary observers of African agriculture are almost unanimously of the opinion that the performance of the agricultural marketing boards has been abysmal and that they are among the major reasons for the continent's agricultural decline. They seem almost universally to be characterized by waste, inefficiency, mismanagement, and corruption. The list of documented administrative shortcomings of many agricultural marketing boards is so extensive that it is sometimes surprising that they function at all. Standards of accountability, for example, are woefully inadequate or nonexistent, with the result that it is often impossible to determine how much revenue is being expended for a particular purpose over a given period of time. Bribery of parastatal personnel is commonplace and since parastatals have an official economic monopoly enforced by the police powers of the state, they have an almost limitless opportunity to extort illicit payments from farmers under their jurisdiction. Parastatals are sometimes viewed by political leaders as instruments of patronage and, as a result, they have been subjected to gross overstaffing. The selection and promotion of key parastatal administrators is sometimes based on political criteria that have little to do with administrative performance. Although parastatal salary scales and fringe benefits are often extremely generous, sometimes exceeding those available in the governmental civil service by a wide margin, there are virtually no incentives for efficient performance or penalties for maladministration....

The policy of industrialization through import substitution has also had disastrous effects on the agricultural sector. The ongoing capital requirements of the new industries have proven to be so great that agriculture has been virtually starved of the capital necessary for its own modernization. In retrospect, it is surprising that so little attention was paid to the amount of hard currency that would be required to launch a series of consumer goods industries and to keep them supplied with up-to-date capital equipment, spare parts and imported raw materials. It may be useful to recall, however, that agricultural commodities had enjoyed an unprecedented price boom during the mid-1950s, following the Korean War and that, as a result, African countries came to independence with foreign exchange reserves that appeared to be fully adequate. Of the many constraints on an industrial strategy that were initially considered to be important, the most important seemed to revolve around the lack of skilled personnel and the absence or relative weakness of the entrepreneurial class. Very few developmental experts considered the foreign exchange constraint to be a major obstacle to successful industrialization, perhaps, in part, because import substitution was considered to be a method of conserving, not expending, foreign exchange.

The agricultural marketing boards dealing with export crops were the principal source of hard currency for financing Africa's new industries. Almost universally, African governments, hungry for the financial wherewithal to launch an industrial revolution, turned to the marketing board reserves as their principal source of investment capital. The operative idea was that the difference between the prices that the marketing boards paid their farmer clientele and the prices they received on world markets would be used as venture capital for the new industrial sector. This decision converted the marketing boards from rurally oriented institutions, whose principal mandate was the economic vitality of export-oriented agriculture, to a wholly new function as the financial launching pad for urban industrial development.

The siphoning off of marketing board reserves can be assigned a great deal of the blame for the steady deterioration of Africa's position as a leading exporter of agricultural commodities. As the capital needs of urban industries grew, producer prices for export crops had to be reduced to a lower and lower percentage of the world market price so as to replenish the marketing board reserves. The capital requirements of urban industries also reduced the capacity of the marketing boards to conduct their other assigned functions such as research and the provision of services. Within a few years, the marketing boards were converted from a position as ally of the rural producer to that of adversary, exploiting the productivity of export farmers but delivering little, if anything, in return.

Linking and Sinking:
Economic Externalities and the Persistence of Destitution and Famine in Africa

RANDALL BAKER[13]

The continent of Africa is trapped by its own history; a history largely shaped by external forces, some originating in the colonial period and some from the inertia which clothed the colonial model of relations in the guise of development once the colors on the flag had changed. That model has not served Africa well but most of Africa's external links were created and fashioned to serve *it*. This chapter examines the proposition that Africa may "develop" itself into its own destruction if external sources of capital and its trading partners do not accept the need for fundamental, systemic change *now*. . . .

It is becoming less and less useful to talk about the Developing World as a concept. Africa seems to stand more clearly apart each year in the World Bank Atlas of indicators. It remains a continent in which per capita food supply continues to decline, [the average African in 1981 had 10% less food than he/she had in 1971], in which dependence upon relief and food imports grows and becomes a regular and widespread feature of life, and where the future prospects for serious and sustainable growth along existing lines over the next decade look grim. Yet, in terms of natural resources . . . Africa has enough land for food self-sufficiency. Even with the assumption of low levels of inputs, the combined potential productivity of all 51 countries could feed nearly three times the people in need...The specific results for the continent as a whole, estimate average potential population supporting capacities of 0.39 persons per hectare [pph] with low levels of inputs, 1.51 pph with intermediate inputs and 4.46 pph with high levels of inputs. These potentials are respec-

13. Baker, Randall, "Linking and Sinking: Economic Externalities and the Persistence of Destitution Future in Africa," in Glantz, Michael (ed.), *Drought and Hunger in Africa: Denying Famine a Future,* (Cambridge: Cambridge University Press, 1987). Excerpts taken from pages 149-157.

Randall Baker is affiliated with the Institute of Public Administration in the School of Public and Environmental Affairs at Indiana University. He is the author of numerous works on the environment and history in Africa, including *Desertification; Cause and Control: A Study of the U.N. Plan of Action and Its Possible Application.* (Norwich, England: School of Development Studies, University of East Anglia, 1980.)

tively 2.7, 10.8 and 31.7 times higher than the average present population density of 0.14 pph.[14]

In trying to reconcile the above quotation with the realities of famine, it may be fair to say that the "development" effort on that continent has not been successful insofar as so many have been left at the bottom of the heap and as the model, in general, seems to have run out of steam. Change is urgently needed. It is relatively easy to ascribe these problems on a temporary basis to dramatic oil price rises, declining commodity prices, adverse shifts in the terms of trade, growing debt, recession in the industrial countries and the absence of any "green revolution" for the basic African staple crops. However, many of these factors—except the last—have been only marginally worse for Africa than for other parts of the world which have shown a better performance. Others point to the succession of natural calamities, principally the droughts, which struck Africa between 1968 and the present. There is little evidence, however, to suggest that the deepening crisis in Africa is a purely natural disaster, despite the unusual length of the drought in many places. The famine and the drought have served only to accentuate and dramatize a much broader and longer-term systemic malaise.

In this chapter, since the concern is with *famine* rather than *poverty per se*, we shall be concerned with the group at greatest risk and not just with those facing—albeit serious—deprivation. [One scholar] estimated the former group at around 15% of the total population and the latter at about 40%. Special problems arise when considering the role of external factors in relation to the 15% since they may well be, through the marginality of their land, their landlessness and/or their joblessness, outside some of the main avenues of development such as better international commodity prices. For these people there are basically only the following options:

- continued support from relief programs (institutionalized destitution);

- improving the traditional option (i.e. better strains of subsistence crops providing little "return" on investment in the conventional financial or economic sense);

- greater incorporation of these people into the commodity sector (through access to land, labor-intensive agricultural programs, and better external prospects for crops);

- diversification: job creation favoring the poorest 15% in new sectors of the economy (incorporating the freeing of world trade and resisting trends towards protectionism).

It is clear that each of these paths involves a strong and determined local policy backed by external understanding and support (e.g. research, more open trade environment, freeing up investment capital). In this effort the aid donors, the multilateral development banks, the International Monetary Fund and the UN agencies all

---

14. Higgins, G.M., et. al., "Africa's Agricultural Potential," in *Ceres* (September–October, 1981), p. 19.

have distinct but complementary roles to play.

To a great extent the problems in Africa derive from its basic models of African development which perpetuate policies from colonial times. This is not a polemic against colonialism, it is simply an acceptance of the realities of that period during which Africa was incorporated into a world system very rapidly, very thoroughly, very one-sidedly and very late. Furthermore, Africa was incorporated after an earlier period of slaving, which had all but beggared the pre-colonial African systems of production, society and exchange, and at a late stage in the development of the economies of those industrial nations which became the metropolitan powers (with the exception of the residual empires of Spain and Portugal). It is with this brief historical perspective that I would like to begin.

Africa is locked into an economic system that obliges it to produce goods it does not consume and to consume goods it does not produce. (*Wall Street Journal*, 28 April 1981)

For most of the time that Africa has been drawn into the world economy the relationship has been a troubled one. It is to some extent the legacy of that period of integration which laid the foundation for many of the problems that presently afflict the poor.

From the time the Portuguese expanded beyond the conquest of Ceuta at the end of the fourteenth century, the African continent went into trauma. Earlier systems of culture, production and exchange were exposed to the ravages of centuries of slave trading by Europeans, Arabs and other Africans. A precondition for such a trade is the stimulation and perpetuation of anarchy, rivalry and internecine strife. Whatever may have been the course of Africa's evolution, this intrusion held it in check.

By the time of the "Scramble" in the late nineteenth century, when the freebooters gave way to the administrators of the dependent territories, Africa already had a legacy of almost 250 years of total mayhem and heemorrhage. Those who came to Africa in the later phase may be characterized by certain qualities which have left their mark:

1. the missionaries who came to replace indigenous belief systems and cosmologies with the Christian ethic in one or other of its many guises;

2. the technologists and entrepreneurs who came to transform Africa into a producer of tradable goods with an infrastructure to market and export these commodities;

3. the administrators who sought ways, through taxation and commoditization, to ensure that the dependent territories "paid their way";

4. the anthropologists who seemed to have, for much of their time in Africa, a preoccupation with the bizarre, the ritual, the deviant and form rather than function.

All these people have something in common: they were either there to effect change according to the principles and ideals they brought with them rather than to understand anything they found, or if they did try, they focused in a descriptive fashion on the ways in which local people seemed to be outwardly different from "us." The approach was *unidirectional*, set upon change rather than on understanding.

To some extent this itself is understandable because the Africa they found had been ravaged and savaged and gave the outward appearance of unsophistication, chaos, and darkness. The fact that this was not an endemic African trait but something wished upon much of the continent by an earlier wave of slavers seems not to have received the attention that it should have. Here again, let us not dwell on the barrenness of "blame" for there is no value in that. Rather, let us try to understand the nature of the process of change and those (and their perceptions) who tried to effect the change.

Thus, there was little interest in ways the Africans had "traditionally" managed to provide a living from the natural environment either by adapting to it or adapting it to them. From the earliest times of systematic European intervention, the ideal was to teach the "dignity of labor" to a people who did not "need to work"; to give agriculture a commercial value and to incorporated Africa into the world system as it was then. Change, or "development," became firmly established as something which came from outside: outside ideas, outside technology, outside capital and (often) outside management and control. This was the reinforcement of the unidirectionalism which has so long dominated the concept of development in Africa.

There were several consequences of this process shaping external links which are briefly outlined here:

1. Change was something overwhelmingly purchased or otherwise derived from abroad in the form of advice, technology, capital, etc., for which you needed the proceeds of foreign-exchange-earning exports.

2. Little attempt was made to research the indigenous subsistence crops or production systems, as the former were not marketed internationally (particularly millet and sorghum) and the latter were considered to have no scientific basis.

3. The subsistence sector was largely left to its own devices and was actually encouraged to remain as it was because it subsidized the cost of labor to plantations, farms, mines, towns, etc. It was, however, subject to pressures from the increased demand for land to grow cash crops, the confinement of population in the "reserves" and the alienation of land for plantations.

4. A dual economy developed in which resources and attention were focused on the "modern" sector. This does not necessarily refer to plantations. Often in Africa the modern sector was simply the field of cotton or groundnuts that the farmer was required to graft onto the existing household garden. Thus, there was little substitution of cash crops for food crops, just an additional demand

on the farmer to increase his or her labor and demand for land.

5. Increasingly, the export-crop earnings became essential nationally to support the often urban-biased development efforts. This was a process which became increasingly important after independence, as public sector expenditure rose and interventionism became widespread. The realities of urban power were such that not only was a tax extracted from the countryside to pay for the towns, but cheap food prices became widely established in order to subsidize the cost of urban labor and urban living. This sent a message of disincentive to the rural population and agriculture has remained the poor relation of development policy ever since. The stagnation of the rural areas then led to increasing urban migration, the increasing threat of political disruption among the growing disaffected poor, and the consequent necessity to retain and even accentuate the policy of cheap food. Thus, at home the towns predominated in policy, though with little productive return; the external economy was seen as the engine of development which, in turn, favored the towns.

The neglect of the subsistence sector and the continued pressure to increase commercial production, accompanied by the growth in human population (among the highest in the developing world) have continued to subject the natural resource base to a process of accumulating pressure. It is doubtful whether the conventional wisdom regarding what has constituted "development" in Africa is going to ameliorate or reverse this pressure. As a consequence, more of the same will result in the periods of stress, acting upon an ever less resilient and overtaxed environment and society, that is, more extreme events and collapse at the margins. What is needed is a *break with history and a re-evaluation of the development process.* As it now stands, an increasing proportion of the really poor population is not only excluded from the development process but also faces the prospect of a growing threat to its survival. Some elements of society, of course, do well from the established model so it may not yield without a struggle. Plans to revitalize the established primary export base—or to diversify it—are not going to reach the potential famine victims, unless a deliberate decision is taken, and practical means are devised, to reach them.

Despite the fact that Africa has been the subject of many economic shocks and reversals over the past decade or so, one of the principal problems derives not from oil or terms of trade (both of which are not much worse for Africa than for elsewhere in the developing world) but from the seemingly structural decline in the volume of traditional primary exports. This is particularly critical for Africa, because 32 major primary exports—with minimal value-added—account for about 70% of Africa's non-fuel exports to the industrial nations, compared to about 35% for other developing countries. Nineteen African countries showed negative rates of export growth during the 1970-80 decade, and the continent's share of non-fuel trade from developing countries fell by more than half during that period. Growth in world trade in major African exports fell from 4.5% per annum in the 1960s to 1.5% in the 1970s, a trend which was then reinforced by the deepening recession in the developed world in the early 1980s. Minerals, on which some countries such as Zambia and Zaire place heavy reliance, declined by 7.1% per annum over the decade.

With the first oil price rises in 1973-74, there was a need in the short run to off-set the extra foreign-exchange demands placed on African nations suddenly faced with current account deficits (excluding grants) which averaged 9% of gross domestic product between 1973 and 1982. This is approximately twice the level of other oil-importing developing countries. Reserves were depleted but the African countries were able to borrow from the international money market with relative ease, because commercial lenders were awash with money and they tended to see the situation immediately after 1974 as temporary, to be offset later by general recovery. However, this was not the case and the second oil shock (1978-79) and the subsequent deepening recession in the industrial nations produced the now-familiar scenario of heavy debt burdens, diminishing foreign exchange earnings to pay the debt interest, a rising dollar, revaluing the debt almost daily, and a fall-off in official development assistance (ODA) which plays so major a part in public-sector capital-investment programs in Africa. Thus, the existing foreign-exchange earnings had to be increasingly redirected toward the payment of debt or the countries had to (a) borrow more or (b) attempt debt rescheduling.

Although Africa is not normally singled out as one of the big debtors, this gives a false impression of the seriousness of the situation. By the late 1970s, and particularly the early 1980s, ODA failed to keep pace with the cumulative effects of the oil price rises, the accumulating debt burden, and the impact of the recession. The importance of this is seen in the fact that in eastern Africa, ODA in 1980 represented 78% of the regional capital inflow and 70% of the region's public capital expenditure. However, since 1980 there has been, at this most critical time, no increase in ODA in real terms. Indeed, between 1980 and 1982, ODA fell from $2.6 billion to $1.7 billion overall. Whereas, at the beginning of the 1970-80 decade ODA covered the current account deficits of most African countries, by the end of the decade it covered less than half. In West Africa's Sahel region about 85% of public financing comes from ODA. This largely bilateral source is (at least in theory) of critical importance because much of it comes in the form of grants and should have a greater potential for use in such areas as improvement of subsistence conditions, sectoral restructuring, food-crop research, etc., where there is unlikely to be any immediate internal economic rate of return large enough to satisfy the commercial lenders and multilateral development banks.

Over the same period, the debt-service ratio (debts as a percentage of exports) of the African countries, which is one of their major links with the external world at the present time, doubled to 12.4% at the end of the 1970s and rose sharply again to 19.9% in 1983. Outstanding and disbursed debts for low-income Africa, taken as a percentage of the GNP (54.6%) are roughly double the percentage of the figure for all developing countries (and 7 times higher than the 8% figure for low-income Asia). As a percentage of exports, the value of debts for low-income Africa is twice that of the developing world and almost three times that of low-income Asia.

Furthermore, the projections show the figure of debts outstanding as a percentage of export value rising from the present (1984) figure of 278% to 328% under the World Bank's "Low" assumption (of global recovery) and only falling to 250% under the "High" assumption. The declining economic performance, existing debt burden and the nervous reaction to debt have generally drastically reduced the prospect of further commercial lending. As more and more foreign exchange has to be directed toward servicing debts, less and less (especially with the decline in real ODA) is available for investment at home to ward off the perils of the future. Unfortunately, also, some of the earlier debt was incurred for consumption of large, nonproductive public investments which generated little to no foreign exchange nor generated much in the way of an economic return. Compounding all this, of course, is the fact that the declining export situation produces a declining domestic savings situation, further reducing the capacity of the home government to dig itself out of its difficulties (domestic savings halved over the 1970-80 decade). This did little to help overcome the shocks that oil prices superimposed on declining export volumes, a 2.7% average annual decline in the purchasing power of exports and a rate of growth of GDP which fell steadily from 1973 through 1983.

The West African Sahel: Human Agency and Environmental Change

JEFFREY GRITZNER[15]

Advanced firearms first entered the Sahel in connection with the slave trade. European traders commonly provided their Moorish associates with guns in payment for slaves. During a visit to West Africa around 1460, the Portuguese traveller Diogo Gomes reported " . . . that there were caravels there which carried arms and swords to the Moors" in exchange for slaves. Writing in the 1790s, Mungo Park notes that the Moors obtained "their fire-arms and ammunition . . . from the Europeans, in exchange for the Negro slaves which they obtain in their predatory excursions. Their chief commerce of this kind is with the French traders, on the Senegal river." James Riley, writing in 1816, recalled that "most of the Arabs are well armed with good double-barrelled French fowling pieces." By 1882, the Mandinka leader Samori Ture had obtained 4000 repeating rifles from the British in Sierra Leone in order to check the French advance into the upper Niger region. By 1892, his forces possessed 8000 such rifles.

Many medieval and modern authors have described the abundant wildlife of the Sahel. The literature of Sahelian peoples, such as Moors and the Kel Tamacheq, frequently refer to camels, wildlife, and hunting but reflect virtually no interest in cattle, sheep, or goats. An appreciation of bush meat is revealed in the commercial importance of *tishtar*, jerked antelope flesh, in Mauritania. Similarly, as recently as the late 1950s, wildfowl and game animals contributed more to the diet of the peoples of the Senegal River Valley than did beef.

Given the appreciation of Sahelian populations for bush meat, it is not surprising that the introduction of improved firearms would result in a dramatic increase in hunting. Indeed, travellers' reports indicate that wildlife populations have declined steadily since the sixteenth century, and Bigourdan and Prunier indicate that the

15. Gritzner, Jeffrey, *The West African Sahel: Human Agency and Environmental Change*, Geography Research Paper, no. 226, (Chicago: University of Chicago Press, 1988). Excerpts taken from pages 64-66, 72-74 and 107-109.

Jeffrey Gritzner is affiliated with the World Resources Institute and has been engaged in travel, research and commercial activity in Africa since the 1960s. He is the author of numerous articles on the ecology and the environment in Africa. He is also the author of *Environmental Degradation in Mauritania*. (Washington, D.C.: National Academy Press, 1981).

addax and oryx populations of the Mauritanian Sahel were already threatened by extinction before the conclusion of the French pacification of the region in the 1930s.

The destruction of wildlife populations in the Sahel has greatly aggravated the problem of devegetation in the region. Birds and browsing herbivores formerly played important roles in the growth stimulation response and seed dispersal of Sahelian trees and shrubs, prominently including large-seeded legumes. . . . The resultant modification of habitat has eliminated additional wildlife species and has also reduced the quantities of seed available for dispersal.

Finally, changes have taken place in herding with the virtual eradication of wild carnivores in the pastoral zone. In the past, young herders were instructed to avoid forests and thickets in order to maintain herd control and avoid livestock losses to predators. The fear of such losses passed with the elimination of the large carnivores, and herds are now permitted to enter wooded areas. The extension of herding into these areas has resulted in the widespread removal of protective understory and seedlings. In consequence, wildlife habitat has been further decreased, precipitation interception and groundwater recharge have been reduced, many wild plants and animals used by rural populations during periods of famine have been eliminated, and critical ecological processes have been seriously disrupted. Reduced carnivore populations also resulted in an explosive increase in rodents and other small mammals, with correspondingly increased pressure upon crops and natural systems.

Wildlife losses are also significant because the potential standing biomass of wildlife populations is much greater than that of livestock populations living under similar conditions. For example, studies undertaken elsewhere in the drylands of Africa indicate that acacia savannah carrying 19.6 to 28.0 kilograms of domesticated cattle per hectare could carry from 65.5 to 157.6 kilograms of wild ungulates per hectare. In contrast to domesticated livestock, wild animals occupy distinct and usually complementary ecological niches. Further, many forms of wildlife eat vegetation that is too coarse for most livestock, wild animals use water more efficiently, and they are more tolerant of stress and disease. Hence, the wildlife of the Sahel could serve as important alternative sources of food during periods of scarcity.

In addition to the devastating impact of advanced firearms, Sahelian wildlife populations have been further reduced through direct competition with livestock and habitat modification associated with agricultural expansion. . . . It is a common assumption that the Sahel is a natural pastureland for cattle and that domesticated cattle have long sustained the populations of that region. This impression is often reinforced by the depiction of cattle in the rupestral art of the neighboring Saharan highlands.

It is true that cattle have long been associated with the Sahara and the Sahel. Wild cattle . . . were prominent among the animals that sustained the ancient hunting populations of these regions. The archaeological record suggests that the concept of domestication entered the area from the north around 6000 B.P. and that the concept was evidently accepted and applied by populations of fisherfolk associated with the many lakes that existed in the central and southern Sahara at that time. The so-called Tenerian groups identified from the excavations at Adrar Bous, Niger, would be representative of these early pastoralists. The expansion of the cattle complex into the Sahel proper was apparently a direct result of the degradation and eventual desiccation of the Sahara region.

The desiccation of the Sahara had an important impact upon cattle because their water requirements are considerable. For example, they require four times as much water, at more frequent intervals, as camels under the same conditions. Also, unlike other animals in which the volume of urine is decreased and its concentration increased with higher temperatures, the increased intake of water by cattle results in decreased concentration and increased water loss through urination. Hence, the intake of water is greater than that required simply to compensate for increased losses. It appears that cattle drink not only to avoid dehydration but to cool the body with substantial quantities of water.

Declining precipitation, a possible shift from a bimodal rainy season to a single-cycle season, the effects of bush fires, deforestation, a reduction in groundwater recharge, and the growing impact of domesticated livestock eventually rendered the Sahel unsuitable for cattle. In response, the prehistoric cattle complexes of the Sahel gravitated southward into the savannah zone, where they are represented by such modern peoples as the cattle-holding Soninke.

The earliest historical records that describe the livestock inventories of Sahelian populations are those of medieval authors such as al-Ya'qubi and al-Muhallabi. These authors describe the Sahel as a region dominated by camel nomadism, and by peoples whose attachment to the camel carried almost religious overtones.

A brief reintroduction of cattle into the Sahel occurred when, in 990 A.D., the Soninke-dominated empire of Gana (transcribed in Arabic as Ghana) expanded into the Sahel to assure their control over the trans-Saharan trade. Al-Bakri, writing early in the eleventh century, describes the dependence of the Soninke cattle upon the wells that had been excavated during the mid-eighth century to support the trans-Saharan trade. His descriptions of the impoverished vegetation around wells and villages contrast vividly with those of al-Muhallabi written in the tenth century, before the expansion of Gana. By 1055, Gana was forced to withdraw southward into the savannah zone, and descriptions of camel nomadism again dominated the writings of the medieval authors describing the Sahel.

Although the occasional presence of cattle in the western Sahel is documented in the fifteenth-century narratives of Ca'da Mosto and later authors, they are few in number and are largely associated with oasis-based Soninke cultivators. The absence of cattle reflected not only the limited carrying capacity of the region for cattle, but also the vulnerability of the herds and herders to the incursions of raiding tribes. In the western Sahel, the problem of raiding was particularly severe following the arrival of the Banu Hilal from North Africa late in the thirteenth century. The problem persisted until the colonial "pacification" of the region early in the twentieth century.

It is possible that this relatively long period (the thirteenth through the nineteenth centuries) of political instability in the Sahel permitted a measure of ecological recovery. For example, an account of an expedition by Sultan Saboun against the state of Bagirmi in central Chad early in the nineteenth century describes "...the unoccupied lands situated between the boundaries of the Waday and the Bagirmi [as] covered with mature forests and dense, thorny undergrowth which served as the refuge of lion, elephant, and rhinoceros." If a measure of recovery had occurred, it was short-lived.

The pacification of the Sahel permitted a northward expansion of agricultural populations early in the twentieth century. They took herds of cattle, goats, and sheep with them. The disenfranchised warrior classes were left with only herding and commerce as acceptable occupations, and economic considerations resulted in a rather abrupt numerical shift favoring cattle at the expense of camels, as the former were more marketable within the context of the new economic order. Furthermore, the French colonial policy of *association*—that is, working through traditional leaders—had strengthened the position of the religious leaders, the *marabouts*, at the expense of the warrior class, and the new wealth acquired by the *marabouts* was characteristically invested in herds of cattle.

Cattle dramatically increased in number following the pacification of the region. In addition to economic incentives, livestock maintenance and veterinary health programs were instituted throughout the Sahel. During much of the colonial period, rainfall levels were unusually high, and therefore, for planners and herders, perhaps deceptively high. According to Jean Gallais, the western Sahel as a whole had witnessed a five-fold increase in cattle during the twenty-five years preceding the 1968 drought.

The introduction of French public-domain law into the Sahel further complicated matters. In many instances, indigenous systems of resource management that were highly regulated and sustainable gave way to the open-access provisions of the colonial system. A prominent example of such indigenous systems was the *herima* system, a system of collective privatization based upon the Qur'an and the Hadith, which regulated animal husbandry and agriculture in the precolonial state of Masina. The transition to open access was accompanied by overexploitation and extensive environmental degradation. . . .

Palaeoenvironmental analysis of the Sahel indicates that the region has witnessed several major episodes of climatic change since the arrival of man around 600,000 B.P. The principal changes were associated with the global climatic fluctuations of the Quaternary period. During the late Pleistocene and the Holocene epochs, the region experienced short- and medium-term oscillations alternately trending toward drier or more humid conditions. Relatively rapid, highly variable climatic change has occurred within these more predictable oscillations. During the last 2,500 years, however, the climate of the region has been relatively constant. It is characterized by unevenly distributed precipitation and frequent drought.

Although the current climatic regime of the Sahel is strongly influenced by the seasonal migrations and interactions of continental tropical and maritime tropical air masses, there is growing evidence that changes of surface albedo and reduced evapotranspiration, both associated with devegetation, are instrumental in reducing precipitation within the region. Devegetation has also resulted in reduced precipitation interception, infiltration, and groundwater recharge; increased erosion; high amplitude soil temperature fluctuations and altered soil-water relationships disruptive of soil ecology; reduced soil fertility; reduced agricultural productivity; reduced livestock and wildlife carrying capacity; the breakdown of human coping strategies; and the reduced availability of economically important, or potentially important, forest products. Furthermore, in the drier areas of the Sahel, the growing absence of dependable in situ water supplies imposes severe economic constraints upon the exploitation of many otherwise accessible mineral deposits.

The evidence examined in this study strongly supports the thesis that human activity, rather than climatic deterioration, is the principal cause of environmental degradation in the Sahel. Environmentally destructive human activities explored in this essay include: (I) the use of fire, (ii) charcoal production in connection with the trans-Saharan trade, (iii) the destabilization of fossil dunes in relation to Arab and Berber settlement preferences, (iv) the widespread loss of *Acacia senegal* stands through the destructive exploitation of gum arabic, (v) extensive losses of wildlife precipitated by the introduction of advanced firearms, (vi) the expansion and transformation of Sahelian agricultural systems, (vii) the proliferation of cattle, (viii) the expansion of transportation networks, and (ix) urbanization.

Indigenous Sahelian social systems were intimately linked to their associated ecosystems through flows of energy, material, and information. Hence, it should not be surprising that, with very few exceptions, the impetus of environmentally destructive change was exogenous to Sahelian social systems: The trans-Saharan trade was largely controlled by commercial interests in Mediterranean North Africa. Many Arabs and Berbers immigrated into the Sahel with commercial and religious motives; some were refugees from areas better suited to their needs and adaptations. The high latitude Sahelian *Acacia senegal* forests were destroyed through intensive competition among the Spanish, Dutch, Portuguese, French, English, and others for gum arabic. Wildlife losses were abetted by the European practice of trading firearms for slaves. The expansion of rain-fed agriculture has reflected both natural population increase and growth acceleration in response to the widespread breakdown of restrictive sexual mores through induced social change. Agricultural change and large-scale irrigation projects were promoted by colonial administrators, often on the basis of inappropriate analogues and an inadequate understanding of environmental and socio-economic context. The proliferation of cattle in inappropriate areas of the Sahel occurred in response to a complex combination of interactive political and economic factors—the colonial pacification of raiding tribes and the acquisition of cattle by these tribes; the development of a market economy that selectively encouraged cattle husbandry; the establishment of veterinary services that reduced livestock losses to highly contagious diseases, such as rinderpest, contagious bovine pleuropneumonia, and anthrax; and the subversion of highly regulated indigenous land-use systems, such as the *herima* system of Masina, by the open-access provisions of French public-domain law. The establishment of modern transportation networks was similarly initiated by colonial administrators. Although many early travellers' accounts describe substantial centers of commerce and learning, such as Awdaghast and Jenne, urbanization is also largely a product of the colonial era.

Many of the activities and policies leading to environmental degradation in the Sahel were simply governed by economic or political expediency. Little effort was made to anticipate the environmental or socio-economic consequences of specific intervention. It is now clear, however, that the cumulative impact of these interventions has been devastating. For example, environmental degradation and destructive social change have progressively increased the vulnerability and powerlessness of rural populations, as traditional coping strategies can no longer be sustained. This, in turn, has imposed the practical necessity of adapting indigenous coping strategies to contemporary circumstances. Unfortunately, the economies and institutions of modern Sahelian states are based upon inappropriate western models and are, themselves, non-adaptive. Hence, the problems persist and intensify. . . .

Suggested Readings

Anderson, David, and Grove, R.H. (eds.), *Conservation in Africa: People, Politics, and Practice* (Cambridge: Cambridge University Press, 1987).

Bates, R., *Markets and States in Tropical Africa: The Political Basis of Agricultural Policies* (Los Angeles: UC Press, 1981).

Berg, E., *Accelerated Development in Sub-Saharan Africa: An Agenda for Action* (Washington, D.C.: World Bank, 1981).

Beach, D.N., *The Shona and Zimbabwe, 900–1850* (New York: Africana Publishing Co., 1980).

Burr, Millard, and Collins, Robert, *Requiem for the Sudan: War, Drought, and Disaster Relief on the Nile* (Boulder, CO: Westview Press, 1995).

Clark, J.D., and Brandt, S.A. (eds.), *From Hunters to Farmers: The Causes and Conse- quences of Food Production in Africa* (Berkeley: UC Press, 1984).

Conah, Graham, *African Civilizations: Precolonial Cities and States in Tropical Africa, An Archaeological Perspective* (Cambridge: Cambridge University Press, 1987).

Hancock, Graham, *Ethiopia: The Challenge of Hunger* (London: V. Gollancz, 1985).

Hyden, Gordon, *Beyond Ujamaa in Tanzania* (London: Heineman, 1980).

King, Preston, *An African Winter* (New York: Penguin Books, 1986).

Kjekshus, Helge, *Ecology, Control, and Economic Development in East African History: The Case of Tanganyika, 1850–1950* (Berkeley: UC Press, 1977).

Lofchie, Michael, "Political and Economic Origins of African Hunger," *Journal of Modern African Studies* (December, 1975): 551-68.

Moll, Eugene, *Dongas and Dogma: Assessing Apartheid's Ecological Impact* (Cape Town: University of Cape Town, 1991).

Munro-Hay, S.C., *Aksum: An African Civilization of Late Antiquity* (Edinburgh: Edin- burgh University Press, 1991).

Nicholoson, Sharon, "The Methodology of Historical Climate Reconstruction and Its Application to Africa," *Journal of African History* 20:1 (1979): 31–49.

Odegi-Awuondo, Casper, *Life in the Balance: Ecological Sociology of Turkana Nomads* (Nairobi: African Centre for Technology Studies, 1990).

Owen, Denis Frank, *Man in Tropical Africa: The Environmental Predicament* (New York: Oxford University Press, 1973).

Rosenblum, Mort, *Squandering Eden: Africa at the Edge* (San Diego: Harcourt Brace Jovanovich, 1987).

Vail, L., "Ecology and History: The Example of Eastern Zambia," *Journal of Southern African Studies* 3:2 (1977): 122-55.

Webster, J.B. (ed.), *Chronology, Migration and Drought in Interlacustrine Africa* (London: Longman, 1979).

EPIDEMICS AND HEALTH CARE IN AFRICA: THE HUMAN AND FINANCIAL COSTS

Africa has been historically afflicted with epidemic diseases. Viruses happen to be non-racial although there are Africans who have lived for many millenia on the continent who have acquired some immunity. As for the Europeans, W.est Africa was known as "the White Man's Grave" where they died mostly of malaria. Nevertheless the Abolitionists, determined to end the trade in slaves and who were politically powerful, convinced a penurious British Government to authorize £100,000, a lot of money in those days of the mid-nineteenth century, to send an expedition in 1841 up the Niger River in the name of Commerce, Christianity, and Civilization. Superbly equipped with three steamers, the expedition sought to open the interior of Africa to "legitimate" trade thus negating the trade in slaves. The expedition was aborted when forty-five of the 150 British scholars and scientists died, almost certainly from malaria. This disaster was followed by the recommendation of a Select Committee of Parliament in 1863 that Britain withdraw its stations and the Royal Naval Squadron from West Africa because of the heavy loss of life. The Abolitionist constituency was sufficiently powerful to negate the recommendation, and Britian remained on the West Coast of Africa despite the losses from disease. There was, however, a dramatic advance in understanding tropical disease in the latter part of the nineteenth century, particularly the antidote to malaria, quinine, which enabled the Europeans to penetrate into the interior of the continent.

Although one can be critical of imperialism, it was the hard core of European medical practitioners who isolated the viruses, developed the vaccines, and mobilized the European administrators to carry out the requirements to contain the spread of epidemic disease. It is now a century and a half since the discovery of quinine and its more sophisticated successors to prohibit the enervating effects of malaria, not to mention other tropical diseases. As an example of imperial tropical medicine, the most powerful official in the Anglo-Egyptian Sudan was the Inspector of Drains who would fine the Governor-General, the Civil Secretary, and the British Chief of Police if they had standing water in their luxurious gardens where mosquitoes who carried the Malarial virus would proliferate. At the end of empire malaria in Khartoum had been extirpated and so had the Inspector of Drains. Malaria has now returned to the capital in epidemic proportions and elsewhere in Africa. That is the Problem.

Health care in Africa has reached crisis and controversy. What is, indeed, the role of medicine in Africa? Una Maclean argues that it is "preventive", rather than "clinical" medicine that can improve the health of the African people. Not surprisingly, most medical care as is understood in the West, is found where the doctors live, which is where the majority of Africans do not reside. Moreover, in many hospitals in Africa one does not go to be cured but to die. Life expectancy is so low because of the staggering rate of infant mortality. McLean argues that to revive the health of Africa in the future lies, not wlth expensive doctors in the cities, but with health care professionals outside.

In the second excerpt, Robert Stock and Charles Anyinam examine the variety of influences shaping the health care policies and delivery systems of African states. Stock and Anyinam argue that African health care systems evolved from complex interactions between colonial legacies, the political ideologies of independent govemments, and local, regional, and international economic forces. The authors discern three general health care models in Africa—colonial, basic health services, and primary health care—functioning simultaneously in all African states. Which model takes precedence depends, the authors maintain, upon the political ideology of particular states. Capitalist states tend to maintain the colonial, urban based curative systems, socialist states append basic and Primary Health Care services models to the existing colonial model, and Afro-Marxist regimes seek to restructure their health care systems entirely away from the colonial model. But goals have seldom been achieved and all African health delivery systems are hybrids with some operating more effectively than others. Thus, unlike McLean, Stock and Anyinam do not support any one solution to Africa's health care needs. However, in line with the Afro-Marxist perspective, they insist that no solutions exist apart from "fundamental political, social, and economic change."

If, as Stock and Anyinam contest, however, health care and economic and political development are intimately bound, given the economic constraints Africa faces, can African nations devise affordable, accessible health care systems? Are the three health care systems Stock and Anyinam identify mutually exclusive? Is one more appropriate to the African context than the others? Is there a single "African health care context"? What are the relationships between political ideologies and health care? What role does international aid play in African health care? What role should it play? These and other questions are present in virtually every country in the world despite their well-being. The problem in Africa is not that there is a pressing and poignant need to relieve suffering, that is obvious in the developed world as well as that known rather arrogantly as the Third; but the issue for the reader is the acute and widespread need for health care when the resources are limited to combat the manifold diseases that debilitate the African people. How best to utilize these scarce resources to rescue the most?

Godfrey Woelk writes with knowledge about Primary Health Care in Zimbabwe. Is Primary Health Care (PHC) going to survive? The issue is stark but simple. At the coming of independence in Zimbabwe there was a great and largely successful effort to extend health care to the African poor mostly in rural areas. This enterprise could not be sustained in a declining economy and spiraling inflation. Primary Health Care for mostly rural Africans was largely ignored by the new African elite and, of course, by the Europeans who were urged by the Zimbabwean Government to remain in the country for their skills were needed but so too were the privileges for health care that their financial position could afford. But the privileged, whether they be black or white, will obviously prevail to the detriment of thr Primary Health Care programs, which have a tendency to get lost in the African bureaucracy at Harare.

There is no more controversial health issue today than that of AIDS (Aquired Immune Deficiency Syndrome) because after two decades and billions of dollars the best and the brightest do not appear to have found a solution to this virulent and emotional problem. Brooke Schoepf addresses this critical Problem as it applies to Central Africa. Her research is focused on Zaire where AIDS has reached epidemic proportions. The public health services in Zaire have virtually disappeared with a devastating impact on those who are ill. Untreated STDS (Sexually Transmitted Diseases) have become common. Women bear the burden of the lack of health care complicated by sexual exploitation whether by partners or in the market place. The flight from the rural areas to the cities and the towns has accelerated the spread of sexually transmitted disease differentiated from the AIDS syndrome. This does not necessarily mean that Zairians are more promiscuous, but that they do not have the public health care to carry out preventive and curative medicine. Needless to say, there is widespread ignorance about how disease can so easily be transmitted by sexual intercourse.

Edward Green raises the question within the context of the AIDS and STDS epidemic in Africa of the relationship, on the one hand, between the Ministries of Health in the independent African states and the traditional healers, on the other. Here is the controversy or the Problem of African health care between the traditional healers and those trained in the medical practices of the West whether they be Africans or Europeans. The elite doctors resent the indigenous practitioners. On their part, the traditional healers appear to want to cooperate with their more scientific medicine men to change their image as "witchdoctors." African civil servants, the elites, were embarrassed by their more rustic and popular healers particularly when they had little use for African socialism and were conservative, steeped in the traditions, religion, and culture of their ethnic heritage. Foreigners clearly dismissed their curative powers. The Problem remains as the traditionalists (THs') and the modernists (TMs') compete not only for patients but for the best health care for the African people.

Medical Expertise and Africa
UNA MACLEAN[1]

At a time when many people in the Western world are questioning the costs and benefits of modern medicine, it is paradoxical that the colonization of Africa with expensive drugs and high technology treatments and the education of specialists should be on the increase. This article will consider some of the medical needs in tropical Africa and alternative ways in which experts could contribute to supplying them. . . .

[H.] Mahler, formerly Director General of the World Health Organization, has called for the demystification of medical technology. Throughout the whole world he has observed "a rising peak of expenditure directed towards the few . . . selected by medical technology" and has called for a major effort to be made, in every country, to describe all the health problems and the alternative approaches to dealing with them in an objective way.

Before leaving this introductory reference to the current heated debate over medicine's role in the developed countries, I would like to stress the point that much of the improvement in our general health and in survival prospects have arisen not from advances in clinical medicine but from the application of the principles of preventive medicine, allied to improvements in nutrition, hygiene and general living standards. It is also noteworthy that, even in the richest countries, paramedical workers of many different sorts and persuasions (health visitors, district nurses, community nurses, nurse practitioners, medical assistants, etc.) are being trained to take over part of what has traditionally been the exclusive preserve of doctors and that we are also witnessing an interesting growth of self-help groups among patients and their relatives.

Essentially it is the misguided use of medical knowledge and the maldistribution of resources which characterize the present situation in Africa. In spite of occasional official pronouncements in favour of preventive measures and some notable success stories for infectious disease eradication campaigns, the provision of care remains grossly unbalanced in most countries.

1. Maclean, Una, "Medical Expertise and Africa," *African Affairs* 78:312 (July 1979): Excerpts taken from pages 331, 332, 333, 334, 335, 336, 337.

Una Maclean taught at the University of Ibadan, and is a Senior Lecturer in the Department of Community Medicine at Edinburgh University. She has edited the journal *Medicine and Society* and is the author of *Magical Medicine: A Nigerian Case Study* (London and New York: Penguin Books, 1971) and *Nursing in Contemporary Society* (New York and London: Routledge and Kegan Paul, 1974).

The point has been put succinctly and strikingly by the pediatrician David Morley [in a November 6, 1976 article in *Lancet*]:

> Although three-quarters of the population in most developing countries live in rural areas, three-quarters of the spending on medical care is in urban areas, where three-quarters of the doctors live. Three-quarters of the deaths are caused by conditions that can be prevented at low cost but three-quarters of the medical budget is spent on curative services, many of them provided for the elite at high cost.

David Morley has gone on to call teaching hospitals in the developing world "disease palaces." They can absorb a quarter or a third of the total health budget of a country without training the appropriate personnel nor undertaking the type of research needed by the surrounding community.

The reason why life expectancy in most African countries is so low is because of the great loss of infant lives. "Over 40 per cent of all deaths in the developing countries occur among children under five years old, from a combination of malnutrition, parasitic infection, diarrhoeal disease and other supervening infections." The only rational approach to health requires environmental improvements allied to the education of local people so that they will alter behaviour patterns which perpetuate the cycles of disease transmission. Maternal and child health programmes with an emphasis on proper nutrition are central to the achievement of these aims. But attention has to be given simultaneously to altering both the macro- and the micro-environment. Pure water supplies, the elimination of places where infective disease agents live, the improvement in domestic sanitary behaviour and the enhancement of resistance to disease by the provision of immunization are all vital. ...

There are a multitude of intestinal infections whose spread is facilitated by contaminated water and food. For malnourished small children and infants whose condition is worsened by dehydration they are easily and rapidly fatal. The state of these children is sometimes unintentionally aggravated by the use of common traditional remedies with a purgative or emetic action.

The significance of widespread ineffective and parasitic diseases is not confined to their effect upon small children. The prevalence of numerous debilitating febrile illnesses, the scourge of blindness from onchocerciases, the anemia caused by hookworm, the crippling effects of tuberculosis all cause an inevitable reduction in the activities of adults. ... Although my review of health problems in Africa has been necessarily superficial and brief there is little dispute over the main issues. Communicable diseases, essentially preventable or at least containable, cause the loss of millions of child lives and at the same time reduce the efficiency and well being of countless adults. ...

So the community diagnoses in Africa are clear. What about the treatments which are currently being applied and what is the current role of experts operating on the patient?

Medical expertise can come in different forms. First, there are the health professionals and health workers of every kind who work directly with clinical problems. Under this heading must be included the manner and place of their training and the relationship of different workers with one another. This is the field of medical education and also the education of nurses, auxiliaries, medical assistants, what the Americans now call "physician extenders."

Then there is the contribution of Western expertise and aid to the solution of basic science aspects of medicine and their part in introducing sound treatments which require special experience in methodology or new techniques.

Thirdly, it is still possible for those who are skilled in operational research to make detailed assessments of health needs and to advise on the optimal utilization of such resources as are available. However, it is ultimately up to national politicians and medical administrators to set their own goals and priorities. Some deliberate decisions which affect health policies may be best taken at a supra-national level.

The application of rational planning to the design and operation of health services and the introduction of simple preventive measures for disease control is in practice regularly frustrated by the desire of African urban elites to secure for themselves and their families living standards and styles of medical treatment comparable to those in the Western world. . . .

Turning now to the training of health care professionals and others, there is no shortage of blueprints and medical expertise on the subject of medical education. For the foreseeable future, doctors, by far the most expensive and expert of the professionals, are bound to be in short supply. It therefore makes sense to use only a limited amount of the total capital available for medical education in training doctors and specialists and to put considerable thought and effort into the preparation of auxiliaries and the development of public health services.

The auxiliary may function either as an assistant to the professional or as a substitute. . . . His or her job is to provide primary medical care for the local community, where ninety per cent of the medical and health needs are to be found. . . . Only by teaching subordinate staff and delegating graded responsibilities can the pressing demands make by patients in African hospitals be met. . . .

There can be little doubt that, wherever we look in the world, many of the leading causes of illness and death are closely bound up with custom, culture and human behaviour. This is true in Africa whether it applies to traditional diets and the ways of disposing of excreta or to the disinclination of professionals, who have adopted western life styles, to leave the towns or to encourage legislation for systems of health care which would deny them what they regard as the natural rewards attaching to high status. . . .

In conclusion, medical experts in Africa still have a place, albeit a limited one; their major contribution should be with advice on the education of all those grades of people whose actual responsibility it will be to prevent illness and care for or cure established disease in their own countries.

National Governments and Health Service Policy in Africa

ROBERT STOCK and CHARLES ANYINAM[2]

Although health conditions in Africa have improved over the past few decades, they remain among the worst in the world. . . . Each of the more than fifty African states has devised a unique combination of policies designed to improve the health of its population. Health policies have varied significantly in terms of the percentage of budgetary resources allocated to health, the mix of private and public sector health care, the relative emphasis given to curative and preventative medicine, the types of health facilities constructed, the kinds of health workers trained, and the degree of integration of health with related developmental sectors. Moreover, health policies have changed over time in response to the changing nature of the state and the growth of our collective knowledge about potential models for improving health care and health. Three basic health policy models may be identified: a colonial model, a basic health services model, and a primary health care (PMC) model. These approaches have emerged sequentially, but have tended to be implemented as add-ons to the existing system. Thus, health systems in Africa are "hybrid" rather than "pure model" systems.

A variety of influences affect the shape of health policies and the ability of the state to effectively implement its vision for development. Health policies strongly reflect the priorities and the self-interest of the ruling classes and are significantly influenced by a self-interested medical establishment. Among other things, the successful implementation of policy depends on the administrative capacity of the state. The quantity and types of available resources which can be mobilized significantly affects the range of choices of health policy and the ability to implement them. The socio-cultural environment, the nature of the existing health care system, and external influences also have an impact on health policy choices. . . .

2. Stock, Robert; Anyinam, Charles, "National Governments and Health Service Policy in Africa," in Toyin Falola and Dennis Ityavyar, (eds.), *The Political Economy of Health In Africa*, (Athens, OH: Ohio University Center for International Studies, 1992): 217-46. Excerpts taken from pages 217-237, and 239.

Robert Stock is an independent medical geographer based in Canada whose particular research interests center on health and underdevelopment and Hausa traditional medicine.

Charles Anyinam, a medical geographer, holds a doctorate from Queen's University, Kingston, Canada, and serves as an assistant professor in the Department of Geography, Brock University, St. Catharines, Canada. His research has focused on traditional medicine in Ghana, and primary health care in the Third World.

The development of health policy is examined in three types of states, namely African capitalist, populist socialist, and Afro-Marxist . . . Although the correlation between political ideology and health policies is far from perfect, it is clear that particular types of states tend to adopt particular approaches to health policy. . . .

Health Policy Models

The Colonial Model. The colonial state had three priorities, namely, the maintenance of social control, the extraction of sufficient funds to cover administrative costs and ideally generate a surplus, and support for European businessmen engaged in trade and production. Colonial expenditure of health care, although severely constrained due to policies emphasizing self-sufficiency, contributed significantly to these objectives.

The first objective of colonial health care policy was to protect European health, Africa having become "the white man's grave." Hospitals were constructed in the major cities to provide health care first for European officials and later for non-official Europeans. Public health measures undertaken in urban areas, including the maintenance of an unsettled *cordon sanitaire* between European and non-European quarters, drainage improvements and vegetation clearance to reduce insect populations, and numerous edicts to regulate the movement and economic activities of Africans, protected Europeans from the perceived health threat of the African masses. Public health measure also served as means of social control; Africans were subject to intimidation and fines for alleged violation of these regulations.

Colonial health services also provided some rudimentary health care for Africans employed by the colonial state, in European companies, and by individual Europeans. Some basic health services, both curative an preventative were also provided in areas of economic development such as mining enclaves and export crop regions to ensure greater levels of labor productivity. However, there were also numerous examples, particularly in the early colonial period and from Portuguese, French, and Belgian colonies, of "development" policies which completely ignored the health of African workers and treated them as a literally disposable factors of production. . . .

Colonial health policy gave scant regard to the health needs of rural Africans in areas with low levels of export crop production. The scattered rural health care facilities were established by local government authorities and financed by tax levies or by missionaries who combined medical care and Christian prosetalization. At the end of the colonial era, most rural Africans had no effective access to Western health care. They continued to rely on traditional medicine which the colonial state either ignored or outlawed, in part because spiritual healers and healing cults could become foci for political protest. In summary, the colonial health system was fragmented in its structure, urban-biased, primarily curative rather [than] preventative and dedicated to serving the diverse needs of the European colonial rulers. The somewhat accelerated growth of health-related expenditure during the last few years of colonial rule brought no fundamental change to this entrenched model.

Following independence, African governments moved to increase the availability of health services primarily adhering to colonial practice. Because few indigenous physicians had been trained during the colonial era, there was a continuing reliance on expatriate doctors. Hence, the training of indigenous medical personnel assumed a high priority. National teaching hospitals were established in most countries for this purpose. Often established as foreign aid projects, these facilities were designed to reproduce the technical medicine of the industrialized countries, rather than to address as a primary concern the most urgent indigenous health problems. These "disease palace" teaching hospitals served to perpetuate the curative, urban, and hierarchical characteristics of colonial health care systems. They also severely distorted national budgets: J. F. Kennedy Hospital in Monrovia, for example takes some 45 percent of Liberia's expenditure on health care.

The Basic Health Services Model. After independence, many countries sought to expand health care services in both rural and urban areas by constructing additional clinics and hospitals. However, the scarcity of financial and personnel resources limited the ability of national government to respond to widespread agitation for improved health care. One response to these constraints was the development of a basic health services model. . . .

The basic health services model focused primarily on rural health care and gave increased emphasis to preventative medicine, to the role of paraprofessional health care workers, and to the integration of the health care service hierarchy. The basic service unit was the rural health center, commonly staffed by a team of paraprofessionals and without a physician. The delivery of curative and preventative medicine was to be integrated; preventative programs such as health education and maternal and child care were emphasized. With the catchment area of each rural health center, several health clinics would be established to deliver basic health care needs to local populations and facilitate the referral of more seriously ill patients to a rural health center. Mobile clinics would take health care to the people in more remote locations. This hierarchy of rural health facilities was designed to replace the simple bush dispensaries of colonial health care systems. The higher echelons of health care hierarchy, the regional and national hospitals where difficult cases could be referred for specialist treatment, remained essentially untouched....

The basic health services model represented a significant change in favor of rural health needs and health education. Nevertheless, it remained very much a delivery oriented model which focused on the role of professional and paraprofessional health personnel. There was no explicit role for traditional practitioners. Moreover, it did not explicitly address broader issues related to health development, such as the provision of safe water and the improvement of agricultural productivity.

Primary Health Care: Health by the People. Primary health care was to reflect the economic, sociocultural, and political characteristics of a community. Promotive, preventative, and rehabilitative care were to be emphasized, with priority being given to those in greater need. Health sector planning was to be integrated into the broader scheme of community and regional development along with agriculture, education, housing, water provision and other socio-economic sectors. Primary health care also stressed community and individual self reliance and

the full utilization of available resources. Community health services were to be delivered by health care workers locally selected and appropriately trained, ideally including traditional healers. This did not imply the creation of a separate health care system. It recognized the important supportive role of health care professionals working in higher order health facilities.

The primary health care model was revolutionary in concept. It redefined health and health policy; instead of viewing them as discrete entities, it incorporated everything impacting on individual and community well-being. It also emphasized local solutions using local resources, and therefore deemphasized the role of medical professionals in local health care. It acknowledged the importance of traditional practitioners. The stress on local control and decision making challenged the predominant top-down mechanisms of control, and pointed toward the development of a more egalitarian society.

Primary Health Care was not a new idea. Rather, it grew from the barefoot doctor model which had been so successful in China, and was subsequently introduced into Tanzania, Mozambique, and various other countries. It also reflected the growing preference of integrated development strategies which stressed the potential benefits of bottom-up, rural-based development in place of the dominant trickle-down approaches. The Primary Health Care model often was adopted for reasons other than a commitment to social justice. The emphasis on self-reliance—local communities were to pay the primary health care worker as well as part of the cost of drugs—falsely suggested that primary health care would be economical for the state, permitting an expansion of rural health care without taking resources from the conventional health care system.

Determinants of Health Policy

The Contemporary African State. Faced with immense demands for improved social services and with the weakness of the capitalist sector African states have had no option but to take the lead in the provision of health care. The state has assumed this dominant role irrespective of whether it has been capitalist, populist socialist, or Afro-Marxist in ideology. The formerly significant mission sector has declined in importance and in many countries has been absorbed into the state sector. The private health care sector has remained small and urban based, although it has recently been growing quickly in wealthier countries such as Nigeria and Kenya. . . .

Empirically the state is composed of the executive, legislative, and judicial levels of government, as well as regulatory bodies, parastatals, and other institutions, all of which enforce national sovereignty and carry out public policy. The ideological orientation of the state influences the matrix of socioeconomic polices which it adopts. Within any particular ideological reorientation, however, a very wide margin of difference arises from the skill, competence, and rationality with which a given strategy is pursued. The ideological framework is significantly shaped by the dominant classes reflecting their self interest. . . .

Theory and Practice: Further Constraints. The choices of African states concerning health care are constrained in relation to resources. Poverty is more pervasive in Africa than in any other continent, with the possible exception of Libya, no African country is prosperous by international standards. Nevertheless, there are significant differences in health between Africa's more prosperous states such a Nigeria and Ivory Coast, a middle group of comparatively poor nations such as Ghana and Senegal, and destitute countries such as Ethiopia and Burkina Faso.

Declining terms of trade for most African commodities and the onerous burden of international debt have meant that the resources available to most governments have declined significantly in real terms. Resources for health have been affected by the polices of the International Monetary Fund (IMF) which have stipulated that governments must severely curtail social service expenditures as a precondition for their support in debt rescheduling. A significant resource for health care development in some countries has come from foreign aid; in Botswana, for example 88 percent of development expenditures for health came from this source. The decline in resources for health care not only limits the possibility of expanded coverage and new program. Cutbacks have caused a shrinkage of existing health systems; some health facilities are without drugs and sometimes without staff.

The shortage of medical personnel of all types also constrains the expansion of health care systems. Educational systems have a limited capacity to train additional personnel, especially in smaller African countries with a small range of medical training facilities. The scarcity of financial and human resources are closely linked. In times of constraint, universities are unable to expand training programs and governments are unable to attract graduates into the state health care system. Instead, physicians emigrate or go into private practice to serve the rich.

Socio-cultural environments vary between and within particular countries, and may impinge upon the development of effective health care delivery systems. For example, the distribution of population constrains choice, particularly in low-density regions. The delivery of health care to nomadic populations has always posed special problems. African countries vary in terms of cultural homogeneity and harmony. To be effective, health programs need to be designed with sensitivity to the cultural milieu in which they are applied. In culturally diverse societies, care must be taken to adapt health care programs to particular ethnic cultural groups. Regional, ethnic, religious, and political-ideological conflicts have occurred, and continue to occur, in numerous African states. Such conflicts may have a profound impact on health; they disrupt economic activity, divert resources from social development to arms purchases, result in the destruction of health facilities, and force people to flee as refugees.

Any existing health care system exerts an active influence on the further development of the system. The existing system exists both as a set of resources and as a familiar model. In Africa the spatial distribution of health care systems remains highly uneven in terms of both space and social class. However, the possibilities for the significant restructuring of the system are limited because of the immobility of existing health care facilities and health-preserving infrastructure such as water supply systems. Other elements, for example human and financial resources, also are relatively immobile, largely because the ruling classes who benefit from the maldistribution of resources are reluctant to sacrifice in the interest of social justice. The medical establishment is a conservative force which resists any move to reduce its professional dominance. Individual physicians are usually reluctant to serve in rural areas.

The development of African health policies is profoundly affected by external influences as well as internal conditions. In recent years the World Health Organization has taken an active role in promoting innovative health polices, especially primary care. However, the options available to African states are constrained by conditions attached to foreign aid and IMF loan guarantees as well as the weak position of African exports in international commodity markets . . .

Health Care Policies in African States

African Capitalist States. The majority of African states have adopted a capitalist model of development, either explicitly or implicitly under the rubric of a mixed economy. African capitalist countries like Ivory Coast, Kenya, and Nigeria are characterized by open economics that are centered on the private sector, although state intervention is generally pervasive. The capitalist states have strong relationships with Western industrialized countries . . . African capitalist states permit very high returns to a relatively small segment of the population, in particular businessmen, top functionaries, ruling politicians, and expatriates. . . .

During the 1960s, theories of development and modernization emphasized macro scale economic growth rather than fulfillment of basic needs such as health services. For example, Nigeria's First National Development Plan (1962-1968) allocated only 2.5 percent of federal expenditures to health; actual expenditures on health were only 1.4 percent during the period. Much of the initial expenditure was on teaching hospitals to train physicians to improve access to health care. These facilities were incredibly expensive to construct and maintain, and contributed little to solving the fundamental health problems of the masses. The early emphasis on teaching hospitals reflected the influence of the medical establishment intent on maintaining their professional dominance, aid donors who saw teaching hospitals as a means of promoting future sales of medical technology, and the ruling classes who demanded international standards of health care for themselves and who viewed these hospitals as important symbols of natural progress.

In some countries, rural communities pressured national governments in the years after independence to improve basic services, including health care. These pressures were especially great in countries with electoral political systems. In parts of Nigeria and Kenya, community groups constructed clinics as self-help projects and then sought government help to staff them. The basic health services model was developed in Kenya during the 1960s as a response to popular agitation for better rural health care. . . .

Despite the increase in rural health care provision, the entrenched urban, regional, and class biases were not significantly altered. In Kano State, Nigeria, the doctor-population ratio was 1:286,000 outside the city of Kano, seven years after the launching of the Third National Development Plan. In Senegal, three quarters of the country's physicians and pharmacists serve Dakar which has only one-fifth of the national population . . .

While the basic health services model had stressed the importance of preventative programs, the reality was different. Staff were overburdened by the demand for curative health care. Commitment to prevention as a first priority remained soft at all levels of the system. It was only with the development of the basic needs approach and integrated rural development model during the late 1970s that greater attention was paid to preventative health care. The construction of water supply systems has taken precedence in many countries. More recently WHO's Expanded Programme for Immunization against the common childhood diseases has brought the first sustained commitment to preventative health care in most of rural Africa. Although the Primary Health Care model had been introduced in may capitalist African states during the past decade, development has seldom proceeded beyond the pilot project phase. There are no African capitalist states where this approach has had any real national impact. These failures reflect a lack of serious commitment to rural mobilization and rural transformation.

With the 1980s financial crises of increasing debt and stagnant revenues which have afflicted all of Africa, health care expenditures have been slashed. Several countries have introduced hospital user fees to generate revenue; such fees have created a significant barrier to health care for all but the rich. Austerity has led to the slashing of national drug purchases. The scarcity of drugs has virtually paralyzed the health care system in many rural areas and added to the cost of care for urban patients who purchased prescribed drugs. . . . Health polices in African capitalist states strongly reflect the self-interest of the urban-based ruling classes who have no interest in dismantling the inequitable health care systems from which they benefit. As for rural areas, they have been served last and least, and have suffered the greatest cutbacks in health services since the imposition of austerity measures.

Populist Socialist States. Populist socialist regimes are those which espouse socialist principles, but which either do not stress or explicitly reject Marxism. The doctrines of African socialism, as espoused by Nyerere in Tanzania, or by Kaunda in Zambia, were typical of the populist socialist pathway. Ghana under Nkrumah and Guinea under Toure provided the earliest models. These states tended to be nationalist, populist, and anti-capitalist. Development policies stressed the role of state enterprises and concentrated on rural reforms designed to achieve mass mobilization. However, despite the use of radical rhetoric, the populist socialist states are non-Marxist, both in terms of self-identification and development policies.

The populist socialist states have a mixed socio-economic development record. The Tanzanian economy, for instance, enjoyed some reasonable successes during the first decade of independence but was badly hit by excesses of the mass village campaign of the 1970s as well as by drought and by deteriorating terms of trade. Ghana under Nkrumah during the years 1981–1988 has a mediocre economic performance because state-run industrial projects intended as the driving force for development proved unsuccessful and socialist-inspired rural polices were unpopular.

Health services remained extremely poor at the time of independence, especially away from areas of economic development. In Zambia for example, health services were highly concentrated in the copper belt where mining companies had established health facilities for their workers, and in the restricted areas of substantial European settlement. There were also great disparities in Ghana and Tanzania between the health services in urban areas and other pockets of modern development and in the underdeveloped rural peripheries . . .

Charismatic leaders—Nkrumah in Ghana, Nyerere in Tanzania, and Kaunda in Zambia—played a crucial role in setting forth national agendas and mobilizing all segments of society to participate in the nation-building process. Their ideologies have been criticized as utopian, vague, and sometimes contradictory, but the far-reaching importance of their visions of independent African development cannot be denied.

Improved health care was an important element in their programs. Following independence, many new hospitals, health centers, and dispensaries were constructed, and many additional medical personnel of all types were trained. . . . Some aspects of their health polices were quite innovative. Nkrumah attempted to revive indigenous medicine by establishing a research institute to study herbal cures and supporting the establishment of a national association of healers. This official recognition of traditional medicine was a significant departure from colonial policy and occurred some fifteen years before international organizations such as WHO began to acknowledge the importance of traditional practitioners. . . .

Tanzania had moved to implement key elements of the Primary Health Care approach. . . . Scattered rural populations were resettle in villages where services such as health care could be provided more efficiently, and where rural people could be encouraged to actively participate in the development process. A program for training Primary Health Care workers, modeled on the Chinese barefoot doctor, was established. National health education programs...used media presentations and community discussion groups to improve awareness of health and stimulate self-reliant health projects such as latrine construction and mosquito control. . . . The relative success of primary health care in Tanzania compared to most countries may be attributed to the favorable political environment, namely the state's commitment to this approach, its implementation as part of a coherent policy of social and economic transformation, and its concern for popular involvement in development. The introduction of primary health care in Zambia, where the state has been much less resolutely committed to rural progress and popular leadership, has been less successful.

Despite a stated commitment in all three countries to a redistribution of health care resources from urban curative medicine to rural health, urban areas continue to receive most expenditures. Tanzania managed to reduce the proportion of the health budget for urban hospitals from 74 percent to 60 percent, and to increase funds for rural health care from 12 percent to 18.5 percent between 1970 and 1980. Nevertheless, this shift fell far short of the stated objective of radically redistributing resources in favor of rural needs. Apart from the reluctance of urban elites, including the medical establishment, to reallocate their own privileges, Tanzania also has been constrained in its planning by the large foreign aid component (80 percent of 1982-1983 budget expenditure) in the health sector and by the considerable influence which foreign donors exert over the allocation of these funds. . . .

The populist socialist states demonstrated a real commitment to improved health care. Health indicators demonstrate the benefits of innovative health policies. However, these gains are threatened by various factors including world commodity markets and international intervention in the planning process. . . .

Afro-Marxist States. Afro-Marxist states are those which maintain an explicitly commitment to Marxism-Leninism as the state ideology. Several such states— Mozambique, Angola, Guinea-Bissau, and Zimbabwe—were forged through a process of armed struggle against colonial regimes, guided by a revolutionary vanguard. . . .

Under this ideological paradigm, there is a consistent thrust to gain control of the "commanding heights" of the economy through state direction. Although these states make efforts to attract Western capital, they generally have extensive ties with communist states. Some of them have performed better economically than their predecessors, but, generally rapid economic growth has eluded them.

Long before their final victories in the anti-colonial armed struggle, the revolutionary Afro-Marxist movements had created distinctive and innovative health care systems. The African Independence Party of Guiné and Cape Verde (PAIGC) maintained a health care system in Guinea-Bissau which was as large as that of the colonial regime. In 1971, they operated a health care system in the liberated areas with over 500 health workers including 70 doctors and with 117 sanitation posts and 9 hospitals. Primary Health Care workers, trained to deliver basic health care at the community level, formed the backbone of the system. Mobile health brigades provided further support. Preventative medicine and health education received particular emphasis. . . . In the liberated areas of Mozambique, the Mozambique Front of Liberation (FRELIMO) maintained an equally developed health care system. . . .

With the collapse of the colonial regime and the nationalization of the health system after independence, five-sixths of the 550 physicians who had worked in colonial Mozambique left. A similar exodus occurred in Angola and Guinea-Bissau.

Doctors from Cuba, the Soviet Union, and other socialist countries were employed on an interim basis. The emphasis on Primary Health Care continued since independence. Mozambique trained some 4,500 paramedical workers between 1975 and 1982, enabling it to provide a spatial coverage of health care comparable to that of Kenya and other countries which had been independent for some time.

The new health care systems of Guinea-Bissau, Angola, and Mozambique were developed specifically in relations to ideas of class struggle. In Guineas-Bissau, urban-based bureaucrats were blamed for giving insufficient priority to rural development and spending half of the national health budget in the capital city. Doctors in Mozambique have been reluctant to work in rural areas, and to fully cooperate in the democratization of hospitals. While those committed to egalitarian development have been disturbed by the continuing urban bias in resource allocation, many physicians claim that resources cannot be reallocated to the countryside if urban hospitals are to function. The improvement of health services of Mozambique and Angola was hampered severely by insurgence fomented by South Africa, as well as by widespread drought and financial crises. In Mozambique, a large proportion of primary health care workers abandoned their posts, sometimes because their communities were too poor to pay them and sometimes because of the dangers posed by the liberation war. . . .

Conclusion

While all African states claim that the health of their citizens is an important priority, there are significant differences in performance. African capitalist states have tended to allocate comparatively small proportions of their budgets to health, and to spend most of their health allocation on urban, curative medicine. The pronounced class biases in access to health care are accentuated by the rapid growth in private sector health care. Populist socialist states have given priority to rural health care and have shown more openness toward non-technological medicine, particularly the Primary Health Care approach, and traditional medicine, than the capitalist states. While some progress was made toward a reallocation of resources toward rural needs and preventative care, urban curative medicine has continued to absorb a disproportionate share of resources. The revolutionary Afro-Marxist states have attempted to restructure their health systems within the larger context of social and economic transformation. While their achievements have been noteworthy, they have fallen far short of objectives. . . .

Since the health of Africans reflects so much more than health policy *per se*, it follows that more efficient management of scarce resources or the adoption of new strategies formulated elsewhere in the world are unlikely by themselves to have dramatic effects. The quest for health and the imperative of fundamental political, social, and economic change are inseparable.

Primary Health Care in Zimbabwe: Can It Survive?

GODFREY B. WOELK[3]

Primary health care (PHC) in Zimbabwe had been hailed as a particular success story. The transition from a situation of a curative, urban-based and minority focused health care system to one which emphasized health promotion and prevention and provided some acceptable level of health care to the majority rural population was in many ways swift and effective. It was a dramatic demonstration of the fruits of a democratic revolution which followed a long and bloody guerrilla war. The majority black population succeeded in wresting political power from the minority white population, and enthusiastically set about organizing services and systems more responsive to their needs and aspirations.

There were soon visible signs of the success of this approach in its effect on the health and access to health care of the population. Infant mortality fell from a rate of between 120–140 per 1000 live births in 1979, to 81 in 1988. . . . The percentage of the population with access to drinking water increased from about 26% at independence, to an average of 52% in 1987. A 1984 survey of 209 families indicated that 71% of mothers were delivering in health facilities, form the 32% in 1979. More than 7000 village health workers had been trained by 1987, from 2000 in 1983.

Yet towards the end of the decade, there appeared to be a tailing off of these achievements, and in some cases even a reversal of successes. Immunization rates, which overall had increased from 25% of children under the age of 1 year being fully immunized in 1982, to 67% in 1988, stagnated; 67% in 1989, and 65% for the third quarter of 1990.

Perinatal mortality showed little change, with 975 deaths reported at Harare Hospital, (one of the central hospitals in the country), in 1980 compared with 882 cases in 1987. . . . Malnutrition is still a leading cause of child death, being consistently among the top three. In 1989, it was in fact the leading cause of death among children between the ages of 1 and 5 years.

This has taken place against a background of a deteriorating economy. Prices

3. Woelk, Godfrey B., "Primary Health Care in Zimbabwe: Can It Survive?" in *Social Science & Medicine* 39:8 (1994): 1027–1035. Excerpts taken from pp. 1031–1033.
Godfrey Woelk is with the Department of Community Medicine at the University of Zimbabwe.

have escalated in recent years, and the average real formal sector earnings (excluding agriculture) of Z$2091 in 1987, were even less than Z$2213 recorded in 1979, and 75% of the 1982 peak of Z$2758. The situation has since worsened especially with the trade liberalization measures and structural adjustment programme, the most immediate effect of which has been a rapid increase in inflation. By the end of June 1991, inflation was estimated to be running at 24.6% per annum. . . .

Underlying the PHC approach in Zimbabwe is an emphasis on three basic ideas: improvement in health status is fundamentally dependent on improvement in socio-economic conditions; that mass participation was the key to over-turning these conditions; and that the health care system had to made to be responsive to the "mass needs of the people", through health activities at primary level. . . .

Thus at the base of the health service was the Village Health Worker (VHW), through whom democratization of the health system was to be attained. The VHWs were to be elected by the community and responsible to them. In addition, various health and development structures were created to facilitate community participation in the health and development systems. . . .

The Role of the State

The struggle against the white minority government had as a clarion call to arms the visible inequality between the majority black population, predominantly rural based, and the minority white ruling class concentrated in the urban areas.

For example, in 1980–81, the average annual per capita expenditure for a private medical aid society member (mostly white and urban) was Z$144, compared with Z$31 for the urban (black) population using the public services, and Z$4 for the majority black population. In the country's second city of Bulawayo, the black population of 410,000 in 1976, was served by a single general hospital, whilst the 69,000 whites had three general hospitals. In the same year, there was one government-provided hospital bed for 255 Europeans, compared to one for 1261 Africans.

The political settlement in 1979 signaled the end of the armed conflict, and with the election of the first recognized democratically elected majority government, the policy of reconciliation was enacted. Industry had to be kept turning, mines to produce minerals, and farms [to produce] agricultural produce to feed the nation. Expectations were high; they could only be met through rapid economic growth and reconstruction of war damaged infrastructure. This obviously could not be achieved through a routing of the white population. Moreover, the much needed aid for this reconstruction was conditional on the existing structural situation being left relatively intact.

Yet this policy of reconciliation contained the seeds that would in time severely inhibit the implementation of PHC. The economic and social structure remained largely intact. This meant the seduction of the party leadership...by these fruits of victory. After all the new leadership had more interests in common with those they replaced than the workers and peasants they were representing. The nutritional status of mothers and children, for example, is profoundly influenced by socio-economic factors. In Zimbabwe's case, these factors do not appear to have changed much, as evidenced by the proportion of low birth-weight babies and the continuing malnutrition problem. Another example is the continued existence of the private medical care sector.

The private sector has not been very easy to control because of its political influence. Reconciliation effectively allowed this to take place through the retention (through political necessity of the prevention of a rapid outflow of skills and needed personnel) of the prevailing institutional and infrastructural status quo. Added to this was the desire of the emerging black middle class to have access to a medical practitioner on demand and to what was perceived to be the best care available reserved only for whites.

This meant that there is in effect a practical recognition of a two-tier system of health care, individualized private medical care for the urban better off, and PHC for the rural and urban poor. Moreover, resources which could otherwise be utilized in the public sector are still diverted to private medical care. Under these circumstances, PHC is seen as inferior health care. This is to some extent related to the phenomenal growth of medical aid society members. The number of medical aid society members in 1990 was 525,139, more than double the 1980 figure of 219,424. (Despite this growth, less than 10% of the population are covered by this form of health insurance.) It is important to note that the private sector is now largely dominated by black providers and consumers and is an indication of rapid class formation and differentiation.

The other factor inhibiting PHC resulting is the centralization tendency. The governments immediately prior to independence and especially the Rhodesian Front governments, beginning in 1962, exhibited a strong tendency to centralize. . . . The incoming black majority government inherited this system and found that it was useful to maintain the controls over the population by the state apparatus that had been put into place by the previous governments. Initially, the centralization tendency was maintained to consolidate the ruling party's power; there was a need to have stability, nation building, reconstruction and reconciliation. More importantly perhaps, the party (at least the leadership) projected itself as the only vehicle through which the aspirations of the majority of the population could be achieved. As a result, development was a process in which government was seen as the main actor, and sometimes as the only actor. The concern with equity too, in a sense, paradoxically added to this process, as government in its attempt to redirect resources to where they were most needed, developed an increasingly large bureaucracy, reinforcing the centralization tendency. . . . Whilst it can be argued that a degree of centralization as necessary at the time of independence to maintain political stability, it soon became increasingly useful as a means for the new rulers to maintain power and privilege. . . .

The Health Workers

For many health workers the introduction of PHC in the context of the political changes at independence in 1980, was seen as a part of this process of the improvement of the status and situation for blacks. The policy of PHC focused attention on the rural areas where the majority of the (black) population lives, and even most urban blacks were supportive of this approach. This was counterbalanced by the expectations that the individual status and situation of black health workers would be markedly improved. However, with the continued existence of the private medical care system, juxtaposed to the public system, many doctors particularly have seen that the real road to their personal advancement lay in the private provision of personal curative care. This perception was especially important as it conflicted with the role of the doctor as the leader of the primary health care team. The doctor was supposed to provide the inspiration and motivation for the movement towards primary health care. . . .

PHC has also been effectively equated with considerable discomfort and hardship for the health workers implementing the policy, especially as PHC in Zimbabwe is very much a rural activity.

There is chronic shortage of accommodation throughout the country. Whereas it used to be worse in the major urban centres, the accommodation shortage now affects all areas, with the shortage perhaps more acute in the smaller towns and outlying areas. This shortage affects both the ability to post staff out in the rural areas and to retain staff already in place. Many health workers are living in overcrowded and difficult conditions. Shortage of accommodation is often cited as a major problem affecting the recruitment and retention of staff in the provinces and districts....

The shortage of transport has severely constrained operations in the provinces and districts, particularly for outreach work. Transport has been cited as the most important constraint to a number of programmes, including the maternal and child health programme, the expanded programme of immunization, the supplementary food production programme and the ability to effectively supervise activities.

Added to this is the chronic shortage of drugs and medicines. A maternal and child health survey carried out in 1988 found that 25% of health facilities never had salt and sugar (for the home-based management of acute mild diarrhoea) available, or it was out of stock. Also, co-trimoxazole, an antibiotic used in the treatment of acute respiratory infection, had been out of stock in 40% of health facilities in the past 6 months. In 1989, only about 56% of the country's drug needs were met.

The shortage of drugs and medicines is fundamentally a reflection of the inequity in the allocation of resources. A wide range of proprietary pharmaceuticals is available in the country, whose differences in effect are minimal. There is also a range of cosmetic and luxury products. Many health workers therefore, must experience a degree of frustration in being unable to carry out their duties properly.

New doctors find themselves rather isolated clinically. They often have to tackle tasks which they might be unsure of without sufficient clinical support. The support is constrained by the lack of transport and the overall shortage of consultants and of those willing and able to provide the necessary backing. . . .

The Population

For the majority of the population, the implementation of PHC had a significant impact. Access was considerably improved as over 300 health centres were built across the country, the Village Health Worker scheme was successfully introduced and highly appreciated, more out-reach activities were undertaken, more nursing staff were deployed into the rural areas. Various programmes were introduced such as the expanded programme on immunization, the control of diarrhoeal diseases programme, the maternal and child health programme and the rural water and sanitation programme.

However, this situation was implemented during a time of considerable political change, where nationalistic fervour and idealism provided the energy to build a *new* nation. Democracy had been the battle-cry during the long years of the liberation struggle, now was an opportunity to implement it. As the centralization tendency, (among other factors), began to be manifest, enthusiasm began to wane and the desire to fully participate in the new developmental structures was lessened. These structures were not effectively allowing for sufficient real decision-making....

As the village health workers programme was also implemented in a centralized manner, the communities perceived it to be a government programme. An evaluation of the programme in 1983 found that the communities felt the VHWs to be accountable more to the authorities rather than the community.

Moreover, government emphasized the fact that the rapid growth and development of the health service after independence was due to the political changes and its enlightened and progressive policies. Whilst this was obviously the case, the emphasis on the success of government provision, (for political credibility), has become contrary to the stated policy of community mobilization and self reliance. Many communities look to government for the provision of health care facilities. Thus PHC is perceived as health care provided by the government and not that which is primarily by and for the community.

The shortage of drugs and medicine has tended to undermine the PHC programme, as the programme loses credibility when patients attend a health centre and are told that there are no drugs, and if in an urban area are given a prescription to obtain the drugs from a pharmacy. This situation has generated considerable anger from the population, as PHC is seen as not being cost-effective. Also, with the cost-recovery policies and high inflation levels, clinic and hospital fees have soared, but there has not been any apparent improvement in the quality of care. . . .

In conclusion the implementation of PHC in Zimbabwe had been constrained by the tendencies of bureaucratization and centralization. There has been a *de facto* lack of support for PHC by government, and the very practice presents an inherent role conflict for the doctor as the PHC team leader. It can be argued that Zimbabwe has not really implemented PHC but instead has expanded basic health services, with a relatively small component of the Village Community Worker.

Women, AIDS, and Economic Crisis in Central Africa
BROOKE GRUNDFEST SCHOEPF[4]

AIDS has emerged and spread in Central Africa as a result of a set of historical-ly specific economic and social relations. Most areas of sub-Saharan Africa have experienced economic crisis, including declining per capita food production over the past decade. In some areas, male labor migration in search of wages which began in the colonial period has intensified.

Zaire's political economy is closely linked to mining and export of strategic min-erals including copper, cobalt and space-age metals. It was one of the first to be rocked by the shock waves of the world economics crisis beginning in 1973. One result of the capital intensive export-led growth strategy followed since the 1950s is a population surplus relative to the labor needs of capitalist agriculture and indus-try.

In Zaire, where per capita incomes are among the world's lowest, many of the poor live in absolute misery. In recent years, Zaire's transfers of foreign exchange to the West (for debt payments, etc.) have exceeded the inflow derived from export production and new loans. Unemployment has been exacerbated by economic stag-nation, hyperinflation, and the crisis of peasant agriculture.

As men become unemployed and hopeless, the entire family may suffer both from material want and psychological stress; marriage ties, already tenuous for many, may become more fragile. The economic crisis is expected to be experienced most severely by poor women and their children, who are most at risk of malnutri-tion and related diseases.

Predominant health problems include nutritional deficits, parasitic and infectious diseases, alcoholism, and conditions related to pregnancy, child-birth and childhood diarrheas. Health services in Zaire reflect their colonial past and contemporary socio-economic conditions. Chronically under-funded, public health expenditures have been reduced to two percent of the national budget, and only about half the allocation actually arrives at destination. While a national primary health care sys-

5. Schoepf, Brooke Grundfest, "Women, AIDS, and Economic Crisis in Central Africa," *Canadian Journal of African Studies* 22:3 (1988): 625-44. Excerpts taken from pp. 626-635, 640.

Brooke Grundfest Schoepf has been the Director of the CONNAISSIDA. This project conducts ethnographic field studies in Zaire. She has also written The *"wild," the "lazy" and the Matriarchal: Nutrition and Cultural Survival in the Zairian Copperbelt* (East Lansing: Michigan State Univerisity Press, 1985).

tem is being organized with foreign donor support, biomedical services of reasonable quality remain limited; their distribution is class and urban based. Among the rural and urban poor, malnutrition is common, and many diseases go untreated. Among women, the cumulative synergistic effects of malnutrition and disease are further complicated by the demands of frequent childbearing and constant physical labor. Untreated STDS are also relatively common in cities and in some rural areas. Many of these conditions compromise the immune system. Data to be presented below indicate that various forms of multiple partner relationships are proliferating in response to economic crisis. Together with the health problems, these factors may help to explain why AIDS has spread so rapidly in the region and why so many women are infected.

During the crisis period increasing numbers of young, overworked and underpaid rural women have sought escape in towns and cities. Sex ratios in most large cities of Zaire are nearly equal, but waged jobs are segregated by gender and educational attainment which is also gender stratified. Although sex discrimination in employment is illegal, the structure of employment opportunity, inherited from the colonial period when women were allocated the tasks of social reproduction, persists.

Outside of agriculture, where women find casual employment at extremely low pay, few waged jobs are available to women without secondary school diplomas. This situation is common throughout Central and East Africa.

Most women still shoulder traditional responsibilities for providing food and other household necessities. However, in both rural and urban areas, many now do so without traditional role complementarity provided by husbands and lineage members. Everywhere women engage in a variety of self-employed income-generating occupations such as food processing, petty trade, sewing, and market gardening. While some (generally those with family capital and connections) succeed, most remain impoverished. Successful women traders may exchange sex for permits and other resources to increase their profits. Even elite women may be required to provide sex as a condition of employment and promotion. Some poor women supplement inadequate incomes by providing occasional sexual services. Although the actual monetary value of such exchanges may be extremely low, they are needed to support poor households. . . .

Despite the high visibility of elite men among the AIDS patient population of Kinshasa, women now constitute the majority of cases and of seropositives. Together with children, they constitute the majority of those at risk. The more sexual partners a woman has, the greater the risk. In Kinshasa twenty-seven per cent of a sample of women soliciting in Matange bars were found to be seropositive in 1985 while forty percent of the first 516 women attending a neighborhood STD clinic in 198 were infected. Since most of these women probably will die of AIDS, what once appeared to be a survival strategy has been transformed into a death strategy. . . .

Nearly one-half the infants of seropositive women are infected, and many die painfully before reaching their second birthday. From six to twenty-two percent of women delivering in hospitals in Central African capitals were seropositive in 1986. Women who become pregnant while infected with HIV may increase their risk of developing fatal disease. Medical advisors recommend that seropositive women abstain from procreation. Even if serotesting were widely available and women were to be informed of their antibody status, this counsel would not be easily followed. Some women say that even if infected they would choose to bear the child on the chance that it might be healthy, in order to have descendants by whom they will be remembered after death. Moreover, a childless wife may be repudiated. . . .

As mothers, women are the major providers of first line health care. They care for chronically ill and dying patients sent home from hospital with advice " to arrange matters within the family." Mothers must be taught to handle body wastes safely. Midwives and birth attendants without formal biomedical training must be supplied with rubber gloves and taught to handle newborns, placenta, blood, and amniotic fluids following basic infection control guidelines. These are only some of the complex issues to consider when developing AIDS control policies. . . .

Zaire and Central Africa sometimes have been represented in the western press as centers where people are too fond of sex, too uneducated, too "primitive," too irrational to protect themselves from AIDS. It is important to emphasize that not everyone is in danger. Some women and men have followed Christian tenets to the letter, married without prior sexual experience, and remained faithful to their spouses. Some men are polygynous and do not seek women other than their wives. Researchers can offer no estimate of the proportion of the population at risk. They did not ask direct questions and might not have gotten truthful answers if they had. However, there is no evidence that central Africans are more "promiscuous" than other peoples. Moreover, even among the most sexually active, access to formally and informally transmitted information can lead to rational reflection and behavior changes. . . .

Since incurable diseases ultimately tend to be categorized as socially or supernaturally caused, people have an added incentive to push the fatal outcome of AIDS from their minds. The process of finding a sorcerer is well-known, unpleasant, and threatening to many. That ultimate causes are occult does not mean that people reject biological causality; even illiterate people can assimilate that information. However, when biomedicine fails, people want to know why a specific person was attacked by the little animal (*nyama munene*) as we have dubbed the virus. Among the many women who earn their livelihood by supplying services to multiple partners, information levels and risk reduction responses vary. The stylish professionals who solicit in the gambling casinos, night cludbs, and high-priced hotels of the city center are best informed, and many have changed their behavior. This is partly a consequence of an AIDS education meeting organized on their behalf by a vocational school director. Some women actually require clients to use condoms. . . . Others, their earning power less secure, propose condoms but will risk infection with non-compliant customers. . . .

Not all women with multiple partners consider themselves prostitutes. Some are mistresses (*bureaux*) regularly supported by married men of means, students, or independent working women who seek extra income when they visit nightclubs for an evening's entertainment. Although they expect to receive gratuities, these women reject the idea of using condoms, for it implies that they might harbor a STD, stigmatized by association with prostitution. . . . One [woman] described herself as the mistress...of a successful married man who pays her rent and other basic expenses. On nights when she expects him to be otherwise engaged, she seeks other partners. Asked if she would use a condom to prevent AIDS infection, she replied vehemently: "I am not sick! If I were my Bwana would know it and he would tell me. He wouldn't come back". . . .

The group most at risk are the low-income prostitutes...who work from rooms in the popular neighborhoods. They charge about US$.50 and report the greatest frequency of sexual encounters, averaging from five hundred to more than one thousand annually. They often suffer from untreated STDs. They are also the least informed about safer sex. . . . While some professionals express doubt about the feasibility of education and behavior change among this cohort, prostitutes in Nairobi are now reported using condoms as a result of education. In October 1987, when one network of Kinshasa sex workers learned that protection is possible, they decided to adopt condoms. In this case avoidance had been fueled by the mistaken belief that they could not do anything to prevent AIDS. . . .

Mass media campaigns have not informed the public about the slow action of the virus or the fact that those now getting sick with AIDS may have been infected for ten years or more. Failure to comprehend the lengthy incubation period contribute to confusion and blame-casting. Interviews conducted over a three-year period with a highly educated official offer a glimpse of the evolution of attitudes widely shared among men.

In 1985 the informant considered AIDS to be a construction by western propagandist seeking to discredit Africans. The imaginary syndrome he believed was intended not only to discourage African lovers but to discourage tourists and investors whose money is needed to redress Africa's economic crisis. . . . In 1986, when the death of some prominent people made it difficult to deny the existence of the disease, it was widely attributed to women's sexual congress with westerners. In 1987 the informant said that since he became aware of the AIDS danger, he limits his sexual relations to his three current wives. If he should find himself infected, he "knows" that it would be the result of their infidelity. He does not believe that he might have been infected by previous partners. Women are the major transmitters of AIDS "because they are more promiscuous than men, who if they desire a woman marry her." By 1988 his fear of AIDS increased to the point where he said that seropositive women should be quarantined. The prospect of interning thousands of women for may years did not give him pause. Nor did he acknowledge that infected men could continue to spread the virus. The identification of AIDS as a STD renders it likely the "promiscuous" women will be held responsible for its spread. . . .

Both elite and working class wives express powerlessness in the face of what they know, assume, or suspect to be their husbands' multiple partners. . . . A restaurant owner in her thirties, married, with a formal sector job, and four young children described the difficulties faced by women with AIDS:

> Society rejects you. When you die you will not even be missed because you have died of a shameful disease. They will say this woman has strayed. They will not see that maybe she has remained faithful while her husband has strayed. Given the status of women in most of our African societies AIDS is doubly stigmatizing for women. . . .

In cultures where a married woman's refusal of sexual services to her husband is grounds for divorce, abstinence is an option only for those who wish to end their marriages. The divorced state now is more precarious than ever, as is widowhood for women who do not have stable waged employment or successful enterprises. Wives cannot always act in their best interests. The parents of a man with AIDS prevailed upon his wife to continue sexual relations unprotected by condoms as a demonstration of her devotion. The wife became fatally ill following her husband's death. A physician who knew he had AIDS kept the knowledge from his wife and continued to have unprotected intercourse. She only learned the nature of his disease at his death. . . .

Paradoxically, risks for young women may be increasing as AIDS consciousness spreads. Some business men reported that they now seek very young partners whom they assume to be free of infection. Their cars can be seen parked at school-yard gates waiting for girls to emerge. Some male secondary school teachers stated that sex is one of the fringe benefits of a poorly paid profession. Since such men are likely to have had many partners in the past, they constitute a risk group. Pupils and students who thus seek to obtain money for school expenses and stylish clothes or to obtain good grades must be helped to understand the risk. At the same time, other means must be found to meet their need for cash. . . .

Unless biomedical breakthroughs, including the discovery of protective vaccines and effective medications, are made and can be delivered rapidly to those at risk, control of the AIDS pandemic will depend mainly on changing sexual behavior . . . [Research] indicates that widespread behavioral change cannot come from education alone, for profound cultural, institutional, and psychological changes are necessary to over come existing cultural constraints. This means, in the final analysis, that effective AIDS control requires changing the economic an social status of women to increase their independence, their personal autonomy, and their control over interpersonal relations.

AIDS and STDs in Africa
EDWARD C. GREEN[5]

Supporters of collaborative programs involving traditional healers constitute a diverse and vocal group, yet by the later 1980s, collaborative health care programs "sanctioned at the national level" appeared limited to Nigeria, Ghana, and Swaziland, at least according to the published literature. . . . In sum, by the end of the 1980s there was not much to show in Africa a decade after the Alma Ata resolution [calling for collaborative programs]. Evidently, there are some powerful counterforces at work. . . . However, with the transition into the 1990s there is evidence that the spread of AIDS has prompted African ministries of health and donors to look anew at the collaboration issue, and specifically to consider ways they might collaborate with traditional healers in AIDS control efforts. In fact, there had been recommendations in the 1980s from anthropologists and others calling for intersectoral collaboration in the area of AIDS and STDs. . . . [T]he major objective of these programs seems to be to develop healers as condom promoters, to prevent HIV infection through sterilization of healers' instruments that come into contact with bodily fluids, to modify healers' practices that put them at risk themselves for HIV infection, to encourage referrals of healers clients to hospitals and social welfare centers, and to counsel healers' clients on the prevention of both HIV infection and other STDs.

Such programs are still very experimental and it may be some time before a model emerges that can be recommended to African health ministries and donors for replication. There seem to be few precedents to suggest detailed ways to involve African healers in programs whose primary aim it is to control common STDs other than AIDS. However, before turning attention to the AIDS question, the constraints to collaborative programs that have emerged . . . ought to be considered, because these constraints still impede and shape AIDS-related and other collaborative programs.

One factor constraining collaborative programs is the logical development of health programs over time. It is understandable that government officials and their foreign advisors would begin with the development of human power that is imme-

5. Green, Edward C., *AIDS and STDs in Africa: Bridging the Gap between Traditional Healing and Modern Medicine* (Boulder and Pietermaritzburg: Westview Press and University of Natal Press, 1994). Excerpts taken from pages 24-28, 30-37, 39.

Edward C. Green is a Washington D.C. based medical anthropologist and consultant. Currently, he is a full-time advisor to the Mozambique Ministry of Health. He has also edited *Practicing Development Anthropology* (Boulder: Westview Press, 1986).

diately available and supervisable, namely government employees. It would be unrealistic to expect that indigenous practitioners—even if they outnumber Western-trained health personnel by hundreds to one and offer far better rural outreach—would be developed as health service providers before Western-trained personnel in either the public or private sectors. . . .

A more basic factor may be "cultural distance" between indigenous practitioners and medically educated Africans and their expatriate advisers: the two groups embrace distinct and perhaps intrinsically incompatible worldviews or paradigms of illness. In the worlds of one observer, traditional healing practice is "frequently premised on supernatural and other belief systems that are distinctly alien to and not easily comprehended by modern-sector practitioners." Resistance to, or rejection of, magico-religious belief systems has been particularly strong in Africa because health care has largely been in the hands of missionary groups which offer competing religious belief systems quite apart from the scientific paradigm. . . .

Another important factor inadequately documented in the literature seems to be economic and prestige competition between the two sectors. Such competition began with the introduction of Western medicine in Africa. When the first missionaries came to Africa, they " . . . recognized in western medicine an instrument for extending their influence among the people," therefore they actively sought patients at the presumed expense of indigenous healers. . . . Yet Africans have continued to consult traditional healers, even when bio-medical practitioners are available and cheaper—or free. . . .

Many contemporary healers have developed financially lucrative practices, some of which are located in urban areas where Western-style medicine is available. Such healers may take patients away from physicians, as can be seen in Lagos where a number of healers have earned enough cash to build multi-bed hospitals with modern equipment and to own one or more expensive cars. The wealthy, successful traditional healer stands as a rebuke to the biomedically trained physician who practices in the same neighborhood.

Resentment of indigenous practitioners by African medical professionals has probably gown in recent years due to the development among African healers of what can only be called professionalization. In this context, the term refers to the institutionalization of more standardized, empirically based indigenous training of healers; the (usually self-initiated) adoption of aspects of Western medicine or other nonindigenous medicine such as homeopathy; and, especially, the formation of professional associations of traditional healers. . . .

A characteristic of the healers that comprise these associations is that they are especially interested in learning more about modern/Western health care, they want to work in cooperation with the modern sector through involvement with ministries of health, they want to change the popular image of traditional healers as "primitive witchdoctors," and they want to become as respectable among government officials as they typically are in their own communities. . . .

For their part, African government officials tend to regard indigenous practitioners as a somewhat embarrassing anachronism, especially when dealing with donor organization officials or other outsiders. Traditional healers project an image of the backward, the primitive, the heathen, even of the illegal. It should be remembered that most colonial regimes supported medical missionary efforts to illegalize or severely curtail the practices of "witchdoctors." Today, Western-educated African elites would prefer to pretend that "witchdoctors" are a thing of the past rather than a genuine force to be reckoned with

Political ideology may also bias government officials against indigenous practitioners. . . . Marxist governments such as those of Mozambique and Tanzania may oppose healers" . . . on the grounds that healers were, and potentially still are, part of the old 'feudal' system, unproductive, giving support to chiefs, furthering 'superstition' and liable to exploit the poor in their need." Traditional healers, as guardians of the traditional moral and religious order, may also be viewed by Marxists as reactionary purveyors of "the opium of the people." . . . In fact, traditional healers tend to be conservative by nature if not by definition. Healers in South Africa describe their role in terms of "securing the stability of the country"; guarding the culture and traditions of the people, and mystically empowering a variety of existing leaders in the region of whatever political persuasion, from Hastings Banda to Nelson Mandela and Robert Mugabe. . . .

In fact foreign donors, planners, and administrators usually have little or no understanding of, or access to, African healers or the worldview they represent. Access to healers may well be subject to the approval of ministries of health that represent local medical establishment views. For example, a high-ranking Ministry of Health official in West Africa told me that he did not believe traditional healers still practiced in his country, except perhaps in remote rural areas. His office was next door to one of a number of prominently advertised clinics run by traditional healers. This same urban neighborhood also had an active branch of a national-level traditional healers association. . . .

Finally, Western development planners and other professionals (including some Africans) tend to think of traditional systems—whether relating to health care, land tenure, communal ownership, kinship obligations, or ancestor veneration—as archaic and dysfunctional, as a way of life to be over come if there is to be progress and development. What such a view fails to recognize is that traditional systems may be well suited to the social, psychological, and other needs of participants in these systems; that traditional systems may be a great source of comfort to Africans undergoing rapid culture change, providing security and continuity in an unpredictable, changing world; and that traditional systems tend to be genuine functioning systems whereas the same cannot as yet be said of the modern-urban alternative. . . .

It may be useful at this stage to summarize in outline form the arguments for and against intersectoral collaboration. . . . (TM will stand for traditional medicine and TH for traditional healer.)

Points Against Collaboration

- Some traditional practices are harmful, e.g., giving enemas for child diarrhea; drinking urine or rubbing urine in eyes for conjunctivitis; douching with bleach for contraception; or making incisions with unsterilized razors.

- Traditional treatment may be ineffective and, even if harmless, serve to prevent or delay patients from receiving appropriate treatment.

- Some Africans charge that outsiders advocate a "double standard of health care," with "second-class medicine for the rural masses" while Western medicine is reserved for urban elite.

- Those who favor collaboration with African healers have a pessimistic, defeatist attitude that the masses cannot be educated to change their tradition-bound thinking and behavior. They are said to advocate "giving up" on the problems of modern sector health manpower and service delivery.

- Traditional healing is a hindrance to progress, development, and "enlightenment." Specifically, it impedes acceptance of scientific thinking and perpetuates magical thinking...

- Patients may undergo traditional and modern treatment simultaneously, posing risk of overdosing or at least of counteracting the effects of Western medicine.

- Traditional medical thinking and behavior holds little or no place for fallibility. Healers must project and protect their image of omnipotence, and therefore make exaggerated and unrealistic claims. Healers seldom admit failure or an inability to understand or treat any problem.

- Dosage of herbal medicines are seldom standardized. Such medicines may be of widely varying potencies due to differences in storage and other factors...

- Extending recognition to traditional healers and initiating any kind of collaboration or training raises expectations and even demands among healers. It's a kind of Pandora's box: today it's oral rehydration salts, tomorrow they'll want antibiotics and a wing of the government hospital.

- Extending recognition and initiating any sort of collaboration also extends at least tacit legitimacy and a measure of government approval to traditional healing practices and practitioners, which doctors and nurses by their training generally do not approve of and do not want to legitimize. Collaboration may also increase patient confidence in traditional healers, causing patients to make even more useless expenditure on ineffective medicines and therapies.

- One reason modern medicine seems to be losing in its competition with traditional medicine is that patients often consult traditional healers first. By the time the healer or the patient gives up on traditional therapies, the patient may be beyond help. When such patients are finally treated at modern medical facilities, they may die, which then reflects badly on the efficacy of modern medicine.

- Traditional healers tend to be nonliterate and therefore not to keep written patient records; this make collaboration difficult . . . THs who join professional associations may be better educated, but skeptics have argued that THs who join such associations are more likely to lack "traditional legitimacy" in their communities. Others assert that THs' competitiveness prevents their associations from functioning effectively.

- There are some priority areas of promotive health care that African healers, by their training, beliefs and orientation, would never promote, for example child spacing or contraception. . . .

Points in Favor of Collaboration

- Whatever biomedical health professionals think of TM, it is largely to THs that people turn in time of illness. THs are generally respected health care provides and opinion leaders in their communities.

- National health services in developing countries lack adequate numbers of personnel, and these are unevenly distributed, with nearly all doctors in the major cities. The resulting rural outreach is poor. THs may outnumber doctors 100 to 1 or more. THs are the de facto providers of primary health care in Africa.

- THs provide client-centered, personalized health care that is culturally appropriate, holistic, and tailored to meet the needs and expectations of the patient. THs share the cognitive understandings and cultural values of those they treat.

- If traditional healers engage in harmful practices, there is a public health responsibility to try to change those practices and try to substitute safer practices. This can only be accomplished if there is dialogue, and some degree of cooperation, with traditional healers. There is also evidence that healers will modify or abandon practices if they are shown that such practices are harmful.

- At the local or village level, traditional healers do not compete directly with physicians, but with village health workers or assistant nurses, whose training and competence may well amount to less than the traditional healer. Almost certainly, the TH enjoys greater prestige and credibility in health and spiritual matters.

- Traditional healers cannot be wished away or legislated out of existence. . . . THs occupy a critically important role in African societies. . . . Traditional healers are priests, religious ritual specialists, family and community therapists, moral and social philosophers, teachers, visionaries, empirical scientists, and perhaps political leaders in addition to being healers in the more restricted, Western sense. Their existence and durability stand as evidence that they meet important social needs, and these needs are in no way diminished as the clients they serve urbanize and undergo rapid sociocultural change. If anything, the needs increase. . . .

- Surveys and limited program experience in Africa have shown that traditional healers are highly motivated to learn about Western medicine, to attend training workshops, and to cooperate with modern health sector personnel. As concluded at a conference on traditional medicine, "Traditional medical systems are open, not closed to techniques and concepts characteristic of cosmopolitan medicine.". . . .

- Since healers have been organizing themselves in recent years, governments and donor organizations can now communicate with healer organizations through professional associations of traditional healers. Healers who belong to—and who occupy leadership roles in—professional organizations tend to be especially eager to collaborate with the modern sector and to learn about Western medicine. They tend to be especially open about new ideas and practices.

- Any efforts toward cooperation seem to improve relations between the two health sectors, which results in earlier and more frequent referrals from traditional healers to clinics. The healer can perform a "triage" function by treating the less seriously ill and only sending the more serious cases on to the clinic or hospital.

- Any efforts that promote cooperation seem to improve communication between the two health sectors, allowing access to the beliefs and practices found among healers and presumably their clients. This, in turn, allows for the development of creative, culturally appropriate, and effective health education strategies. It also facilitates interventions aimed at discouraging practices proved to be harmful. . . .

- An efficient, cost-effective training-of-trainers approach is possible by focusing public health training efforts on leaders of healer associations and on senior healers under whom novice healers apprentice. Members—and especially leaders—of traditional healer associations may be especially open to new ideas. In some countries (e.g., Swaziland and Nigeria), the "traditional" training of healers has become more formalized, empirically oriented, institutionalized, and influenced by the rise of biomedical professionalism in Africa.

A great and unprecedented opportunity now exists for adding public health ideas and methods into the "traditional curriculum" of healer training. . . .

In view of all these factors, it would seem that if the cooperation of indigenous practitioners can be enlisted in public health programs, there can be no more potent impetus for improvement in the public health. Although actual collaborative programs have been few and far between, surveys of African healer attitudes and limited programmatic experience have consistently shown willingness on the part of the healers to learn more about Western medicine and to cooperate and collaborate with Western-trained practitioners.

Suggested Readings

Arhin, Dyna C., "The Health Card Insurance Scheme in Burundi: A Social Asset or a Non- Viable Venture?" *Social Science & Medicine* 39:6 (1994): 861-870.

Bassett, M. T.; Mhloyi, M., "Women and AIDS in Zimbabwe: The Making of an Epidemic," *Journal of Health Services* 21:1 (1991): 143-156.

Bigger, R. J., "The AIDS Problem in Africa," *Lancet* (January 11, 1986): 79-82.

du Toit, Brian M.; Abdalla, Ismail H., *African Healing Strategies* (New York: Trado-Medic Books, 1985).

Essex, Max; Mboup, Souleymane; Kanki, Phyllis J; Kalengayi, Mbowa R, (eds.), *AIDS in Africa* (New York: Ravan Press, 1994).

Gilson, Lucy, "Management and Health Care Reform in Sub-Saharan Africa," *Social Science & Medicine* 40:5 (1995): 695-710.

Kelly, Joe, *Finding a Cure: The Politics of Health in South Africa* (Johannesburg: Institute of Race Relations, 1990).

Kikhela, N.; Bineau, B.; Corin, E., "Africa's Two Medical Systems: Options for Planners," *World Health Forum* 21 (1981): 96-99.

Last, M; Chavunduka, G. L., (eds.), *The Professionalization of African Medicine* (Manchester: Manchester University Press, 1986).

Namboze, Josephine M., "Health and Culture in an African Society," *Social Science & Medicine* 17:24 (1983): 2041-2043.

Oberender, Peter; Diesfeld, Hans J.; Gitter, Wolfgang, (eds.), *Health and Development in Africa: International, Interdisciplinary Symposium 2-4 June 1982* (Frankfurt and New York: Verlag Peter Lang, 1983).

Saunderson, Paul R., "An Economic Evaluation of Alternative Programme Designs for Tuberculosis Control in Rural Uganda," *Social Science & Medicine* 40:9 (1995): 1203-1212.

Sempebwa, Joshua W., "Religiosity and Health Behaviour in Africa," *Social Science & Medicine* 17:24 (1983): 2033-2036.

Sobatier, R., *Blaming Others: Prejudice, Race, and World Wide AIDS* (London: Panos Institute, 1988).

Turshen, Meredeth, *The Political Ecology of Disease in Tanzania* (New Brunswick: Rutgers University Press, 1984).

Williams, Olefemi A., *AIDS: An African Perspective* (Boca Ratan: CRC Press, Inc., 1992.

DEMOCRACY AND THE NATION STATE

Perhaps the most succinct and perceptive comment on democracy was made by that unrepentent imperialist, Winston Churchill, who was not about to preside over the dissolution of the British Empire when he declared that "Democracy is the least efficient form of government but every other form is worse". In 1960, "the year of African Independence" most, but not all, of the colonial powers had left behind what may be described as a vestige of democracy that history has shown was too fragile to withstand the ethnic, religious, and cultural tensions that the departing imperialists hoped could be subsumed by the beneficent introduction of democracy, a political ideology that has been accepted in the West, some states in Asia, and hesitantly in the former Soviet Union. But what of Africa? The Problem of Democracy and the Nation State is disfigured by its demise before the intervention of the military who argue, not without credence, that they and not the competing civilian ethnic groups, have the interests of the nation. They come out of the barracks, certainly not in any crusade for democracy, but to bring order and sanity to government. This has clearly not been the case, but there is no doubt that democracy has turned in many African states to autocracy where "kleptocracy" and local disputes have initiated deadly cycles of violence that have demolished the concept of democracy in much of Africa.

The academics, politicians, and the masters of the media have agonized over this question dissecting why the Africans did not accept the political inheritance of their colonial rulers and behave as good democrats. David Goldsworthy has examined the two years of civilian government in Ghana from 1969 to 1971. Kwame Nkrumah, the leader of the independence movement in Ghana was forced into exile in 1966 by the military. Civilian rule returned in 1969, which inspired hopes for democracy that were crushed by the military's second seizure of power in 1972. There are few who believe that soldiers, in any society, can provide better government than that by the people whom they govern. The military, however, have familiar themes, whether in Ghana or elsewhere. Virtually every military seizure of a democratic governnnent justifies its action by ridding the state of those who are corrupt and have mismanaged the affairs of government, alienated important civil servants, farmers, unions, the business community, and just about everybo else.

Finally, there is the ultimate justification employed by the military for their forceful acquisition of power at the expense of democracy. In Africa the military will argue that they are the only national institution transcending ethnic and religious rivalries. With ill-disguised innocence they have pleaded tnat they had no option but to intervene. And so the military came out of the barracks. Moreover, the Ghanaians were like rural people everywnere: suspicious of government particularly in hard times. Nor was the small but influential business community encouraged to support the continuation of democracy in a declining economy. But has Goldworthy corrctly identified the challenges to democratic rule? Are they primarily national in scope and indigenous in character?

Michael Crowder, writing nearly fifteen years later, locates the problem in a scathing indictment of the colonial legacy itself. The colonial state, which Africans inherited, perpetuated itself, according to Crowder, through liberal use of violence and coercion, ignored the will of the majority to pursue elite perrogatives, and exacerbated ethnic divisions to maintain power. Furthermore, Europeans denied Africans meaningful political roles and barred them from exercising power except when in the direct service and control of colonial agents. Liberal democracy played little role in the African past and thus has little chance of lasting success now. Democracy, Crowder concludes, was a European dream, not an African one. However, were African leaders so shackled by the colonial legacy that democratic constitutional rule was impossible? Do Africans bear so little responsibility for their governing systems as Crowder implies? Or is blaming the colonial past only one more example of Eurocentric analysis that places Europeans, not Africans, at the center of the story? What is the relationship between the colonial past and post-independence struggles over governance?

Robert H. Jackson and Carl G. Rosberg assert in their analysis of democracy in tropical Africa that liberal democracy has little chance of success in Africa in the face of the numerous ethnic and social groups contending for power within the modem African state. The solution, they argue, may be in one-party rule within democratic forms. They note that parties often define themselves and their power ethnically, and thus heighten divisions that produce instability. A single party state, they concur, might be able to create a sense of nation that would transcend ethnic cleavages. By 1985, the date of this article's publication, one party states proliferated. Yet, questions remained. Were Rosberg and Jackson's vibrant grass-roots participation and voter "fickleness" really signs of democracy or of instability? If the electorate could not substantially change the course of governance because they could not vote the leadership out of office, was there anything democratic about one-party rule?

Kathleen Staudt in a study of women and the African state, and Molara Ogundipe-Leslie in her book on African feminism, point out that women have been largely excluded from political power no matter what form the post-independent state takes. Staudt links this marginalizing of women to the colonial legacy. Colonialism, she maintains, not only defined patterns for political rule, but it also imposed gender constructions that left African women with few avenues of political influence or power. Ogundipe-Leslie insists that not only are women denied power, they are often denied the rights of citizenship that might form the basis for a claim to power. Both authors raise the question of legitimacy: Can any rule be accepted as legitimate if women are effectively excluded? In addition, Staudt and Ogundipe-Leslie open the door to other considerations. Would women in governance stabilize regimes? Expand democratic potential? Weaken the negative influences of the colonial past? Who should decide what women's political roles should be?

After fifty years of observing, analyzing, and describing Africa, Basil Davidson wrote what he called "a meditation on the nature of the African experience" in which he locates the problem of African governance in nationalism itself. The nation-state, according to Davidson, subjugates African to European history and thus alienates Africans from one another. In a poignant, wide ranging comparison of Africa with the dissolution of the Soviet empire, Davidson despairs over much— terming the 1980s the decade of the AK-47, then the most available automatic weapon. Yet, Davidson cautions that despair is only for those who can afford it and finds some hope in regional cooperative organizations. But given the depths of the divisions that Davidson chronicles, the extent of the alienation of Africans from the African political leadership, and the profound economic crisis gripping the continent does such a hope for regional cooperation have any realistic foundation? Is there any basis for thinking that nations will put aside their parochial vision for a broader one that would impinge on national sovereignty and personal power? Is Davidson's hope any more "affordable" than the despair he rejects? But if hopes for regional cooperation remain groundless, can there be any basis for optimism?

Africa does possess stable nation-states. Botswana, as Patrick Molutsi and John Holm point out, has had competitive elections for twenty-five years. They concede Botswana's exceptionalism: relative ethnic homogeneity, shared language and cultural norms, and minimal (by African standards) impact of British colonialism on indigenous rule. Yet, the authors note that, as with the rest of Africa, disputes in Botswana are often perceived according to tribal divisions, urbanization tears at the social and political fabric, and foreign influences through multinational corporations and aid programs shape economic development. Given that Botswana shares similar challenges with other African states, can Botswana serve as a model for African democracy? Or does Botswana's past limit its utility as a prototype?

Finally, Timothy Sisk attempts to evaluate South Africa's transition to democracy. On May 10, 1994, Nelson Mandela was inaugurated as president of the national unity government in South Africa bringing to an end forty years of apartheid and three-and-a half-centuries of white minority domination of that region. Democratic hopes flourish once again. Sisk, however, cautions that it is less clear whether or not democracy can be sustained. Like Molutsi and Holm, Sisk points out that a shift to democracy is only possible after a transitional period—a period marked by doubt, uncertainty, and risk. How a nation negotiates this period determines the democratic possibilities. South Africa has succeeded in passing through the first transitional phase, but formidable hurdles still confront South Africans before their fledgling democracy can be declared secure. Given the post-independence history of democratic failures that often define western understanding of Africa, the willingness of South Africans to defy the odds of their own history, and the ability of black and white South Africans to accommodate former enemies—however fragile that accommodation proves to be—provides hope that other divided African nations may also travel paths leading to good and stable governance.

Ghana's Second Republic: A Post-Mortem
DAVID GOLDSWORTHY[1]

Ghana's second military coup followed a characteristic African pattern. It took place early in the morning, early in a new year, and at a time when the Prime Minister was absent from the country. It was bloodless; the simultaneous toppling of constitution, government, parliament and parties was accomplished by a few strategic detentions and the deployment of soldiers at major buildings. There was no discernible public protest. . . .

The stated motives, too, had a familiar flavour. . . . From the copious indictments issued by Colonel Acheampong and echoed by the press, three particular themes may be distilled. First, the Progress Party regime had been guilty of extreme economic mismanagement so that by the end of its truncated term of office the problems of inflation and overseas debt were even greater than they had been at the outset. Second, it had consistently acted against the interests and wishes of one important social formation after another: the civil servants, the farmers, the business community, the unions, the press, the students, and the armed forces themselves. Third, it had been acting in defiance of the democratic constitution which it had sworn to uphold. In short, all the ills characteristic of the Nkrumah era "still existed under the Progress Party Government," and the army therefore had no option but to intervene. . . .

In turning to the private sector it is useful to keep in mind Dennis Austin's reminder that "if there is a pervasive concept in Ghanaian politics it is that of 'patronage' or 'clientage'." Ghanaians "give their support to those who can look after them." It is at the same time a politics of the marketplace: "When the goods run out, the traders are discredited. They lose not only their customers but the trust that the customers once placed in them."

In the villages, for example, what people noticed about government policy were not the long-term plans—for roads, piped water, electrification and so on—but rather the short-term intensificaitons of hardship: the rising prices, the imposition of

---

1. Goldsworthy, David, "Ghana's Second Republic," *African Affairs* 72:286 (January 1973): 8-25. Excerpts taken from pp. 8, 15, 16, 19, and 23.

David Goldsworthy received his Ph.D. from Oxford and has been affiliated with Monash University in Clayton Australia. He was the editor of *Australian Outlook*, and is the author of *Colonial Issues in British Politics 1945-1961: From Colonial Development to Wind of Change*, (Oxford: Oxford University Press, 1971).

fees for medical treatment at country clinics, the re-imposition of school fees abolished by Nkrumah. And for the cocoa farmers in particular, things kept getting worse. Prices for their products were falling. The Cocoa Marketing Board, aiming to head off over-declarations of purchases, declined to extend loans to buying agents. Accordingly the farmers continued to receive chits and not cash for their crops, despite government promises to terminate chit payments....

Ghana's business community is numerically small, yet it has always exercised influence beyond its apparent strength if only because of its potential for patronage in the creation of employment in a slowly developing economy. It is also, true to the spirit of clientage, opportunist in politics. It generally supported . . . Nkrumah, and supported the Progress Party at the 1969 election less because of the party's anti-socialist image than because it seemed likely to win. As time passed and economic injury grew, its enthusiasm for the Progress Party diminished very markedly....

The Busia government's accession to office in 1969 had seemed the finest moment of Ghana's liberal intelligentsia. A painstakingly devised democratic constitution had been promulgated. In a free election the country had returned a government of educated professional men led by the University of Ghana's first African professor. Many government members had had their liberal bona fides solidly established by years of opposition to Nkrumahism.

By the republic's end, little more than two years later, this liberal image would hardly have been recognized. Its many critics (especially among the liberal intelligentsia) saw the government's rule as increasingly paranoid, destructive of the constitution, in parts corrupt, and even—as Colonel Acheampong implied— reminiscent of a kind of politics from which the officers had once already delivered the country. . . .

In other words . . . developments in Ghana can well be accounted for in generic terms. . . . Among the typical factors involved we may cite first the basic attitude of the elite towards political power. In a developed country the careerist's normal route to advancement lies through the economy. In a poor country with a markedly underdeveloped private sector, it lies perforce through the polity. And where the political system provides the major means of access to wealth and influence, and where both commodities are, in absolute terms, in short supply, the attitudes of those seeking entry will be intensely opportunistic and of those who have gained it, intensely defensive. The stakes are seen as total, in zero-sum terms: to be ousted is to sustain total loss for oneself and one's clientele. . . .

Second, we may cite the generic fact that civilian African governments tend to have low executive capacity. This is partly a function of a low level of legitimacy. In a poor country characterized by multiple communal divisions and a very wide social, economic and educational gap between urban elite and rural mass, it is natural that much of the population should feel primary allegiances to groups and leaders other than those who sit in the national assembly and the cabinet room. Accordingly no African government—not even the exceptional one elected by universal suffrage—can afford to assume that its "legitimacy" will suffice to secure general compliance with its decrees. But in addition, the actual physical resources of state authority tend to be few and brittle. The writ of many an African leader has run no further than his capital city and/or ethnic base, not only because of low legitimacy but also because of the state machinery's basic ineffectiveness—itself a product of poverty, divided communal loyalties and so on. From the regime's point of view, such factors give its incumbency a sense of precariousness. Consolidating one's grip on office becomes much more difficult than gaining it in the first place, since consolidation depends so much on governmental effectiveness. And lacking authoritative capacity, regimes have often tried to compensate in the only available way—by use of such force as they command. . . .

Whose Dream Was It Anyway?
Twenty-Five Years
of African Independence
MICHAEL CROWDER[2]

When the Union Jack was lowered at midnight and the green white and green flag of Nigeria raised in its place on October 1st, 1960, there was considerable optimism in the British press about the future of that erstwhile British colony. The leaders of its three political parties were all by their own declarations committed to the practice of liberal democracy, Westminster-style. The constitution that enshrined the ideals of Westminster had been patiently negotiated over a decade between the British and the leaders of the three main political parties. . . .

Despite the many internal strains which the country experienced in its first few years of independence, including the suspension of the constitution of one of its three constituent regions and the jailing of the leader of the opposition for treason, the British press appeared to share the belief that as one Nigerian newspaper put it: "Nigerians seems to have perfected the art of walking to the brink of disaster without falling in." Indeed the British Prime Minister and his officials were apparently so ignorant of the real breakdown of law and order in the country that in January 1966 they flew to Lagos to attend the Commonwealth Prime Ministers Conference on the Rhodesian question. A day after they flew back to London the Prime Minister of Nigeria was assassinated and the first military regime was installed. In the twenty years that followed, Nigeria has suffered four more military coups, at least one failed coup, a three-year long civil war, a brief return to an elective form of government that made a mockery of liberal democracy, and an oil boom that permitted lavish spending and corruption on a massive scale, followed by the near bankruptcy of the country, which today is economically on its knees. As a result, Nigerians of all classes have developed a deep cynicism about their leaders, both civilian and

2. Crowder, Michael, "Whose Dream Was It Anyway? Twenty-Five Years of African Independence," *African Affairs* 86:342 (January 1987): 7-24. Excerpts taken from pp. 7-8, 10, 12-13, 15, 17, and 19.

Michael Crowder had a distinguished career as an editor, a scholar, and a teacher. He taught, among other places, at the University of Botswana, and the Nigerian Universities of Ibadan, Ife, Kano, Zaria, and Lagos. He was the editor of *Nigeria,* and of the *Journal of African History*. His numerous publications focused primarily on West Africa and include *West Africa: An Introduction to its History* (London: Longman, 1977) and *West African Resistance* (London: Hutchinson, 1978).

military, and certainly have little faith in the liberal democracy and mixed economy that were the legacy of their colonial rulers. . . . The story everywhere else has been the same. Majority parties voted to establish one party states which western apologists were quick to justify as reflecting true African democracy encouraging the politics of consensus where two or multi-party democracy was divisive. In reality, such moves usually proved but a cloak for the establishment of personal rule...Even military regimes that intervened were seen by optimists as mere correctives or temporary aberrance in the practice of democracy by young nations. Military coups were invariably started in the name of cleansing the state, after which the soldiers would return to the barracks. And this they did in Sudan, Ghana, the former Upper Volta and Nigeria, only to fling wide the barrack gates again as it became clear that the politicians had learnt nothing except how to abuse power more successfully. . . .

And yet, grasping at straws, westerners refused to see their dreams shattered. Nigeria's return to democracy in 1979 was seen as a vindication by those who believed that Africans could and would adhere to the ideals of Western liberal democracy. Similar optimism attended the return to civilian rule under Obote [Uganda], with the British government even helping to train the army he used to establish a worse record with Amnesty International than [Idi] Amin. . . .

Was not this dream of a model Africa in which Africans would faithfully adhere to the liberal democratic institutions transferred at independence and uphold a mixed economy in which the interests of the ordinary people would be served in reality a pipe dream in the context of a plethora of states that had for the most part only been cobbled together fifty odd years before?. . . . Given the little attention that any of the European colonial powers gave to building national political and economic structures during the period of their rule will not historians of the future see the very survival of these states as something of an economic and political miracle?

The Colonial Legacy

The colonial state was not only conceived in violence, but it was maintained by the free use of it. Any form of resistance was visited by punitive expeditions that were often quite unrestrained by any of the norms of warfare in Europe. The bloody suppression of the Maji Maji and Herero uprising in German East and South West Africa are well enough known. . . . The bloody massacre of Tirailleurs Senegalais protesting against delays in paying their benefits and effecting their demobilization at Thiaroye in Dakar in 1944 sent shock waves throughout the French African empire, as did the revelations about the brutal treatment of Mau Mau prisóners by the British at the Hola Camp in Kenya through the British African colonies. The colonial state, it must be remembered, maintained troops for internal security, not for defense against external aggression. . . .

The colonial state was certainly not run for the benefit of its inhabitants. . . . In the white settler colonies the best land was appropriated from the African farmer who was crowded into less fertile reserves often with disastrous ecological results.

Where the main agent of exploitation was the African farmer, he was forced to produce the crops that the colonial rulers required rather than those he needed. Through taxation, compulsory crop cultivation, forced labour and requisition, and in the case of the Portuguese territories physical coercion, the farmer produced the cash crops that the big companies over-seas required even at the risk of impoverishment of the land and famine. . . .

[W]e must remind ourselves how little opportunity Africans had of participating in the machinery of government of the colonial state until a few years before its demise. In British Africa only a few chiefs under British indirect rule were allowed any initiative in the administration before 1945. Otherwise all Africans in the administration, whatever the colonial regime, fulfilled a purely subaltern role without executive initiative. As to legislative functions, again these were limited to local government under the system of indirect rule, and to a handful of elected Africans in Nigeria, Senegal and the Gold Coast. . . . Even where some effort was made to prepare African administrative cadres, they were often treated as second class members of the administration. In the 1950s, newly appointed African administrative officers in Uganda were specifically barred from access to the confidential files, a point that led to much bitterness on their part. In many African countries not a few inhabitants exercised the right to vote for the first time at the elections that brought their independence governments to power. . . .

No aspect of post-independence Africa has drawn more criticism by scholars and journalists of the West than the personal power exercised by its leaders. Again it is instructive to look at the colonial model. Colonial governors enjoyed very wide powers without brakes from below. Even in British Africa where some territories had legislative councils these were dominated by an official majority which could be relied on to vote as solidly for any new policy or programme introduced by the Governor as the legislators in today's one party states. The Governor also enjoyed to the full the outward trappings of power, living in an imposing palace, driven in large limousines flying the flag, deferred to by all, and on ceremonial occasions dressed in cocked hat and plumes and a quasi-military uniform. In the British territories, he alone was allowed to use red ink to minute or sign official documents. . . .

A final point concerning the colonial legacy to Independent Africa concerns the state structures that were handed over at independence. The borders of these states, it may be tedious to remind ourselves, were erected without reference to African realities in the chanceries of Europe. But having created them, colonial powers did little to foster a sense of national unity within them. The French territory of Upper Volta for instance was not created until 1920, was dismembered in 1932 and divided up among its neighbours, only to be re-established in 1947, thirteen years before it became independent. . . . The two French federations of Equatorial and West Africa were broken up by the French against the wishes of the majority of the constituent colonies on the eve of independence. Furthermore it has been argued, convincingly, that the system of indirect rule, employed by the British, was a divisive one in that it emphasised the integrity of the pre-colonial political unit as against the new colonial state. And up until the mid-forties there were still powerful advocates in the Colonial Office who saw the native authorities as the building blocks of independence.

This had been a deliberately selective view of the colonial past but, I hope, a corrective one that the cassandras of contemporary Africa would be advised to take into account.

Whose Dream Was It Anyway?

We come now to my second theme: how far did Africans share the dream of the colonial rulers for Africa? In the first place, it has to be remembered that the liberal democratic ideal was espoused only by the British and the French for their African colonies. Though at home the Belgians shared these ideals, they only very belatedly suggested that might be appropriately transferred to their colonial subjects. In both Spain and Portugal liberal democracy had succumbed many years since to Fascist regimes, so for their overseas subjects there was not even a metropolitan model of democracy to aspire to. In the case of the Portuguese their African colonies were considered integral parts of the metropolis and, far from instruments of power being transferred to African subjects, control of the state was seized by them by force of arms. There was thus no obligation placed on the victors to maintain any particular form of government. . . .

African leaders may have skillfully pressured the British and French to transfer their models and when finally they agreed to do so accepted them as a condition of gaining independence, just as Nkrumah had to accept a final election as a precondition of independence for Ghana. But did this mean that they implicitly believed in them as anything other than as a means to an end? The answer is surely "No". Only thus can we explain the rapid dismantling of these constitutions in form or spirit by nearly all who were party to the independence agreements. . . .

But democracy remained, in the eyes of the Western press, the panacea for Africa. Thus there was general rejoicing at Nigeria's return to civilian rule in 1979 and general hostility to the military coup that brought it to an end in December 1983, even though there was rejoicing by the general population at the demise of a corrupt and increasingly oppressive regime. . . .

What African leaders surely appreciated more perceptively than those who wished liberal democratic constitutions on them was that liberal democracy had only worked in those countries of Europe where there was relative lack of inequality, a deep-rooted sense of national identity, and a consensus as to the ideal model for the government of the state. Where, as in Zimbabwe, such conditions did not obtain, and where there were two major ethnic groups vying for power, the operation of the liberal democratic constitution became very close in character to the operation of democracy in Northern Ireland. There was certainly genuine belief on the part of those African leaders who advocated the one-party state, however much later they were to pervert it to their own ends, that it would be less divisive than the two-party model of the British or the multi-party model of the French. Nor were African leaders particularly committed to the equitable distribution of resources that their election manifestoes promised and their talk of African socialism may have suggested. Since the means to independence was to be through the ballot box, they had necessarily to persuade the electorate by offering to implement programmes that would benefit them. With independence won, the behaviour of African politicians has differed little from that of the majority of office-seekers in promoting personal advancement and profit, with some pork barreling for their homeboys. Africans were much more hard-nosed, realistic and even cynical about what independence portended. Rosy dreams were left to the departing colonial masters and the metropolitan press. . . .

Democracy in Tropical Africa: Democracy versus Autocracy in African Politics

ROBERT H. JACKSON and CARL G ROSBERG[3]

Once it became clear to the colonial powers that decolonization was inevitable, independence democracy came to be seen as both a vindication of colonialism and a political expedient. African nationalists, who saw it as an acknowledgment of their dignity, equality and humanity, would accept nothing less than democracy. However, African nationalists gradually began to treat the democratic institutions as an expedient to gain power. Rarely did independence democracy last as long as a decade, and, in only two countries—Botswana and The Gambia—has it been retained, owing to somewhat special circumstances.

Once sovereignty had been transferred and the colonial authority had departed, the independence constitution of the new African government was usually either amended, ignored or discarded by those in power, or was undermined or violated by those seeking power. Constitutional government was rapidly transformed into personal rule, and the *coup d'état* became the usual means of changing governments. Military intervention in politics was endemic by the late 1960s. Civil wars occurred in Sudan, Ethiopia, Zaire, Nigeria, Angola and Chad, which in some cases have recurred or have never fully been resolved. Genocide has been practiced in Rwanda and Burundi, and major ethnic conflicts involving bloodshed have occurred elsewhere. In short, violence and political instability have dominated the politics of these countries. In most Tropical African countries, the postindependence era has been marked by substantial political turbulence. If the introduction of liberal democracy is conceived as an institutional substitute for civil warfare and other

3. Jackson, Robert H.; Rosberg, Carl G., "Democracy in Tropical Africa: Democracy Versus Autocracy in African Politics," *Journal of International Affairs* 38:2 (Winter 1985): 293-305. Excerpts taken from pp. 295-297, 302-305.

Robert Jackson teaches in the Political Science Department of the University of British Columbia and has published numerous works on state systems in Africa. Along with Carl Rosberg, he edited *Personal Rule in Black Africa: Prince, Autocrat, Prophet, Tyrant,* (Berkeley: University of California Press, 1982).

Carl Rosberg is Professor of Political Science at the University of California, Berkeley and directed the Institute of International Studies there. Rosberg is widely published with his most recent work being colaboration with David Apter, *Political Development and the New Realism in Sub-Saharan Africa,* (Charlottesville: University Press of Virginia, 1994)

forms of political violence and disruption, then it is clear that liberal democracy has not been established in postindependence Tropical Africa. In most countries, civil institutions have proved to be weak and brittle.

Such political difficulties were not generally expected by either Africans or Europeans at the time of decolonization, but in retrospect their occurrence is not surprising. Modern Africa, like most of the world outside the West, has no experience of liberal democracy. There is no tradition of constitutional democracy, or even constitutionalism, at the national level. Although there were checks on the power and discretion of rulers in many traditional African chiefdoms and kingdoms, most of these societies were incorporated into larger multi-ethnic states by the colonial powers and never became states in their own right. Thus for traditional African constitutionalism to become established at the level of the state, the political traditions of one ethnic group would have to be accepted by all, which was very unlikely. . . .

African circumstances and cultures have almost invariably undermined imported liberal democratic constitutions: the indigenous societies and exogenous institutions are often sharply at odds. Plural democracy has proved to be ill-suited to the "plural society" which is a significant feature of most African countries. . . . Strictly speaking, a plural society is not a society because the social bonds and shared values that constitute a society are absent. Under such conditions, the social base needed to support an imported liberal democratic constitution—which postulates a radically different, individualistic, national society—is lacking. The imported democratic institutions are therefore likely to remain, at best, forms without substance.

In such circumstances, it is relatively easy for political actors to contemplate unconstitutional actions—certainly much easier than in states with well-established constitutional traditions. The temptation to disregard or violate the constitution is likely to increase if one believes that one's political rivals are planning illegal acts. Since most African countries are extremely poor, and the only significant source of power, wealth and privilege is the national government, it is easy to understand how the temptation to violate the constitution can be overwhelming both for those who now control the government and those who desire to gain control. Once the first unconstitutional acts occur and the ice is broken, so to speak, they are likely to be followed quickly by others. This eventually leads to the end of constitutionalism and the emergence of a system without rules—a zero-sum game of winner-takes-all know as authoritarian power politics. This is in fact the standard scenario of postindependence African politics. . . .

Of the forty independent countries in Tropical Africa, currently more than half are one-party states and more than one-quarter are military regimes. Fewer than ten of the one-party states are democratic to some degree, with varying restrictions on the capacity of electorates to determine who shall rule. Only three have comparatively open and energetic competition among large number of candidates for national legislative office: Kenya, Zambia, Ivory Coast. Kenya is the only country that has operated as a one-party democracy for a significant length of time—since the election of 1969—and is therefore a model for other African countries. Tanzania is also often considered to be a substantial one-party democracy. However, the ruling party exercises control in that the candidates compete for election to political office only after they have received the National Executive Committee's seal of approval. Tanzania has operated under such a system since 1965, and has become an alternative, more restrictive model of one-party democracy.

Unlike multiparty democracy, which is equated with capitalism and colonialism—an equation based more on ideology than on history—one-party democracy has a good press in Africa. The most frequently offered rationale for one-party democracy is national unity: the one-party system is believed to promote the unity of the state, whereas the multiparty system is thought to undermine it. . . . The negative version of the rationale for one-party democracy calls attention to the danger of multipartyism in multiethnic African countries. In attempting to justify his recent establishment of a one-party state in Sierra Leone, President Siaka Stevens said: "We have banned a system...(of) institutionalized tribal and ethnic quinquennial warfare euphemistically know as elections....We have done away with an unnecessary system." He maintained that a one-party system was not only desirable but also necessary "if the country is not to disintegrate into tribal faction." . . .

These arguments can serve as a rationale for authoritarian rulers to retain power by denying rival leaders and parties any opportunity to compete for election. It would be ingenuous to believe otherwise. However, the rationale should not be assumed to lack validity because it is self-serving. The fact is that multipartyism does present a serious risk of instability, disunity and even violence in African multiethnic countries owing to the unusual intensity and inflammatory character of ethnic division, combined with lack of self-restraint. Where the layer of social toleration and civility is very thin and fragile, a multiparty system may not be in the best interests of a country. . . . One-party government can foster unity by eliminating political contestation. The question is: can it be democratic?

If the political experience of Kenya in the last fifteen years is any evidence—and we believe it is—then, with a major qualification, the answer would seem to be "yes." Using Robert Dahl's terminology, the problem of democratic politics in Kenya is to invite "participation" of ethnic localities while avoiding the danger of unrestrained "contestation" between the country's large ethnonations. Kenya has tried to resolve the problem, with considerable success to date, by permitting almost unrestricted local involvement in one-party election to the National Assembly which are held on a regular basis and are reasonably fair. The result is an amazingly vigorous grass-roots democracy. The Kenyan electorate is as fickle as any, and at every election since 1969 many members of Parliament—including ministers and assistant ministers—have been turned out of office. For example, in the September 1983 election 40 percent of nonappointed MPs were defeated, as well as five ministers and twelve assistant ministers. A remarkable 991 candidates competed for 158 seats. If a Kenyan MP hopes to retain his seat, he must cater to his constituents with as much diligence and know-how as any member of the U.S. House of Representatives. . . .

Of course the major limitation of African one-party democracy is the exclusion of the presidency from electoral competition. This means that the electorate is unable to bring about a basic change of government. Even in Kenya the presidency is not occupied by a democrat who won a general election, but by an autocrat who came out on top in an authoritarian struggle for power. Trough his extensive powers to appoint MPs to a large number of cabinet posts and through other forms of patronage, the Kenyan president is able to exercise substantial control over parliament in much the same way English monarchs did before the democratic age. However, while the Kenyan electorate cannot change the government, it can cause large turnover in political offices by defeating incumbents and obliging the president to make new appointments.

The majority of African politicians have not been democrats—if willingness to submit to relatively free, open, fair and regularly held popular elections is the basis of definition. Only a very few rulers have been prepared to do this. Of those African politicians who are "democratic," most have been skeptical of liberal democracy and have experimented with more restrictive, usually one-party democratic institutions which are considered better suited to African political conditions. Liberal democracy is unlikely to develop in the foreseeable future. In contrast, one-party democracy . . . is more likely to find acceptance by rulers who quickly become aware of the political advantages of have the electorate dismiss unpopular politicians.

However, in many countries the problem of establishing democracy is secondary to the problems of establishing order, stability and civility. The historical development of democracy in the West has shown quite clearly that it is necessary to establish law and order, political stabiltiy and standards of civility before it is possible to provide democratic rights and opportunities. In more than a few African countries, this basic foundation is still lacking.

Women's Politics, the State, and Capitalist Transformation in Africa

KATHLEEN STAUDT[4]

Africa is a world region in which women, whether producing and processing food, trading on both large and small scales, or carrying water and gathering firewood, visibly participate in a wider economy, beyond that of domestic household units. Moreover, Africa stands out above other world regions with its widespread female-solidarity organizations, suggesting women's vital and collective voice in the polity. However, the modern state has diminished women's voice and power.

The modern state artificially divides society into public and private spheres. The public sphere consists of extrahousehold affairs; the private sphere, internal household matters. This division of reality into public and private comes to parallel the male and female worlds, even though the indigenous precolonial reality did not always conform to that division. Over time, the state, through its policies and systems of participation, *creates* that reality.

Historically, those who control or protect property and capital have comprised the modern state's active participants and decision makers. With the gradual expansion of political participation to men or through male authorities, women have come under the control and protection of men. The moral and legal foundations of this state define men as authorities over and representatives of women and children. This penetrates the private sphere and profoundly affects male-female power relations within it. . . .

The economic and ideological components of state-created public and private spheres meant that no policy and program supports were relevant, or even justified, for women, whatever their breadwinner or economic activities, because they were the responsibility of male breadwinners. State decision makers formulate policies

4. Staudt, Kathleen, "Women's Politics, the State, and Capitalist Transformation in Africa," in Irving L. Markovitz, *Studies in Power and Class in Africa,* (New York and Oxford: Oxford University Press, 1987): 193-208. Excerpts taken from pp. 193-197, 202-203, 205-208.

Kathleen Staudt teaches at the University of Texas at El Paso in the Political Science Department. She has written extensively on women and development. Her publications include *Agricultural Policy Implementation: A Case Study from Western Kenya* (West Harford: Kumarian Press, 1985), and *Managing Development: State Society, and International Contexts,* (Newbury Park, CA: Sage Publications, 1991).

and conduct politics with men in mind, or with the picture of reality in which men control and represent women. Once in place, the gender distinction undermines women's economic base and the political means to protect that base, thereby generating and perpetuating gender inequality.

Not surprising, women lack much interest in "official" politics and policies, which are seemingly irrelevant to them. A partial extension of the political agenda and of participation rights offsets this tendency somewhat. Women, as the last category to be incorporated into the chain of participants in the modern state, compete with the well-endowed, politically experienced, and other late entrants. Moreover, the few women activists, often *among* the well-endowed, voice concerns compatible with the modern state. Almost invariably, those activities reinforce and reproduce the power relations that the state protects. Even under socialism, the state has so deeply embedded public and private spheres which correspond with gender that real transformation of male-female reality is unlikely. . . .

Women's political functions in prestate and community politics were rich in variety and broadly representative of all sub-Saharan Africa. In southeastern Nigeria, women's authority structures paralleled men's to function as women's courts, market authorities, and overseers of village welfare. Women managed their own affairs in kinship institutions, age grades, secret and title societies. In markets, women fixed prices, settled quarrels among traders, and imposed fines to enforce their will. Ibo villages had women's councils at various territorial levels. Among the Mende in Sierra Leone, women's secret societies, called *Bundu*, protected women's rights and served as political support bases and training grounds for women chiefs, such as for Madam Yoko of the Kpa Mende Confederacy. In Cameroon, Bamileke female farmers belonged to the *Mensu*, a women's society composed of the best cultivators. The *Mandjon* was a group of important women who administered village work done by women, such as clearing paths. Among the Kikuyu in Kenya, women's age-segmented organizations matched those of men's and performed a wide variety of functions, including judgment, mutual aid, initiation into womanhood, cooperative farm labor, religious ceremonies, and disciplinary action among women. . . .

However prevalent women's participation, African societies were not unstratified by gender, class, or status. Not all societies had women's associations or authority structures, and in rigidly stratified societies with titled female leaders, ordinary women were often excluded from politics. In the rich variety of African precolonial state societies, such as the Baganda, rulers recruited men to participate in large-scale social labor, such as corvée public works, conscription, or collective labor, in order to accumulate surpluses to maintain their states. Karen Sacks argues that such labor made men "adults" in society's eyes, thereby denying adulthood to women and defining them as wards of men. Regardless of stratification patterns, the material accumulation of most African societies prior to colonialism limited the scope of existing resources, which were distributed unevenly (or evenly) by gender, class, and status. The colonial state hastened and aggravated this stratification, setting the stage for an expansion in the totality of resources to distribute unevenly, with men accumulating a disproportionate share of opportunities, wage employment, mobility, and credit. . . .

With the imposition of European colonialism in Africa, groundwork was laid to conceive of work, its value and reward, in ways already present in the highly differentiated and sex-segregated industrializing world. The best and the brightest of administrators selected for the colonial service were products of late-Victorian middle-class society in which women preserved the home refuge for men, who in turn insulated women from the pressures of public life. In this ideological model, men are the family breadwinners and men's work in the wage economy or in commercializing agriculture is viewed as necessary for "modernization." Policies were thereby established to pressure men to enter the wage economy through taxation, to train men for a commercial economy and civil service, to put property in men's names through land reform, and to subsidize men's farming through credit and extension.

While women remained active participants in economic production, that production was not valued with rewards in the same way as other (wage) work. With the spread of market economic systems, labor was redefined "so as to make it virtually synonymous with work for which cash or other forms of remuneration were paid." Other productive activities, once recognized as work, eventually were regarded as not quite "economic." A general obliviousness to women's indigenous political authority eliminated women's political agenda and women as political actors. . . .

Nationalist movements drew initially from the educated, urbanized World War II veterans and from the wage-earning populace, most of whom were men. As mobilization extended in the 1950s, women became active participants, both in protest activity and in guerrilla movements. African nationalist leaders such as Modiko Keita (Mali) and Sekou Touré (Guinea) publicly praised women's participation in militant action. Touré even exhorted women to deny sex to husbands unless they joined the party. Women collaborated in the famous Guinea 1953 strike which weakened the French colonial government. Women traders refused to sell chickens, eggs, and milk to the French; they, and peasant women, collected rice for the strikers. Ghanaian women were actively involved in the nationalist struggle, providing financial support and organizing trade boycotts. Madame Quezzin Coulibay (Ivory Coast) mobilized Abidjan women to invade prisons where party members were jailed at 3 A.M., surprising guards; a jolted government released party leaders two days later. Women also were active in guerrilla movements in both support and military functions from Algeria, Guinea-Bissau, Mozambique, Zimbabwe, and Angola to Kenya. . . .

Who benefits form the kinds of measures women advocated? Equal pay and maternity leave for work in *wage* labor exclude the overwhelming majority of ordinary women workers. Elsewhere on the continent there is a dismal regularity to this cycle of narrow goals that serve select interests and that result in political vulnerability and the replacement of leadership.

The implantation of male government under colonialism, its continuation, and the simultaneous depoliticalization of most women's issues to the private sphere became institutionalized at independence and thereafter. Former women's issues disappeared form the public or political agenda. Women's agricultural and trade activities were neither viewed as economic nor measured in national statistics, the indicators for which were developed in states with long-standing gender dichotomies.

Deprived of public resources to build on and extend their economic base in this commercialized economy, or deprived of even the "need" for those resources given the prevailing gender ideology, the resource gaps between men and women became aggravated. Any and all studies which examine the comparative male-female distribution of agricultural services, from Ghana and Senegal to Tanzania, Kenya, and Botswana find that women get less extension, training, and credit than men. Such distribution patterns are bound to reduce women's comparative productivity. Yet these phenomena are not viewed as "political." . . .

On the whole, women face a political system whose agenda they neither control nor influence systematically. With the historical legacies of their issues (becoming nonissues) and their minute representation in the largely male activist pool, women's politics is fairly ineffectual. Women activists play pluralist politics but often lose pluralist political games, being late joiners, voicing social issues not seen as economic, or threatening male interests. Women's political marginality in various kinds of regimes is illustrated in the following examples.

Abidjan women trades unsuccessfully utilized various strategies to reduce market rental fees, including delegations and fund-raising to facilitate entree with officials. Past support women gave to the mayor, party, and president was forgotten. Women beer brewers in Nairobi, while successful in securing some household units for women in a relocation project, piped water for their community, and delays in slum unit demolishment, have no access for formal jobs and education and face constant police harassment and consequent insecurity at the margin of survival. Still, there is some evidence of women voting the interest of their specific occupation's interests, such as women traders, bread-bakers, butchers, and fishmongers in Ghana. However important franchise rights, voting does little to expand political agendas or control officials in between elections or when there are no elections.

Women are no better in corporatist or authoritarian regimes, which absorb women (and sometime dismiss them at whim) or accommodate them in minimal ways. To centralize voluntary associations and subordinate them to the ruling party, Nkrumah replaced the Federation of Ghana Women (thought to support the opposition) with the National Council of Ghana Women. Political parties following Nkrumah have also had women's party wings but they are little more than paper organizations during elections. . . .

Public-private distinctions are social creations which seemingly create the proper setting for capitalist transformation and the long-term interests it serves. Much of precolonial Africa, while gender stratified, had no such distinctions. As such, gender issues were political issues, reflected in organizations and authority structures, and both relevant and central to society. The colonial state actively created gender distinctions, however much they diverged from indigenous reality. In so doing, men became the public actors, both economic and political, and women the private, apolitical guardians of the household. The dichotomy was a hierarchical one, allocating to men greater social valuation, and to women, subordination.

After decades, this ideology gradually penetrated educational institutions, law, policies, and government programs, thus making its way into people's consciousness and political participants' agendas. While the notion of public itself extended somewhat into the private sphere through social policy both the state and politically active women negotiated demands compatible with the public-private distinction, thus reinforcing that distinction. As one of many competitors in the political process now, women face overwhelming odds, against further extending the political agenda and women within it. Besides, women's politics, like other politics, is dominated by class interests which perpetuate a political agenda inimical to comprehensive gender redistribution. Periodically, however, women rise to assaults against their interests and reveal either visions of indigenous female institutions or the severe affronts to their sense of justice. Such activities prompt curiosity, too, about just how deeply the public-private ideology has penetrated or how long it will take to incorporate all women.

In this article, the state is viewed as a relatively autonomous actor, forging gender identities and institutionalizing them in law and policy. The processes synthesized here raise questions about whether the state can ever accommodate women's comprehensive gender concerns, or whether women can transform this edifice responsible for undermining their economic and political activities. Reformers seek redress from the state, but can the contemporary state, which undermined women's centrality to politics, be part of the solution for women? Many women remain aloof from politics, preferring autonomy or resisting incorporation, however much the state envelops them ultimately.

In Search of Citizenship: African Women and the Myth of Democracy

MOLARA OGUNDIPE-LESLIE[5]

There seems to be an almost superstitious (or perhaps just constructed) belief that multiparty systems will lead Africa to the political utopia that she needs. This belief appears implicit in the tying of aid to political stability of the parliamentary type. The populations of Africa themselves seem tired of the proliferation of military rule on the continent as they claim to be tired of the particular forms of governance handed down by soldiers. Between November 1958 and April 1984, 56 successful military coups were counted by one political scientist. Since then, more successful military coups have taken place in several countries, including Nigeria. While there is some general hope placed on democratic rule under civilians, even as marionettes, some voices are already warning that weak political parties can impede the installation and consolidation of democracy. One voice has warned . . . of "the danger that multipartyism will reflect, in the end, merely a consensus among the "elites" on the re-allocation of prebends." I feel that care needs to be taken that multipartyism does not promote ethnic division and hatreds while it ensures a further balkanization of the continent. . . .

Very often, too, on the continent, other nationalists, thinkers and political adventurers have harked back to our indigenous forms of government which some of us would argue guaranteed true democracy (if democracy is understood as the representation of the will of all the people who are encompassed by a political organism). Care has to be taken, however, to identify truly democratic procedures and structures in indigenous African governmental practice.

The term, "democracy," which is sometimes defined as "the assembly of the citizenry for the conduct of public affairs" should not in this day and age, be applied to village gatherings and assemblies which exclude women and slaves, which recognize only adult men, men with wives, and the freeborn only, or male elders exclu-

---

5. Ogundipe-Leslie, Molara, "In search of Citizenship: African Women and the Myth of Democracy" is a chapter in her book *Recreating Ourselves: African Women and Critical Transformations,* (Trenton: Africa World Press, 1994): 243-250. Excerpts taken from pp. 244-249.

Molara Ogundipe-Leslie is a widely published Nigerian poet and feminist. Together with Carole B. Davies she has edited *Moving Beyond Boundaries,* (Washington Square: New York University Press, 1995).

sively. Such gatherings should not be panegyrised, as some of us are doing, as fine examples of democracy. . . .

Fundamental questions first need to be posed, in my view, before we can even begin to discuss women and democracy in Africa. To get down to brass tacks, is the African women, in fact, a national of her own country? In how many countries does she have legal citizenship? Research shows that some countries have still not re-written their inherited colonial or settler constitutions (and not only Southern Africa) wherein and whereby women were legal minors. Ruling classes who are now enjoying the benefits of total control of their female counterparts may be loathe to change these outmoded laws. Do not internationally accepted laws and human rights conventions support the idea of a woman's adulthood (like that of any man) at eighteen or twenty-one when she is considered able to be responsible for herself? Some countries employ other social and religious traditions to keep women in a state of legal and social minority. Imagine the trauma and the confusion of African women, who are considered adult at puberty within indigenous laws and who have been adult in their social comportment in traditional realms within the dictates of their cultures, suddenly finding themselves incredibly handicapped by legal minor-ity in the modern state?

In how many countries can a woman sign her own forms to attain her own pass-port as a bona fide member and national of her own country of birth? The ability to acquire a passport is not a simplistic right, considering that a passport is one of the basic proofs of one's nationality. The woman's right to acquire her own passport without passing through a husband, father or male relative is often dismissed as a distractive and unnecessary introduction of foreign avant-garde ideas into Nigerian civil discourses. But if some African women are not, in fact, basic citizens of their countries through their own recognized will, how can we speak of democracy with regard to them?

Following right on the heels of the issue of citizenship are the rights of liberal democracy to which the African woman is supposed to be heiress. Does she have rights which the power classes in her country feel they are *bound* to respect? Is she considered an inalienable participant in the project of building democracy in the modern nation state or simply a means to an end, "a tool to democracy", an instru-ment for the mobilization of resources and rights to the male population? These are not idle questions as the experience of women demonstrate and the theories of development experts corroborate. Being instrumentalized has been the fate of African women in many countries. Established rights like freedom of movement or freedom of association are not so guaranteed as to make the African woman every-where a free political actor.

Experience in several African countries has demonstrated that women are not only included as tokens and sops to the demands by women for representation and participation in national projects, they are also basically conceived of as instruments to galvanize their husbands and children. Women are not in themselves conceived of as subjects in political discourse and action or direct recipients of the benefits of both. In general, women are seen to exist as instruments to be used for the political purposes of men. The woman in herself is not thought of as a citizen to be mobilized to attain political rights, benefits and advantages *for herself*. This reductive attitude to women is to be found, strangely enough, even among the most verbally progressive of the menfolk.

The attitude toward women's claim to liberal democratic rights is often one of charity couched in benign patronization. "We shall *confer* some rights on you if you behave yourselves, and certainly do not talk feminist" sums up the attitude. In some circles, the saying: "Women do not have rights that we as men are bound to respect" is often laughingly interchanged with: "The poor do not have political rights that we are bound to respect." The institutionalization of the habit of appointing one token woman to cabinets, commissions and committees to represent 60% of the populace confirms the attitude of patronization that men are being "kind" to women by including women at all.

Throughout Africa, a natural tendency seems to be towards the exclusion of women from national events, institutions and exercises, including *the writing out of her contributions* to the modern efforts at nation building, whenever these contributions are given space to occur at all. In addition, women are frequently not acknowledged for their ideas nor recognized as intellectual producers of ideas. When they have ideas, these are often pirated, appropriated and used without acknowledgment, recognition, or compensation. These politics of exclusion, unacknowledgment and appropriation help to ensure the silencing of women needed to shore up the hegemony certain men in the power classes derive from knowledge or the affectation of epistemic superiority.

Not only are African women sometimes not citizens or not considered as citizens in *themselves* (i.e., not as wives and mothers only), in the modern sociogony, planning is often not made with women in mind, neither are they called upon to participate in planning and policy. Some marginal spaces have been created by certain women in some countries where we also see an urgent haste for the usually phallocratic governments to co-opt these women's spaces and activities. Sometimes women's energies and organizations are used to work against women's interests. . . .

African women are not only written out of constitutions, commissions and committee reports, they are often erased out of the national canvas of power brokering and resource-sharing. Middle class women are often excluded and vilified because they are said to be too Westernized to represent the "true African woman," that is the romanticized, rural and unlettered African woman. At the same time, this rural and unlettered woman is naturally excluded and derided (in private, when the middle class woman is not being opposed) because she is too rural and too unlettered. So by this clever maneuver of excluding both the lettered and unlettered African woman, African women remain unconsulted and erased from the realm of events while African men maintain hegemony. The contemporary African nation state sails happily ahead as the exclusive preserve of middle class, lettered and westernized men. . . .

In politics, however, women are supposed to participate fully as "instruments to power" for men; as entertainers, campaigners, and party workers. They are not naturally accepted as candidates or considered candidates of the calibre of men. Most men still somehow resent women in a position of authority over them. Sometimes Christianity and Islam are evoked to support these attitudes. Meanwhile, modern democracy is supposed ideally, to function irrespective of gender and other variables.

The Black Man's Burden: Africa and the Curse of the Nation-State

BASIL DAVIDSON[6]

What follows, essentially, is a meditation on the nature of the African experience but, centrally, since Africans began to emerge from foreign rule, from colonial rule, in the 1950s. This has been an experience which inspired high hopes and promised liberating freedoms, and these were justified and real in their results. They gave new life to a continent of peoples long reduced to silence and subjection. That this should be so cannot surprise the historian, for the history of Africa's self-development, before foreign rule began, has shown that these peoples achieved much in the past, and will in all likelihood achieve much again.

But the actual and present condition of Africa is one of deep trouble, sometimes a deeper trouble than the worst imposed during the colonial years. For some time now, deserts have widened year by year. Broad savannahs and their communities have lost all means of existence, or else are sorely threatened. Tropical forest such as the world will never see again have fed the export maw. Cities that barely deserve the name have spawned plagues of poverty on a scale never known in earlier times, or even dreamed of. Harsh governments or dictatorships rule over peoples who distrust them to the point of hatred, and usually for good and sufficient reason; and all too often one dismal tyranny gives way to a worse one. Despair rots civil society, the state becomes an enemy, bandits flourish. Meanwhile the "developed" world, the industrialized world, has continued to take its cut of Africa's dwindling wealth. Transfers of this wealth to the "developed" countries of Europe and America have annually expanded in value: in 1988, for example, to what was then a record figure, an immense figure, paid out to "developed" creditors. And multitudes starved.

And so the historian, emerging from the study of past centuries when Africa generally knew no such misery and crisis but, generally, a slow expansion of wealth and self-development, meets questions not to be avoided. What explains this degradation from the hopes and freedoms of newly regained independence? How has this

---

6. Davidson, Basil, *The Black Man's Burden: Africa and the Curse of the Nation-State,* (New York: Random House, 1990). Excerpts taken from pp. 8-13, 162-164, 181-185, 262-263, 319-322.

Basil Davidson remains one of the most widely published and read historians of Africa. Many of his numerous books appear on course syllabi around the world and his widely aclaimed eight part television series "Africa" continues to reach a wide audience. His publications include *African Genius,* (Boston: Little Brown, 1969), *The African Slave Trade,* (Boston: Little Brown, 1980), and *Modern Africa,* (London: Longman, 1982).

come about? Where did the liberators go astray? . . .

We have to be concerned here with the nationalism which produced the nation-
states of newly independent Africa after the colonial period: with the nationalism
that became nation-statism. This nation-statism looked like liberation, and really
began as one. But it did not continue as liberation. In practice, it was not a restoration of Africa to Africa's own history, but the onset of a new period of indirect subjection to the history of Europe. The fifty or so states of the colonial partition, each
formed and governed as though their peoples possessed no history of their own,
became fifty or so nation-states formed and governed on European models, chiefly
the models of Britain and France. Liberation thus produced its own denial. Liberation led to alienation. . . .

A meditation of this kind provokes knotty questions, and tribalism is one of
them. A terrain full of pitfalls opens out beyond it. In a large historical sense tribalism has been used to express the solidarity and common loyalties of people who
share among themselves a country and a culture. In this important sense, tribalism
in Africa or anywhere else has "always" existed and has often been a force for good,
a force creating a civil society dependent on laws and the rule of law. This meaning
of "tribalism" is hard to distinguish in practice from the meaning of "nationalism."
Before the period of modern imperialism Europeans visiting and reporting on Africa
seldom drew any such distinction.

But the "tribalism" that we see today is evidently quite another thing. This modern tribalism flourishes on disorder, is utterly destructive of civil society, makes hay
of morality, flouts the rule of law. It is the reverse of the civil society revealed by
the records of history increasingly and intensively inspected, since the 1950s, by
historians from many cultures and countries. This was the civil society undermined
and finally brought down by the decades of alien rule after Africa's imperialist partition in the 1880s, leaving as it seemed no valid structures for the future. And this
of course was why British colonial policy claimed that its task in Africa was "nation
building," it being supposed in London that the task had been beyond the capacity
of Africans themselves. At first, the British set themselves to the work of inventing
tribes for Africans to belong to; later, with possible independence looking ahead,
they turned to building nation-states. Because, according to the British, there were
no African models, these states would have to be built on European models. So
these, being alien models, failed to achieve legitimacy in the eyes of a majority of
African citizens, and soon proved unable to protect and promote the interest of those
citizens, save for a privileged few.

Left with the shells of a fragile and fallible civil society, the majority have sought
ways of defending themselves. The principal way they have found of doing this is
through "tribalism," perhaps more accurately, clientelism: a kind of Tammany Hall-
style patronage, dependent on personal, family, and similar networks of local interest. Insofar as it is a "system," clientelism has become the way politics in Africa
largely operates. Its rivalries naturally sow chaos. Like the economic misery now
afflicting much of Africa, this tribalism—the term is always slippery—"reflects, in

significant part, pathological characteristics of the contemporary [Africa]state": of the postcolonial or, as some prefer to call it, the "neocolonial" nation-state which came from decolonization.

These quoted words are Crawford Young's, and here he was thinking especially of the neocolonial nation-state of Zaire, once the Belgian Congo. But his words apply widely, as we shall discover. . . .

So an analysis of Africa's troubles has also to be an inquiry into the process—the process, largely, of nationalism—that has crystallized the division of Africa's many hundreds of peoples and cultures into a few dozen nation-states, each claiming sovereignty against the others, and all of them sorely in trouble. . . .

The activists of the 1950s plunged into their chosen road of nationalism, seeing this as the only available guarantee of a route open to progress. They accepted the aim of building nation-states on the British model (or later, on the French) because, as it seemed to them and as they were strongly advised, there could exist no other useful objective. Nkrumah's advice that they should seek the political kingdom, and all would then be added to them, expressed a central maxim of which the truth appeared self-evident: once sovereignty was seized by Africans no matter under what conditions, the road to freedom and development would be their s to follow.

That this acceptance of the postcolonial nation-state meant acceptance of the legacy of the colonial partition, and of the moral and political practices of colonial rule in its institutional dimensions, was a handicap which the more perceptive of the activists well perceived. They foresaw some of its possible perils, and they armed against these perils. In accepting the British government's offer of 1951 to make him leader of a Gold Coast (Ghana) government pledged to an eventual African independence—a long step forward at the time—Nkrumah told his voters that "there is a great risk in accepting office under this new constitution which still makes us half-slaves and half-free." There would be a great need for "vigilance and moral courage" to withstand the consequent temptation of "temporary personal advantage." This was because "bribery and corruption, both moral and factual, have eaten into the whole fabric of our society and these must be stamped out if we are to achieve any progress."

No doubt it was inevitable that such warnings fell on deaf ears. Along with the nation-state as necessary aim and achievement, the legacy of the partition was transferred practically intact, partly because it seemed impossible to reject any significant part of that legacy, and partly, as one is bound to think in retrospect, because there was as yet no sufficient understanding of what the legacy implied. There were political thinkers, true enough, who understood that the colonial partition had inserted the continent into a framework of purely artificial and often positively harmful frontiers. There were others who perceived that a petty-bourgeois nationalism was bound to remain a nationalism subordinate to external powers organized on a capital-owning and capital-commanding basis. But they were few, and their voices feeble in the great resounding chorus of anticolonial agitations that was now heard on every side. . . .

In its essence, this 1950s nationalism had far less to do with any national cause than with demands of a social nature and content. "One thing's certain," wrote Jacques Rabemananjara, the Malagasy nationalist, in 1958, "in today's political vocabulary the word nationalism means, generally, the unanimous movement of coloured peoples against Western domination. What does it matter if the word doesn't really describe the phenomenon to which we like to apply it?" What fired the activists, in short, was never an imagined spectacle of the beauties of the sovereign nation-state, but the promise that the coming of the nation-state would strike away the chains of foreign rule and all that these had meant in social and moral deprivation. . . .

Critics have said that the pioneering nationalists of the 1950s should have better considered where they were heading and should have understood that nation-states fashioned from the structures and relationships of colonial states, and thereby produced from European and not from African history, were bound to be headed for trouble. This is asking a great deal of men and women to whom the lessons and examples of European history had been invariably presented as the sum and summit of all useful experience; moreover, as far as the crucial economic structures and relationships were concerned, these in the 1950s were little understood anywhere. . . .

[I]t is a misreading of history of those years to suppose that the nationalists, or at any rate the best of them, nourished any great illusions as to the obstructive nature of the colonial legacy they were going to accept. Its economic implications may have largely escaped them, just as these escaped their imperial rulers; but they thoroughly understood its political and moral implications, for it was from those implications that they, as the object of colonial rule, had suffered. At the same time it needs to be recalled that any informed "looking ahead" was difficult or impossible if only because, to the very last, colonial governments in all the empires hugged closely to their chest whatever sound information their administrative files might contain. They camouflaged their social and economic problems with clouds of condescending propaganda. Or they simply denied that these problems existed. . . .

Some among the leading nationalists, as I have indicated earlier, demurred. They argued for a different destination in multistate sovereignties of a regional or subregional nature. This would be widely forgotten in the futile anarchy that began to develop in the 1970s, and the anarchy would be laid at the doors of a purely African irresponsibility or incompetence. There would certainly be much of both, but not during the 1950s. It might be "trouble-making" for Julius Nyerere, years before national flags were hoisted over new sovereign states, to look ahead and recommend steps in preparation for an East African federation of Uganda, Kenya, and Tanganyika. And it might e "idealist chatter" for nationalist movements in 1958 to launch a regional organization, the Pan-African Freedom Movement of East and Central Africa, aiming first at independence and then at federation. But these were nonetheless political initiatives of foresight and imagination. Nothing came of them. But with active official support and promotion, something might have come of them. That something, one can argue, might have averted a measure of the sorrows which came after. . . .

And it did not happen then because the social aspects of anticolonial struggle still had command of the national aspects. Down the line of agitation and organization, among the mass of rural and urban supporters of the anticolonial movements, there was small sign of any developing loyalty or attachment to this or that colony-turned-nation. What the multitudes wanted, by all the evidence, was not a flag for the people or an anthem for the people, nearly so much as they wanted bread for the people, and health and schools for the people, while caring precious little, as these same multitudes would overwhelmingly prove in the years ahead, about winning frontiers for the people. The jubilant crowds celebrating independence were not inspired by a "national consciousness" that "demanded the nation," any more than were the Romanian peasants and their coevals in the nation-states crystallized some decades earlier from Europe's old internal empires. They were inspired by the hope of more and better food and shelter. . . .

Meanwhile, the problem of the 1990s, as thoughtful men and women in a good many African countries had begun to see and even to say, was the absence of a clear political catalyst that could break into the stagnation so as to set new ideas moving and new hopes stirring. Just as evidently, this catalyst, whatever it might turn out to be, was not going to take the form of some grand ideological "breakthrough." The ideas for that were not at hand, or were not sufficiently mature; or else, in the measure that these ideas emerged in the participatory schemes and policies of the anti-Portuguese liberation movements of the 1960s and 1970s, they were ideas that seemed defeated by the middle of the 1980s. All that was otherwise available, in terms of teleological salvation, as one or another manifestation of a religious fundamentalism, chiefly Islamic, from which nothing fruitful of peace and progress could be expected.

Social revolution meanwhile had vanished into a verbiage become absurd by empty repetition, even though, in practice, revolution of existing structures of stagnation remained ever more urgently desirable. If "inventing the future" had so far failed, this was certainly not from any lack of the need for it. . . . For what may after all be most deplorable about these fruitless years was not the hunger and frustration on every side, bitterly painful though all that might be, but the absolute hostility between rulers and ruled.

Notwithstanding all the manifold linkages of kinship, the gap between "have and have not," even between "have-something and have-nothing," appeared to become uncrossable once the power lines were set. It was as though these nation-statist structures had functioned and must function so as to rob the best-intended wielders of power—and these, here and there, were far from lacking—of any real capacity to share their power with those it was supposed to benefit. The continent whose past development had rested on a real participation in the use of power was now in this dead-end where power and participation had become sore enemies of one another. . . .

All such miseries of malice and incompetence or greed could be blamed for "the prime failure of this government." But they were not the cause; they were the effects. The cause was to be found elsewhere. It lay in "the failure of our rulers to reestablish vital inner links with the poor and dispossessed of this country." It was the failure of postcolonial communities to find and insist upon means of living together by strategies less primitive and destructive than rival kinship networks, whether of "ethnic" clientelism or its camouflage in no less clientelist "multiparty systems." . . .

No doubt, generally, there were and will remain plenty of well-nourished reasons for despair. All objectively expert judgments—whether on Africa or Eastern Europe, the two great zones I have compared in this book—shared in subscribing to these reasons. It appeared as good as certain that no kind of easy and prosperous future could now be achieved anywhere in the poor man's world, the ex-colonial world: existing system of wealth exploitation, with their ever-continuing transfer of resources from the impoverished to the privileged, stand too solidly in the way. But while despair is all very well for those who can afford it, despair comes too dear for those who can't. For those who can't, a ground for hope is a necessity.

I find it obvious that this necessity is far from assured. No matter what strivings for democracy there may be in the upheavals of the 1990s, there is no guarantee that a culture of tolerant consensus, a culture able to promote a politics of self-development, is going to be possible. . . . If one or other pirate falls in Africa, what promises that another will not take his place? And so on down the line, always looking over our shoulders at the old devils of nation-statist violence. . . . From this analysis it emerges that the ground for hope for those people who can't afford despair, meaning most people as things now stand, lies in one or another mode of politics of participation. This politics claims to raise a means of defending all those people who lie now on the losing side of the existing world system, the poor and the very poor, and offer them a means of survival.

On past showing this may seem to be claiming more than any such politics can deliver. And yet times have changed. No matter how old devils may posture and threaten, the two great contests of our epoch have gone against them: the crushing of Nazi-Fascist imperialism and the subsequent curtailment of other imperialisms; and then, against old devils become younger devils, the peaceful winding down of the East-West Cold War and its drive to terminal disaster. These tremendous facts build no new world, but they give sure scope for building one. And the core of this scope, it seems, lies in this building of a new politics, a postimperialist politics such as has not been possible before. If this has to mean new developments in democracy, as the evidence suggest, then the democracy of the early twenty-first century will be the politics of participatory self-commitment—or else it will be empty rhetoric, mere soapbox verbalism with different words.

What the analysis then goes on to demand, all this being so, is the invention of a state appropriate to a postimperialist future. To those who prudently reply that it can't be done, the answer will be that it can certainly be thought of. Cases spring to mind. It was already beginning to be thought of, even during the dreadful 1980s, in the projects of the sixteen-country Economic Community of West African States, and potentially again, in those of the nine-country Southern African Development Coordination Conference launched a little later. Each set of projects has supposed a gradual dismantlement of the nation-statist legacy derived from imperialism, and the introduction of participatory structures within a wide regionalist framework. And if it is objected (as it often has been) that these are aims beyond realistic reach, because these are nation-states which will never accept a lessening of their sovereign powers and privileges, another confident answer is that such aims were already in process of being reached in that most unlikely of regions, Western Europe, the very seat and cradle of nation-statism. As things were moving in the 1990s, even those most nationalist of peoples, the English and the French, might before long find themselves without sacred and sovereign frontiers between them. It could sound improbable; to many it must sound impossible. And yet as Galileo said in another dawn of dizzying change, *Eppur si muove*. And the earth, it has turned out, really does move around the sun.

Developing Democracy When Civil Society is Weak: The Case of Botswana

PATRICK P. MOLUTSI and JOHN D. HOLM[7]

Botswana has had competitive elections regularly for 25 years. The ruling Botswana Democratic Party (BDP) has won every time, but opposition parties are becoming stronger. They now control four local councils and are close to a majority in others. Many observers believe the opposition's national Parliamentary vote, 35 per cent in 1989, could be close to a majority in the 1994 election if the leading party in the opposition, the Botswana National Front (BNF), applies itself to developing a more expansive coalition. Critical to the openness of partisan conflict in Botswana is a climate of freedom of speech, press, and assembly. Secrecy of the ballot is rigorously observed.

Contrary to the conventional theory regarding the development of liberal democracy, Botswana's political tradition offers minimal support for organized group activity, and its rapid economic growth has spawned few such groups. In lieu of a pluralist structure to civil society, organized citizen influence has taken the form of a series of village based participatory institutions. The Botswana experience thus provides evidence of an important alternative path to democratic politics in Africa. As such, the country could be a model for some countries which do not have an indigenous pluralist culture.

In some ways Botswana's cultural, historical and economic development has been unique in Africa. In comparison with most other African countries, Botswana is ethnically homogeneous. Somewhere between 80 and 90 per cent of its 1-2 million people belong to one of the eight major Tswana tribes. An even higher per cent speak the same basic language and have similar cultural norms. British colonialism

7. Molutsi, Patrick P.; Holm, John D., "Developing Democracy When Civil Society Is Weak: The Case of Botswana," *African Affairs* 89:356 (July 1990): 323-340. Excerpts taken from pp. 324-325, 327-329, 331, 333-335, 337-340.

Patrick Moutsi teaches sociology and serves as coordinator of the Democracy Research Project at the Univeristy of Botswana. Together with John Holm he edited *Democracy in Botswana: The Proceedings of a Symposium Held in Gaborone,* 1-5 August 1988, (Gaborone, Botswana and Athens, OH: Macmillian and Ohio University Press, 1989).

John Holm teaches political science at Cleveland State University. He served as the first coordinator for the Democracy Research Project and has written extensively on Botswana.

had minimal impact by African standards. London established a protectorate in 1895, but the Tswana chiefs ruled almost unrestrained into the mid-1950s. The only major economic change during this time was increasing labour migration to South Africa. At independence in 1966 the new government could tap so few economic resources that over 40 per cent of its funds came from foreign governments.

During the last two decades Botswana's fortunes have dramatically changed. It has become one of Africa's economic miracles, averaging over ten per cent real growth per year. This development has been largely fueled by diamond mining. The country is currently the largest exporter of diamonds in the world in monetary terms. Cattle ranching has also expanded greatly in the post-independence period so that this sector is able to produce 15 to 20 per cent of the total export revenues.

The foregoing unique features aside, Botswana is typical of many African countries. Both the mass and the elite often perceive political disputes in ethnic terms. Consequently, the BDP government assiduously seeks tribal balance wherever possible. Literacy is low. Primary education has only become available to the entire population in the last decade. Urbanization is rapid. The capital city of Gaborone will triple its population of 120,000 within this decade. Migration is extensive. Somewhere around 10 per cent of the adults work in neighbouring South Africa. An equal number are temporarily absent from their permanent residences working within Botswana. Foreign influences in the form of aid organizations and multinational corporations play a major role in economic terms. Finally, as in the rest of Africa, a bureaucratic class largely based in the civil service and parastatal corporations presides over not only government but society and the economy as well. . . .

Government is assuming some corporatist characteristics: policy initiation takes place within government ministries; persuasion is presented as consultation; limits are placed on participation in politics; government dominates communication processes; and ministries create and control most organized groups. For the most part, this transformation has proceeded by default because civil society lacks the capacity and initiative to organize itself. Specifically, it does not have a group political culture; few politically oriented groups exist; elected representative rarely feel compelled to engage the public in policy discussion; private newspapers are weak; and the political parties do not reflect grass roots opinion on policy questions. . . .

If civil society is to organize itself against the state, persons who are knowledgeable must be available to do so. The nature of the employment structure in Botswana limits this possibility greatly in that most educated citizens work for government or one of its parastatals (one-third of the formal sector work force of approximately 150,000 is employed by government as civil servants or teachers). As is usual in developed liberal democracies, public employees are not allowed to participate in most political activity, the only exception being that employees of parastatals and those in government's industrial class can attend party meetings and run for local councils. The result is that a very high proportion of the politically attentive public in Botswana cannot engage in open political activity, particularly relative to national issues. . . .

The state even dominates the group formation process. Ministries initiate and finance many groups at the local level, including cooperatives, farmers organizations, and parent teachers associations. In many cases, government has imposed a model constitution on these associations. The new trade union act has greatly constrained trade unions, allowing the Commissioner of Labour to impose his own appointments on recalcitrant unions and permitting his representatives to attend almost all union meetings. To this point, these powers have not been used, but in the minds of union leaders the threat is real.

Groups do arise on their own, particularly in the urban areas, and they have some impact on politics. Most prominent are churches, women's and youth groups, service clubs, and sports organizations. However, government manipulates these groups through sizable financial grants. Well over 50 per cent of the budgets of some of these more autonomous organizations come from government. Such groups are hesitant to challenge prevailing arrangements. . . . None of the groups we studied participated at all in the politics of elections. An important factor inducing groups to stay out of election politics is that many voters do not make their choice on the basis of economic interests. It is rather tribal and personalistic loyalties which are critical. Politicians thus have little to gain by carrying the support of organized interest groups.

The absence of politicized social groups in Botswana means that elected officials must solicit public opinion directly if they are to keep informed in this regard. For this reason, the *kgotla* has enjoyed a resurgence as a medium through which consultation occurs. There is a general expectation among the attentive public that councilors and MPs will tour *kgotlas* in their districts both before and after a legislative session. The MPs are given an allowance, which in the larger constituencies is close to $1000 per month, to make these tours. . . .

The argument in this section is twofold. First, the state has organized itself to control group activity in Botswana. Second, it is relatively successful because civil society remains immobilized. The corporatist tactics of the government exist with little in the way of organized group challenges. This leads to the question on which the next section of this article is focused: Is it possible that, within such a semi-corporatist context, there are alternative means of citizen control not suggested by the pluralist model of democracy? The answer we propose is that a number of community based institutions have exercised important, if not continuous, limits on elected politicians.

The problem in a democracy is to find devices by which public officials are compelled to respond to citizen needs and concerns. Elections in themselves are not sufficient. In a pluralist system, group leaders mobilize their publics on issues of concern to them. In Botswana a different process of opinion formation takes place. Political activist at the local levels use community meetings to educate the populace as to its grievances and to legitimize criticism of the government. The focus is different from a pluralist system in that citizen mobilization deals with local problems rather than the national allocation of resources.

This approach builds on the associational relationships, including those in the family, which are most significant to people in the rural areas. It takes advantage of existing community leadership. It also reflects a tension which exists between "us", the community, and "them", mainly outsiders, most particularly the central government. At present three forums are most important to this process: *kgotlas,* freedom squares, and party primaries.

As we have already noted, elected officials and civil servants have adopted the traditional Tswana *kgotla,* the meeting place in front of the chief's residence, to mobilizing the public for various government programmes. They do not always succeed, however, in controlling the meetings. Sometimes the community may reject a project; in other cases it may propose an alternative course of action. . . .

To accommodate party politics, a new type of community meeting called the "freedom square" emerged just before independence. Any political party or group of political activist had a right to call a freedom square. With few limits (it is not acceptable, for instance, to insult the President), there is freedom of speech at these meetings. The resulting dialogue is highly emotional, personalistic and partisan. At most of these rallies activists from parties not organizing the meeting are present to heckle *and* to observe public reactions. However, there is some policy discussion.

. . .

A third important community forum is the party primary, which is better described as a nomination caucus. The BDP and the BNF hold primaries around six month before the national election. Members of the party in a constituency or delegates for subsection of the constituency meet on an appointed day and select their party's candidate for the next election. While the vote in these meetings is not binding on the national organization, almost all caucus decisions prevail. . . .

Critical to the establishment of a democracy is that autonomous basis of influence arise over time in response to social change and political events. This is what has happened in Botswana with respect to the community based institutions we have just discussed. In the nationalist period, the political parties were denied access to the *kgotlas* by the chiefs; so they established freedom squares as a comparable means to reach the people. The post-independence government decided to legitimize its local policies through the use of the *kgotla.* The BDP created primaries in the early 1980s as a means of ousting the first generation of party leaders who were becoming too old and out of touch with their communities.

This process of institutionalizing democratic controls takes time and includes experiments that fail. It involves political debate where the problems with the present structures are identified and various solutions are considered. The motivation for change will often come from those excluded form power. They must demand their inclusion. . . .

The argument of this paper is that a pluralist democracy cannot emerge in Botswana and in many parts of Africa except through a period of transition, which most probably will be measured in decades. The same barriers to group formation that other more developed democracies have confronted, and continue to have in some form or other, are bound to be present in the African context.

Botswana's problems of an authoritarian culture, a powerful state structure, an absence of organized and politically oriented groups, paternalistic representation, a submissive mass media, and elitist party structures are not unique. They are to be found in even those countries which are labeled more "progressive" such as Tanzania and Senegal. Coping with these problems is a reality of democratic development in Africa.

The instructive aspect of the Botswana experience is the possibility of making use of community based institutions of popular influence during a period of transition to democracy. At a minimum these institutions can establish a tradition of popular control. The impact of these institutions may in most cases be minimal in that they largely affect policy implementation and rarely lead to leadership change. In the long run, however, community based participation forums in countries such as Botswana may be critical in facilitating institutionalization of pluralist forms of accountability. These forums can be places where the rights of new groups can be defended and where group leaders can seek grass roots control over national leaders and their policies. The specific institutions that have developed in Botswana may not work in other African countries. What is important is that such transitional controls by civil society be sought.

South Africa and the Politics of Divided Societies

TIMOTHY W. SISK[8]

Negotiation in South Africa entailed redefining the new rules of the political game for both the transition and the new political order. Driving negotiation forward to a settlement was the central lesson of conflict in deeply divided South Africa as it entered the postapartheid era: No single actor could unilaterally impose its rule preferences on others, given the balance of power. As a result, the institutional choices converged through strategic interaction among the major parties. Institutional choices were formulated and reformulated with an acute appreciation for what was possible, given the preferences and bargaining power of others. Clearly the dramatic transformation of politics in South Africa from the centrifugal impasse of 1984-89 to the centripetal pull of 1993 deserves careful inspection for its implications for the potential management of conflict in other deeply divided societies. Above all, this experience shows how the politics of discord in a deeply divided society can conceivably evolve toward conflict-regulating institutions through negotiation.

Although transition in South Africa was and will remain very turbulent, the prospects for a postapartheid democracy are far beyond the expectations of even the most optimistic observers just a few years ago. The underlying social conditions for conflict clearly remain; the patterns of conflict will be managed, but not eliminated. The reorientation of the conflict away from legally sanctioned and enforced racial segregation toward a multiethnic, democratic outcome occurred because a critical mass of centrist actors' interests were best served so. . . . Democratic institutions will in all likelihood emerge out of the South African transition; the unresolved issue is whether they can be sustained and whether a truly participatory democracy will evolve. . . .

The South African case shows how the interests of political parties can converge on democratic institutions through negotiation as they pursue their common interest

---

8. Sisk, Timothy W., "South Africa and the Politics of Divided Societies", is a chapter in his book *Democratization in South Africa: The Elusive Social Contract,* (Princeton: Princeton University Press, 1995): 284-299. Excerpts taken from pp. 284-290, 298-299.

Timothy Sisk is the Program Officer in the Special Program in Middle East Peacemaking and Conflict Resolution at the United States Institute of Peace. As a 1991 Fulbright Scholar, he went to South Africa and did the initial research for this book. Sisk has also published *Islam and Democracy: Religion, Politics, and Power in the Middle East.* (Washington D.C.: U.S. Institute of Peace, 1992).

in escaping stalemate in an intractable social conflict. If this is true of South Africa, it may also be true of other divided societies. How can a settlement that creates democratic institutions result even when the underlying conditions for sustaining democracy—tolerance, civil and political liberties, a culture of human rights—are absent?. . . .

In divided societies, a recognition of a shared or common destiny is a recognition of interdependence. The interdependence relationship is heightened when there is a perceived balance of power among actors. Interdependence in an unbalanced power relationship leads actors either to believe that they can subdue their opponents (if they perceive the imbalance to be in their favor) or to fear their opponent will subdue them (if they perceive the imbalance to be unfavorable). In both instances, an unbalanced power relationship leads to a zero-sum view of the conflict: dominate or be dominated, submit or withdraw from the common society. The South African conflict moved from a zero-sum to positive-sum perception when the balance of power between the dominant white minority and the increasingly empowered black majority reached a level of approximate parity.

These important determinants of change in South Africa—interdependence and a changing balance of power—which laid the underlying conditions for the onset of negotiation toward democratization, may not be present in other divided societies. Where an incumbent regime perceives that it can maintain its dominant power position or where an insurgency believes that it can prevail through armed force, negotiated democratization is an inherently limited possibility. . . . But when a balance of power and interdependence do exist, the possibility of moving beyond deep-seated conflict to a positive-sum alternative is present. . . .

When negotiation does begin, so does a period of intense uncertainty...The onset of transition means the impending adoption of a new set of rules, rules that are unpredictable, uncertain, and untested. Expectations, either of demise or aggrandizement, flourish, So, too, do aspirations for a better future. During this initial period of transition from authoritarianism toward a new, negotiated democracy, mobilization occurs as open political activity is first tolerated or resurrected. Political parties and actors mobilize in order to demonstrate their power in anticipation of the creation of the new rules of the political game. What makes democratic transitions so difficult is that this mobilization occurs during a period in which there is a vacuum of well-defined rules of the political game, a time of intense uncertainty. . . . The uncertainty of transition can yield the fear of political extinction, a fear strong enough to cause some to turn to violence for their own survival. . . .

A mutual security pact, such as South Africa's National Peace Accord, can potentially provide sufficient assurances to parties that their political future is secure. It can eliminate the immediate source of uncertainty over whether the new game will result in permanent political exclusion. But the Peace Accord did not immediately succeed because the uncertainty of transition continued to reign.

Whereas uncertainty over a political party's vital interests, over political survival, can potentially prevent a settlement (and it nearly did in South Africa), uncertainty over how a political party may fare under the future rules is a different matter. Uncertainty following a successful mutual security pact is the hope of winning the game, if not all of the time, at least some of the time. . . . Minority parties will continue playing the game within the new institutions if the can win on some issues by their ability to prevail over the will of the majority. They must not always win elections, but they must be able to win on some critical issues some of the time. . . . When they continue playing, political conflict is reoriented from an anarchic, violent arena to the political institutions of the state. . . .

Centrist political actors in divided societies are locked in a mutually dependent power relationship; this was especially true of the newly emerging center in South African politics. . . . When the power relationship is balanced, collusive decision making becomes an enterprise in the interests of the parties themselves. As de Toit writes, "Power sharing is necessary not only because the antagonistic groups see each other as potential enemies, but because they are in fact each other's only potential *allies*." Centripetal institutions are potentially viable for conflict-regulating democratic institutions in divided societies, and can evolve out of a stalemate if mutual dependence is sufficiently strong. This leads to another important conclusion: Institutional choices in divided societies can converge on a social contract which eschews ethnic politics if there exists a centrist core of political parties with sufficient uncertainty about their potential to win outright in the new game, and if there is a roughly balanced, mutually dependent power relationship among them. . . .

Given sufficient consensus, a just political system can evolve out of situations rife with ethnic or racial conflict when political parties, pursuing their own self-interest in the course of transition, derive a set of fair principles of justice that command the consent of all those committed to living by them. The substantive principles of justice are those which emanate from the choices of the political actors themselves pursuing their own interests. . . .

In divided societies, democratization settlements need to be exceptionally broad and inclusive. Complete consensus is not only unobtainable given empirical conditions, it may not be desirable. The objection to consensus government is a deeper one that arises from the structure of it as a decision-making rule itself. A universal right of consent . . . is tantamount to "pure autocracy" if every individual has the right to veto every government policy. Therefore the need arises to arrive at non-consensual rule that allows for a broad enough base of support that allows the new rules to survive. How inclusive should it be? A consolidated moderate center, choosing centripetal institutions to protect its own interests as it perceives them, can survive over time under conditions of democracy if it can use the very institutions of inclusive democracy to marginalize extremist opponents through the ballot box rather than through the coercive forces of the state. At first, severely limited democracy—hegemonic exchange—may be all that is possible; after all, the democratization pact was a settlement among elites. In order to govern a still-divided society, moderate elites may need to initially establish an inclusive hegemony. Friedman writes that:

> [I]t is possible to envision a prolonged period of limited democracy, partial stability, and contradictory interaction between the parties. In this phase, conflict that seemed to hasten disintegration would be mixed with cooperation whenever the abyss really yawned. Given the way the parties have interacted so far . . . this may be the most realistic projection."

For this reason, Friedman correctly refers to a long transition before the final outcome of the democratization process in South Africa is fully known. . . . .

The events between the adoption of the democratization pact in late 1993 and the highly successful founding election in April 1994 reinforce the essential themes that emerged during the transition. First, the centripetal force of the political system was reaffirmed as one after another of the rejectionist parties responded to the incentives of inclusion and participation and the disincentives of spoiling. The IFP [Inkata Freedom Party] chose brinkmanship over spoiling and jumped aboard the train at the latest of moments. Second, political violence—an endemic feature of the transition—would not disrupt the process. As the election neared, tensions soared and many lives were lost as uncertainty and anxiety gripped the country. Yet heightened political violence reinforced the determination of the moderate parties to proceed with the transition. Third, the transition was based on pact making. For example, bringing in the IFP entailed a pact that assured its vital interests—perpetuation of the traditional and tribal authority structures—would be protected in the new order. Finally, the institutions chosen by the parties themselves proved to have conflict-mitigating effects. The election, fought under proportional representation, generally met the parties' expectations of how the electoral system would perform and allowed each of the major protagonists to gain a share of power in the new order, both at the national and regional level. Their expectations of how they would fare were also met.

The successful conclusion of South Africa's transition does not mean that underlying conflicts have been resolved. Real conflicts of interest remain. Indeed, the campaign itself reflected the fact that the society remains deeply divided. The ANC [African National Congress] earned very few white votes, and the NP [National Party] won very few African votes (although it carried a majority of Coloured and Indian votes); the IFP mobilized on ethnic chauvinism. The building of truly integrated political parties, and of civil society, must await the era of nation building. And racial and ethnic outbidding will remain a constant danger, especially if strong economic performance is not forthcoming. Yet with a successful founding election, South Africa's negotiated transition—and the institutions created in the course of those negotiations—are imbued with legitimacy. The challenge ahead will be to use that legitimacy to create a set of permanent postapartheid institutions that perpetuate the moderation, borne of necessity, that arose during South Africa's transition from apartheid to democracy.

Suggested Readings

Anyang'Nyong'o, Peter, "State and Society in Kenya: The Disintegration of the Nationalist Coalitions and the Rise of Presidential Authoritarianism 1963-78," *African Affairs* 88:351 (April 1984): 229-251.

Bayart, Jean-Francois, *The State in Africa: The Politics of the Belly* (London and New York: Longman, 1993).

Bienen, Henry, *Armies and Parties in Africa* (New York and London: Africana Publishing Company, 1978).

Chabal, Patrick, (ed.), *Political Domination in Africa: Reflections on the Limits of Power* (London: Cambridge University Press, 1986).

Chazan, Naomi, "Africa's Democratic Challenge," *World Policy Journal* 9:2 (1991): 279-307.

Cheru, Fantu, *The Silent Revolution in Africa: Debt, Development and Democracy* (Harare, Zimbabwe, and London: Anvil and Zed Books, 1989).

Davidson, Basil, "Questions about Nationalism," *African Affairs* 76:302 (January 1977): 39-46.

Decalo, Samuel, "African Personal Dictatorships," *Journal of Modern African Studies* 23:2 (1985): 209-237.

———, "The Process, Prospects and Constraints of Democratization in Africa," *African Affairs* 91 (1992): 7-35

Fatton, Robert Jr., "Bringing the Ruling Class Back In: Class, State, and Hegemony in Africa," *Comparative Politics* 20:3 (April 1988): 253-264.

———, *Predatory Rule: State and Civil Society in Africa* (Boulder, CO, and London: Lynne Rienner Publishers, 1992).

Geisler, Gisela, "Troubled Sisterhood: Women and Politics in Southern Africa, Case Studies from Zambia, Zimbabwe and Botswana," *African Affairs* 94 (1995): 545-578.

Graf, William, "Issues and Substance in the Prescription of Liberal-Democratic Forms for Nigeria's Third Republic," *African Affairs* 88:350 (January 1989): 91-100.

Holm, John; Molutsi, Patrick, (eds.), *Democracy in Botswana: The Proceedings of a Symposium held in Gaborone, 1-5 August 1988* (Gaborone, Botswana, and Athens, OH: University of Botswana, and Ohio University Press, 1989).

Jackson, Robert; Rosberg, Carl, *Personal Rule in Black Africa: Prince, Autocrat, Prophet, Tyrant* (Los Angeles and Berkeley: University of California Press, 1982).

Kpundeh, Sahr John, ed., *Democratization in Africa: African Views, African Voices.* (Washington D.C.: National Academy Press, 1992).

Lewis, Peter, "Endgame in Nigeria? The Politics of a Failed Democratic Transition," *African Affairs* 93:372 (1994): 323-340.

Macmillan, Hugh, "Swaziland: Decolonisation and the Triumph of 'Tradition'," *The Journal of Modern African Studies* 23:4 (1985): 643-666.

Markovitz, Irving Leonard, (ed.), *Studies in Power and Class in Africa* (New York and Oxford: Oxford University Press, 1987).

Nzongola-Ntalaja, "Presidential Address, The African Crisis: The Way Out," *African Studies Review* 32:1 (1989): 115-128.

Ogbuagu, Chibuzo S. A., "The Nigerian Indigenization Policy: Nationalism or Pragmatism?" *African Affairs* 82:327 (April 1983): 241-266.

Parson, Jack, (ed.), *Succession to High Office in Botswana: Three Case Studies* (Athens, OH: University of Ohio Press, 1990).

Shaw, William H., "Towards the One-Party State in Zimbabwe: a Study in African Political Thought," *The Journal of Modern African Studies* 24:3 (1986): 373-394.

Tripp, Aili Mari, "Gender, Political Participation and the Transformation of Associational Life in Uganda and Tanzania," *African Studies Review* 37:1 (April 1994): 107-131.

Willame, Jean-Claude, "Political Succession in Zaire, or Back to Machiavelli," *The Journal of African Studies* 26:1 (1988): 37–49.

Wiseman, John A., *Democracy in Black Africa: Survival and Revival* (New York: Paragon House Publishers, 1990).

PROBLEM V

DEVELOPMENT IN SUB-SAHARAN AFRICA FAILURE OR SUCCESS

Since the independence of the African states, their economic development has generated much controversy as to resources, methods, motives, and results. Each one of these could result in a separate problem in this volume, for which there is neither space nor purpose. To elaborate on the many and diverse aspects of development would not necessarily provide clarity, for many have already confused what is meant by "development." There is, however, one fundamental issue about which there is no ambiguity but a clear and sharp division of opinion—who must bear the burden of responsibility for the widespread failure of development in independent Africa, the colonial powers of the past or the African governments of the present?

As the majority of the European African colonies gained their independence early in the 1960s, there was a general euphoria by Africans and Westerners alike who shared an optimistic view of the continent's future. Independence promised to mobilize the Africans' energies and their resources in the service of the African people. Today the expectations at the beginnings of independent Africa have turned to despair, and the heady years of the 1960s now appear hopelessly naive. Social unrest, economic stagnation, and political instability have become endemic throughout the majority of African states. At the heart of Africa's plight is the question of development. Why has African economic development lagged so far behind that of other nations on other continents? Who is to blame, the imperialists and their legacy or the Africans in power since the coming of independence?

Crawford Young asserts that the current development crisis in Africa has its roots in the colonial occupation. He argues that the nature of the post-colonial African state is a product of the past, the colonial era, and is responsible for many of the economic and social problems of the post-colonial state. These independent

African states inherited, with little modification from their colonial rulers, systems that have contributed significantly, whether they be political, social, or economic, to their instability and are the root of the current development crisis. In his view, the colonial powers created a unique state in Africa, which has proven incapable of providing the social and political environment necessary for sustained growth.

Elliot P. Skinner has long been a critic of colonial rule and places the responsibility for the current failure of African development on the colonial experience. He argues that the colonial economies placed African societies at the mercy of global forces and Western interests over which they had little control. Despite political independence, these forces and interests continue today to dictate and shape economic development. Western development programs in Africa, particularly since independence, imposed a scale of size, pace, and financial demands that are often inappropriate to African conditions. "The present concern about the 'inability' of African countries to develop as rapidly as other countries is as much due to cultural perceptions as it is a concern with the actual rate of cultural change there." For African development needs to take place at a rate commensurate with local realities, using indigenous methods and judged by local standards and not those imposed by the West.

The Ghanian, K.E. Agovi, strongly supports the arguments of Crawford Young and Elliot Skinner, but shifts his criticism more to the present than the past. This is the age of "neo-colonialism" in presumably an independent Africa where the presence of Western resources for development are far from altruistic. He argues that donor nations and organizations use aid to manipulate Africans to their detriment, undermining their cultural and economic integrity and essentially perpetuate the attitudes towards the Africans by the colonialists. This dependence on Western aid stifles African development and, like the past, benefits the West more than Africa. "Independence of mind and initiative," he believes, "were completely eroded by the kinds of aid proposed by Western countries." He, like many African critics of Western aid, appeal for new approaches to development that free Africans from Western initiatives and models.

There is, however, another side to this Problem whereby many argue that the time has passed for "bashing the colonialists" and after forty years of independence the Africans themselves must assume responsibility for the decay of the quality of life in Africa symbolized by the failure of development. This is not an idle charge and has been at the center of debate by Western governments, humanitarian agencies, and such institutions as the World Bank and the United Nations, which have been the principal financiers of African economic development.

The nature of African development and its future has been an eternal debate at the World Bank, the principal lending agency to Africa. Robert S. Browne summarizes the most recent exchange in this debate as to the proper role of Western aid in promoting economic growth in Africa. The African position (as presented in the 1989 report "African Alternative Framework to Structural Adjustment Programmes") is strongly critical of Western demands for "structural adjustment," calling them callous and failing to take to account the "human factor." The World Bank is disinclined to be portrayed as inhuman but emphasizes that the African states cannot ignore economic or fiscal reality. The World Bank's response to "African Alternative Framework to Structural Adjustment Programmes" was a position paper entitled "Sub-Saharan Africa: From Crisis to Sustainable Growth" in which the rapid pace and scope of painful adjustments are necessary to arrest what the Bank perceives as Africa's downward spiral into economic crisis. Implicit in the Bank's policy is that it is the Africans themselves through corruption, mismanagement, and political and fiscal ineptitude who are responsible for decay. To place the blame on the colonialists of the past is irrelevant to the current failure of development. Browne ends on an optimistic conclusion that hopefully the two protagonists, Africa and the West, can move toward a consensus on strategies for future development.

Andrew M. Kamarck provides a different interpretation of the failure of African development from that of the bankers but comes to the same conclusion. He argues that the expectations of the Africans as to development have been inflated beyond the realities of the current available resources of the continent. Climate, geology, disease, and an insufficient understanding of what the natural resources of Africa can support has not only determined the glacial pace of economic development in Africa, but created the myth that Africa actually possessed "enormous and easily exploitable resources." Certainly, this myth was peddled by the imperialists, but more important, it was fervently believed by African national leaders who roused the expectations of their constituents by placing the blame on foreign exploitation. The myth continues to this day, shaping the attitudes and policies of African leaders irrationally and irresponsibly.

Finally, David Fieldhouse examines the economic history of Africa from the 1940s to the late 1970s, wondering why political independence did not lead to economic autonomy and sustained development predicted at the coming of African independence by both Western economists and particularly the African nationalists. After discussing the economic dynamics of decolonization (the Europeans transferred political power when they no longer needed to govern the colonies to ensure opportunities for metropolitan capital), he turns to the economic consequences of decolonization. He points out that African development varied greatly within black Africa, but by the 1970s there was general decline in development throughout the continent. Exaggerated expectations were common whereby African states were incapable of carrying out sophisticated development, but these expectations often led African governments to emphasize industrial development when they did not possess the human or material resources to achieve it. Sustained development in Africa had to be built on agricultural productivity, not the myth of an industrial revolution, which was compounded by the increased dependence on foreign borrowing to finance flawed development policies. " . . . [T]he broad interventionist strategies adopted by almost all states were undesirable." Nor were the development policies of the African states in regard to agriculture any better than those applied to industry. In fact they were worse. The agricultural policy of African states, fixed by "monophonic marketing boards," discouraged the development of indigenous agricultural production. State farms were a disaster to development. The failure of these development policies lies with a bankrupt political system, incompetent and corrupt African management, and the greed of the self-seeking African elite. Fieldhouse recognizes environmental factors (see Kamarck's previous views on Africa's natural resources) that have inhibited economic growth in tropical Africa. But in the last resort, African economic development has been restricted by low productivity, "stagnation," in peasant agriculture, the development of which was largely ignored by African politicians and governments.

Bula Matari and the Contemporary African Crisis

CRAWFORD YOUNG[1]

We are not interested in the preservation of any of the structures of the colonial state. It is our opinion that it is necessary to totally destroy, to break, to reduce to ash all aspects of the colonial state in our country to make everything possible for our people.

The problem of the nature of the state created after independence is perhaps the secret of the failure of African independence.

—AMILCAR CABRAL, "THE STATE IN AFRICA"

In 1879–1880, Henry Morton Stanley, an American in Leopoldian livery, forced a small army of porters bearing dismantled steamers over the tortuous terrain separating tidewater in the Zaire estuary from the vast pool of the Congo (Zaire) River above the rapids. Beyond lay the huge network of navigable waters along which the meager yet sufficient "tools of empire" projected the developing power of the colonial state in formation. Stanley's logistical feat engendered mingled fear and admiration in the Congo regions through which he passed, reflected in the nickname Bula Matari (he who crushes rocks) by which he became known.

Over time, as the new state on whose construction Stanley had surreptitiously embarked ceased to be his personal undertaking as Leopoldian emissary and burgeoned into an impersonal embodiment of oppressive European power, Bula Matari came to represent this intrusive alien authority more generally. The metaphor captured well the crushing, relentless force of the emerging colonial state in Africa. "For all Bakongo," wrote a Zairian sociologist, "the name of Bula Mata(r)i signified terror."

European administrators found this semiotic imagery congenial, as it suggested the irresistible hegemony deemed necessary to performance of their guardian role.

1. Young, Crawford, "Bula Matari and the Contemporary African Crisis," in *The African Colonial State in Comparative Perspective* (New Haven: Yale University Press, 1994): pp. 1-292. Excerpt taken from pp. 1-15, 283-288, 290-292.

Crawford Young is a Professor of Political Science at the University of Wisconsin, Madison, and has served as President of the African Studies Association. He is author of numerous books including *The Rising Tide of Cultural Pluralism: The Nation State at Bay* (Madison, WI: University of Wisconsin Press, 1993).

In the everyday informal discourse of rule, the prefectoral agents of Belgian colonial power widely employed the term as a synonym for "state"; a summons from Bula Matari was an order from the government. In the symbolism of Bula Matari the colonial state is stripped naked: the term did not apply to the layers of African intermediaries who in a number of settings partially concealed it from village view; it referred solely to the alien, white domination that was the energizing force in the superstructure of imperial hegemony.

Bula Matari as specific lexical rendering of the colonial state was particular to the Belgium realm. Yet its evocative imagery can be projected onto the much larger domain I explore: the African colonial state in its variant forms throughout the continent. In its ultimate teleology—the vocation of domination—are embedded the behavioral imperatives that marked its operation.

Bula Matari as a codeword for the superstructure of alien rule brings us back to Cabral's normative appeal in the epigraph above "to totally destroy, to break, to reduce to ash" the colonial state, to repay Bula Matari in his own metaphorical coin. The empirical Cabral sounds a more somber note than does his moral exhortation; the colonial state lives, absorbed into the structures of the independent polity. A state, once institutionalized, has a formidable capacity for its own reproduction across time and in the face of systematic efforts by new regimes to uproot prior forms and build new blueprints. Residues of Czarist Russia and the Middle Kingdom remained within the state socialist forms constructed by revolutionary design in the Soviet Union and China. Nationalist revolution in Africa had less sweeping goals, and thus by silent incorporation it retained more of the operational code of its defeated enemy in the postcolonial polity. In metamorphosis the caterpillar became butterfly without losing its inner essences.

Some will find Cabral's categorical pronouncement of the "failure" of the African state too sweeping: not in all places, one might demur, not in all ways. For those states whose disarray and decay were most striking at the beginning of the 1990s—the Sudan, Somalia, Zaire, Mozambique—the label fits reasonably as a global judgment, although even here on close inspection some positive elements mights be discerned. For the most capably ruled states—Botswana and Mauritius stand out—the progress we once believed immanent in modern historical process has occurred and been widely shared with civil society. But for most African states the 1970s and 1980s were years of disappointment and often decline; by the 1980s the term *crisis* had achieved general currency as a description of the African condition.

African independence in the 1960s coincided with a time of immense self-confidence in the world at large. In the West the prolonged post-war prosperity was at its apogee; Keynesian theory had conquered the business cycle, and Western Europe had recovered from the ravages of World War II. In the Soviet Union, Nikita Khruschev was promising to bury capitalism and to surge triumphantly into full communism by 1980. China's "great leap forward" then under way was not recognized as a lethal catastrophe until many years later. With hubris resonating throughout the world and exhilaration at the unanticipated swiftness of African independence, the high optimism that attended the transfer of power is not surprising. An influential pan-African assembly of intellectuals at Ibadan in 1959 reflected the general mood: supreme confidence in the capacity of the intelligentsia to lead new nations through socialist policies to social justice; "to throw off the imperialist yoke, and end discrimination and the exploitation of man by man"; to gain "freedom, and respect for the dignity of the black man."

A few discordant voices were heard from the outset. In the exquisite polemics of Frantz Fanon are some memorable passages warning that a new ruling class drawn from the petty bourgeoisie might engross the benefits of independence. The irascible French agronomist Rene Dumont warned in 1962 that Africa was off to a poor start. But these were isolated views; a handful of Cassandras did not suffice to shake the robust confidence of the early years. . . .

By the end of the 1970s, a sense of alarm had percolated into the economic realm. The Nigerian director of the United Nations Economic Commission for Africa (ECA), Adebayo Adedeji, wrote in 1979, "How have we come to this sorry state of affairs in the post-independence years which seemed at the beginning to have held so much promise?" A report prepared for the 1979 Organization of African Unity (OAU) summit in Monrovia offered the dispiriting conclusion that "Africa . . . is unable to point to any significant growth rate or satisfactory index of general well-being." The deepening pessimism led to the preparation of two key documents, at the initiative of the African leadership: the Lagos Plan of Action, reflecting OAU thinking, and the World Bank report drafted under the leadership of Elliot Berg. The contrasting demonology of these rival reports (the ravages of the world economy, for the OAU; African state policy and performance, for the World Bank) formed the intensifying debate on the African development impasse; the common ground in both was the severity of the economic crisis afflicting the continent. The gentle and understated cadences of Jacob Ajayi epitomize the transformed perspectives: "The optimism of development plans of the 1960s has given way to increasing frustration in the 1970s and disillusionment in the 1980s. The general lament is that this is not what was expected from independence."

Throughout the 1980s, a drumfire of disheartening statistics deepened the apprehensions. The African external debt, insignificant in 1970, had ballooned to well over $200 billion by the beginning of the 1990s. In proportion to the scale of the economies, it extracted an even heavier ransom than the better publicized Latin American debt. Before the late 1970s, only Ghana had ever had recourse to an International Monetary Fund (IMF) stabilization program; in the 1980s most IMF clients were African. Per-capita income continued to decline, in many countries to below 1960 levels. Carl Eicher, in an influential article, demonstrated that Africa was the only major world region to experience declining per-capita food production after 1960.

The state found itself the object of growing opprobrium. The Zairian bishops declared in an angry 1981 pastoral letter that the state had degenerated into "organized pillage for the profit of the foreigner and his intermediaries." Michael Crowder, while pointing to the colonial origins of state autocracy, exorbitant extraction, violence, and personal despotism, notes that "Nigerians of all classes have developed a deep cynicism about their leaders, both civilian and military, and certainly have little faith in the liberal economy and mixed economy that were the legacy of their colonial rulers. . . . ."

Jean-Francoise Bayart, in his magistral summation of the African state, echoes Mbembe:

> The under-remuneration of agricultural labor, the brutality of the territorial administration, of the chiefs and of the armed bands which control the countryside constitute . . . reasons for...desertion as the sole pertinent response to the arbitrary action and wasteful consumption of the state . . . exit [by the subjects] . . . continues to sap civic space, to constrain the process of accumulation of power and wealth, and to render predation easier than exploitation. . . .

A phenomenal parastatalization of the economy had occurred in states of all ideological orientation. Zambia had 134 parastatal enterprises by 1970, the Ivory Coast nearly a hundred by the late 1970s, Nigeria approximately 250 by 1973; Zaire by 1975 had vested most of its economy in public enterprises. In Tanzania 75 percent of the medium and large enterprises were parastatals in the early 1980s. The ubiquity of the parastatal led Sudanese African Development Bank economist Lual Deng to characterize the African state as a "policed economy," with comprehensive administrative rationing its most salient (and negative) feature.

The state security apparatus contributed as well to hypertrophy. In 1989 an estimated 20 percent of the $230 billion African external debt was incurred for armaments. Until the mid-1980s, African arms expenditures were high relative to those of other regions; during the 1970s they rose faster than anywhere else.

The hegemonical ambitions of the state were imposing, measured in its "policed economy," the scale of its apparatus, and the weight of its consumption. But its quantitative expansion was not matched by qualitative improvement in services to civil society. Educational systems and health networks expanded numerically but often deteriorated in performance. The parastatal sector became the target of the gallows humor that helps make everyday survival bearable: NEPA (Nigerian Electrical Power Authority) was rendered "Never Electric Power Again"; the Zairian Office des Routes was better known as "Office des Trous." The option for radical quantitative expansion carried an unanticipated trade-off in qualitative decline.

As the African crisis deepened in the 1980s, so did the contrast between Africa's aggregate developmental performance and that of most other third world regions. The emergent phenomenon of the "newly industrializing country" (NIC) stood in particular counterpoint to African trends. The increasingly sharp discrepancies in outcome in different spheres of what had been conceptually globalized as the third world punctured the credibililty of such explanatory frameworks as "dependency theory," which postulated uniformly operating determinants on a world scale. By the 1980s, the specificity of regional patterns within the world political economy came to dominate the problematics. The NIC heartland of East and Southeast Asia towered over the others—although only two decades before, the international development community had regarded South Korea as hopelessly corrupt and singularly unpromising; the Pearson Commission report had concluded that it "seemed doomed to permanent dependence on foreign aid with *no possibility* of achieving a high growth rate from its own resources. Critics could point to almost every abuse in the catalogue. There was serious corruption, there was inflation, the aid dialogue was most acrimonious, and exports of the country's own products were low.

No other third world area could match the Pacific Rim, but the severity of the crisis in Africa compared to other regions was underlined both in repeated World Bank reports and in Economic Commission for Africa documents. India—which a quarter century earlier seemed destined to absorb the globe's grain surpluses—became self-sufficient in food and found ways to manage the world's most complex cultural pluralism through constitutional governance and open political competition. The Middle East, although dominated by an array of autocracies (theocratic, monarchical, or military), survived its endemic regional conflicts with a modicum of prosperity (partly through an informal secondary distribution of the oil windfall to such non-oil states as Yemen, Jordan, and Syria). Latin America was severely damaged by its debt crisis in the 1980s but nonetheless enjoyed a strong trend toward political democratization. Here and there were polities afflicted with decay or even disintegration: Afghanistan, Burma, Haiti. But the pattern of regionwide decline of the political economy was particular to Africa.

The quest for explanation leads one down a number of pathways. Natural calamities have struck much of the continent with distressing regularity, above all the prolonged droughts in the Sahel zones in the first half of the 1970s, then, in the early 1980s, both there and in much of southern Africa. Some observers argue that the African physical environment is more unfavorable than any other. The dialectics of colonial partition and decolonization spawned a proliferation of sovereign units— fifty-two in 1990, many small and weak (thirteen had fewer than a million people, and only thirteen had populations of more than ten million; a mere four had a GDP as high as Hong Kong's). Population growth—about 3 percent since independence—produces huge younger generations to educate and employ, growing pressure on historically abundant land, and the necessity for relatively high growth rates to avert a per-capita decline. . . . No continent has suffered more from the AIDS epidemic that became visible in the 1980s; by the turn of the century, countries like Tanzania and Uganda will have well over 10 percent of their population HIV positive, and a wide swath of eastern and central Africa faces a comparable threat.

Although the terms of international trade were very favorable to Africa in the 1950s, and reasonably so in the 1960s, the pattern changed during the 1970s and by the 1980s had become heavily unfavorable for most African states. The debt issue became serious at the same time, and by the late 1980s outflows in debt repayments exceeded aid inflows and new credit. External investment had all but ceased, private and public financial institutions offered little but debt reschedulings with costly charges, and aid levels stagnated. . . .

Political calamities too have played their part in African distress. . . . Persistent regional conflicts in northwest, northeast, and southern Africa triggered spiraling arms races, unleashed refugee flows that made the continent home to half the globe's displaced populations, and put many rural communities at the mercy of marauding armed bands. Above all, the deliberate South African strategy of aggressive destabilization during the 1980s took a terrible toll on vulnerable neighboring states, especially Mozambique and Angola. . . .

Thus, the various contemporary pathways supply important elements to understanding the African crisis: core-periphery interactions in the world political economy, political logic and class dynamics of the postcolonial polity, angered gods of climate and environment. Yet one broad trail leads us backward to the historic determinants that have molded the contemporary state and shaped its behavioral imperatives. The colonial system created the African states in most instances; only a handful have a more distant ancestry, and even fewer have decisive institutional continuities with a precolonial past. . . . [A] retrospective examination of the African colonial state can illuminate some of the frailties of its postcolonial successor and perhaps even suggest avenues of escape from its more burdensome legacies.

The colonial state in Africa lasted in most instances less than a century—a mere moment in historical time. Yet it totally reordered political space, societal hierarchies and cleavages, and modes of economic production. Its territorial grid—whose final contours congealed only in the dynamics of decolonization—determined the state units that gained sovereignty and came to form the present system of African polities. The logic of its persistence and reproduction was by the time of independence deeply embedded in its mechanisms of internal guidance. . . .

The incorporation of Africa into colonial space was a continental phenomenon; the dialectics of partition in the last quarter of the nineteenth century operated from "the Cape to Cairo." We thus take the entire continent as geographical referent, while at once acknowledging the importance of regional variations. In particular, the white-settler zones of southern Africa and the Arab tier of states whose historicity was never wholly extinguished on the northern rim stand somewhat apart from most sub-Saharan polities. Nonetheless, I believe that there are enough common patterns in the construction of colonial states to justify a common analytical framework for all. I hope to suggest overarching patterns as well as ranges of variation within them. . . .

By the 1980s, the plight of the African state seemed distinctly worse than that of other world regions formerly subject to imperial rule. If the African colonial state bore the pathologies of the contemporary polity, at least in part, then comparative examination of its counterparts in other zones of the once-colonized world should reveal significant contrasts. This requires difficult comparisons across historical time; the colonial state in the Americas was ascendant from the sixteenth to the eighteenth centuries, well before the European presence in Africa was anything other than a few coastal outposts. Nonetheless, I believe that the comparison helps draw attention to dimensions of Africa's colonial state legacy that have been detrimental to the postcolonial polity.

In conclusion I suggest some ways in which the legacy of the colonial state remains deeply embedded within its postcolonial successor. Not only the state: the forms taken by the civil societies that crystallized in the postwar years to challenge European rule...bore the imprint of Bula Matari in unsuspected ways. The opening epigraph drawn from Cabral, composed before Africa's past two dismal decades, is a prescient acknowledgment of the contemporary weight of the colonial state legacy.

The modern colonial state wore many masks during its half-millennium of existence. Some had scowling features as intimidating to the subject as Bula Matari (like early Peru, Mexico, and Vietnam). Some were stern and distant in demeanor (like British India). Still others were almost featureless, so concealed behind the throne of the ostensible suzerain as to be unfathomable to the subject (as in the Persian Gulf sheikdoms). Let me suggest by way of conclusion seven salient characteristics of the African colonial state that I believe mark it as a distinctive species.

First, the impact of the dynamic of partition was singularly important. The imperial irruption into the African interior came suddenly, after 1875, and acquired formidable interactive momentum. The sheer number of colonial claimants redoubled the intensity of this dialectic: in most areas only two or three competitors were active in any one time or place, whereas in Africa there were six (Britain, France, Germany, Italy, the Belgian monarchy, and Portugal). The forces of conquest were under a pressure unusual in imperial annals to give muscular effect to the doctrine of effective occupation, exhumed and sanctified at the Berlin Congress. In the longer history of European subjugation of Asia and the Americas, imperial atavism was the twin brother of international anarchy. But the drama played itself out over much longer time frames; only in Africa were the occupying powers under the compelling, immediate requirement of confirming proprietary title by forcible demonstration of dominance.

Second, driven by this compelling necessity for rapid conquest, the interactive dilemmas of the hegemony and revenue imperatives made survival of the fledgling colonial states contingent on ruthless extractive action. The promoters of imperial expansion enjoyed only tenuous support from the parent states; for the most part, the future gains were speculative, and the immediate costs and risks real. Thus, the managers of the colonial states were required to find the resources to finance the consolidation of conquest within the subjugated societies. . . . In Africa, newly created colonial institutions required for survival the simultaneous imposition of authority, extraction of resources to pay for it, and invention of intermediary mechanisms to organize the collection of tribute. The combined logic of these imperatives produced the ruthless brutalities so widespread in the construction phase.

Third, both revenue and accumulation imperatives propelled the colonial state into an active role in forcing rural Africans into labor service. The imposition of head taxes had this objective as well as revenue generation. The basic necessities of the colonial state, and the initial public infrastructure, were often met by conscription: porters, road workers, construction teams for administrative stations. European mines and plantations, whose development was presumed to benefit colonial treasuries through customs on their exports, demanded an assured labor supply at wages few would accept voluntarily; this drew the colonial state into labor conscription. In this respect the African colonial state has companions, such as early Latin America and Vietnam. But in comparative terms the degree to which the logic of colonial state construction was rooted in the control, conscription, regulation, and use of African labor stands out.

Fourth, the sequencing of decolonization, the assimilation by the late colonial state of a welfare ideology as doctrine of legitimation, and the nature of its developmentalism produced a curious syndrome of citizen attitudes and expectations. Welfare, in the terminal colonial era, was bestowed from above in the characteristically paternalist mode: borrowing a John Ayoade expression, and mixing gender metaphors, the colonial polity became a "Mother Theresa" state. But at the same time the state remained external to the citizen, an alien and predatory other. Ayoade writes:

> The inheritors of the postcolonial state [tried] to outbid their colonial predecessors by exaggerating the benevolence of the state. . . encouraged the growth of public spending by emphasizing the benefits, rather than the costs, of the welfare state as if benefits are costless.

In the Nigerian case, the flow of oil revenues after independence permitted abolition of most forms of local taxation, a pattern not matched in most other African states. Oil was viewed as a "national cake," for whose slices contending private actors and groups engaged in relentless struggle. Nearly everywhere the curious terminal colonial state blend of long-standing autocratic paternalism and a newfound social beneficence engendered a *mentalite des assistes* among the subjects.

Fifth, the technologies of dominance in the terminal period were far more advanced than earlier. The degree of sheer military supremacy from advances in weaponry affected the texture of domination. The ready availability of the punitive expedition as an auxiliary medium of administration and its frequent use—especially in the early period—reflected the magnitude of the military imbalance. Particularly after World War I, colonial states were somewhat constrained by the risk of provoking a rebellion on a scale they could not master on their own. But the everyday supremacy of colonial power was of exceptional weight. Its capacity for mobility and communication rapidly expanded; motor vehicles became available early in the colonial era, replacing the hammock, and the telegraph and radio tied the superstructure together into a grid of domination not available in earlier centuries.

Sixth, the creation of the African colonial state coincided with the historical zenith of virulent racism. The colonial construction of the African as savage other permeated all spheres of policy thought. Racism was always present in colonial encounters, to be sure; imperialism is the parent of race as an ideology of human difference. But the arrogance of race was never stronger than at the moment of colonial onslaught on Africa. African culture had no redeeming value; only a wholly new African might be worthy of the colonial order, tailored from imported cloth.

Seventh, the cultural project of the colonial state confronted societies not only subjected to a pervasive domination but—outside the Islamic zones—also lacking the insulation provided in Asia by the major religious systems. The remarkable expansion of Islam in sub-Saharan Africa during the colonial period partly reflects a search for a cultural shield that indigenous religions alone could not easily provide. In its initial colonial version, Christianity, writes Mbembe, in claiming a "civilizing mission," sought to "impose recognition of the West as the sole center of meaning, the unique location competent to engender a discourse on the human and the divine." The struggle for hegemony is carried out as a contest for meanings, as well as through material forces. The colonial state was unsparing in its efforts—through the Christian missions, the educational systems, and language policies—to monopolize the production of meaning and thus the construction of culture. Christianity became contested terrain, a vehicle for reassertion of the indigenous through syncretization. When the battle was first joined, however, Bula Matari demanded unconditional-surrender terms of settlement, which went well beyond the imperial norm.

No claim is made that the African colonial state is in all respects unique. In one or another of its aspects, similarities can be found elsewhere. But when we assemble its traits, examine its trajectory, and weave together the determinants of its structure and behavior, a singular historical personality looms before us.

Development in Africa:
A Cultural Perspective

ELLIOT P. SKINNER[2]

The debate about the role of culture in development, especially in Africa and in Third and Fourth World countries, had become so sterile that no new insights appeared possible. Now, a number of factors have stimulated a renewed interest in the role of culture in the development process. Chief among these factors is the emergence of Japan as a global giant whose success is said to be due not only to its cultural characteristics, but retrogressively, to the "racial homogeneity" of its population. Second, the publication of Paul Kennedy's book, *The Rise and Fall of Great Powers* has raised the Spenglerian conundrum: the possibility that the core state in the West (US) is in danger of losing its *elan vital* and, like Ninevah and Tyre, doomed to disappear. The issues here are not only didactic, but social, cultural, and philosophical. It is probably only a matter of time before it is suggested that Gorbachev's call for *glasnost* and *perestroika* in the Soviet Union, in conjunction with the growing economic anxiety in the United States, might not only end the Cold War, but free the Third and Fourth Worlds to develop, independent from today's outworn economic and especially cultural-philosophical dogmas.

The notion that culture is important to development, as well as to all aspects of human life, has been long recognized by social scientists. Culture is important for human beings because it provides the necessary designs or models for living, indicating what is considered proper, or moral, or even sane. It provides a body of knowledge and tools by which people adapt to their environments, rules by which they relate to each other, and a veritable storehouse of knowledge, beliefs, and formulae through which humans attempt to understand the universe and their place within it.

Through the use of shared cognitive symbols, culture provides the distinctive way in which each societal system orders the world. It tells people what to expect from others in their society and why, thereby furnishing them with a degree of mastery and confidence in most social situations. The cognitive claim as to what is "fact" or "data" or "reality" is not always readily explainable and while these

2 Skinner, Elliot P., "Development in Africa: A Cultural Perspective," in *The Fletcher Forum of World Affairs* (1989): pp. 205-215. Excerpts taken from pp. 205-215.

Elliot P. Skinner is the Franz Boas Professor of Anthropology of Columbia University. From 1966-69, he served as US Ambassador to Upper Volta/Burkina Faso.

processes are ultimately judged against experience, people have difficulty sharing experiences with persons of other cultural traditions. Those societies which are the result of largely endogenous processes and forces and have cultural characteristics unique to themselves and their people often find it hard to share their experiences with others. Nevertheless, all human societies are capable of borrowing cultural traits from each other even though, given the opportunity, they modify them to suit their own traditions and circumstances .

The present concern about the "inability" of African countries to develop as rapidly as other countries is as much due to cultural perception as it is a concern with the actual rate of cultural change there. Non-African as well as Western-educated Africans complain about the slow rate of change, whereas many rural Africans believe that they are living in a "runaway world." It is a fact that Africa has never been immune to fundamental change. The continent is a veritable museum of past and present cultures in all stages of complexity and development, and Africa's role in the development of humanity and culture now is recognized fully. That this was not recognized earlier is due as much to racism as to the state of paleontology and archaeology. Moreover, in prehistoric as well as historical times, Africa gave, as well as received, cultural traits from the Fertile Crescent, the Mediterranean, Southeast Asia, and even the New World. In fact, many parts of Africa at times had been integrated into the political, economic, and cultural systems of the Mediterranean, the Middle East, and Asia. Nevertheless, some parts of the continent retained a basic African cultural system, modified to suit regional ecological realities, while other parts exhibited multiple cultural heritages when Islam arrived in the seventh century, and Western Christendom in the fifteenth century.

Africa shared the fate of most of the world in being conquered and colonized by Western Europeans from the fifteenth century until recently. Again, as for many societies, the European impact was so shattering that it will take generations of people to cope with its effects. Arnold Toynbee once wrote that future historians reviewing the emergence of the modern world would note:

> [T]he terrific impact of the Western civilization upon all other living societies of the world of that day. They will say of this impact that it was so powerful and so pervasive that it turned the lives of all its victims upside down and inside out—affecting the behavior, outlook, feelings, and beliefs of individual men, women, and children in an intimate way, touching chords in human souls that are not touched by mere external material forces—however ponderous and terrifying.

Later on, Sekou Toure of Guinea was to remark that it was easy to build railroads, ports, and towns; what was more difficult to change were the minds of the colonized persons.

Many European colonizers recognized that they had to change the culture of their victims if colonialism would suceed. Colonel Trentinian, the governor of French

Sudan in 1897, sent this circular to his subordinates:

> Here in the Sudan, we confront a population which has been defeated
> militarily, it must now be conquered intellectually and morally. We
> must therefore draw the people to us, work with them constantly so that
> we can curb their spirit, impose our ideas upon them, and brand them
> with our particular stamp.

This cultural "policy of assimiliation" was spelled out in the first lesson the African
pupils learned in school: "My new country from today is France. I am French. And
when I grow up, every Sunday, I shall place the Tricolor on the top of my house and
say to my subjects, 'There is a beautiful flag.'" These African youngsters were also
taught that their ancestors were Gauls with blond hair and blue eyes!

By the 1920s and 1930s, a small but later influential group of Africans had
acquired aspects of Metropolitan cultures and considered themselves to be
"British," "French," and "Portuguese." These were the products of an effort "to literally make of the native an object in the hands of the occupying nation." They not
only considered Europe as "home" but adopted European names, clothing, speech,
and mannerisms (some went as far as to practice throwing back their heads when
speaking so as to prevent their actually short hair from tumbling down before their
eyes, in imitation of their European teachers). The colonial African elite "judged,
condemned, abandoned his cultural forms, his language, his food habits, his sexual
behavior, his ways of sitting down, of resting, of laughing, of enjoying himself."

The ultimate reaction of many Africans to the colonial situation involved both
anger at their psycho-social and cultural dependency, as well as a determination to
end it. They often attempted to "return to the source," and embrace their original
culture with what Fanon called "the desperation of a drowning man." He observed:

> This culture, abandoned, sloughed off, rejected, despised, becomes for
> the inferiorized an object of passionate attachment. . . . The customs,
> traditions, beliefs, formerly denied and passed over in silence are vio-
> lently valorized and affirmed. . . . Tradition is no longer scoffed at by
> the group. The group no longer runs away from itself. The sense of the
> past is rediscovered, the worship of ancestors resumed. . . . The past,
> becoming henceforth a constellation of values, becomes identified with
> the Truth.

To counter this cultural dissonance, many African leaders developed such cultural slogans as "negritude" and the "African personality" to liberate themselves
psychically as their countries moved toward independence in the 1960s.

Because of their cultural ambivalence *vis-a-vis* the West, most African leaders
had no clear view of the programs to be used to develop their countries. It was not
so much the sting of economic exploitation as it was the yearning for human digni-

ty that loomed very large in their thinking. Marxist-derived "socialism" was attractive not only because it postulated a relationship between the twin evils of capitalism and colonialism, but also because it predicted a socialist millennium without those scourges. As important, however, was that Marxism was linked to the Soviet Union, a nation-state system which was distrusted and feared by the West. By adopting the rhetoric of Marxist communism, Africans were able to plug into a symbolic system which alarmed the people who had only scorn for their indigenous movements and ideas. "African Socialism" became for them the economic analogue of such cultural terms as "negritude" and the "African personality."

Fanon was troubled by the cognitive dissonance between the needs of independent states for the appropriate technical, economic and highly differentiated modes of thinking, and the emotional fervor of some African nationalists. He believed that what he considered to be the archaic cult of "negritude" had no relationship to technical development. Moreover, he felt that the institutions which the Africans were attempting to valorize no longer corresponded to the elaborate methods or actions that were needed. Instead of "mystification," Fanon wanted a thorough understanding of the relationship among technologies, social structures, and culture. But neither "negritude" nor the "African personality" consciously affected African economic behavior. Paradoxically, the few attempts made by African leaders to utilize traditional institutions as guides with which to develop their societies received no intellectual or public support.

Central to the development problems of African states has been the fact that their economies remain under the control of their erstwhile colonizers. Amazingly, given the harsh rhetoric of many African nationalists, very few took steps to sever their feeble economies from Metropolitan control. It also was partly because of these ties that African leaders were unable to agree on the possibility of political federation in 1963. The result is that an area representing only about 12 percent of the world's surface and less than 9 percent of the world's population controls thirty-five largely economically unviable states with populations below ten million, and ten states with a population under one million. Large multinationals, such as United African Company, Societe Commerciale de l'Ouest Africain, Unilever, and Lohnro have remained intact and battened on the bilateral and multilateral funds destined "to develop" the African countries. To complicate matters, these states have been pulled along by the West into an increasingly consumer-oriented economy, which initially attracted the African elites and proved increasingly seductive to the urban masses and rural peasants.

Ghana, Guinea, and Mali, which aspired to "socialist" economic development policies and left the sterling and franc zones respectively, found their new currencies worthless on the world market, and their states cut off from aid and loans for development from the capitalist international community. Ironically, the world's major socialist states, claiming adherence to the orthodox Marxist view that Africa had to go though a capitalist phase before socialism was possible, refused to help. For them, such a notion as African Socialism was a chimera developed by bourgeoisie still cognitively Western. Discouraged by both East and West, a number of leaders attempted to halt the importation of consumer goods which diverted dollars or francs needed for endogenous development. Such politics angered both the masses and the elites. The peasants smuggled their products to neighboring countries to obtain hard currencies, and the urbanites plotted revolutions. These groups refused self-sufficiency and African Socialism when these policies cut rather than enhanced their living standards. The experience of Ghana is a case in point.

Francis (later) Kwame Nkrumah, was not only an American and British-trained intellectual, but a fervent pan-Africanist and creator of the concept of the "African personality." He wanted to change the thinking of colonial Africans, to unite the peoples of the continent politically, and to change their mono-product economies. In order to do so, he was prepared to abandon the colonial structures which united British West Africa, and use part of the substantial amount of money garnered during World War II by the Gold Coast Cocoa Marketing Board. He built monuments hailing the "Black Star" and created an airline whose decals projected the "Black Star" over African and European skies. Ghana became the site of cultural festivals honoring the African past and the home of revolutionary exiles plotting how to expel the European invaders from the continent.

Foremost among Nkrumah's dreams was to indigenize and to diversify Ghana's mono-crop economy so as to develop his country. In an early effort to convince Ghanaians that the ideological concept "African personality" implied endogenous development, Kwame Nkrumah decided to manufacture a local gin to replace the Ghanaians' gustatorial favorite, *London Dry Gin*. The reaction was furious. Ghanaians feared that their social status would be jeopardized if they used a local product instead of a prestigious, imported one. They also complained that they preferred American cars to the Bristol cars assembled in Ghana as an example of import substitution which ultimately would lead to a full-scale automobile industry. One can argue that if Nkrumah really wanted to indigenize, be might have suggested that the locally produced palm wine be improved and used as Ghana's national drink. This, however, would have raised a greater storm—one involving charges of retrogression, paternalism, and cognitive dissonance Ghanaians were intoxicated by the desire to modernize. A preference for palm wine contradicted this need to move ahead.

Nkrumah's major problem was that he had absolutely no control over the international price of cocoa. His country experienced hardship during the postwar economic recession when the price of cocoa fell, and that made him more determined than ever to industrialize Ghana. He decided to use his scarce resources to build the Akosombo Dam and with the power produced electrify all of Ghana, provide power for local industries, and most important of all, fuel the conversion of local bauxite into aluminum. His ideological stance did not endear him either to the United States or to Great Britain, and therefore, he had difficulty in getting loans to build the dam. Through political pressure exercised in the United States by African Americans and others, Nkrumah did get an American loan but it was conditional: he had to permit an American multinational to use Akosombo's electric power to smelt bauxite brought all the way across the Atlantic to the Guianas.

Psychologically more devastating to Nkrumah was the local Ghanaian reaction. His attempt to use the scarce dollars for development by curtailing the importation of consumer goods was not accepted. Both the small elite group and the larger, market-women constituency were infuriated by not being able to purchase the goods they desired. Later, when Nkrumah could not get an emergency loan from the West because he criticized US policies in Vietnam, the military overthrew him and seized power. Even so, Nkrumah's fall did not solve Ghana's problems.

Due to a continuing decline in the price of cocoa and corruption in high places, Ghana could not repay the debts incurred during the attempts to endogenize its economy. Desperately short of food, subsequent military governments in Ghana launched programs such as "Operation Feed Yourself" and "Industrialize Yourself." But the country's economy continued to decline. The elite and the masses fled abroad to more prosperous countries, only to be later expelled. After a succession of military and civilian leaders who could not solve Ghana's problems, Flight Lieutenant Jerry Rawlings seized power. Initially, he attempted to use his own methods to rescue the country's economy. Pressure from the International Monetary Fund (IMF) and the Reagan regime forced him to adopt a rural strategy and even to advocate privatization. The Ghanaian economy improved for a time, but there is strong feeling that Rawling's experiment will have difficulty in succeeding.

Africa's lamentable experiences with the use of exogenous models have forced some scholars to suggest development strategies more in keeping with their own traditions and current realities. The question is: What strategies will succeed after African economies and societies have been linked so long to the West ? Samir Amin, among others, has advocated "uncoupling" from the capitalist West, and seeking salvation in autonomy and "development from below or from the masses." This is how Samir Amin puts it:

> In order to serve the mass of the peasantry, industrialization must first be made to concentrate on improving rural productivity. Similarly, in order to serve the urban masses, it is necessary to give up luxury production for the local market and give up exporting, since they are both based on the reproduction of a cheap labor force.

There are a number of technical, environmental, and cognitive/ideological problems involved in such strategies. First, there is a difference between endogenous or culturally-specific development (starting from an autonomous base), and industrialization (a set of interrelated processes, tools, and ideas characteristic of the West). How to meld those two approaches is worthy of serious philosophical debate. A second concern is the question of whether the people in many African urban areas are prepared to undertake such experiments. Paradoxically, few Africans, even those who are anti-Western, or Marxist, display any interest in endogenous development.

Either they believe that endogeneity is so much nationalist humbug or suggest that "development by the rabble" would fail. These persons insist that the Japanese success with development, instructed by tradition, is due to their having not been colonized by the West.

The ambiguity that many Africans feel toward strategies of development is due mainly to the failure of so many development projects in their countries, whether attempted from the "top-down" or from the "bottom-up," or whether in the hands of Western-trained developers, Africans or Europeans, or American expatriates. The epithet "WAWA" (West Africa Wins Again) still is used to express the frustration of developers in the face of project failures. Whether judged either in theoretical or practical perspective, however, it is clear that "WAWA" is symptomatic of a gross misunderstanding of the cognitive universes in which developers and Africans have found themselves. Africans have always adapted to changes in their physical and sociocultural universes. People in urban and coastal areas have adapted more readily than those in rural interior regions. The issue is that contemporary adaptation cannot be comparable to that of the colonial or immediate post-colonial epoch, but must take into consideration the spread of an all-embracing, planet-wide civilization.

What a carefully crafted approach to development should take into consideration is that African traditional cultures can provide the philosophical justification for looking to their own culture and existential condition for the strength to modernize. This would involve a systematic and judicious analysis of the worthwhile elements surviving from the past, those of the complicated present, and those elements of the global civilization that are impinging on the entire world. Many of these elements can be beneficial to all humanity; others are harmful; and still others are neutral. Faced with the need for new institutions, Africans should look to their own societal systems for the answers, and adopt or adapt local ones whenever possible. On the other hand, when given the opportunity to contribute what Alfred Kroeber called their "own proper peculiarities and originations" to the contemporary world, they ought to do so.

Consensual Politics and Development Aid in Africa

KOFI ERMELEH AGOV[13]

Since independence, postwar Africa has experienced various forms of aid. These have been mostly concentrated on select areas of the African economy. Aid meant to develop agriculture, for example, has often been designed to promote efficiency in the production of cash crops and raw materials for industrial purposes. Technical advisers and equipment are normally provided to strengthen the mining industry so as to ensure continuity on the production lines of industrialized countries. Even in the seemingly innocuous sector of local manpower training and development, educational exchange programmes, short-term travel grants and study tours, there has been a calculated objective to use it as avenues for political influence in the award of public contracts and projects of great financial value. Loan agreements have released foreign exchange components that have encouraged the consumer orientations of urban populations in Africa to the extent that nowadays part of Africa's political heritage is for each successive government to renegotiate its debt burdens. In all these designs, the initiative for such forms of aid has quite often not originated from African countries themselves.

Although, admittedly there was a lot of goodwill towards African states during the independence period, and this was reflected in both the number and variety of aid at the time, independence also created a certain atmosphere of competitiveness and anxiety in trade and diplomatic circles in accordance with the cold war situation of postwar geopolitics. Consequently, one can say with a fair amount of certainty that goodwill as a political expression of aid was obviously hopelessly outweighed by the calculated motive of gain and self-interest in aid components to Africa before the eighties.

The consequences of such aid initiatives have since become part of the fixed image of Africa in international relations. The political instability, intractable corruption, increasing involvement of multi-national corporations and banks, debts, a picture of abject poverty and helplessness. A people unable to salvage their economies let alone possess the will to live. In a world accustomed to value judge-

---

3. Agovi, Kofi Ermeleh, "Consensual Politics and Development Aid in Africa" in *Culture and Development in Africa* (Africa World Press, 1990), excerpts taken from pp. 177–186.

Kofi Ermeleh Agovi is an Assistant Professor at the Institute for African Studies of the University of Ghana.

ments and fixed images of other cultures in their international protocol arrangements, dealings and debates, a further proof of Africa's loss to world civilization
and development was provided in the eighties with the onset of drought, famine and
desertification. Once again, Africa was treated to the historical bout of Western
humanitarian Band Aid, and the new civilizing "imperialism" of the World Bank
and the international Monetary Fund, who insist on the moral discipline of Economic Recovery Programs.

But, African states have consistently, since independence, sought to change their
economic relations with Europe. They have consistently sought to change the character of aid to Africa. They have sought to complement political nationalism with
economic nationalism.

They have always sought to create a condition where political nationalism and
economic nationalism will be fused as complementary forces to meaningful development on the Continent. If African nationalism had the immediate aim to liberate
African colonies from political and economic exploitation, it also had definite aspirations towards modernization. There was the need to create new socio-political
institutions, expand educational establishments and diversify the horizons of the
national economy in order to take into account the quality of life of African citizens.
On the eve of independence therefore, Africa ushered in a new determination—in
the words of Dr. Kwame Nkrumah in 1957—that the African given the chance
(emphasis mine) will "prove to the world that he is capable of managing his own
affairs." For some inexplicable reason, Western nations have never been willing to
understand or support the aggregate character of the postwar nationalism in Africa.
In their anxiety to maintain the colonial status of African economies at independence—as suppliers of raw materials and industrial inputs—Western countries have
never demonstrated the political will to come to terms with the political and economic implications of African nationalism in its drive towards modernization.
Moreover, unfortunately handicapped as African countries were in terms of technical expertise and finance capital, they were compelled to make hard economic bar-
gains and painful political compromises in order to embark on their modernization
process. In such a context, the industrial countries used the factor of development
aid to neutralize African economic nationalism. Independence of mind and initiative—two basic factors in any drive towards modernization—were completely eroded by the kinds of aid proposed by Western countries. Equally exacerbating was the
fact that African states did not have sufficient time to develop an agreed program or
strategy of development that aid could effectively support in its implementation.
There was no coherent or efficient state machinery for scrutinizing aid, accepting it
and channeling it through the most productive fields. Then added to that state of
affairs was the total absence of management values and principles to promote efficiency in aid disbursement. In this situation, aid in Africa became, in effect, the
most potent denial of whatever modernization had connoted in the experience of
other countries.

Lessons of history have clearly established the fact that although political and economic factors are important considerations in nation building and therefore have to be tackled simultaneously as a unified process, it is most obvious that political consensus in nation building and modernization is primary. Jack Greene has argued in a recent lecture on "The American Revolution and Modern Revolutions" that the 1776 Constitution of the American people was "a modern instrument, the expression of the modern society out of which it came. Consequently, the American Revolution did not have to contend with socio-economic problems, hence its overriding concern and preoccupation with political issues. Thus, a central concern of these political issues, what he terms as an "unfinished agenda" was the "continuing movement toward an expanding conception of citizenship, of who should be included in the political category of people." This problem led to a civil war to determine whether a nation such as America could afford to remain, in the words of Abraham Lincoln, "half-free, half-slave." The historicity of that civil war did not only lie in the will towards complete nationhood but in its principled drive towards a consensus of values of nationhood, of what ought to constitute an ideal modern society in which considerations of race and colour will not determine social relations and the pursuit of life and liberty. Indeed, it was the resolution of this central issue, and perhaps more important, the creation of a consensus based on the constitutional document of the American Revolution which really enabled America to release its energies towards effective modernization in terms of industrial, scientific and technological development.

Similarly, the historical experience of Britain in this respect is equally instructive. By the time of Queen Elizabeth I, a single and powerful monarchy supported by a disciplined aristocracy had become the basis of a strong, united and stable country, whose successful maritime ventures instilled added confidence in her people. Yet, soon afterwards, it became obvious by the time of Charles I in 1625, that there was need for a civil war to resolve the political question concerning the values and institutions which should symbolize and represent, without reservation, the popular will of the people of the United Kingdom. The turmoil of that struggle is now history. But its resolution enabled the Victorian era to undertake massive imperial ventures, radical social transformations and industrialization at home. Thus, as we find in the American situation, the struggle to elevate and establish "popular representation" as a framework for national consensus on everything became the most important political decision for true development to emerge in Britain.

The Japanese experience is even more telling. After the consolidation of the shogunate, the Imperial Monarchy felt powerful enough to cut Japan off from the rest of the country by 1630. For over two hundred years, Japan became "the closed country." It sought to control all factors that might threaten political stability, while it consolidated and defined its primary political values and institutionis. One result of this isolation, wrote Reischauer and Craig in 1981, was Japan's ability to develop its "native characteristics" and "native Japanese traits. " Further, as a consequence of this isolation, the Japanese "have developed a larger proportion of their culture themselves than have most nations." By the time of the Meiji Restoration in the 19th Century, Japan had made up its mind on the effective values and institutions to promote its development. A favourite slogan at that time was "Western Science, Japanese Mind." Thus, as Gregory Clarke has observed, the miracle of the Japanese economic growth "is the mystery of its value system. . . . It allowed the sophisticated sense of consensus, the human relations values such as giri and so on. Combined with outside rationalism, it resulted in rapid growth." For Japan therefore, "cultural consensus" became the most important factor for development.

From the experiences of the countries we have alluded to so far, it seems that a historical paradigm emerges. There is first a situation of instability and chaos, when the fragmented realms or estates within the country have to be forced into a central direction or identity. This is followed by a phase of stability in which the collective inner forces of strength within the society are released towards national unity. Side by side with this is a search for a "national ethic" or a body of ideals and aspirations and values which clearly define the country's collective urges towards progress and development. It is a situation of commonly agreed principles and assumptions of state which are intended to motivate and define the society's sense of development. An enunciation of consensual values, in all spheres of life, that invigorate collective behaviour and guide the conduct of state institutions.

We in Africa have not been able to determine whether this kind of consensus should be built around cultural, political, or economic necessity. Historically it must be emphasized that the colonial intervention put an end to the effective and systematic establishment of nation states in Africa and disrupted its people's sense of values. Consequently, the postwar Revolution in Africa and its urgent nationalism had to deal with political, cultural and socio-economic problems at the same time. Not only did the individual African states have to be ushered into the scientific, industrial and technological age, but they also had to develop corresponding values and institutions that will make such a transformation permanent and meaningful and constitute for Africans a way of life. In the face of the fairly obvious complexity of Africa's historical past, including the need to come to terms with modern systems of advanced economies and market forces, the only choice open to Africa was to develop quickly a consensus on all fronts at once within a given framework of priorities. Nkrumah's dictum for Ghana's Independence struggle, "seek ye first the political Kingdom, and all other things shall be added unto it" was a profound metaphor for such a framework. His subsequent attempts at Continental Unity through the pursuit of political goals were all profound expressions of the need to establish politics as the "framework of priorities" for Africa, a framework through which Africa can build up its consensus on all fronts. Paradoxically, after his death, African leaders in their collective wisdom decided that national and continental economies of Africa should be the framework for such a consensus. Thus, even as recent as 1985, West Africa magazine, in its editorial of 15th July 1985 asserted that indeed Africa needs "political clout to deal with the challenges of the modern world.... And that begins with economics. "

This view reflects a mood in Africa since the 1970's, which perceived Africa's problems exclusively in the economic mould. Accordingly, that period witnessed a marked concentration on economics and the establishment of economic institutions and groupings, particularly at the level of O.A.U. forums. Coincidentally, it also marked a period when development aid became a craze on the continent, an essential commodity that every country and government in Africa needed in order to exist or survive. Multi-national banks and their collaterals such as the World Bank and the IMF became the central agencies of "aid for development" in Africa. In the words of one commentator, they cashed in on the African situation with a "vengeance." They established conditionalities for loans which very often trespassed "into the exercise of (state) sovereignty." They created situations which raised disturbing arguments about "the unjust economic system in which (African states) are mere appendages of the rich countries." And worse still, even under such difficult conditions, aid was offered and utilized without any real effect, impact or result on African societies. As Edward Hirabayashi et al. observed in 1976, International development aid in Africa has suffered "reversions" whose reasons are in most cases "unclear." Some have attributed the ineffectiveness of aid to "a lack of understanding of the local population's socio-cultural systems along with a lack of local participation." People have pointed to the evidence of massive corruption in the body politic of African countries from the governmental level to the level of implementation bureaucrats, a situation that has led to the misappropriation or misdirection of aid funds. Political instability in the form of chronic coup d'etats and frequent changes of government has also led to the abandonment of development projects and lack of zeal or consistency in the prosecution of agreed development programs. Others have drawn attention to inefficiency in administrative and bureaucratic structures owing primarily to a lack of infrastructural development and the non-existence of a sharp business-like attitude and management expertise among African program implementors.

In my view, a more telling reason is the use of aid as a manipulative device by donor countries and multinational banks to maintain economic, political and diplomatic leverage in African countries. "Aid without strings" either in the form of securing raw materials or sustaining a sphere of political and military influence is completely unknown in African's post-Independence history. Under this category may also be mentioned the binds of aid, whose cumulative effect in terms of bank interest rates, has tended to cripple the ability of African countries not only to develop but to pay for their original loan components. Thus, it is not unusual, at the change of government in African countries, for the new leaders to "reassure" donor and creditor countries of their willingness to fulfill repayment schedules and obligations as the first act of winning international acclaim and support. In this very act, the Western mass media and their diplomatic channels have always responded most favourably and most encouragingly even where suspicions of the ultimate political allegiance or ideology of the incoming regime are obvious in their reports and bylines. A more recent scenario in the attitude of donor countries is the fact that contract awards under aid proposed by such countries are invariably "won" or given to firms and contractors who originate from the donor country. The ritual of open tenders may be performed, but at the end of it, the receiving country has no say in who ultimately wins the contract at a lower or higher cost. The receiving country has no control on where to order particular equipment, even if it wishes to do so for purposes of standardization. Indeed, the attitude here is that firms and contractors from donor countries must be made to keep a firm grip on spare parts supply as a definite avenue of continued economic dependence.

Also, a more fundamental issue is the fact, already suggested, that aid has been concentrated in sectors of life that completely exclude development in terms of building up ideas and institutions that can integrate the country on a more continuous, stable and permanent basis. It has taken Africans themselves more than two decades to realize that they have no cultural consensus, no social consensus on anything within their modern independent boundaries. It has taken them the same period of agonizing experiences to realize that they have been promoting, through emphasis on trade and import habituation, an artificial divorce of political and institutional development from economic development. They have tended, in fact, to give primacy to economic development—notwithstanding the manipulations and constraints in that sector—when they should first and foremost give priority to the creation, establishment and perpetuation of political consensus as a condition for economic development.

Fortunately, the nineteen-eighties has seen a determined effort on the continent to reverse this trend with a concentration on political development, particularly in the area of consensus politics. If Ghana's example can be cited here, there have been fundamental attempts to restructure economic relations to correspond with reforms in the educational, cultural and political sectors. Indeed, African countries are now faced with the search for a grand "national ethic," a hard core of permanent values that define a collective temperament or a national spirit and vision of goals and aspirations that can support systematic development. This search has involved mental and psychological changes, the introduction and acceptance of concepts such as "self~reliance," "social justice," "mass participation in the decision-making process", "grassroots democracy" and "decentralization." It has also involved the mobilization of development initiatives at village, town and district administrative levels in terms of providing new skills and new forms of knowledge that can lead to the physical transformation of the environment. Quite clearly, then, Africa is on the verge of releasing her peoples' inner forces for real development.

The attempt to lay emphasis on political development now or at least complement economic initiatives with a new framework of political action does not, in my view, seek to project the white man, his culture and money as centres of emulation or excellence. It does not encourage development initiatives that do not originate from African traditional thought and practice. It is an inner search for strength to forge a national consensus on a common image and identity for the continent while creating corresponding values that ought to give meaning to the concept of a self-reliant people. It is only in this context that development aid in Africa can become effective, meaningful and significant. Development aid that merely opens our eyes to possibilities in other lands and cultures to the total neglect of ours, a situation that creates "dependence development" in the thinking and behaviour of our people is bound to end in failure. Development aid that recognizes the responsibility to promote a coherent strategy for national consensus and, in the end, motivates and mobilizes the collective energies of African people towards their own vision of positive transformations in the environment; development aid that opens a people's eyes to their inner strengths and makes it possible for them to exercise initiative and sense of responsibility towards themselves and others certainly constitutes development to mankind.

In effect therefore, African states today are caught up in the whirlpool of developing basic ideas, values and assumptions in the political, cultural, social and economic fields, that may unite all shades of opinion, and which in turn, may significantly shape the basis for collective national policies and development strategies. Consequently, although aid for development, particularly in the industrial, scientific and technological fields in Africa is important and desirable, it may nevertheless have no impact on African societies unless the primary question of consensus has been settled by Africans themselves. Development aid that is not designed to support such efforts towards institutional stability and ideological coherence based on consensual values, may prove to be futile in the end. This paper would therefore suggest that aid in Africa should recognize that the most important developmental issue in Africa today is the establishment of a national consensus. When development aid becomes a force of fusion, a point of integrating and translating both the political and economic aspirations of Africans into reality in their modernization process, only then will it be effective. Thus, unless development aid is emphasized along such lines, it will continue to fail in its obsession with manipulative designs.

Alternative Policy Frameworks for African Dvelopment in the 1990s

ROBERT S. BROWNE[4]

In 1976 there were eleven sub-Saharan countries classified as "middle income" by the World Bank's categories, but by 1990 only six of these eleven were still so classified. The others had all slipped back into the low income category with the rest of the African countries. At independence, most African countries had per capita incomes far in excess of those in South and Southeast Asia. Today, however, these Asian incomes have leaped far ahead of Africa's, and if present trends continue, Africa's per capita income will be about half of Asia's by the year 2000. Clearly, Africa is doing something wrong. The decade of the 1980s was a difficult one for much of the Third World other than Asia, but for Africa it was a disaster of such catastrophic proportions that the very fabric of the society is now, in many places, under severe strain.

The massive scale of Africa's economic deterioration did not come as a surprise to Africa-watchers. The Economic Commission for Africa (ECA) had been sounding the alarm since the late 1970s, and the seminal *Lagos Plan of Action* (LPA) [written by the ECA but published as a document of the Organization of African Unity (OAU)] released in 1980, plus subsequent ECA reports, including the "nightmare scenario," published in 1983 under the title *ECA and African Development 1983-2008*, have been landmark documents designed to alert both Africa and the donor community to the gravity of the African situation. The World Bank has also monitored this growing deterioration and issued a stream of reports and prescriptions intended to call attention to the problem and suggest how best to address it.

During the early years of the 1980s, the development community's attention was drawn to a debate of sorts which grew up around the LPA and the World Bank's basic analysis of Africa's poor economic performance, a document entitled

---

4. Browne, Robert S., "Alternative Policy Frameworks for African Development in the 1990s," in Julius E. Nyang'oro and Timothy M. Shaw (eds.), *Beyond Structural Adjustment in Africa: The Political Economy of Sustainable and Democratic Development,* (New York: Praeger Publishing, 1992): pp. 71–82. Excerpt taken from pp. 71–82.

Robert S. Browne is the author of *The Lagos Plan of Action vs. the Berg Report: Contemporary Issues in African Economic Development* (Lawrenceville, VA: Brunswick Publishing Co., 1989).

Accelerated Development in Sub-Saharan Africa: An Agenda for Change, popularly known as the Berg Report. These two documents were antithetical, both in identifying the principal causes for Africa's dismal performance and in prescribing the cure. The World Bank placed principal blame on the inefficient and irrational behavior of African governments, whereas the LPA attributed Africa's dismal results primarily to Africa's colonial heritage and to external factors, such as drought, oil prices, the unfavorable terms of trade, and similar factors beyond Africa's control.

The most stark difference between the two documents, however, lay in the prescriptions they offered for reversing the grim situation. The LPA called for a radical change in Africa's development strategy—a shifting of emphasis from export-led growth to a strategy of collective self-reliance, akin to import substitution. The World Bank, on the other hand, continued to push the Africans toward the traditional export-led development strategy but called for massive reforms in how African governments were pursuing this strategy. A litany of policy changes was prescribed, with great stress being placed on decreasing the role of the public sector, on the devaluation of currencies, on balancing domestic budgets, on restricting the safety net, on allowing the market to operate more freely, and on liberalizing the trade regimes.

The debate which ensued was a very unequal one, given the disparity in the power of the contenders: on the one hand, a handful of African intellectuals, majestically armed with the endorsements of Africa's fifty heads of state but virtually all of which states had empty coffers; and on the other, the developed county bureaucrats who control the financial resources to which those African states must have access for their development. It was easily predictable that the donor community would win the debate, and since the early 1980s the Africans have been increasingly obliged to accept policy reforms of the type described, which have come to be known as "structural adjustment." The LPA continues to receive rhetorical support from the Africans, but the refusal of the World Bank and the general donor community to accede to the Lagos Plan concept has ensured that the LPA would remain at best a dormant issue.

By the end of the 1980s, the resistance to structural adjustment had become muted yet controversy continued unabated as to its effectiveness. Structural adjustment programs were being attempted in some twenty-four African countries, and the World Bank was making frequent evaluations of these programs. It was within this atmosphere that the ECA introduced its report, the *African Alternative Framework to Structural Adjustment Programmes* (AAF) in 1989 (ECA 1989a). In this report the ECA called again for Africa to shift its emphasis away from export-led development toward a strategy of self-reliance, but the ECA develops the argument within the context of a response to the structural adjustment programs (SAPs) being imposed by the donor community.

In the wake of the appearance of AAF, and in a virtual reenactment of the events of the early 1980s, the World Bank a few months later published its second thoroughgoing analysis of the African economic situation, entitled *Sub-Saharan Africa; from crisis to sustainable growth* (SSA). Once again, the closely timed appearance of two in-depth analyses of African development by the preeminent institutional voices of the donor and recipient communities created a splendid opportunity for a comparative airing of the basic issues of African development. What follows is an overview of this second debate.

AAF, like the LPA which preceded it, strongly reflects the views of Dr. Adebayo Adediji, the Nigerian economist who has served as the Executive Director of the Addis Ababa-based ECA, and the views of the team of mostly African economists who worked there with him. Both of the African documents, however, carry the approval of the Planning Ministries of the fifty member states of the Organization of African Unity, and the AAF also carries the endorsement of the African Ministries of Finance, who reviewed it in draft form and appear to have removed some of the stridency which characterized an earlier version.

The theme underlying the AAF is that the orthodox economic policy prescriptions which the donors devise for the developing countries are generally inappropriate for Africa because they fail to take into consideration the special circumstances which prevail in most of the African countries. For this reason, the reforms often fail and, more objectionable, they sometimes leave the countries even worse off than before.

The report identifies several "structural characteristics" which impart a particularity to the African economies sufficient to disqualify orthodox economic analysis from being applicable to them. These include, among other things, the predominance of commerce over industry, the absence of linkages within the productive sectors, the small size of most of the African countries, the excessive dependence on exports (and on a very limited umber of export items), the general policy bias in favor of urban and wealthier residents, and the weakness of African institutions. Given these structural bottlenecks, the AAF argues that policy reforms aimed at improving financial balances and price structures—the reforms that typify orthodox structural adjustment programs—are inadequate to the task of redressing Africa's problems, and that what is needed are reforms which will *transform* Africa's societies into entities which are capable of carrying out sustainable development programs.

The development of the individual is afforded top priority in the ECA's approach to transforming Africa, which means that the AAF places great emphasis on alleviating poverty and on improving the welfare of the people as well as on ensuring the people have a significant voice in shaping how the development process proceeds. The provision of health care, education, and training are the basic building blocks of this approach. This implies a priority role for food production and distribution, together with some concern for assuring not only that food is available but also that the populace has the means to acquire it. This in turn leads to the need for providing either employment or accessibility to productive land, which in turn implies the necessity to provide physical infrastructure, especially in rural areas.

The foregoing description quickly begins to sound like a shopping list of things to be done in a standard development program. The distinguishing feature, however, is the emphasis placed on the need for keeping human development always at the forefront, even more forcefully than was the case with the "basic human needs" approach to development which was so popular in the seventies. It is this emphasis which places the AAF on a collision course with structural adjustment programs (SAPs), which have become the current vogue of the orthodox development and lending agencies. The essence of the SAPs is insistence on budgetary balance, on the ending of subsidies, on currency devaluation, on the levying of user fees, on reduction in the numbers of public employees, and other economies which too often strip the poor of such amenities as free education and free water and of whatever flimsy safety net they may have had, and expose them to unemployment, malnutrition, and other social ills. This is all directly contrary to the process of human development and transformation which the ECA sees as the essential condition for self-sustaining growth and development. Such programs are rendered even more unpalatable because the immediate impetus for them is to improve the balance of payments so as to permit the servicing of foreign-held debt.

The Africans do not charge that the donors' structural adjustment prescriptions are necessarily wrong (although they sometimes are). Budgets do need to be balanced, and excess numbers of public employees must be eliminated. The AAF does not deny this. But in the view of the Africans, the SAPs of the eighties have pursued these reforms single-mindedly, blind to the deleterious effects which they were having on both the human and the physical infrastructure of Africa, a deterioration which is no less serious merely because it may not be immediately reflected in the economic and financial variables which are the traditional benchmarks of SAPs. In the view of the ECA, African development objectives are measured by what is happening to the people, not by what is happening to the GDP, the balance of payments, or the budget deficit. Thus the AAF argues that, along with SAPs which the donor agencies are demanding, it is necessary to implement far more profound adjustments—transformations—in the African economies. Lacking these transformations, the SAPs are useless, or worse.

Structural bottlenecks and donor-imposed conditionalities are not the only villains in Africa's faltering development effort: African governments and African cultural practices are not exempted from the ECA's critical analysis. Along with the physical and economic deficiencies which handicap Africa, the AAF identifies a number of sociopolitical traits of the African societies which require transformation as well. There is, for example, a tendency for African governments to obstruct rather than to encourage the informal business sector. This largely unorganized but nevertheless quite extensive sector is perhaps the most dynamic facet of many African economies and constitutes African entrepreneurship in its most energetic and productive manifestation. Yet, rather than provide these entrepreneurs with support and assistance, most African governments at best ignore them and, in too many cases, pursue policies which actually drive them underground.

The practice of slavishly imitating Western consumption patterns is another such trait, leading to a debilitating dependence on luxury consumer imports financed at the expense of vitally necessary producer inputs. Nigerian President Babangida's recent decision to ban all wheat imports and to urge his people to "eat what they can grow" was an exemplary step in this direction. It is regrettable that the United States chose to denounce this courageous initiative merely because it promises to lose the United States some agricultural sales. The ECA document also attributes Africa's poor performance in part to the poor leadership which has plagued the continent. Corruption is specifically mentioned as a negative factor, as is the elitist orientation of public policy. The document calls for "wide-ranging changes in the democratization of society within the social and economic framework as well as in development strategies and policies."

The very heart of any transformation of the African economies, however, rests on the reversal of the bankrupt export-led development strategy. Ending Africa's dependence on the export of a few unprocessed agricultural and mineral commodities, both by expanding the variety of exports and, more importantly, by shifting the focus of production from exports to the satisfaction of needs, is seen as indispensable for the building of a self-sustaining African economy. This implies both self-sufficiency in food plus the creation of an industrial sector based on the utilization of local inputs and designed to meet basic needs, not to satisfy consumption patterns copied from foreigners.

Such goals are meaningful only within a continental, or Pan-African, framework. Substantially increased inter-African trade must replace much of the external trade, which is not only increasingly less profitable but also increasingly vulnerable to technological displacement and to the emerging regionalization of trading patterns. The implementation of such a strategy contains an imperative for much greater effort in the direction of sub-regional cooperation and integration than has taken place thus far. The African governments are criticized for not having afforded greater priority to the strengthening of Africa's key sub-regional organizations, such as the Economic Community of West African States (ECOWAS), the Preferential Trade Area for Eastern and Southern Africa (PTA), the regional clearinghouses and other instruments of the LPA.

The AAF offers comments on most of the key conditionalities which are generally included in orthodox SAPs, endorsing some and rejecting others, generally either because they would be unlikely to achieve the intended result in the African situation or because their negative side effects would outweigh their benefits. Currency devaluation, a perennial element in most SAPs, is viewed as being sometimes inappropriate for African countries. It may not raise export earnings because prices of Africa's exports (and oftentimes quotas as well) are set by external forces. It does not lead to substitution of local inputs for imported ones because African economies lack the necessary technological capacity. Although it may decrease imports, this can do more harm than good by eliminating the inputs necessary for maintaining production. Furthermore, devaluation is inflationary and it increases the burden of debt servicing. These negatives must be weighed against the obvious positives before a rational assessment can be made as to whether or not devaluation is called for in a specific case. The IMF and World Bank are alleged to lack sufficient awareness of and sensitivity to these African realities.

The same applies to the currently fashionable drive for "privatization," which has become a standard conditionality of contemporary reform programs. The AAF admits that public enterprise in Africa has been inefficient and costly, but it suggests that a blind embrace of privatization makes no sense within the African context. The problem is that Africa has no cadre of experienced people in the management area nor are there market sectors to complement the privatization efforts in many activity areas.

In the area of trade policy we find the traditional liberal trade policies of the Western democracies (policies which are honored more in the breach than in actual practice) are imposed on Africa, using both the classical economic arguments that free trade provides better competition, more efficient production, and lower priced goods to consumers, and also on the grounds that import licensing encourages corruption. AAF responds that while this may be true, an excessive liberalization of African trade policy would lead to the destruction of whatever incipient industrial sector Africa has managed to build as well as stifle any expansion of this vital sector, which is obviously not at a stage to compete with manufactured products from more advanced countries.

In sum, then, the AAF calls upon the lending agencies and the donor countries to become more knowledgeable about Africa's economies and to be more sensitive to their vulnerabilities before they impose upon them conditionalities which are more likely to be harmful than helpful. At the same time, it calls upon the African governments to adopt a broader view of the development problem and of the approach which must be taken to it. African governments must commit themselves to creating the environment and the institutions which will permit the effective implementation of the adjustment with transformation programs. Such adjustment with transformation must be designed and produced by the Africans, although with considerable input and support from the donor community. The AAF is to be seen as offering guidance in the shaping of programs tailored to each country, not as a boiler plate formula to be applied indiscriminately to all countries.

One of the major criticisms levied against the World Bank's landmark 1981 report, *Accelerated Development*, was that it was prepared with only a minimum of African input. As a consequence, the new World Bank document, SSA was widely exposed within the African development community at various stages of its development (World Bank 1989a). The results are self-evident. SSA is a far more sophisticated, sensitive, and valuable document than was its predecessor. Its tone is humbler. Clearly, the Bank had learned that it does not always have the correct answers and it seems to be prepared to pause and listen to what the Africans are saying about their countries. In sharp contrast to *Accelerated Development*, which ignored the LPA, SSA is not only responsive to the AAF, it virtually plagiarizes it in places. Not literally, of course, but in the sense that there has been a remarkable convergence of views between the two camps over the past decade. This is not to suggest, however, that there is total agreement as to what is to be done, or even as to which are the major and which the minor causes for Africa's economic plight. But the prescriptive gap is greatly reduced from where it was at the beginning of the decade and there is clearly a greater willingness for accommodation on the part of both the Bank and the Africans.

A principal cause for the tension between the two earlier documents was a difference in their time horizons. Whereas the LPA had taken a long-term view of what needed to be done in Africa, the World Bank's report had focused more on short term reforms. That dichotomy reappears in the two current reports under the labels of "structural adjustment" and "transformation," although it may seem odd to characterize structural adjustment as short-term in nature when in reality it may require several years to achieve. In both of the African documents it is mainly transformation which is being emphasized, although the term is only introduced in the latter volume. In the World Bank reports, shorter term policy reform is the dominant theme of the earlier report, where it is only occasionally described as "structural adjustment" because that term was then not yet in wide usage. In SSA, short-term policy reform, or "structural adjustment," continues to be the dominant theme, but its importance is tempered by frequent reference to the need for simultaneous attention to the type of longer-term changes which the Africans call transformation. Without them, the structural adjustment is described as being of limited usefulness.

Somewhat surprisingly, the Bank is fairly restrained in the claims it makes for its SAPs in Africa, acknowledging that the success ratio has not been very impressive. This restraint is in sharp contrast to the triumphant tone which had characterized a report on structural adjustment in Africa which the Bank had issued in early 1989 and whose optimistic findings the ECA had challenged as false. This acrimonious exchange had brought into the public forum a dispute which had long smoldered privately among development experts as to whether SAPs were actually achieving any measurable success in Africa or not. Throughout the latter half of the decade of the eighties, World Bank and IMF officials had boasted of the success which SAPs were having in specific African countries, successes which were viewed with considerable skepticism by many, and whose durability was open to question. When the Bank published these success stories as a public document (World Bank 1989b), the ECA challenged the validity of the Bank's statistical techniques (ECA 1989b) and went on to suggest that the improvements which the Bank attributed to the SAPs could just as logically be attributed to other factors. Although the Bank continued to maintain the validity of its findings, it was henceforth more subdued in its claims for SAPs, at least in Africa.

The final word on the effectiveness of structural adjustment lending in Africa will not be known for some time. Within the staffs of the World Bank and the IMF there is a wide range of opinion as to the effectiveness and appropriateness of SAPs for Africa, and the trend seems to be one of growing skepticism. The doubts do not derive primarily from loss of faith in the concept of SAPs but from a growing feeling that they cannot be implemented effectively in Africa. The factors which generate these doubt are in large part the very characteristics which the AAF delineates as requiring "transformation" if the African economies are to achieve a self-sustaining growth path. The Bank has become aware of this reality and SSA's exhortations for structural adjustments are interspersed with caveats which acknowledge the necessity for transformational type reforms if the SAPs are to be successful.

Indeed, much of the SSA is in fact a call for the type of transformation which the AAF highlights: human centered development; agriculture as the primary foundation for growth; expansion of the physical infrastructure, with the emphasis on infrastructure which directly raises productivity; enhanced intra-African trade and accelerated regional integration and coordination; involvement of the populace in the planning and implementation of development programs; improved governance, including the reduction of corruption and increased accountability on the part of African leaders.

With these priorities common to both documents, there is some basis for hoping that a consensus of views is finally emerging as regards African development. It is not the millennium, of course, not only because it remains to be seen what will be the depth of commitment to these very ambitious goals but also because there remain some areas to which the consensus does not extend. It's a fairly useless exercise to speculate over the depth of commitment which an institution will bring to a program. In the case of the World Bank, there are three power centers which interact to produce policy, the major donor countries, the Bank's leadership, and Bank staff. The SSA is at present just a Bank publication, a publication whose appearance long remained in doubt because of disagreements over what it should ultimately say. Although the average reader might find it to be an unexceptional document, in World Bank circles it is perceived as leaning toward the radical side because of its tentative tone as regards SAPs, its call for involvement of non-professional persons and organizations in the development process, its open allusions to corruption among recipient governments, and for other heresies. Merely because the forces of enlightenment succeeded in obtaining publication of the document does not guarantee that the bureaucracy will be mobilized to implement it, a task which would be Herculean even with the best of intentions.

As for the areas where consensus does not yet exist, reference has already been made to the major item: the appropriateness of devaluation in specific situations; the wisdom of instituting fully liberalized trade regimes; the extent to which privatization should be pushed; and the suitability of an export-led versus a more domestically focused development strategy for the continent as a whole. These are all fairly fundamental policy choices and it is consequently regrettable that the African and the donor communities remain far apart in their views on these items.

Logic would seem to be on the African side on all four of these items, although with differing degrees of force. The African resistance to privatization and to devaluation is by no means absolute, and in large measure the Africans are, in principle, actually supportive of substantial privatization. They just fear that there is as yet little in the way of an adequately capitalized and experienced private sector available to take over the many public sector enterprises which the donor nations would like to see privatized. They are not, of course, eager to see large segments of basic industry and public works falling into foreign ownership and control. Insofar as devaluation is concerned, their position is that one should proceed with caution, and on a case by case basis rather than across the board and without an adequate weighing of what all the consequences are likely to be.

With respect to the liberalization of the trade regime, the Bank's rationale for it rests on (a) an ideological attachment to open markets and free trade; (b) the inefficiencies which arise from protected markets and protected producers; and (c) the encouragement of rent-seeking and the opportunities for corruption which arise from import and foreign exchange licensing systems. The appropriate response would appear to be to attack the inefficiencies and the corruption directly rather than by the removal of all restraints and the imposition of pure market relationships. The latter approach might bring lower prices to the consumer but it would almost certainly destroy Africa's fledgling industrial sector and probably flood the countries with luxury imports as well.

As for the World Bank's continued emphasis on an export-led development strategy for Africa (even while it admits that the market outlook for Africa's main export products is not encouraging), it makes no sense at all. The Bank's call for support for industry linked to agriculture and for expanded intra-African trade deserves priority over the development of exports, a position which the Bank seems to be reluctant to support. This is the essence of "self-reliant" growth, which is clearly what Africa needs. Until Africa breaks its near total dependency on the sale of its commodities to foreigners it will not have achieved a position of genuine economic independence. With the global trading system breaking up into regional trading groups such as the European Common Market, the United States-Canada Free Trade Agreement, and an incipient East Asian trading bloc under the leadership of Japan, Africa will find itself becoming ever more vulnerable and isolated if it chooses (or is obliged) to remain a collection of 50 small, competing exporters, dependent on these regional giants to purchase its output and to supply its needs.

Africa enters the decade of the nineties under relatively inauspicious circumstances. The litany of economic ills from which it is suffering is staggering, to say nothing of its non- or semi-economic problems such as civil strife, AIDS and other debilitating diseases, and a host of miscellaneous problems. Meanwhile, the fast pace of technological change in the world is causing Africa to fall ever further behind from a materialistic point of view.

With per capita incomes no higher in 1989 than they were in 1960, Africa is facing a critical juncture. The World Bank report projects a potential growth rate of four to five percent for the decade of the nineties, but soberly points out how difficult such an achievement is likely to be. And even if such an ambitious target were achieved it would still leave the bulk of sub-Saharan Africa's population living at subsistence levels and below.

Previous World Bank projections for Africa's growth have generally proved to be overly optimistic, and should that again prove to be the case, one shudders to imagine the conditions likely to prevail on the continent by the end of the century. One can, however, derive some encouragement from the greater degree of consensus which now seems to exist within the donor and the African communities as to what needs to be done by way of development efforts. There remains cause for concern over the key areas in which no consensus has been achieved, notably, the debate over the wisdom of continuing to rely on an export-led development strategy as the proper route to self-sustained growth and development for Africa. In addition, the chronic uncertainty regarding the adequacy of the flows of external assistance casts a growing shadow over African development efforts in the face of the growing attraction which Eastern Europe holds for the donors.

The burgeoning technological progress and the breathtaking geopolitical realignments which are presently restructuring our globe are leading to an alarming marginalization of Africa, which has arrived too late to the technological party and brings too little to the political table. Africa has no choice other than to use this decade to transform itself while resisting a plethora of overwhelming forces from the powerful neighbors with which it shares the planet. In the final analysis, only the Africans can transform Africa, but the chances that they can do it without substantial external help are virtually nil. The hope is that this external help will be available in sufficient volume and on terms compatible with African aspirations. Only the passage of time will reveal the outcome of this agonizing drama.

The Resources of Tropical Africa

ANDREW M. KAMARCK[5]

The most important fact about the natural resources of tropical Africa is that we are still profoundly ignorant about them. First, relatively little is known of the minerals Africa possesses, and second, there is only slight knowledge and little in the way of technology concerning how African agriculture can best exploit the continent's soil and climate conditions. In minerals, finding, delineating, testing, and making an appreciation of the costs and benefits of exploiting the minerals hidden in the African countries are problems that have yet to be solved. In agriculture, because the existing advanced technology was developed mainly to handle the problems and characteristics of temperate zone agriculture, we still have not developed the optimum varieties for most African crops, nor do we know the best cultivation practices and how to cope with tropical weeds, pests, and other predators.

Two other important constraints on the development of African resources are transport costs and "security." High transport costs, which from the beginning of modern times have inhibited development of African resources, persist. The scarcity of natural harbors; the lack nearly everywhere of navigable river access to the interior; the African plateau, cut by deep valleys, that dominates most of tropical Africa and makes the building of roads and railways very costly; the fierce tropical rains that threaten the rapid erosion of road and railways—all require massive investment in transport facilities if any appreciable volume of cargo is to be moved. The result is that even on those rare occasions when a particular mineral can be exploited with a relatively small investment in the mine, the total investment in likely to be high—often in the range of hundreds of millions of dollars—because of the need to invest in a railroad, road, or port.

In Gabon in northwest Central Africa, there is a very large deposit of nearly a billion tons of proven reserves of rich iron ore. It is separated from the ocean, however, by some four hundred miles of tropical rain forest and swamps. A detailed study, financed by the United Nations, was begun in 1960 to study the economic feasibility of building a railroad across Gabon to make possible the exploitation of the iron

5. Kamarck, Andrew, "The Resources of Tropical Africa," in *Daedalus,* vol. 111, no. 2, (Cambridge, MA: American Academy of Arts and Sciences, Spring 1982): pp. 149–163. Excerpts taken from pp. 149–151, 151–163.

Andrew M. Kamarck served as an associate fellow at the Harvard Institute for International Development. His books include *The Economics of African Development* (New York, Praeger, 1971) and *The Tropics and Economic Development* (Baltimore: John Hopkins University Press, 1976). He has worked with the World Bank for 29 years.

ore and to help develop the practically uninhabited interior of the country. After years of work, it became clear that the economics of such a railroad were dubious at best, and the World Bank and other international financial sources refused to finance it. Taking advantage of its oil resources, the government of Gabon decided to build the railroad on its own. The first hundred miles were completed in 1978; the second are expected to be finished by December 1982. By 1986 or 1987, a branch is expected to reach Gabon's manganese mine, which now exports its ore by cable car to the Congo Republic's railroad. Sometime in the mid-nineties or around the year 2000, if the government persists in this endeavor, and oil prices remain high, the railroad should reach the iron ore. By this time, the costs will total in the billions of dollars—this, for a country that is estimated to have a population of well under one million.

To combat high total investment costs—except in the case of high unit values like diamonds or gold—a large volume of minerals must be transported to achieve unit costs that are low enough to make a mining operation economically justifiable. Further, for the extraction of a mineral deposit in tropical Africa to be economic, it has to be several times richer in content (that is, in percent of the desired metal contained in the raw ore) compared to deposits in the United States or Canada.

Because the size of mining investments tends to be so large in Africa, governmental prices vis-à-vis investment and the treatment of company staff have even more than usual importance. For example, no corporate management with any feeling of responsibility for corporate shareholders or the future of the corporation will embark on an investment of hundreds of millions of dollars in any country where the risk of expropriation without adequate compensation appears to be unduly high. Consequently, an additional inhibiting factor to the development of Africa's mineral resources, for at least the last twenty years, has been the political-administrative environment over most of the continent.

As we shall see, the extraction of oil is the exception, for at least two reasons. The major oil companies, and even those classed as minor, are so colossal, that even an investment of several hundred millions of dollars in a single project is relatively small compared to a company's total resources. For Exxon, the biggest, an investment of $1 billion is less than one percent of annual gross receipts. Standard Oil of Indiana, a "minor," invests around $7 billion a year. Giants such as these can risk African-size projects without jeopardizing the life of the company. Second, the timing of the risk in oil is different from that in mining. Oil-extraction requires huge capital outlays early in the game, and with success, there is a rapid payout. Thus high and continuous investment to sustain output over the entire life of the mine is required.

A belief in the richness and easy exploitation of African resources has persisted from early times, beginning with the stories of King Solomon's mines and the gold of Ophir. Despite repeated discouragements, the myth endures. The exploration of the coasts of Africa began shortly before the discovery and exploration of the two Americas. Yet North America was thoroughly explored, opened up, settled by immigrants, and the United States was well on its way to becoming an industrial power before the sources of the Nile and where the Niger came to the sea were even *known.*

Africa remained an unknown, undeveloped continent for so many centuries, and so little is known even today about Africa's resources and how Africans can best exploit them, for good reasons. Excepting only the North African countries at the top of the continent and South Africa, Swaziland, and Lesotho on its southern tip, Africa, with over 75 percent of its 30 million square kilometers in the torrid zones, has a climate that is predominantly tropical. The equator almost exactly bisects the continent, there being about 4,000 kilometers (2,500 miles) from the equator north to the shores of the Mediterranean and 3,800 kilometers (2,300 miles) to the southern tip. The tropical climate and its effects, added to the other difficult geographical features (scarcity of harbors and of rivers navigable from the coast) isolate tropical Africa from the rest of the world and most Africans from one another. Yellow fever and malaria levied a heavy toll of death on all visitors to tropical Africa. Trypanosomiasis (sleeping sickness), carried by the tsetse fly, killed horses and cattle, and thus made travel to the interior impossible using animal transport. Commerce depended on human porters, the most costly and inefficient of all transport systems. Consequently, little commerce other than in gold and diamonds (commodities of high value and small bulk) and slaves (a commodity with legs) was economically possible with the interior in most of tropical Africa before the invention of the costly, but disease-impregnable, iron horse.

The tropical climate still inhibits the discovery of mineral resources. Although there is no rational basis for believing that countries in the tropics have poorer or fewer mineral resources than those in the temperate zones, a relatively small portion of the known reserves of the world's minerals has in fact been found so far in tropical countries. . . .

Although mineral development in tropical Africa has been slowed essentially by technological reasons, as the technology—knowledge, techniques, and instruments—improves, it will become easier to discover the mineral resources of Africa. There remains, however, one other highly inhibiting element—the governmental - administrative environment. Investors prefer to invest in countries with stable governments, at least those with a minimum level of administrative competence and predictable legal systems.

Up to 1960, technological factors and high transport costs were the main factors retarding African mineral development. Since that time, insecurity has been the major factor keeping new material exploration and development in tropical Africa to such a slow pace. In 1960, African bauxite reserves and hydropower potential clearly pointed to Africa as the place where the major expansion of the aluminum industry sector (bauxite, alumina, aluminum) of the world would take place, and some promising starts were made—aluminum in Ghana and Cameroon, and bauxite and alumina in Guinea. But investor interest soon shifted to the discovery and exploitation of bauxite and the development of aluminum output in Australia.

Similarly, virtual stagnation of copper output in Zambia and Zaire over the last decade contrasts strongly with the rapid growth in earlier years and the continuing growth in Latin America.

Africans do not yet have the critical mass of managerial and technical skills in mining that are necessary if their mineral resources are to be found and developed without help from abroad. South Africa and Zimbabwe have been exceptions, and here, white Africans have provided the necessary skills. Elsewhere, and also in Zimbabwe if the whites migrate, reliance has been placed on expatriates. Since independence, previously existing mines have been nationalized in nearly all countries. Yet despite nationalization, expatriates, whether recruited as individuals or provided as a team by an international mining company, still form the key cadre that keeps the operation going. . . .

Although forecasting is always dangerous, it is possible to assert with reasonable confidence that there will be no major increase in the exploitation of nonfuel mineral resources of most of tropical Africa before the year 2000. The lead time between discoveries and the beginning of large-scale mining usually is measured in decades. Since 1960 there has been a drastic decline in exploration in most of tropical Africa. American and Canadian mining companies in recent years have been spending over 80 percent of their exploration expenditures in the United States, Canada, and Australia. European mining companies similarly have turned their main attention away from Africa, toward finding mineral resources in industrialized countries. Brazil, which itself is rapidly becoming industrialized, and a few other Latin American countries are the main exceptions to the present aversion of the large mining groups to exploration and investment in the less developed countries.

Even if a sea change in the investment atmosphere in the African countries, and in the willingness of the large mining companies to undertake exploration in tropical Africa, were to occur in the next few years, substantial increases in output of any newly discovered minerals could not take place before the year 2000. Some increase in output could take place sooner, of course, from the exploitation of mineral deposits that were discovered up to the mid-sixties and that have not reached the stage of exploitation as yet.

It is only in energy, mainly oil, that any appreciable progress has been made since independence in beginning to identify and exploit new African resources. But what has been done to date as far as tropical Africa as a whole is concerned is merely a beginning. . . .

Hydropower is one of tropical Africa's most important potential assets. The physical formation that helped keep interior Africa isolated from the coast for millennia—the great central plateau with rivers plunging off it near the coast—gives Africa the greatest undeveloped hydroelectric potential of any continent in the world. The World Energy Conference in 1974 estimated the gross theoretical hydroelectric capacity of tropical Africa at over 400 million kilowatts, or about four-fifths of the grand total potential of all the developed market countries (United States, Canada, Western Europe, Japan, Australia, and New Zealand). With practically all of the major sites in the United States and Europe—where cheap hydropower can be produced in substantial volume—already utilized, what was once an obstacle to African development has become an important potential asset. . . .

Hydropower can eliminate the need to use expensive imported oil for the production of electricity. The problem, however, is to find a market for this potential electric power. The domestic market being too small to utilize the huge block of power that a large project must generate to be economic, the solution is to look toward exporting it. Either the power itself or power-intensive commodities must be exported. In the latter case, new industries must be created that depend on consumption of large quantities of cheap power, such as aluminum, other electrometallurgical industries like ferrochrome, and the electrochemical industries.

Kariba, on the Zambezi River between Zambia and Zimbabwe, which created the world's largest man-made lake at the time, provides power for copper mines and electrolytic copper refineries in Zambia, for ferrochrome production in Zimbabwe, and for the copper industry in Shaba province in Zaire, as well as for other purposes. The Volta project in Ghana is largely devoted to providing power for an aluminum smelter as well as for exporting power to Togo, Benin, and the Ivory Coast. Cabora Bassa, one of the world's largest hydroelectric plants, in Mozambique, downstream from Kariba, exports power 850 miles to the power network in South Africa, and provides around a tenth of South Africa's electricity.

These projects and the few others that already exist use only a small fraction of the total potential. The problem here again is the need to put a large amount of investment capital at risk for a long period of time, in places where there are reasonable doubts as to its security. To utilize economically the power potential of a large project, hundreds of millions of dollars must be invested in the power project itself, and hundreds of millions more in building the highly capital-intensive industry to use the power. In the event of trouble, it is not possible to uproot a dam, dig out the underground power house, and evacuate them both by helicopter. . . .

Farming is the dominant economic activity of tropical Africa; it provides everywhere the means of livelihood to the vast majority of the population. It also produces between 40 and 60 percent of the gross national product in all countries, except Botswana, Gabon, and Zambia, where mining is particularly important. Around three-quarters of the African people still live on farms; in Burundi, over 95 percent. African exports are still largely products of agriculture. For most of tropical Africa, economic development is closely tied to progress in exploiting its agricultural potential. Yet, a principal problem in such exploitation is the lack of knowledge, except in the case of a very few crops, of how best to farm efficiently in the tropics.

Tropical Africa does not have a single homogenous tropical climate. There is, in fact, a continuously variable succession of climates that blend and overlap. A wet equatorial climate, in which rain falls in all months, and total 200 to 300 centimeters (75 to 120 inches) a year on the average, is the rule across most of the center. North and south from this area there is an alternately wet and dry tropical climate, the dry periods tending to grow increasingly longer as one goes farther north or south. Finally, there is the dry tropical climate, characteristic of the Sahara and the Namibia deserts.

All of these different tropical climates are characterized first by the fact that they are not temperate—that is, moderate. Rainfall is usually too much or too little, and at most one can be certain only of its unpredictability and violence. It is not surprising that we call torrential showers "tropical rains." Second, there is no frost; the average temperature in the coldest month is at least eighteen degrees Celsius (64 degrees Fahrenheit). Continuous heat and the absence of frost mean life and reproduction are not stayed by the great executioner of nature, winter. Life in most parts of the tropics thus takes on an infinite multiplicity of forms, and there is fierce competition for survival. The conditions are right for rapid evolutionary change as species adapt to new opportunities, with a consequent high probability that any new plant or animal, introduced by man and grown in considerable numbers, will soon be attacked by a new enemy adapting rapidly from some existing form.

Cultivated plants are threatened by weeds, parasitic fungi, insects, spider mites, eelworms, and virus diseases. After harvest, storage pests and rats move in. In some areas, millions of weaver birds attack crops. Gigantic swarms of desert locusts in Western and Eastern Africa, and red locusts in Southern, Central, and Eastern Africa, are a major, recurrent threat to crops. Constant research against new threats is therefore necessary if any major increase in agricultural output is to be achieved.

Tropical soils, with the exception of alluvial or recent volcanic soils, are poor and contain little organic material. Even in dense forests, soils are thin, although equilibrium is maintained by the return of elements to the soil by decaying plants and trees. If the forest is cleared, the soil is soon exhausted by two to three years of crops. For this reason, African farmers in the humid tropics developed "shifting," or seminomadic, cultivation. A farm is hacked out of the forest, cultivated for a few years, and allowed to revert to bush again.

Most African farmers still have to depend on human muscle power to cultivate their fields. Over most of tropical Africa, the transition to ox or horse-drawn mixed farming, with the resulting enormous gains in efficiency and output, could not take place because of the tsetse fly. Typanosomiasis, the disease carried by this fly, is deadly to cattle and horses, and has still not been mastered. Where the fly has been pushed out, constant vigilance and control measures are necessary to keep the fly from coming back. Where the fly is absent, there are innumerable other parasitic, infectious, nutritional, toxic, metabolic, and organic diseases that affect livestock. Intestinal parasites result in retarded development of young animals, reduce yields of meat and milk, and diminish the working capacity of draft animals.

Not only are the farmer's crops and livestock damaged by tropical diseases and predators, but the farmer is as well. The average farmer in tropical Africa is infected by at least two different types of parasites. He or she will usually have had, or be currently subject to, attacks of malaria or schistosomiasis (bilharzia, or liver fluke), a debilitating disease that may affect up to half the African farmers. Hook worms, round worms, pinworms, and whipworms are widespread. Millions have filariasis, spread by the bite of mosquitoes, onchocerciasis (river blindness), spread by the bite of a black fly, or guinea worm, spread by infected drinking water. Sleeping sickness (trypanosomiasis), kala-azar (leishmaniasis), dengue, trachoma, cholera, and leprosy are also economically significant. Most of these diseases have not been brought under control; in fact, the necessary research effort to do so has barely started. Only in 1975 was a coordinated international effort begun to try to discover, develop, and apply new technologies for the control of six of these diseases. The Special Program on Research and Training in Tropical Diseases, co-sponsored by the World Health Organization, the United Nations Development Program, and the World Bank, is concentrating on malaria, schistosomiasis, sleeping sickness, filariasis (including river blindness), leishmaniasis, and leprosy.

It is not only these "exotic" tropical diseases that blight African life. When tropical Africa was opened up to the rest of the world, among the first immigrants were diseases new to the continent such as measles, smallpox, and tuberculosis, and these were as devastating to human life as Arab slave traders or colonial punitive expeditions. A large part of the mortality and sickness in tropical Africa today is caused by diseases that also exist in temperate climates. Many of the diseases are more difficult to resist in the tropics because of the warm temperatures the year round. These temperatures allow large populations of insects to live for most or all of the year and permit a much more rapid multiplication than in colder climates. The house fly, for example, spreads bacillary dysentery and other diseases. It takes forty-four days for the fly to develop from egg to adult at sixteen degrees Celsius (62 degrees Fahrenheit), but only ten days at thirty degrees Celsius (88 degrees Fahrenheit). The difference in the number of days means a difference in the potential birth of millions of flies. But that is not all. Parasites, such as malaria, that carry out a part of their development within an insect carrier (such as the mosquito) are also "ecothermic"; that is, the speed of their development and multiplication within the insect host varies directly with the temperature.

Most of the African rural population, consequently, are dragged down by parasitic diseases and constantly besieged by other sicknesses. It is hard for anyone from an industrialized, temperate climate to have a real sense of what most African farmers must endure. Probably the closest anyone can get to this is to imagine having to work day in and day out while in the grip of a perpetual, severe cold or the first stage of flu.

The African farmer has had to survive by using human muscle power in a difficult environment, coaxing crops out of a soil that is rapidly being depleted of its nutrients, and surrounded by the enormous fecundity of minute life that is trying to feed off big life. It is no wonder that the exploitation of Africa's agricultural potential still awaits accomplishment.

The picture I have painted of Africa's agricultural potential thus far is bleak, since I have presented only the main causes that keep African farmers poor. This is largely because existing agricultural technology, which was developed mainly for temperate zone agriculture, cannot cope with the problems of tropical African agriculture or exploit the particular tropical advantages. These do exist. First, sunlight energy for plant growth in the humid tropics is 60 to 90 percent higher than in humid temperate regions. Consequently, plants in tropical rain forests produce as much as three to five times more organic matter each year than do plants in temperate forests. The absence of winter, once pests are controlled, can extend the length of the growing season, and if water is available, may make it possible to grow as many as three or four crops a year. The very multiplicity of species could help in developing new and better crops and livestock. . . .

Owing to the many variation in climate and soils, and the small stock of scientific knowledge available, progress in taking advantage of African agricultural potential is bound to be very slow. Considerable success, however, has already been attained in developing improved strains of maize and sorghum. A great deal has been accomplished also in the tree crops, such as bananas, cocoa, coffee, oil palm, rubber, and tea. Tree crop cultivation has few of the problems of tropical agriculture mentioned above. The plants shade and protect the soil, and come close to achieving the same equilibrium with the soil and climate as did the original forest. Since tree crops provide a permanent farm, the results of research to increase productivity and income can be applied more easily. Perhaps even more important, there has been a great deal of research on these crops usually elsewhere in the tropics, but also, in some cases in Africa, beginning in the colonial period.

An outstanding example is rubber. The trees and the system of cultivation and processing developed in Malaysia made natural rubber competitive with synthetic rubber made from oil even before oil jumped in price. Similar technological opportunities exist in the other tree crops. Cocoa is grown in the Ivory Coast, Ghana, Nigeria, Cameroon, and other African countries. Coffee is grown in many African countries, but principally in the Ivory Coast, Kenya, Uganda, and Tanzania. Oil palm is a West African crop, but is also grown in Cameroon and Zaire. Tea is mostly an East African crop. Bananas come from the Ivory Coast, Cameroon, and Somalia; rubber is a long-time export from Liberia and Zaire, but now is also being developed in other West African countries.

While the cultivation of tree crops provides and opportunity for many African countries to develop their agricultural resources, only a few governments have encouraged their farmers to do so. The Ivory Coast and Kenya in Africa, like Malaysia in Asia, have paid attention to their agriculture, and in doing so, have made impressive progress, compared to their neighbors, in exploiting their agricultural potential for local consumption and for export.

The myth that Africa possesses enormous and easily exploitable resources is likely to survive any balanced objective appraisal of the facts such as this discussion has attempted to be. The myth has served a useful purpose—and continues to do so—for many different interests over the last century. In the late nineteenth and early twentieth century, it was diligently peddled by European imperialists and colonial officers to persuade reluctant ministries of finance and parliaments to back the grabbing of African territory and to pay for the minimum of infrastructure required. At the same time, financiers and stock market speculators, busily floating African concession companies at handsome profits for themselves, led the investing public into the shearing shed with similar fabrications of easily exploitable African riches.

After World War II, the myth was picked up by African nationalist leaders, who roused the people by placing the blame for their poverty on foreign exploitation. That Great Britain, France, and Belgium relinquished their tropical African colonies, from which they were supposed to be drawing so much wealth, with so little reluctance disturbed the myth not a whit.

The myth continues. It is now sustained by the apologists for the Republic of South Africa. These people clothe their support for South Africa by greatly exaggerating the importance of South African minerals to the noncommunist world. A second group of myth-sustainers are the radical "neo-colonialists" and "dependency" theorists. African governments discovered that nationalizing foreign-owned companies did not result in an outpouring of wealth for their peoples; the "dependency" theories serve the useful purpose of placing the blame on the industrialized world for the disappointment of pro-independence expectations. According to this set of theories, the African countries are kept poor and under the control of the industrialized world by their continued economic dependence on it, through their exports of primary products and their imports of manufactures. There is no doubt that countries that are exporters of primary products (such as minerals and agricultural products) have special economic problems. But most of tropical Africa's problems are more fundamental and closer to home than this particular aspect of their economies. The hard economic reality is that the countries of tropical Africa have major real problems in developing their resources. As I tried to make clear in this paper, the indications are that the resources exist to make substantial African economic development possible, but that they are not easily exploitable. There are real difficulties to overcome—both natural and man-made. It is no service to the African nations to ignore or make light of them.

Arrested Development in Anglophone Black Africa

DAVID FIELDHOUSE[6]

There are two basic questions that have to be asked about the role of economic factors in African history between the mid-1940s and the late 1970s. First, why did the metropolitan states transfer political power, despite their very considerable economic stake in African territories? Second, why did political independence not lead to that economic autonomy and sustained development which was confidently predicted by many development economists and nationalists in the 1950s and 1960s? Neither question can now be answered with any confidence, since the primary official sources are not yet open for research and insufficient work has been done on economic development during the last two decades. But the issues are so important that they demand assessment. The aim of this essay, therefore, is to identify some of the major questions and to indicate in which direction the available evidence is pointing. . . .

Historians must always be aware of the dangers of a *post hoc ergo propter hoc* argument. To describe the dominant patterns of economic development in tropical anglophone Africa after decolonization—that is, from about 1960—is not to suggest that what happened was necessarily the direct consequence of the transfer of political power. There were both continuities and discontinuities, and it is in most cases impossible to draw a hard line between them. Successor states and development economists may point to dramatic increases in national incomes or to rapid industrialization, and claim that these were only possible because of the beneficent forces liberated by decolonization. On the other hand critics of "third world" regimes may suggest that in fact the best years for Africa were just before independence, perhaps in the booming 1950s, and that the almost universal economic disasters of the 1970s and 1980s demonstrate the unwisdom of adopting the types of "managed" economies most common in tropical Africa. There is no way of adjudicating between these standpoints. The basic question must, therefore, be whether it is possible to

6. Fieldhouse, David, "Arrested Development in Anglophone Black Africa," in Prosser Gifford and W. Roger Louis (eds.), *Decolonization and African Independence: The Transfer of Power, 1960–1980,* (New Haven: Yale University Press, 1988): pp. 135–158. Excerpts taken from pp. 135, 145–158.

D.K. Fieldhouse is the Vere Professor of Imperial and Naval History and Fellow of Jesus College, Cambridge University. His books include *Colonialism, 1870–1945* (London: Weidenfeld and Nicolson, 1981), and *Economics and Empire, 1830–1914* (Ithaca: Cornell University Press, 1973).

pinpoint specific factors that may, at least partially, explain the fluctuating fortunes of these states since about 1960. . . . These were, nevertheless, excellent years for most parts of Africa. The later 1970s and early 1980s saw a serious slowing down of the rate of growth. According to the World Bank, the rate of growth of GDP for the whole of sub-Saharan Africa slowed from 3.9 percent in the 1960s to 2.9 percent in the 1970s (excluding Nigeria, from 4.1 to 1.6 percent), while per capita income growth overall slowed from 1.3 percent to 0.8 percent. . . . Thus the basic question with which all students of recent African history must be concerned is why the apparent promise of these earlier decades appears to have evaporated.

Within this generalized picture, however, there are marked contrasts between different sectors of African economies. In most countries industry grew fast, with a growth rate of 3.3 percent in the 1970s, rising from 16 percent to 31 percent of GDP in sub-Saharan Africa between 1960 and 1979. General infrastructure and welfare indicators also suggest a quite impressive performance. For example, energy consumption per capita rose from seventy-six kgs coal equivalent to 128; life expectancy rose from an average of thirty-nine at birth in 1960 to forty-seven in 1979; and between 1960 and 1978 the proportion of the appropriate age groups in education rose from 36 percent to 63 percent in primary schools and from 3 percent to 13 percent in secondary education.

Other aspects of economic development were, however, much less promising. Most serious was the trend of agriculture. . . .

Declining exports (except from Nigeria) and increasing dependence on imported food in many countries, coupled with large imports of goods and extensive borrowing abroad, inevitably resulted in an increasingly adverse balance of payments and thus in foreign indebtedness. . . . For many African states this meant virtual bankruptcy, postponed by foreign aid and further borrowing, which in turn implied greater dependence.

Thus the general picture, ignoring the vast differences between countries that are obscured by these aggregate statistics, is of very considerable growth from the 1950s, which was slowing up by the later 1970s and appeared to be seriously at risk in the early 1980s. Within this, however, there were marked sectoral contrasts. Industry and the provision of infrastructural and welfare services grew very fast; but this was offset by a serious lag in the growth of agriculture. Food production was not keeping up with population growth, and many of the staple commodity exports were in decline. The result was increasing dependence on imported food and international aid, coupled with balance of payments deficits, heavy overseas borrowing and deteriorating debt-service ratios. By the early 1980s, most parts of black Africa were in varying degrees of crisis. The golden dreams of the independence era were in ruins: It was no longer possible to hope that black Africa would be able to sustain rates of growth and patterns of development which might enable her to close the gap on the affluent West. It has become a main preoccupation of those concerned not only with African history but specialists in many related fields to find an explanation.

Broadly, there appear to be four main types of explanation, and these will be examined in turn. First, that there is in fact no cause for surprise at failure to sustain the high growth rates of the earlier decades, because great expectation were based on false premises. Second, that the check to growth was caused by Africa's relationship with the international economy and, in the thinking of the Left, with international capitalism. Third, that limited success was due to unwise policies adopted by the African states, whose consequences were merely accentuated by adverse international trends from about 1973. Finally, that there are major obstacles to rapid and sustained growth in tropical Africa which are not found to the same degree in other parts of the world. These explanations are not mutually exclusive. They will be considered in turn merely for clarity, and at the end an attempt will be made to measure their relative importance.

The first point to emphasize is that, insofar as one can trust the statistics provided by national governments to multilateral agencies such as the World Bank and the United Nations, African development has been neither disastrous nor exceptionally poor in comparison either with long-term trends or with other contemporary societies. The average growth rate of per capita incomes over the period 1960-1979 was 1.6 percent, which was the same as for all low-income countries for the same period.

Never, probably, in the past has such a performance been achieved by Less Developed Countries (LDCs). Hence, the disappointments and complaints concerning black Africa relate either to particular countries or groups of countries; to different period within these twenty years; or, finally, to Africa's performance compared with that of more developed countries. Again, to recapitulate, using these headings, development has certainly varied greatly within black Africa: a number of states, including Ghana, Senegal, Angola, and Uganda, had negative per capita growth rates during these twenty years. Conversely, the weighted average is greatly affected by Nigeria's oil-based growth rate of the 1970s. Moreover, the most serious feature of these decades seems to be a marked downturn in growth in the early 1970s, which suggests that whatever steam the development process may have had earlier was running out by then. And so one could go on. How should one look at or explain all this?

There is, of course, no single or certain answer: No one knows enough about the dynamics of economic growth fully to explain success or failure. For what it is worth, here is a personal amalgam of elements of arguments currently in play.

The starting point must be exaggerated expectations. The optimistic projections of the mid-1950s and thereafter were based more on hypothesis than on fact or historical experience. In many cases they took the favorable conditions of the 1950s, the first development decade for any country since the 1920s, as their model for the future. As Killick and others have since pointed out, most of their basic assumptions were as false as the very pessimistic projections being made ten years earlier, which were themselves based on the equally untypical 1930s. Black Africa had no capacity to put infinite amounts of capital to good use. Young African states were quite incapable of carrying through the highly sophisticated development schemes the experts drew up for them. Industry could not, given the size and character of most of these states, take the rest of the unmodernized economy along with it: Certainly import-substituting industry could not generate an efficient intermediate or capital-goods industry in the short term. Agriculture could not indefinitely bear the weight of penal taxation to provide the necessary investment surplus for modernization, nor would it necessarily respond to the stimulus of industrial demand or be tempted into greater productivity by the availability of locally manufactured consumer goods.

It is significant that among those economists who were most critical of the typi-cal approach of this period were two who had more direct knowledge of the facts of "third world" and black-African economic life than those who spun theories in Europe and North America. Both W.A. Lewis and S.H. Frankel (who had studied African conditions for many years) held that sustained development in black Africa had to be built on improved agricultural productivity and could not be conjured up by ingenious economic theorization. Thus the principles on which most African development schemes and expectations were based may have been theoretically correct, given their prior assumptions, but they were essentially misleading in terms of African realities. Their signposts to the promised land pointed in the wrong direc-tions, and we should not be surprised that African states who obeyed them ended up in Doubting Castle.

If, however, we ignore these over-optimistic projections, we are still left with the fact that many African states are now much less well placed for future development than it would have been reasonable to predict in the 1950s, even on the assumption that they continued on the relatively orthodox paths marked out by colonial author-ities in that first, and last, decade of energetic colonial development. Colonies that then had large overseas credits, favorable trade balances, expanding agricultural and industrial production, modest unemployment, and public services that were both cheap and comparatively efficient, now have few of these things. Can this decline be ascribed to black Africa's unchosen place in a hierarchical international econo-my?

At least in terms of raw dependency theory it cannot. As P.J. McGowan argued in 1976, by the three standard measures of economic "dependence" (the proportion of aid received from the major donor country; the proportion of exports to the largest market; and the share of total exports taken by the three leading commodity exports), African countries were in no sense "dependent." Indeed, most of them greatly diversified their external relations during this period. But if one looks at the effects of broad trends in the international economy since the 1950s, the picture is somewhat different. It is true that the trends in the terms of trade, while variable, were not particularly adverse, that there were few effective inhibitions on exports to the West, and that aid flows did not fall off to any great extent. Nevertheless, African countries could not avoid the effects of the business cycle, which was cer-tain to affect both the return for their exports and the cost of imported goods and credit. The 1950s and early 1960s had been a boom period for the world economy.

The downturn came in the early 1960s. The all-item dollar commodity price index fell from about 1964 to 1967, then recovered in 1969, only to fall again in 1971. It was then raised by the 1973 OPEC oil price increase, only to fall to a new low level in 1975. After a rise in 1977 and subsequent fluctuations, it fell to a low level again in the early 1980s.

Within these global fluctuations particular commodities followed their own paths. Of the main black-African commodities, copper did well in the 1960s but suffered an annual price decline of 18.7 percent in the 1970s. Iron-ore prices declined by an average of 13 percent in that decade. Sugar prices declined during both the 1960s and 1970s, as did prices for tea, groundnut oil, and palm oil. Virtually all African export commodity prices declined during the 1970s and were joined by oil in the early 1980s. These trends were in no sense special to black Africa, affecting also Asia, Latin America and the developed countries. African countries, however, were particularly vulnerable at that stage of their development, heavily dependent on export prices and the price of foreign imports and credit to sustain their ambitious development programs. The effects were bound to be comparable with those of the slump of the 1920s and 1930s. The main difference was that black Africa was now much more exposed because of its increased dependence on foreign borrowing and on the imports necessary for its new industries and public-works programs. Just as exceptionally favorable international conditions in the 1950s and early 1960s had made possible high rates of growth, so less favorable conditions thereafter held back development until the next upturn of the international business cycle.

What, then, of the effects of the policies adopted by African states and the way in which they were executed? The evidence suggests that in varying degrees the effects of these policies were either unfavorable or, at best, neutral. Without rehearsing the evidence, it seems clear that the broad interventionist strategies adopted by almost all states were undesirable roughly to the extent that they were "open" or "closed" economies. Ghana and Tanzania, which adopted highly structured and allegedly socialist policies, did worse in most respects than Kenya or Nigeria, though the latter was admittedly helped in the 1970s by oil revenues. Within this general framework, policies that aimed at the most rapid and complete import substitution for manufactured imports, especially by means of state or parastatal enterprises, were most wasteful of national resources: They added little or no value at international prices, had minimal impact upstream or down on other sections of the local economy, cost a great deal in foreign exchange and tended to be capital intensive, creating very little employment.

The use of multinational corporations (MNCs), commonly in partnership with government or private indigenous capital, was more efficient economically, but resulted in liability to provide foreign exchange for transfer of dividends, royalties, etc. as well as an "invasion" of national autonomy and an extended commitment to capitalism. Finally, there is debate over the extent to which these industrializing policies stimulated a genuine indigenous bourgeoisie. Ghana and Tanzania discouraged this development, Nigeria and Kenya encouraged it; and the evidence suggests that in Kenya at least there are the roots of what may grow into a genuine industrial bourgeoisie, able ultimately to challenge the MNCs for control of the modern sector of the economy.

If industrial policies seem to have had few if any beneficial results, agricultural policies (with Kenya a partial exception among the states considered here) were worse still. Low producer prices, fixed by monopsonic marketing boards, discouraged established export staple and also the marketing of domestic food products. Only Kenya, probably because of the continued influence of large-scale farmers and conventions established by earlier white settlers, gave producers a reasonable share of the value of their efforts; and there alone the adoption of a reasonable foreign-exchange policy protected producers from a further erosion of their returns resulting from over-valued currencies. Nor were state attempts to compensate for the decline or stagnation of peasant production by other means generally successful. State farms in Ghana were a disaster; subsidized capitalist farming there and in Nigeria was, for the most part, a highly inefficient use of scarce resources. Tanzania's various schemes for restructuring peasant communities and modes of production had precious little economic value, whatever the political return.

State policies in these fields (and one could of course add in most other fields, such as exchange policy, licensing of imports and production, the provision of credit and the distribution of economic goods) were thus almost uniformly unhelpful to economic growth. Where they were most constructive was in providing a range of infrastructural and welfare services, notably education and medicine, on which a greatly increased proportion of the national income was spent after independence. In the long term such expenditure may pay off; but in the short run its effects could be seen largely in rapid increases in population growth and in the number of literate people searching for jobs in overcrowded towns.

As to the roots of these public policies, the current consensus, which includes many on both the Left and the Right of the ideological spectrum, is that the basic cause of error lies in the character of political systems and the self-seeking of the successor elites. Whether seen as an indigenous petty bourgeoisie accumulating capital by engrossing the national surplus and by collaborating with foreign capital or, in socialist states such as Tanzania, as a state bourgeoisie accumulating through control of the state apparatus despite the principles laid down at Arusha, the verdict is almost universally adverse. The most common reason lies in the special needs of new political elites in ethnically divided societies to establish and maintain a viable power base for themselves, their families, their ethnic groups, or their class. In such a situation men cannot afford the luxury of public abstinence or probity: To survive they must subordinate national needs to private ones. Hence macro-economic strategies and micro-economic tactics are both designed to concentrate control of power and wealth. Once established, such systems and networks become self-perpetuating, though not usually with the same individuals at the top. Regimes may change and incoming governments announce high-minded self-denying ordinances; but underneath the bureaucrats, state managers and party functionaries cling to power and profit.

Solutions to the problem of incompetent and corrupt state management are legion: The Right generally proposes more genuine democracy plus a progressive dismemberment of systems of economic and social control that provide excessive scope for public malpractice; the Left demands true revolutionary socialism and the exclusion of the corrupting influence of foreign capital. Yet both prognosis and pre-scription are open to the same basic criticism: Could things be otherwise in societies situated as African states were situated after decolonization? Could any regime sur-vive without controlling whatever sources of public income existed? Conversely, could the most public-spirited and wisely advised regime have produced substan-tially better economic results? The answer to the first question must be no: The real-ities of immediately post-colonial Africa made it necessary for the new rulers to engross power in order to maintain the viability of their proto-nation states. To the second, however, the answer may be that better calculated policies, particularly in Ghana, might have prevented the huge waste of resources that made a mockery of Nkrumah's promise to make his country a paradise.

Yet it is difficult to believe that even in the best of all possible worlds black-African economic development would have been as substantial and sustained as the optimists of the early years predicted. This, therefore, brings us to the third of the main explanations of limited development outlined above: The existence of special obstacles to growth in tropical Africa in the second half of the twentieth century.

On the whole I find this an attractive approach. The fact that Africa's postwar performance, at least in terms of growth rates and the difficulty of carrying agricul-tural productivity along with industrial expansion, had much in common with that of much of Asia in the same period, suggests that there may be something in the belief that the tropics are peculiarly difficult terrain for the developer. Clearly many of the problems experienced in Africa stem from the factors listed by Kamarck: Variable rainfall resulted in discontinuities in food and commodity production; cli-mate, plant disease, water shortages, and poor soils had much to do with the failure of attempts at large-scale schemes for mechanized agriculture, ranging from the groundnut fiasco in colonial Tanganyika to capitalist farms in northern Nigeria. Again, disease and malnutrition may have reduced the mental and physical effi-ciency of both the rural labor force and the urban. Although such environmental problems can theoretically be overcome or mitigated by sufficient investment and effort, in the short run they have undoubtedly helped to make many development plans unworkable.

The proposition that limited human resources slowed down developments is also obviously correct, particularly in the field of industrial management and public administration. All the studies suggest that at independence all African societies, though in varying degrees (the Belgian Congo being perhaps the most extreme example) were seriously lacking in men educated or trained in the higher levels of management and government. At the level of the factory floor, while African labor is adaptable, it has proved a slow process to develop many of the basic skills and attitudes to work that are taken for granted in the West. Ironically, urban labor was much quicker to develop attitudes and organizations based on Western trade unions than to adopt Western work ethics; and this made it possible for them to demand rates of pay and conditions of work that were often unjustifiable in economic terms. This is one reason why both private and state industrial enterprises have preferred capital-intensive methods of production, despite the need for greater urban employment and the nominally low cost of wages. In the countryside it is the same. Even quite large capitalist farmers and managers of state enterprises have proved incompetent or careless in using the more sophisticated equipment and organizing their labor force. This is, of course, only to say that it took centuries to evolve that range of attitudes and skills which are characteristic of industrial societies in the West and which constitute its main asset. African countries possessed few of these assets at independence, and it was quite unreasonable to expect high levels of efficiency until they had been created by education and work experience. Until then the return to any form of investment is likely to be much lower than might be predicted by economists who take no account of such contrasts.

But ultimately the main check on the rate of African economic development has probably been, and remains, low productivity in peasant agriculture and, closely related to that, the social structures and attitudes of Hyden's "uncaptured peasantry." It is significant that at critical parts of any analysis of limited African development agricultural production seems to constitute a major bottleneck. A very large proportion, usually above 60 percent, rising to more than 90 percent in the poorest countries, is engaged in agriculture; but agriculture is responsible for a very much lower proportion of the domestic product. In 1979, 78 percent of the Kenyan population was engaged in agriculture and was responsible for 34 percent of GDP. In Tanzania the figures were 83 and 54 percent, respectively. Low productivity in turn reduced the market for domestic manufactures below the minimum economic level for large-scale production of many things, provided inadequate food for the cities, and reduced commodity exports, so putting a strain on the balance of payments. Agriculture was unable to provide many of the raw materials needed by industry, nor could it generate a sufficient surplus for public investment, despite all efforts to seize its profits. In short, Lewis was surely right when he wrote of agriculture in the Gold Coast in 1953 that "this half of the economy is almost certainly stagnant" and that "a vigorous agricultural programme is needed, not because food is scarce, but because this is the road to economic progress."

How far "stagnation" was or remains a necessary feature of the peasant mode of production remains a matter for debate, and assumptions have fluctuated over time. Prewar colonial governments believed that peasants, at least in West Africa, could and would produce all the market demanded, given enough professional guidance. Postwar colonial and the independent governments lost faith in the peasant in their preoccupation with rapid expansion. In the early 1980s the general failure of large-scale mechanized agriculture has led to the rediscovery of the merits of the peasant, again assuming he is given sufficient help and stimulus. Structured smallholder production systems along the lines of the Ghezira cotton scheme in the Sudan have come into vogue as a means of combining the efficiency of industrial management with peasant autonomy and flexibility.

Yet fundamentally the problem remains. Peasant modes of production necessarily mean relatively low levels of productivity. To raise productivity, should the state invade the peasant domain and impose higher standards, at the risk of serious, counterproductive resistance, or bypass the peasant by establishing modernized state or capitalist agro-business? If the latter, it would be safe to continue to mulct the peasantry through monopoly purchasing organizations, since they would in any case be destined to marginalization. Ghana and Nigeria broadly adopted this approach. Kenya, in the end, did not; and, despite the relatively large proportion of "large" farms, occupying some 2.5 million hectares to the 3.5 million hectares of "small" farms, the smallholders' share of total marketed agricultural production increased from 41 to 51 percent of the total from 1964 to 1972. Smallholders produced some 58 percent of the food crop in 1974–75, increased production of coffee from 16,300 to 39,000 tons from 1964 to 1974 and of tea from 11,000 to 27,000 tons from 1971–72 to 1976–77. How much productivity has improved and the extent to which productivity increases with the size of holdings is not apparent from the statistics; but Kenya at least suggests that, given the right stimuli and sufficient state help, peasants can respond to market forces.

Hyden and others, however, have pointed out that Kenya is a special case in that many black farmers learned modern farming techniques from and benefited from the demonstration effect of white farming. Moreover, the post-independence political elite was predominantly landowning and prepared to encourage agriculture. In Tanzania also there was initially a thriving capitalist agriculture, based on plantations, white settlers, and a growing class of African capitalists. In the first years of independence production of the main export crops (there are no useful statistics for food) expanded well or, in the case of sisal, was static. But from 1966–67 to 1976–77-1977–78 the index of the standard of living of rural producers declined from 100 to 72.8. Official statistics claimed a growth rate of 6.5 percent in subsistence agriculture, but this is highly suspect, since large amounts of food had to be imported in the same period. Thus in Tanzania, as in most of West Africa, the peasant mode of production failed to expand, despite its initial impetus; and the standard explanation is low producer prices and the turmoil associated with Nyerere's successive attempts to reconstruct the peasantry as an alternative to relying on large-scale capitalist agriculture. Kenya looks increasingly like an exception to the general rule.

The question therefore remains whether an unreconstructed African peasantry is consistent with sustained growth in the economy as a whole. The conservative view seems to be that with sufficient stimulus from a realistic pricing policy and adequate state help of all sorts this can be done. Others, including Hyden, are less certain. In his view it is of the essence of the peasant to put limits to the extent of his effort and production, however great the incentive to produce more. Only if he ceases to be a peasant and in fact becomes a capitalist with the capitalist's urge to accumulate, will his production rise indefinitely.

It is not the purpose of this chapter to produce policy conclusions but to examine reasons for limited African economic performance in the past. From this standpoint the evidence suggests that, so far, Lewis is right: You cannot build a modern industrial state or maintain the momentum of economic development in a predominantly agricultural country whose agricultural productivity is not rising as fast as the growth of the population. In most parts of black Africa, and certainly in the four countries considered in this chapter, the per capita index of food production declined significantly in the 1970s and this was not compensated for, on the principle of comparative advantage, by sufficient increase in commodity production and exports to pay for imported food. Agriculture was not performing its essential development functions. We have seen many reasons for this failure, many of which could be eliminated. But it is difficult to avoid the conclusion that at root the problem was one of scale and technology.

As Lewis argued in 1953, how extensively a peasant can cultivate is determined by the means at his disposal; that is, whether he can improve his productivity. To replace hoes by a bullock and plow meant "multiplying by four the amount of land a family can cultivate in one year." Beyond that lay mechanization, which was expensive and difficult. "But this is without doubt the line of progress." By 1984 very few African peasants had bullocks or a plow, let alone tractors or access to them on satisfactory conditions. The failure to supply them or to make their use generally possible (for example, by eliminating tsetse fly) and economically worthwhile was probably the main economic failure of post-independence African states, as of their colonial predecessors.

Suggested Readings

Adedeji, A. and T. Shaw (eds.), *African Perspectives on Development Problems and Potentials* (Boulder, CO: Lynne Reiner, 1985).

Apter, David E. and Carl G. Roseberg (eds.), *Political Development and the New Realism in Sub-Saharan Africa* (Charlottesville: University of Virginia Press, 1994).

Barrett, Hazel, "Women in Africa: The Neglected Dimension in Development" in *Geography* v. 80 (3) (1995): pp. 215–224.

Callaghy, Thomas M. and John Ravenhill (eds.), *Hemmed In: Responses to Africa's Economic Decline* (New York: Columbia University Press, 1991).

Fidelis Ezeala-Harrison, B-S.K. Adjibolosoo Senyo (eds.), *Perspectives on Economic Development in Africa* (Connecticut: Praeger Publishers, 1994): pp. 3–21.

Ferguson, James, *The Anti-Politics Machine: "Development," Depoliticization, and Bureaucratic Power in Lesotho* (London: Cambridge University Press, 1990).

Momsen, Janet Henshall and Vivian Kinnaird (eds.), *Different Places, Different Voices: Gender and Development in Africa, Asia, and Latin America* (London: Routledge, 1993).

Kamara, S., M.T. Dahniya, and P. Greene (eds.), *The Effect of Structural Adjustment Policies on Human Welfare in Africa South of the Sahara* (Freetown, Sierra Leone: UNICEF, 1990).

Nyang'oro, Julius and T. Shaw (eds.), *Beyond Structural Adjustment: The Political Economy of Sustainable and Democratic Development* (New York: Praeger, 1992).

Taylor, D.R.F. and Fiona Mackenzie (eds.), *Development from Within: Survival in Rural Africa* (London: Routledge, 1992).

PROBLEM VI

COLLAPSED STATES

Since the end of the colonial era the inviolability of national sovereignty has been an article of faith for all African nations that, ironically, made sacrosanct the irrational boundaries established during the "Scramble for Africa" by the European powers in a "fit of absence of mind" at the end of the nineteenth century. The tenacity with which the independent African states have defended their boundaries as defined by the European powers was enshrined in the Charter of the Organization of African Unity in 1963 in Addis Ababa, the subsequent headquarters of the OAU, whose Charter was emphatic in Article III that "The member States, in pursuit of the purposes stated in Article II solemnly affirm and declare their adherence to the following principles:

1. The Sovereign equality of all Member States.

2. Non-interference in the internal affairs of States.

3. Respect for the sovereignty and territorial integrity of each State and for its inalienable right to independent existence.

The optimism for the future of Africa in the 1960s gradually turned to cynicism twenty years later in the 1980s both within Africa and without as the state systems left behind by the Europeans dissolved before African initiatives, ethnic, military, political, which were not in the best interests of the inhabitants. Many Africans, both from the elite and the non-elite, began to question the defense of national sovereignty by the OAU and defined by boundaries established by ignorant Europeans. There is concern by the international community about the instability created by irrational frontiers and artifical nationalism, and today no country, no matter how remote or impoverished, can remain aloof from the community of nations. International interventions into Liberia, Somalia, and Rwanda have forced Africans and their sympathizers in the West to reconsider the question of national sovereignty and the boundaries that protect it. What caused the collapse of the state in Africa? Is this an African problem or is it one that involves the international community and humanitarian organizations to intervene when the state has lost control over civil society? Which organizations, African, the United Nations, or foreign powers are prepared to render assistance to states in trouble and with what conditions? There are no easy answers to these questions as the following selections regarding this emotional and very pragmatic controversy make very real and very clear.

Writing in 1992 the long-serving observer of African political affairs, Aristide Zolberg, ponders upon the origin of the anarchic conditions of several African states. He sets out to answer the fundamental question "under what conditions do normal attachments of human beings to their communities become pathological?" Zolberg argues that the nature of African states renders them vulnerable to the anarchic collapse of the state which the world has witnessed in Liberia and Somalia. He describes these states as "ethnically based predatory states" and attributes their nature to both the pre-colonial and the colonial experience. There are, of course, specific conditions within each state that have determined whether or not it will remain a national community, but every African state is at risk. He calls for "an enduring commitment from the international community to assist in the political reconstruction of destroyed countries." Reconstruction, he warns, will be a complicated and lengthy process, one which requires a complete reformulation of the political system. Some will argue that such intervention is unrealistic and in fact "neo-colonial," but Aristide Zolberg has always been optimistic about Africa.

William Pfaff, writing in the wake of the 1993 genocide in Rwanda, pleads for "a disinterested neo-colonialism" to end further bloodshed. Pfaff, like Basil Davidson the most influential popular writer of the African past, blames the crisis in Africa on the failure of colonialism to create viable nation states. Like Zolberg, he sees the collapse of the African state as not limited to a few but an infection that could potentially spread throughout most of Africa. And like Zolberg, he proposes that the former colonial powers, who did so much to contribute to the collapse of the present African state but who possess the resources, administrative, and technological skills, lead a recolonization of the African states in their crisis.

Like Pfaff, the Nigerian Nobel Laureate, Wole Soyinka, blames the former colonial powers for leaving the continent unprepared for independence. In a recent interview, he expounded on his belief that the arbitrary borders drawn during the colonial occupation created disfunctional nation states. But Soyinka does not limit his critique to bashing the colonialists. To him and others the Organization of African Unity must bear a portion of the reason for the decay by their "failure of will" in meekly accepting the frontiers established by the colonial powers. He presents an African point of view.

> If we fail to understand that all this stems from the colonial nation-state map imposed upon us, there will be little chance to correct the situation over the long term. . . . [W]e should sit down with square rule and compass and redesign the boundaries of African nations.

In Soyinka's opinion the Addis Ababa Charter of the OAU of 1963 can no longer apply to the chaotic conditions created by the collapse of African states. "The horror of Rwanda is too high a price to pay for a very vaporous and whimsical notion of what constitutes inviolable boundaries." Unlike Pfaff, however, Soyinka believes that ultimately the initiative to save these states must come from within the continent and not from the intervention of Western nations.

In "The Blood of Experience" Ali Mazrui considers the history of the collapse of the African state. Like Aristide Zolberg he seeks to explain Africa's current dilemma as to the structure of the post-colonial state. He provides some strategies for reconstructing and reintegrating collapsed states into larger federal communities. He follows "The Blood of Experience" with another article, "Development or Recolonization?," in which he expands his previous strategies for coping with the Problem of the collapsed states. He presents several possible approaches to rebuild collapsed states. Some, such as the proposal for a "trusteeship system—like that of the U.N. over the Congo in 1960—which would permit the mutual cooperation of African and Western nations to administer territories where civil society has disintegrated. His proposal that Egypt "might re-establish its big brother relationship with the Sudan" appears not only controversial but naive.

Ibrahim A. Gambari begins his article with an overview of foreign intervention in Africa. Historically, these incursions into the continent have caused more problems than they have resolved:

> In almost all the cases of foreign intervention in Africa, the evidence suggests that they do not generally provide early or full solutions to the perennial problems of stability and state cohesion. On the contrary, some unilateral interventions, be it from Africa or elsewhere, have exacerbated and prolonged the crisis, introducing extraneous ideological and political dimensions to what were essentially local conflicts.

He concludes that multi-national intervention is the most likely to succeed in restoring order to a collapsed state but acknowledges that the task of reconstructing states in disarray will be a complicated and protracted process.

Francis Deng argues that foreign intervention, which does not react until a state dissolves, inevitably arrives too late. He insists that the international community must prepare strategies for diffusing the potential collapse of a state by identifying nations at risk. "It would be preferable to have in place a preventive strategy to apply before the crisis of collapse." Preventive measures rather than "crisis-induced reactions" are the key to averting state collapse. Deng further argues that such intervention should not be perceived as purely altruistic or humanitarian. The industrial societies of the West "cannot prosper in an irreversible international economy if large contiguous populations descend into endemic violence and economic disorder."

The Spectre of Anarchy: African States Verging on Dissolution

ARISTIDE ZOLBERG[1]

Beset by a horrendous economic predicament, Africa is today also haunted by a dreadful political nightmare: now that the winds of democracy are sweeping the continent, it looks as if tyranny might give way to anarchy. The term is used here in its literal sense, to denote a nearly total absence of constituted authority that leaves a country's contentious elements to fend for themselves. Anarchy is no mere figment of the white racist imagination, but a realistic description of the conditions that have emerged among a disparate group of African countries. Should these be dismissed as highly exceptional cases, or do they reflect in a more extreme form problems common to sub-Saharan Africa generally?

Serious consideration of these matters has been blocked by the self-censorship of well-meaning observers, reluctant to furnish ammunition to those who proclaim that Africans are but one step removed from savagery. But the crisis has now become so severe that we must abandon such niceties and stare reality in the face. The purpose of this analysis is not to demonstrate that the tragic fate experienced by a handful of sub-Saharan countries is ineluctable; rather, it seeks to establish how, despite their bad prospects, Africans might avoid such outcomes, and what obligations this entails for the rest of us.

One thing should be clear from the start: although Africa's troubles are commonly laid at the door of "tribalism," this is a gross oversimplification. True, ethnic solidarities play a major role in its political life, but this does not always lead to violent conflicts. Most countries consist of a fairly large array of diverse groups, making for a very large number of possible confrontations; but severe clashes are in fact relatively rare. Yet ethnicity does play a role. The question we must therefore ask is: Under what conditions do normal attachments of human beings to their communities become pathological?

The first instance of an African country falling apart, which evoked headlines in the springtime of African independence some thirty years ago, was the ex-Belgian Congo—today's Zaire. The Congo's problems were thought to be unique, attribut-

---

1. Zolberg, Aristide, "The Spectre of Anarchy: African States Verging on Dissolution," in *Dissent* (New York: Dissent Publishing Corporation, Summer 1992): pp. 301–311.

Aristide Zolberg is the author of *Escape from Violence: Conflict and the Refugee Crisis in the Developing World*, (New York: Oxford University Press, 1989).

able mainly to an especially exploitative colonial power that failed to prepare the country for self-rule and then responded to pressure by quickly getting out of the way. The consequences of this negative legacy were said to be compounded by an unusually divisive array of "tribes," exacerbated by cold war confrontations involving the United States, the Soviet Union, and China.

Following the death, possibly at the hands of the CIA, of Patrice Lumumba, leader of the sole Congo-wide and multi-ethnic political organization, the country quickly fragmented into localized movements, headed by ethnic leaders backed by rudimentary militia, sporting either a vociferous Marxism or an equally strident "Westernism." However, Humpty Dumpty was unexpectedly put together again when the United Nations intervened to reestablish the country's territorial integrity and the CIA, in one of its greatest feats, transformed an army clerk named Joseph-Desire Mobutu into a Hobbesian sovereign. Thanks to this patronage, which brought him unstinting military assistance, and to the world's continuing interest in the country's mineral resources, the CIA's creature emerged as one of Africa's cruelest tyrants, and certainly the richest.

For two decades, stability prevailed. Then, with Zaire subject to the geopolitical devaluation occasioned by the end of the cold war, Mobutu was dropped by his American and European patrons as overly embarrassing and enjoined to sanitize his economy. With tyranny going out of fashion everywhere, he also faced internal demands for political reform. The accumulated wherewithal of repression enabled him to fend off these demands, at least for a time, but only at the cost of escalating violence. Then, once the tyrant was no longer able to properly reward his henchmen for their services, they went into business for themselves. Matters came to a head in September 1991, when the soldiers brought to the capital to repress demonstrations on behalf of a National Conference of Democratic Forces, belatedly convened by Mobutu to alleviate international criticism, devastated the city instead. Kinshasa was pacified by French and Belgian troops sent in to evacuate their citizens; but it was clearly the beginning of the end. Mobutu now agreed to an opposition leader as prime minister, but subsequently replaced him with a more amenable personage, who proceeded to suspend the National Conference; this provoked an intervention by "pro- democracy" elements of the army, in turn put down by Mobutu loyalists.

There is no doubt the tyrant will soon be gone; but given that for the past quarter of a century government in Zaire has meant almost nothing but depredation, the country will be back at square one—with the added burdens of a much larger population, the plague of an HIV epidemic, a huge international debt, and a long list of accounts to be settled between ethnic groups and institutional factions that worked with Mobutu or suffered as his victims. A large stock of weapons will be used as currency.

In the past two years, chaos has also engulfed the region's two oldest independent states, Liberia and Ethiopia, as well as Somalia. While almost totally ignored in America, Liberia should be of special concern because of its relation to our own racial history, and its use as an instrument of U.S. policy for over a century. It has been proudly displayed as Africa's only independent republic, a little black America constructed by volutarily expatriated ex-slaves. In reality, however, the ex-slaves were mostly duped and intimidated into going back, and Liberia evolved into a quasi-colonial client state, found on racial inequality. Until well after World War II, it was governed under the umbrella of the U.S. Navy by a tiny minority of American-Liberian families, organized as a one-party machine, fueled by rake-offs from concessionary companies, among which Firestone Rubber was paramount, until the discovery of rich iron and bauxite deposits brought in a number of others. The hinterland's heterogenous peoples, formally designated as "natives," were left under the rule of their traditional leaders, turned into clients of the American-Liberian machine. With less access to education than in any European colony, they were mobilized by the chiefs for plantation and mine labor, and as with many other "backward" peoples, also provided rank and file for the constabulary.

Liberia's ancien regime lasted until 1980. Its downfall began when President William Tolbert's decision to increase the price of rice, the major staple of the "natives," triggered massive protest; brought in to repress the populace, the army joined them instead. With the officer class restricted to American-Liberians, the coup was staged by a band of noncommissioned officers under the leadership of Master-Sergeant Samuel K. Doe. Ten days later, the foreign press was invited to witness the public execution of a dozen senior government officials.

Despite historic ties to the American-Liberians, the Reagan administration cynically accepted the fait accompli and Doe's perfunctory promise of democratization. Over the next five years, Liberia was turned into a bastion of the American security system, and thereby emerged as the leading African recipient of U.S. aid on a per capita basis. The sudden influx of military goods and the launching of major construction projects raised the level of corruption to unprecedented heights. Predictably, elections held in 1985 under American supervision produced a majority for Doe. He proceeded to scavenge the state on behalf of his own Krahn people, a small group located in the southeast alongside the Côte d'Ivoire border, who dominated the army's enlisted ranks. But this triggered growing resentment among the groups he excluded. After an attempted coup in 1986, the last American-Liberian in the government, Charles Taylor, was dismissed, and fled into exile.

As with Mobutu, Doe's value dropped precipitously with the waning of the cold war. Invoking his corruption and violations of human rights, the United States in 1987 placed Liberia into receivership. In late 1989 Charles Taylor led a guerrilla force of about 250 into Nimba county, Liberia's primary agricultural, mining, and logging region. He had backing from a combination of strange bedfellows: Mischief-making Muammar Qaddafi and Burkina Faso's radical leader Blaise Compaore, but also Côte d'Ivoire's conservative President Houphouet-Boigny, who worried about Doe's irredentism. Welcoming the invaders as liberators from Krahn rule, Nimba County's population swelled the ranks of Taylor's force. This in turn triggered retaliatory violence by Doe's army, propelling some two hundred thousand refugees into Côte d'Ivoire and Guinea, and others south into Monrovia.

As Taylor pushed on toward the capital, all of Liberia's peoples were engulfed in the confrontation; the Mandingo aligned themselves with Doe, while the Gio and Mano split off from Taylor to form yet another movement, under Prince Johnson. With the various forces stalemated around Monrovia, where civilian deaths escalated, in August 1990 leaders of the Economic Organization of West African States (ECOWAS) decided on an unprecedented intervention, on the grounds that the war was no longer an internal conflict because thousands of their citizens were trapped in Liberia, while neighboring countries were swamped by Liberian refugees. After the multinational force landed, Doe was assassinated under mysterious circumstances. In October the peacekeeping forces established an interim government under political science professor Amos Sawyer; but its authority was limited to the capital, while Taylor controlled most of the country.

Negotiations dragged on, chaos set in. As of early 1991, half of the population was uprooted, with over seven hundred thousand abroad; the death toll rose to some twenty thousand, mostly civilians; agriculture was totally disrupted, creating a danger of famine. Seasoned observers asserted the situation was much worse than anything they had seen in Lebanon, and Liberia's ubiquitous Lebanese traders were themselves fleeing back to Beirut. Although in mid-September the antagonists agreed to stop fighting and turn in their arms to ECOWAS, it is unlikely that this will prove to be a permanent settlement. Exiled Krahn forces are continuing to stage attacks from Sierra Leone, and Taylor is receiving new military assistance from Burkina Faso and Côte d'Ivoire.

Where the prospect for Liberia is for a protracted, multisided civil war, Ethiopia faces a disintegration into a number of successor states. Its roots in the legendary Abyssinian Empire notwithstanding, the Ethiopia we know is a relatively recent and fragile amalgam. Throughout its history, Africa's Coptic Christian realm stagnated at an extremely low level of organizational development, owing to material and technological constraints; its two main kingdoms, Tigre in the north and Amhara-speaking Shoa in the south, contended for supremacy but were themselves subject to recurrent disintegration. In the late nineteenth century, following the scramble set off by the collapse of Egypt, the Shoan king Menelik astutely exploited European rivalries over the Horn, whose geopolitical value was enhanced by the Suez Canal, to more than double his holdings. The new lands provided coffee, gold, and slaves; but the expanded realm was more difficult to manage because Menelik's new subjects were culturally very different, Negro animists, or Oromo, and Somali Muslims —the Christian empire's traditional enemies.Throughout the first half of the twentieth century, despite intermittent attempts at modernization from above, including those launched by the Italian occupiers from 1935 to 1941, Ethiopia's administration remained rudimentary. and there was little economic development. After expelling the Italians, Britain assumed control over their colonies, Eritrea and Somalia, awaiting their disposition by the international community. Eritrea is a relatively well-developed territory, whose population, according to the British census of 1950—the last to date—consists about equally of Copts, closely related to

Ethiopia's Tigreans, and Arabic-speaking Muslims. Although Britain at first advocated partition, as in India or Palestine, in 1950 bargaining among the great powers prompted the United Nations to entrust the country to Ethiopia, on condition that it be allowed to retain its own representative institutions and its distinct cultural identity. But once international attention waned, Emperor Haile Selassie violated all these conditions and moved steadily toward annexation.

Especially hard on Muslims, Ethiopian rule provoked the formation of an Eritrean liberation movement initially based in Cairo. Annexation triggered dissent among Christians as well, and in 1961 the movement launched an armed struggle. Soon the conflict was highly internationalized. Ethiopia was firmly backed by the United States, which assumed Britain's succession in the Red Sea region, as well as by Israel, concerned to prevent the emergence of a Muslim-dominated independent state. As for the Eritreans, they gained access to money, weapons, training, and staging bases from a variety of Arab states; their supporters included Sudan, but also Syria from 1964 onward, and, after 1969, Libya and Southern Yemen.

As in any empire, the Ethiopian armed forces constituted a double-edged sword. Their first challenge to Haile Selassie's authority, in 1960, was defeated with U.S. help. In the following decade, the country underwent substantial economic growth, mostly by way of generous concessions to foreign investors, and education was expanded as well; but this brought few benefits to the urban masses, and none whatever to the peasantry, whose margin of survival was steadily reduced by demographic expansion and galloping erosion.

During the drought that swept the continent in the early 1970s, Ethiopians were deprived of aid because the emperor insistently denied there was any famine. This abdication of responsibility destroyed the regime's last vestige of legitimacy among the educated of the new generation. The stresses of the unending Eritrean war undermined discipline among the armed forces; in early 1974, yet another string of mutinies culminated in a generalized uprising. With the military out of commission, protestors with long-accumulated grievances could act with impunity. The cities were taken over by workers and students, the landed estates of the nobility and the church by peasants. Waiting for the government to disintegrate of its own accord, the armed forces finally deposed Haile Selassie and proclaimed a Provisional Military Administrative Council (PMAC). The coup then evolved into a social revolution, punctuated by a radically egalitarian land reform in March 1975.

The PMAC clashed simultaneously with defenders of the ancien regime and more revolutionary organizations, as well as subjected peripheral groups taking advantage of the empire's collapse to increase their autonomy; and it was torn also by tensions between Amharas and other groups. By 1976 the PMAC had managed to transform itself into a tightly structured body dominated by Amharas, under the leadership of Major Mengistu Haile Mariam. Although this radical junta controlled the capital and the major towns, it faced uprisings in nine out of fourteen provinces in addition to Eritrea. Those in the south were supported by neighboring Somalia, then a client state of the Soviet Union. With the Carter administration unwilling to intervene actively on its behalf, the PMAC turned to the Soviets, who quickly decided that Ethiopia was more valuable. The Somalis invaded Ethiopia on July 23, 1977, and rapidly seized the coveted Ogaden territory, but were expelled the following March by Ehiopian forces under the leadership of Soviet officers, with the support of Cuban troops. The Eritrean insurgents had taken advantage of the diversion of the Ethiopian army to the Ogaden in order to gain control of most of their province; however, after the victory in the south, the Ethiopians were able to roll them back, again with direct Soviet assistance. The conflict then turned into a devastating war of attrition, causing recurrent waves of refugees.

With his survival and Ethiopia's integrity assured thanks to the Soviet commitment, Mengistu undertook to transform the ancient empire into a People's Republic; but the ruthless strategies he deployed over the next decade exacted a heavy cost in human suffering, and probably aggravated the population's economic predicament. These developments again fostered massive flight as well as renewed uprisings. Almost totally dependent on the Soviet Union and East Germany, the regime was doomed from the moment the Gorbachev government decided to sharply reduce its involvement in the Third World. The Mengistu regime ended where it began, in Eritrea. The turning point came in February 1990, when after nearly three decades of struggle, the Eritrean People's Liberation Front took Massawa, Ethiopia's major port, and the delivery point for relief food as well as military supplies, and laid siege to the regional capital. The government's war effort was fatally hampered by the Soviet Union's refusal to provide aircraft to transport troops to the besieged city. Concurrently, the Tigrean People's Liberation Front advanced southward toward Addis Ababa. With the treasury empty and a critical shortage of fuel, in early 1991 the army disintegrated and Mengistu prepared to leave.

Seizing the opportunity provided by the Soviet withdrawal, the Bush administration then undertook to create an orderly succession, as well as to negotiate the evacuation of some 14,000 Ethiopian Jews who had fled to the encircled capital. Mengistu flew off on May 24, and three days later representatives of the opposition forces as well as remnants of his government gathered in London to negotiate the transfer of power. Hitherto opposed to Eritrean independence, Washington now accepted the battlefield outcome and acquiesced to a referendum, to be held within two years; at American insistence, the opposition coalition agreed to hold a conference by July 1 to form a broad-based provisional government. Meanwhile, with American blessing, the Tigreans entered the capital to restore order.

Although the conference did produce some democratic guarantees and a timetable for political reconstruction, Ethiopia continues to implode. The Council of Representatives has decided to give each of the country's fourteen regions its own parliament and control over internal security. While designed to foster a viable confederation, this framework may signal the beginning of the end.

In effect launching their existence as an independent state without awaiting the referendum, the Eritreans have turned their back on Ethiopian affairs, while nevertheless retaining control over its lifelines. With the external struggle over, divisions between Muslims and Christians are ominously moving to the fore. Although in control of the capital, the Tigreans are isolated amid hostile Amhara territory, with their home base hundreds of miles to the north; moreover, they constitute a mere 10 percent of the Ethiopian population. The Amharas, who make up some 25 percent, remain firmly committed to Ethiopian integrity but are themselves deeply divided by the conflicts of the past decade and a half; convinced that the Tigreans have no choice but to share power with fellow Christians, they are seeking to exact the maximum price for their cooperation. The collapse of central authority has redounded once again to the benefit of the periphery, now in the hands of well-armed guerrilla forces. With Eritrea gone, the main challenge comes from the Oromos, some 40 percent of the Ethiopian population, a majority being Muslim. They view themselves as an enslaved people, who can now legitimately exact bloody retribution from their defeated Amhara masters.

A the beginning of 1992, the most extreme situation anywhere in Africa was to be found next door in Somalia. In the past year the country has split in two, and is now so torn by violence as to be inaccessible to even the most dauntless international humanitarian organizations. A Muslim pastoral people, in the pre-European period the Somalis were organized into loosely associated clans sharing many cultural elements but without an overarching political organization; in the twentieth century they ended up under four colonial jurisdictions: Ethiopia, French Djibouti, British Somaliland, and Italian Somalia. In the postwar period nationalists in the British and Italian possessions advocated reunion of all Somalis; although this was partly achieved in 1960, when the two territories merged into a single state, independent Somalia continued to voice irredentist claims, especially toward Ethiopia's Ogaden province. The pursuit of this objective was initially constrained by the need to maintain a balance among the clans and by Ethiopia's military superiority. Exploiting the resulting frustrations and the civilian regime's notorious corruption, in 1969 the army took over. Major General Siad Barre, a member of the Marahan clan, whose domain encompasses the Ogaden, then astutely exploited superpower rivalries to obtain Soviet aid for a vast military buildup.

In 1977 Barre successfully invaded the Ogaden, but was ultimately routed. In addition to losing most of its military equipment, Somalia was faced with a heavy burden of refugees from the Ogaden, supplemented in the mid-1980s by new waves driven by hunger. The defeat precipitated an attempted coup by disgruntled army officers from rival clans; but Siad Barre, now receiving military assistance from the United States, survived through severe repression and relying increasingly on his own kin. This in turn fostered a proliferation of opposition groups, including a secessionist movement in the north (former British Somaliland). In 1982 the various groups united as the National Somali Movement and began staging raids from Ethiopian bases.

In the late 1980s the northern insurgents gained control over most of their region; Barre's clannishness precipitated a rebellion in the central part of the country as well; and in the south disgruntled army commanders began to go into business for themselves. Severely injured in an automobile accident and abandoned by the United States, the seventy-year old despot turned toward Libya, but to little avail. The accelerating collapse of authority left a vacuum filled by young warriors with automatic guns. Thousands fled the ravaged countryside to the capital city, only to land amid bloody chaos. Barre escaped in January 1991, leaving seven well-armed groups jockeying for power. Now in effect an independent country, Northern Somalia is itself being torn asunder by clan-based bands of juvenile bush fighters. Negotiations among the warlords have so far led nowhere, largely because they hardly control their men; outside powers are no longer interested, UN agencies fear for the safety of their personnel, and the Organization of African Unity is reluctant to take on a desperate case in a problematic region. The situation at the end of 1991 was summed up by a headline in *The New York Times* (Dec. 12): "Somalia Self-Destructs, and the World Looks On."

One suggestive indicator of Africa's predicament is that as of the end of 1990 it had over five million refugees, nearly one-third of the world's total. The violence that produced international flows also occasioned massive internal displacements, with current estimates reaching over nine million. Leaving aside the special situation of southern Africa, which accounts for about one-third of the internal and external refugees, these displaced populations are all victims of violent conflicts in sovereign African states. Since the dawn of independence bloody implosions have taken place also in Uganda, which appears to have somewhat recovered, and Chad, which is perennially on the brink of yet another catastrophic episode. Major civil conflicts have erupted as well in Nigeria, Rwanda, Burundi, and Sudan.

What distinguishes these unfortunate countries from the rest of the continent? Altogether, they constitute a highly disparate group, with very different pre-European cultures, dissimilar colonial experiences, and varying economic situations at the time the conflicts got under way. Nor do these countries share a particular pattern of ethnic groups, beyond heterogeneity; but this is a feature they share with many others. Pre-1980 Liberia, however, did have a configuration that is especially explosive, involving political and economic domination by an ethnic or racial minority. Fortunately, this is quite rare; aside from white-settler countries, which indeed experienced violent decolonization, it was found also in Rwanda and Burundi (Tutsi-Hutu), as well as Zanzibar (Arabs-Africans), all of which have by now in fact blown up.

Besides ethnic heterogeneity, what the countries under consideration have in common is that they can all be described as *weak predatory states*. But since this is again a characteristic they share with the rest of sub-Saharan Africa, it does not by itself provide an adequate explanation of their predicament. The solution to the quandary is that *all* such states hover on the brink of disaster; whether or not they go over the edge depends on circumstances, especially the emergence of a sinister syndrome found in all the cases considered: a coincidence of tyranny with external military patronage.

The extreme weakness of the African state was initially hidden from view because it displayed a considerable capacity for engaging in repressive action; but this entails a confusion between two types of power, which Michael Mann has termed "despotic" and "infrastructural." Although the African state looms large in relation to other organizations, it has a limited capacity for managing society and directing change—a paradox captured by Thomas Callaghy's apt characterization of that state as a "lame Leviathan." A further source of confusion is the assumption that the persistence of an organization can be attributed to its capacity to perform tasks required for survival. Since most African states have kept going, it is taken for granted that they meet "system-maintenance requirements." However, states do not exist in a vacuum, and their fate depends substantially on the character of the international environment. The weakest of states may persist if that environment is supportive, as Robert Jackson and Carl Rosberg have suggested with regard to the international political community's stance toward the new African states. But they neglected to point out that the international environment can also make things worse, either by way of destructive intervention, as in southern Africa, or indirectly by making it possible for tyrants to expand their power well beyond what they might do on their own.

The African states' generally weak infrastructural power stems from the combination of distinctive precolonial and colonial structures. In contrast with states in other parts of the developing world, which were often carved out of larger empires, most of them consist of small-scale societies that were bundled into entities designed by European colonial entrepreneurs in response to imperial rivalries of the late nineteenth century. These societies had a low ratio of population in relation to land and lived close to the level of subsistence; under conditions of slash-and-burn agriculture, their domain was not fixed. Chiefship tended to be over people rather than over land, and political dynamics focused on competition among clientelist factions. The absence of political centralization and the low population density left open the possibility of "exit," giving rise to a process of segmentation whereby new social clusters were constantly being established by emigrants on available land.

Consequently, precolonial political structures could offer relatively little resistance to the formation of a new system of domination, and the remnants of traditional societies appeared in the newly formed colonial territories mostly as "ethnic groups," which were sometimes newly constructed amalgams altogether. Governing their possessions with traditional imperial techniques, the Europeans exploited tensions among these groups to enhance their own power; existing differences were sharpened also by the uneven impact of social and economic change. Ethnic groups became "advanced" or "backward," rich or poor.

African movements for self-determination are usually referred to as "nationalist"; but the term is somewhat misleading in that it evokes *national* identities. Whereas it is true that established colonial territories were generally taken for granted as the relevant political unit, and that a number of organizations sought to encompass its entire population, democratization also sparked ethnic solidarities. Party competition as well as the high value of office fostered a proliferation of political entrepreneurs, who cast their appeal in parochial terms.

The postcolonial elite's project has been aptly characterized by Frederick Cooper as "self-aggrandizement combined with enough redistribution to maintain its tenuous and vital hold on the state" ("Africa and the World Economy," *African Studies Bulletin,* 24: 2-3 [June/Sep. 1981]). However, Africa's predatory rulers are severely constrained by extreme poverty, and the prevalent structural weakness makes it as difficult to increase extraction by way of state action as of capitalist exploitation. Takeover of the apparatus of the colonial state provided resources for organizing the initial array of clientelist networks by which the state was managed, and there was also aid from the former colonial power, and grants and loans from international actors seeking to establish a sphere of influence within the African arena. In a few instances the new elites had access to mineral royalties; but more commonly, they could squeeze income only by fostering a shift from subsistence to export agriculture, while stepping up exactions from primary producers.

Some of the loot was redistributed to relieve pressures from the urban sector, to which rulers were most vulnerable, but much of it was appropriated. In the face of demands occasioned by broader mobilization and rising expectations, resources had to be expanded and demands managed. Beleaguered governments relied heavily on the instruments of despotic power, namely the police and military forces inherited from the colonial state. But the strategy proved self-defeating, for the agents of repression quickly learned where true power lay; hence within a few years a majority of the new states experienced military coups.

Although foreign policy "realists" in the United States welcomed military rule as a harbinger of political stability, of anticommunism, and of development policies attuned to capitalist imperatives, this rested on a profound misunderstanding of African realities. During the colonial period, soldiers were frequently recruited from minority groups in hinterland regions, "unspoiled" by dawning political consciousness; hence they tended to be even more parochial than the civilians they replaced and, with no experience of statecraft, quicker to fall back on brute force. Far from inaugurating an era of stability, the advent of the military often exacerbated the very conflicts that had provided the pretext for intervention.

Africa's difficulties were aggravated in the 1970s by the deterioration of its already extremely marginal position within the international economy, the energy crisis, the mounting burden of debt, the corruption of economic managers as well as of their foreign patrons, and the disenchantment of investors. A number of countries also experienced a crisis of subsistence, occasioned not only by catastrophic climate, but also the degradation of marginal agricultural environments as the result of overgrazing and overcultivation, as well as the expanding production of commodities for export at the cost of subsistence farming. Amplifying the effects of these factors was Africa's runaway demography. Overall, food production per capita decreased by nearly 20 percent from 1960 to 1986, with the prospect of continued decline.

It was during this very period that Africa moved to the fore as an international strategic arena. This reflected the evolving relations between the superpowers in the epoch of "Mutually Assured Destruction," with cautious stability at the center and confrontational probings throughout the periphery. The United States early on planted itself in Zaire, Ethiopia, and Liberia, while leaving French-speaking territories to be managed by Paris, and the southern part of the continent by Portugal and South Africa; the Soviet Union established itself in ex-French Guinea as well as Somalia, and invested in futures by sponsoring insurgent movements in the Horn, Portuguese Africa, and Namibia. Even after the countries of Portuguese Africa gained their independence, these probings and confrontations were accompanied by vast flows of weapons. Wherever these deadly supplies landed, conflicts between rulers and ruled, and between contending groups, increased. Even as the superpowers worked out ways of averting the dangers of thermonuclear proliferation, they poured out streams of firepower, mostly automatic and semi-automatic personal weapons, that fostered a rapid escalation of misery and dread among the world's least fortunate.

Weak predatory states with a large supply of firepower, which they tend to misuse but cannot monopolize, are subject to two distinct kinds of deterioration. In the face of shrinking resources and an absence of institutional restraints, desperate authoritarian rulers degenerate into kleptocratic tyrants, which under African conditions takes the form of ethnic exclusiveness, as seen in Liberia and Somalia. This occurred also in Uganda, Chad, the Central African Republic, Equatorial Guinea, and Burundi. Without resources to fight back, oppressed urban and rural masses have little choice but to try to get out from under. If the international configuration allows, this may result in a massive exodus. Another path is internal withdrawal, where peasants concentrate on production for subsistence while withholding from the state what it claims as its due. But because extortion is their only way of making a living, rulers in turn have to engage in violent repression of such challenges.

Ethnocracy can also trigger a violent implosion, a disaggregation of both rulers and ruled into primary solidarity groups vying with one another in a desperate search for security. Even if its existence is externally assured, the state may be reduced to little more than an arena where groups vie for survival. Under these conditions, life is reduced to two fundamental activities: food production and war. But since weapons are widely available and warriors can secure their subsistence without engaging in production, war making gains the upper hand. As violence becomes the leading means of survival, it tends to feed on itself. The process fosters the emergence of a warlord system, as in seventeenth-century Germany or China at the beginning of the twentieth, verging on a murderous Hobbesian war of all against all. Should the preservation of existing borders no longer be of concern to the international community, tenuously amalgamated countries may be allowed to disintegrate altogether into their component elements.

The present diagnosis suggests that the greatest threat to the lives of contemporary Africans arises not from what is loosely called "tribalism," the deep attachment of ordinary people to their communities, but rather from the emergence of ethnically based predatory states. How can this be met? To begin with, the cases considered highlight the key role and heavy responsibility of foreign sponsors in sustaining the ethnocrats. In this light, despite the catastrophic present, Africa's prospects have improved somewhat since the United States and the former Soviet Union relinquished their callous adventurism. But withdrawal is not enough; the wounds that murderous conflicts have inflicted on fragile societies are unlikely to mend of themselves, and Africa remains fair game for other international birds of prey—especially in the northeast, which is linked with the Middle East theater.

All these problems call for an enduring commitment from the international community to assist in the political reconstruction of destroyed countries, to provide protection against nefarious intruders in vulnerable regions, and even to intervene directly should the state take on a completely pathological character. Although this appears to violate conventionally held notions of "sovereignty," in such cases sovereignty has in effect ceased to exist.

The appropriate approach is multilateral, preferably under the umbrella of some regional organization, as in Liberia. Africans should help one another, but cannot shoulder this additional burden entirely with their own resources. Beyond this, it is especially urgent to bring about general disarmament, and to establish a tight embargo on the further supply of automatic weapons, which constitute an even deadlier plague in Mogadishu, Monrovia, or Moroto than in the Bronx or Dallas.

While international restraints would limit the tyrants' destructive capacity, they would not prevent their emergence in the first place, which is attributable to deepseated, historically determined flaws in the political configuration of contemporary Africa. Although I have emphasized the infrastructural weakness of the state as a major problem, this is not to argue on behalf of the reinforcement of state power alone, since Africa's predicament arises also from the fact that societal institutions are insufficiently developed to hold potential tyrants in check. As increasingly emphasized by a new generation of African intellectuals, priority must be given to the development of "civil society"; but this should not be viewed as an alternative to state formation.

Infrastructural power, as against despotism, is fostered by organic exchanges between state and society, and this in turn can take place only if the economic environment is relatively favorable. But this is clearly not the case among the countries of sub-Saharan Africa, which are extremely poor to start with, and have deteriorated further as the result of a fatal combination of inauspicious world realities and political misdeeds. The resulting debt burden is enough to swamp Africa's fledgling democratic forces. Hence this is not the time to impose on them harsh remedies, but rather to wipe the slate clean.

A New Colonialism?
Europe Must Go Back Into Africa

WILLIAM PFAFF[2]

The destitution of Africa has been an all but forbidden topic in political discourse for reasons as comprehensible as they are disabling. The time has arrived, however, for honest and dispassionate discussion of this immense human tragedy, for which the Western countries bear a grave if partial responsibility and which will worsen if not addressed.

Much of Africa needs, to put it plainly, what one could call a disinterested neo-colonialism. Africans acknowledge the immensity of their crisis and the need to consider hitherto unacceptable remedies. The democracy movement, which in the past few years produced a series of national conferences to end dictatorships, is foundering. Fewer than a third of sub-Saharan Africa's nations have anything resembling multiparty politics. The Congolese author Ange Severin Malanda says, "From now one, the danger in several parts of the continent is of pure destruction or generalized destabilization. The destabilization is already evident in Somalia, Liberia, and Angola. The pure destruction began to be realized in Rwanda on the sixth of April 1994, annihilating every contemporary African standard of reference. Genocide there accomplished the unimaginable and the unlimited." A spokesman for the International Committee of the Red Cross says of Liberia that "no moral barriers remain . . . every reference to the principles and values which found and bind a community of men have disappeared . . . virtually nothing remains except horror and cruelty." The Nigerian Nobel laureate Wole Soyinka, writing in anguished response to the repression of minorities in Nigeria, has questioned—as have some Western commentators—the postcolonial convention that frontiers must be left as they are. Any program, however, for redrafting frontiers on the principle of ethnic self-determination must explain why the equitable redivision of Africa on ethnic lines would be more feasible than it has proven in the Balkans, where the pursuit of this principle has engendered war after war, from the Serbian uprising of 1804 to the present war in the former Yugoslavia.

2. Pfaff, William, "A New Colonialism? Europe Must Go Back into Africa," in *Foreign Affairs*, (New York: The Council on Foreign Relations), January/February 1995, pp. 2-6.

William Pfaff writes a syndicated column for the *International Herald Tribune*. His latest book, on nationalism, its origins and its consequences, is *The Wrath of Nations: Civilization and the Furies of Nationalism* (New York: Simon & Schuster, 1993)

In Africa, any attempt to redraw borders on ethnic lines would seem certain to accelerate political disintegration and inspire new conflicts. It is now the convention in right-thinking Western circles that Africa's tribes and ethnic groups are repressive colonial inventions and that nothing significant distinguishes Zulu from Xhosa, Masai from Kikuyu, or Tutsi from Hutu, notwithstanding the reactionary Western sciences of ethnology and anthropology.

Nor does the idea of a new form of colonialism stand much chance of acceptance, but in the absence of an alternative it must be considered. It has separately been proposed by the Kenyan historian Ali A. Mazrui, editor of the final volume of the *UNESCO General History of Africa*, and by several Western observers of Africa, including the present writer.

Most of Africa, I have argued, lacks the crucial educated middle and professional classes and the mediating private and public institutions that compose a "civil society." Civil society makes democracy possible; without it democracy has failed and will continue to fail in Africa.

The history of the continent since the great wave of decolonization in the late 1950s and early 1960s includes a shameful series of self-interested foreign interventions and ruthless exploitation of indigenous African conflicts by the Soviet Union, its proxy, Cuba, and the United States, with deliberate instigation or intensification of wars in Katanga, Ethiopia, Eritrea, Angola, and Somalia. But this history is also a chronicle of anarchic breakdown within African societies, some of which are manifestly worse off now than under colonialism, heading toward the type of social collapse and genocidal struggle that has occurred in Rwanda and Burundi.

The anarchic struggle for factional power in Somalia goes on, with both the United Nations and the United States humiliated. Before that came horrors in Liberia and Sierra Leone, as well as in Equatorial Guinea, Mozambique, and Sudan. A part of West Africa today suffers insensate and feral struggle, devoid of political or ideological purpose, conducted by uprooted, ignorant, anomic young men serving Caligulan warlords. This is a postmodern barbarism unconnected to any African past. The Uganda of Idi Amin and the Central African "Empire" of the egregious Jean-Bedel Bokassa seem rational enterprises compared with the inadvertent and apocalyptic nihilism practiced there and in Rwanda. . . .

What can be done? Mazrui wants the old League of Nations trusteeship system reestablished, with African and Asian nations among those appointed by the United Nations to govern certain countries, under the guidance of a council of major African states, which would possess a peacekeeping army. (France proposed the creation of such an inter-African force at the French-African summit in Biarritz in November 1994 and offered logistical support, but this evoked little response from the African participants.)

The feasibility of one-nation trusteeships seems slight, and the probability that any nation would take on such a thankless responsibility seems near zero. An internationalist U.N. trusteeship, as Mazrui wants, seems equally unlikely. The United

Nations, even now, is overburdened. It has great difficulty finding peacekeeping troops. It is all but bankrupt, with the United States the principal defaulter on pledged payments. It has no apparatus for actually governing a country, and the politicking of its membership makes it all but impossible to acquire one. It is the agent of the Security Council, and the policies it would follow in any nation-building enterprise would be dictated by the Security Council majority. Neither the Somalian nor the Bosnian experience encourages confidence in such an undertaking.

What is left? The answer seems to lie in the responses to three questions. Who is principally responsible for this catastrophe? Answer: the European powers who colonized Africa, out of a complex mixture of good and bad motives, destroying Africa's existing social and political systems and its customary institutions and law.

Who outside of Africa has the most urgent material interest in its condition? Clearly, the former European colonial powers. Africa's continued foundering means the exodus of hundreds of thousands, even millions, of desperate people headed to the closest place where they can find order, jobs, security, a future. Their scarcely controllable migration to Europe has already created immense social problems and serious political tensions there. Europe is also the principal consumer of African mineral and agricultural exports.

Who is competent to supply not only peacekeeping and peacemaking in Africa but serious support for building administrations, economies, and infrastructure? Neither the United Nations nor the United States, as we have seen. Both Italian and French peacekeepers in Somalia vainly warned the United States and United Nations against their ill-conceived attempt to impose American-style solutions there. As its former colonial ruler, the Italians know Somalia, just as the French know West and Central Africa, the British, East Africa, and the Portuguese, Angola and Mozambique. They know the languages. They still have among them not only former colonial administrators but specialists and scholars concerned with these regions. If anybody is competent to deal sympathetically with these countries, the Europeans are.

It is true that in some respects Europe has never left Africa. France's persisting presence in Western and Central Africa still evokes hostility from American and British commentators and many non-Francophone Africans, and there undoubtedly is much to criticize in a policy whose ruling principle has been stability above all else. However, the overall judgment must also be that French Africa for more than three decades has been the Africa that worked, the place where life for ordinary Africans has been markedly better than where the old colonial powers, as one commentator put it, "absconded with no forwarding address."

France today is probably the only European country that might, if invited, consider a major commitment to the rehabilitation of a former colony. It would be better if the European Union as an institution, which insists it wants an international role for "Europe," would collectively assume such responsibilities in cooperation with Africans in an effort to arrest the continent's decline and put it on a progressive course.

The components of such a program are easier to imagine than how European opinion could be mustered to support it or African authorities persuaded to accept it. There would have to be a cooperative Euro-African trust organization to which the majority of African governments would assign a defined (and irrevocable) authority to keep or restore order in troubled societies, establish regimes of political and social rights, rebuild health and educational institutions, develop national economic infrastructures, and develop and support competent government administrations.

This would be the project of a half-century, perhaps a century. But it could mean a great deal for Africa and be a deeply constructive accomplishment for Europe. It would eventually end, and that would have to be understood from the start. The European pledge to the Africans would be: We imposed this ordeal of modernization on you, which you are determined to complete. We are prepared to rejoin you and support you in that enterprise.

There need be no moralization or condescension. Europeans can also say to Africans: You are divided by hysterical tribalism and suffer anarchical social upheavals? Some among you have committed genocide? You have practiced ethnic murder? We know all about that. Look at our history in this same century. There are no invidious moral distinctions to be drawn between us. Let us now work together to find a way out of this, toward higher ground.

HOPE AND HORROR IN AFRICA

WOLE SOYINKA[3]

NPQ: Africa today is living a moment of hope and horror. A young multiracial democracy has been proudly born in South Africa while countless corpses from tribal war clog the sad rivers of Rwanda. Which fate will win out?

Wole Soyinka: South Africa is our dream, Rwanda our nightmare. The dream can be our fate, but not tomorrow.

Rwanda is clinically dead as a nation. The international community, in this case the Organization of African Unity (OAU) and the United Nations, should have the courage to pronounce this fact. What we should concern ourselves with is the humanity which is trapped in this abattoir. We are not dealing with a nation, but a slaughterhouse.

When a nation is able to lose in a few days a quarter of a million of its people, when its so-called government lacks the means to protect its citizens from being slaughtered en masse by machetes, that government, whether by acts of omission or commission, dooms that space recognized by the world as sovereign.

I do not know an instance in our contemporary world where humanity has been so degraded, so nullified, so treated with total contempt, as it is today in Rwanda. Two years ago there was the Rio summit on the environment. There have been global meetings in Japan to discuss threatened species of elephants, rhinoceros, or wart hogs. Everyone is worried about the gorillas in Rwanda. A great stir has been made about the fact that poachers are killing a few thousand elephants a year, laws are made, commodities are banned.

But we are talking here today about a human decimation. To talk about an endangered species is to talk about the Tutsis in Rwanda today.

NPQ: We've seen the Rwanda kind of unraveling before in Africa, in Liberia a couple of years ago and more recently in Somalia. Now it threatens to engulf the entire horn of the continent. What is the underlying connection in this trend?

3. Soyinka, Wole, "Hope and Horror in Africa," in *New Perspectives Quarterly,* (Los Angeles: Institute for National Strategy), Summer 1994, pp. 61-62.

Wole Soyinka was awarded the Nobel Prize for Literature in 1986. He is the author of many books and plays, including *Death and King's Horseman* (New York: Norton, 1975), *Ake: The Years of Childhood* (New York: Random House, 1981), and *Isara* (New York:Random House, 1989). He was interviewed in London by the editor of *New Perspectives Quarterly,* Nathan Gardels.

Wole Soyinka: One hundred years ago at the Berlin Conference the colonial powers that ruled Africa met to divvy up their interests into states, lumping various peoples and tribes together in some places, or slicing them apart in others like some demented tailor who paid no attention to the fabric, color or pattern of the quilt he was patching together.

One of the biggest disappointments of the OAU when it came into being more than 20 years ago was that it failed to address this issue. Instead, one of its cardinal principles was non-interference and the sacrosanctity of the boundaries inherited from the colonial situation. That was a foreboding failure of political will. And now we see in Rwanda what that absence of African self-redefinition has wrought. If we fail to understand that all this stems from the colonial nation-state map imposed upon us, there will be little chance to correct the situation over the long term.

NPQ: But you can't blame it all on the colonial powers. You, yourself, wrote just a couple of years ago that Africans must accuse Africa's failed leadership for "the trail of skeletons along desiccated highways . . . the lassitude and hopelessness of emaciated survivors crowded into refugee camps . . . the mounds of corpses." Africa, you wrote, had been betrayed "from within."

Wole Soyinka: You cannot, of course, dismiss the context for our failures. At the same time, you are right. So many decades of so-called independence have passed since the end of colonial rule. Unfortunately, African leaders have been so concerned with maintaining their power and authority within these artificial ponds created by colonialism, they have been so eager to preserve their status as king toad, that they've never really addressed the humanity which is entrapped within those ponds.

It is incredible that, with these horror-stricken events taking place right here on our soil, the OAU has not to date even called an emergency meeting. There has been no meeting on Rwanda, nothing at all. Instead, our leaders allow this hemorrhage to go on. In Africa today there is an absolute failure of vision and leadership. Yet, the initiative must come from within the continent. Why, for God's sake, should Americans or others be asked to send their troops to the continent when we in Africa have not been sufficiently agitated to do anything about this blot on our sense of humanity?

We just can't sit idly and tolerate this. Africans should assess the situation to see what humanitarian needs must be met, what political situation must be proffered and what kind of intervention must take place. Africans should take the lead in forcing the UN to act, not the other way around. And African soldiers should take the lead in intervening to end the carnage. The do-good world should follow and get as worked up (about the loss of human life) as they do about saving the endangered wildlife of this continent.

All notions of sovereignty with respect to Rwanda should be completely forgotten and we should just go in and stop the killing. Tanzania marched into Uganda to get rid of Idi Amin's legacy. I don't recall that many tears were shed. The same moral imperative applies for Rwanda, even more so because the situation is so grotesque.

NPQ: Are you, then, proposing redesigning the "spaces" in Africa into a more harmonious quilt, or at least one less prone to tribal bloodletting?

Wole Soyinka: Yes, we should sit down with square rule and compass and redesign the boundaries of African nations. If we thought we could get away without this redefinition of boundaries back when the OAU was formed, surely the instance of Rwanda lets us know in a very brutal way that we cannot evade this historical challenge any longer.

The horror of Rwanda is too high a price to pay for a very vaporous and whimsical notion of what constitutes inviolable territorial boundaries. How can we accept the brutal decimation of a quarter of a million people in a couple of weeks for the preservation of boundaries that aren't even ours?

NPQ: South Africa was the last nation in Africa to be liberated, but the only one in which liberation came through the ballot box, through democracy. Will this special quality enable South Africa under Nelson Mandela to provide the leadership role Africa's king toads are so sorely unable to offer?

Wole Soyinka: It seems that a kind of political chemistry brewed by Mandela and (F.W.) De Klerk gives that nation a very good chance to make it. What has happened there through the democratic process is a rebuke to the rest of the African states for their failures. It should make Nigeria, the other African nation with great economic potential, ashamed at its betrayal of its people and the squandering of their promise.

The tension and contradictions faced by South Africans were far more intractable than those in the rest of Africa. Yet, they were overcome and a democracy has been born. That gives the rest of Africa no excuse. No excuse whatever.

THE BLOOD OF EXPERIENCE

ALI A. MAZRUI[4]

We used to think that decolonization consisted of the nationalist struggle against colonialism, the granting of independence, and the replacing of colonial symbols of authority with national flags and national anthems. Decolonization was complete, we thought, when colonially educated members of the African elite, the author included, came to the fore, and when some of us, as, for example, Kwame Nkrumah of Ghana and Leopold Senghor of Senegal, inherited the reins of the colonial state from our colonial masters.

The question that has arisen lately, however, is whether real decolonization is not the winning of formal independence, not the changing of the guard on independence day, the raising of new flags, or the singing of new national anthems, but the collapse of the colonial state itself, the cruel and bloody disintegration of colonial structures. Liberation and decolonization can no longer be equated.

Are Somalia, Rwanda, Liberia, Angola, and Burundi experiencing the death throes of the old order? Is the colonial order being washed away with buckets of blood? Or are we witnessing the agonizing birth pangs of a genuinely postcolonial order? Is the blood in fact spilling in the maternity ward of history as a new Africa is trying to breathe? Until we know whether this is the birth of a truly decolonized Africa, we cannot celebrate. In any case, who can celebrate in the midst of all this blood and carnage?

But before we can decide whether or not the colonial state is dying, we need to understand what constitutes state failure, as opposed to less catastrophic political collapse.

In order to assess whether a state has failed, we must first identify the basic functions of the state. Six functions seem to be crucial: sovereign control over territory; sovereign supervision (though not necessarily ownership) of the nation's resources; effective and rational revenue extraction from people, goods, and services; the capacity to build and maintain an adequate national infrastructure (roads, postal services, telephone systems, railways, and the like); the capacity to render such basic services as sanitation, education, housing, and health care; and the capacity for gov-

---

4. Mazrui, Ali A., "The Blood of Experience: The Failed State and Political Collapse in Africa," in *World Policy Journal*, Vol. 12, No. 1, Sring 1995, (New York: World Policy Institute): pp. 28-34.

Ali Mazrui is the Director of the Institute of Global Cultural Studies and the Albert Schweitzer Professor in the Humanities at the State University of New York, Binghamton, Albert Luthuli Professor-at-Large in the University of Jos, Nigeria, and senior scholar and Andrew D. White Professor-at-Large Emeritus at Cornell University.

ernance and the maintenance of law and order.

When we look at Africa with these functions in mind, it is clear that many states are in trouble. The government of Angola, for example, has lost sovereign control over a large proportion of the country, with the result that it has also lost control of resources, infrastructure, revenue, social services, and governance. Do governments sometimes lose control at night and regain it during the day? Some reports claim that certain suburbs of Algerian cities are under the control of the authorities during the day and under the control of Islamic militants at night.

On the issue of sovereign oversight of a nation's resources, it is arguable that very few African states have effective control over their country's resources. The activities of mining and oil companies, the distant setting of coffee and cocoa prices, and rampant corruption have all drastically diluted the concept of resource sovereignty in Africa. Political apartheid in South Africa may be dead, but economic apartheid is alive and well. Most of the best land and the mineral wealth is owned by and most of the best jobs go to whites, local or foreign.

The tax systems are also in shambles in one African country after another. The state without the capacity for the rational collection of revenue is a state headed for ever-deepening decay. It will also be ever looking for handouts from foreign donors. African states also lag behind in providing essential services and infrastructure. The state that falls further and further behind in providing services and infrastructure engenders massive popular discontent and is headed for either regime failure or total collapse.

But it is the sixth stage in state failure—a crisis in governance, sometimes leading to the collapse of law and order—that is often catastrophic.

Every African government walks the tightrope between too much and too little government. An excess of government becomes tyranny; too little government becomes anarchy. Either can lead to the failed state. Indeed, either may lead to the collapse of the state. Somalia under Siyad Barre was a case in which tyranny ultimately led to the collapse of the state; anarchic conditions in the Congo (now Zaire) in 1960 nearly destroyed the new postcolonial state, which was saved by the United Nations.

A major unresolved dilemma for African states is that of civil-military relations. Military rule almost always leads to too much government. On the other hand, civilian rule, as in Nigeria and Sudan, with politicians squabbling among themselves and sometimes plundering the nation's resources, has sometimes meant too little government. In either case, the countries of Africa have to find solutions for the future.

Nnamdi Azikiwe, the first president of Nigeria after independence, once proposed a constitutional sharing of power, or diarchy, between the military and civilians. At the time that Azikiwe proposed the dual sovereignty idea in 1972, he was roundly denounced, especially by intellectuals and academics who were against military rule. Some would contend that Egypt, whose government was controlled by the military following the revolution of 1952 but which has become increasingly civilianized, has evolved into (or is in the process of becoming) just such a diarchy. But the dilemma of how to bridge the gap between the ethic of representative government and the power of the military persists in Nigeria, as it does elsewhere in Africa.

Another dilemma of too much government versus too little hinges on the party system. There is little doubt that one-party states tend toward too much government. This has been the case in most of Africa. On the other hand, multiparty systems in Africa have often degenerated into ethnic or sectarian rivalries resulting in too little control. This tendency was illustrated in the l980s in Ghana under Hilla Limann, in Nigeria under Shehu Shagari, and in Sudan under Sadiq el-Mahdi.

Although diarchy may be a solution to the civil-military dilemma, another approach is needed to address the problems presented by the party system. Uganda is feeling its way toward one solution: the no-party state. Under both the administration of Idi Amin (1971–79) and the second administration of Milton Obote (1980–85), Uganda experienced, simultaneously, some of the worst excesses of both tyranny and anarchy. Although the state did not actually collapse, the government lost control over a large part of the country and was unable to perform many of the basic functions of a state. Concerned that a multiparty system would lead to a reactivation of the ethnic and sectarian rivalries that had brought Idi Amin to power in the first place, President Yoweri Museveni lent the weight of his name and the prestige of his office to the idea of a Uganda without political parties for at least five years. In an election held in March 1994 to choose members of a constituent assembly, candidates apparently favoring a no-party Uganda won a majority of the seats. However, the constituent assembly is now debating whether to amend Uganda's 1962 independence constitution or to draw up a new one.

There are other possible solutions to the dilemma of multiparty anarchy versus one-party tyranny. One possibility is a no-party presidency with a multiparty parliament. A strong executive with extensive constitutional powers, one who is elected in a contest between individuals rather than between party candidates, could counterbalance the anarchical tendencies of a multiparty parliament. Such a system may give undue advantage to Africa's millionaires—to such "black Ross Perots" as M.K.O. Abiola, the multimillionaire Nigerian entrepreneur and philanthropist (who, by all accounts, won the June 1993 presidential election in Nigeria but was prevented from taking office by the military government, which refused to either announce or confirm the election results). That may well be the price to be paid for the stability conferred by a no-party presidency in a multiparty society.

Although the state succeeds or fails in relation to the nature of its political institutions, it also succeeds or fails in relation to wider societal configurations. In postcolonial Africa, ethnicity continues to be a major factor in the success or failure of the state.

Yet, here too Mother Africa presents contradictions. A state may collapse either because it has too many ethnic groups or, paradoxically, because it has too few. The failures of the state in Uganda in previous decades were partly due to the very ethnic richness of the society—to the striking diversity of Bantu, Nilotic, Sudanic, and other groups, each of which is itself internally diverse. Uganda's political system was not able to sustain the immense pressures of competing ethno-cultural claims. Ethiopia under Mengistu Haile Mariam, who came to power in 1977, also drifted toward state failure partly because the system was unable to accommodate the country's rich cultural and ethnic diversity. Mengistu's tyranny did not foster free negotiations, or compromise, or coalition building among ethnic groups.

But how can a state fail or collapse because it has too few ethnic groups? At first glance, it looks as if Somalia has been just such a case. George Bernard Shaw used to say that the British and the Americans were divided by the same language. It may be truer and more poignant to say that the Somali are a people divided by the same culture. Its cultural homogeneity notwithstanding, Somalia is also a plural society. The single culture of the Somali people is misleading because Somalia's pluralism is at the level of subethnicity. Its culture legitimizes the system of clans that is one of the central causes of discord. And it legitimizes interclan feuds and the macho response to interclan stalemates. These interclan rivalries would decline if the Somali themselves had to compete with other ethnic groups within a plural society, if, for example, the Amhara and the Tigre were members of Somalia's society. Somalia's disguised pluralism was exploited by Siyad Barre, who played one clan against another. Siyad Barre's tyranny, which lasted from 1969 into the 1990s, turned out to be the road to destruction of the Somali state.

In contrast to the threats to the state presented by the plural society are the threats presented by the dual society. The plural society endangers the state by having more sociological diversity than the political process can accommodate. The dual society endangers the state by having *less* sociological diversity than is necessary for the politics of compromise.

As we grapple with new levels of strife in Africa, from Kigali to Kismayu, from Maputo to Monrovia, we ought to at least try to identify which socio-political situations are particularly conflict-prone. A good deal of work has been done on the plural society in Africa—Kenya and Tanzania, for example, and their multiplicity of ethnic groups and plurality of political allegiances. What has yet to be explored adequately is the phenomenon of the dual society—in which the fundamental divide within a country is between two groups or two geographical areas. In such countries, the state is vulnerable in a different way than in plural societies.

Rwanda is a dual society. So are Burundi and Sudan. Rwanda is an ethnically dual society, whose fatal cleavage is between the majority Hutu and the minority Tutsi. Burundi is similarly bifurcated between majority Hutu and minority Tutsi. Sudan is a regionally dual society, divided between an Arabized north and a Christian-led south. (Sudan is also ethnically plural. Both northern and southern Sudan are culturally diverse regions.)

The most risky situations with respect to dual societies are not those involving a convergence of ethnic duality and regional (territorial) duality, as in Cyprus or Czechoslovakia. It is true that when the two ethnic groups are concentrated in separate regions, it increases the risk of territorial or political separatism and secession. But, in human terms, that may not be the worst scenario. The most risky form of duality is that of pure ethnic differentiation *without* territorial differentiation, because there is no prospect of even a Cyprus-type stalemate, in which the conflicting ethnic groups can live separate but peaceful lives. Nor is there the prospect of creating separate countries, as with Czechoslovakia's "gracious parting of the ways." Rather, the two groups are so intermingled in neighborhoods, at times so intermarried, that a soured ethnic relationship is an explosive relationship—a prescription for hate at close quarters. There is no question, for example, of partitioning Northern Ireland into a Catholic sector to be united with the Irish Republic and a Protestant sector to remain within the United Kingdom. A second Irish partition is not in the cards, not least because the population of Northern Ireland is too geographically intermingled. Intercommunal hate thrives in such close quarters.

Rwanda and Burundi also fall into this latter category. Hutus and Tutsi were intermingled from village to village, from street to street. Rwanda is also the most densely populated country on the African continent (its population was estimated to be about 540 persons per square mile in the 1980s). Ethnic duality, population density, geographic intermingling, and the legacies of colonial and precolonial relationships—all contributed to the tragedies in Rwanda and Burundi.

Sri Lanka, divided between the majority Sinhalese and the minority Tamils, may also be considered a dual society. Its population is intermingled to a substantial extent, although the Tamil Tigers rebel group is fighting for a separate Tamil homeland in predominantly Tamil areas. Such ethnically dual societies are vulnerable to polarization. The absence of other groups makes the possibility of forming mediating coalitions difficult, if not impossible.

Sudan is also a country at war with itself, but its duality is regional rather than ethnic. Both northern and southern Sudan are multi-ethnic, but the south, led by Christianized Sudanese, is less Islamized and culturally more indigenous. The civil war between the two regions that broke out in 1955 ended with the Addis Ababa Accords of 1972. A second Sudanese civil war erupted in 1983 and has raged ever since. The first civil war was clearly secessionist, with the southern rebels wishing to form a separate country (the Czechoslovakia solution). This time around, the southern military leader, Col. John Garang, has emphasized that he stands for the democratization of the whole of Sudan rather than for southern secession.

Although there is some nationwide intermingling between southerners and northerners in Sudan, the numbers are modest. The real divide is region-specific and can be territorialized—unlike the division between Hutu and Tutsi in Rwanda. The state has not collapsed in Khartoum, but it has no control over parts of the south. Nor has Sudan's national army sought out helpless civilians for slaughter. The speed of the killing in Rwanda in April 1994 was much faster than almost anything witnessed in the Sudanese civil war—some 200,000 people were killed in Rwanda within a two-week period. However, both civil wars have been very costly in terms of human lives and human suffering. Sudan has yet to find a solution to its violent dualism. Its split cultural personality—the division between north and south—has so far proven to be more deadly than its split ethnic personality.

The dual society casts a long shadow over plural Africa—from Zimbabwe (Shona versus Ndebele), to Algeria (Arab versus Berber), from Nigeria (north versus south), to Rwanda and Sudan. Yemen presents a case of territorial dualism (north versus south) without significant ethnic dualism. It is unclear if the distinction between the self-styled Republic of Somaliland and the rest of Somalia is a case similar to Yemen's, or if there is a subethnic dualism between the two parts of Somalia that makes it more like Cyprus, where there are two ethnically distinct and territorially differentiated groups. Alternatively, the two parts of Somalia may be equally prone to internecine conflict. This third, or intermediate, category of dualism will probably prove to be the most prevalent in the coming decades.

The United Republic of Tanzania represents a more artificial case of dualism, between a small geographical region—the island of Zanzibar, and a larger region—the former Tanganyika. There have indeed been heated political disputes between the two parts of the United Republic, separatist sentiments at times being expressed by Zanzibarians and at other times, paradoxically, by mainlanders. There are ominous ethno-religious warning signs in Tanzania that ought to be monitored. It is a situation to which the present secretary general of the Organization of African Unity (himself a Tanzanian) might pay special attention.

The big story of the 1990s in Africa may turn out to be the painful redefinition of what constitutes decolonization. Three decades ago, decolonization was equated with liberation. Now, decolonization appears to require the collapse of colonial structures. If this is so, instability may be the real engine of decolonization.

Just because almost all African countries are unstable in varying degrees, however, we must not assume that they are unstable for the same reasons. Put differently, just because all patients in a hospital are sick does not mean that they all suffer from the same disease. Conflict prevention requires greater and greater sophistication in *diagnosing* conflict-prone situations. Unfortunately Africa is full of contradictions: conflict generated by too much government versus conflict generated by too little; conflict generated by too many ethnic groups as distinct from conflict ignited by too few ethnic groups. It is dark outside and Africa is waiting for the dawn. Let us hope the wait is not too long.

In the meantime, how can the problems of acute state failure or political collapse be addressed? One option is *unilateral intervention by a single neighboring power* in order to restore order. Here the precedent is Tanzania's invasion of Uganda in 1979. Tanzania's troops marched all the way to Kampala and put Uganda virtually under military occupation for a couple of years. Tanzania's intervention was very similar to Vietnam's intervention in Cambodia to overthrow Pol Pot and the Khmer Rouge, except that the Vietnamese stayed in Cambodia much longer than the Tanzanians stayed in Uganda. The question arises whether Yoweri Museveni's Uganda should have intervened in Rwanda in April 1994, the way Julius Nyerere's Tanzania intervened in Uganda fifteen years earlier.

Another possibility is *intervention by a single power with the blessing of a regional organization*. There is no real African precedent for such a scenario, but there is an Arab one: Syria's intervention in the Lebanese civil war with the blessing of the League of Arab States.

A third option is *inter-African colonization and annexation.* Such action is not unprecedented in Africa; witness Tanganyika's annexation of Zanzibar in 1964, partly as a result of pressure from the United States and Great Britain. The West wanted to prevent the clove island on the east African coast from going the way of Marxist Cuba. Nyerere was persuaded that an unstable or subversive Zanzibar would be a threat to the mainland. He got the dictator of Zanzibar, Abeid Karume, to agree to a treaty of union—very much as the British used to convince African chiefs to "accept" treaties by which they ceased to be sovereign. Nobody held a referendum in Zanzibar to ask its people if they wanted their country to cease being a separate independent nation. But the annexation of Zanzibar was the most daring aspect of what became, de facto, Pax Tanzaniana.

Still another option for dealing with political collapse is *regional integration.* In the longer run, one solution to the problems of Rwanda and Burundi may well be federation with Tanzania. Under such a federation, Hutus and Tutsi would no longer be able to maintain their own ethnic armies, and their soldiers would be retrained as part of the federal army of the United Republic of Tanzania. This is not a new idea. Before the First World War, Germany had leaned toward treating Tanganyika and Ruanda-Urundi as a single jurisdiction. For Rwanda and Burundi, union with Tanzania would, in the short run, be safer than union with Zaire. Even though they are linked to Zaire by their historical connection with Belgium and the French language, Tanzania's society is less vulnerable than Zaire's and a safer haven for Hutu and Tutsi. It is indeed significant that Hutus and Tutsi on the run are more likely to flee to Tanzania than to Zaire, despite ethnic ties to Zaire. Moreover, Hutus and Tutsi are becoming partially Swahilized and should be able to get on well with "fellow" Tanzanian citizens.

In terms of conflict resolution, the *establishment of an African Security Council,* complete with permanent members in the style of the U.N. Security Council, would be useful. The permanent members could be Egypt, representing north Africa, Nigeria, representing west Africa, Ethiopia, representing east Africa, and the Republic of South Africa, representing south Africa. There should also be three to five non-permanent members. The makeup of the permanent membership could be reviewed every 30 years. Three decades from now, it may be necessary to add Zaire as a permanent member to represent central Africa. Other issues would also have to be worked out. In times of crisis, for example, should the African Security Council meet at the level of heads of state? Should each permanent member have a veto?

Conflict resolution at times of political collapse would also be aided by the establishment of a pan-African emergency force—a sort of fire brigade that could be rushed to the site of conflagrations in collapsed states or at the outbreak of civil war and that would teach Africa the art of maintaining peace. Should such a force be independently recruited and trained in a specialized manner? Or should it be drawn from units of the armed forces of member states? And who would pay for its training, maintenance, and deployment? Certainly the successes of ECOMOG—the military arm of ECOWAS, the Economic Community of West African States—in Liberia should be studied carefully in preparation for this new venture.

Ad hoc conflict management with an emphasis on mediation and a search for peaceful solutions to crises also has a place in this overall picture. Such ad hoc efforts are definitely much better than doing nothing and could constitute a major part of Africa's search for a Pax Africana—an African peace established and maintained by Africans themselves. In this more modest tradition of intervention is the Organization of African Unity's Mechanism on Conflict Prevention, Management, and Resolution, which for the first time gives the regional organization a more active role in internal civil conflicts. Modest as the mechanism is, it signifies a qualitative shift in the position of African heads of state with respect to intervention.

Still, behind the search for solutions, behind all the pain and the anguish, is the paramount question: are we witnessing the death throes of decolonization, as the colonial structures decay and collapse? Is the colonial state being washed away with the blood of victims, villains, and martyrs? Or is the blood from the womb of history, from the painful birth of a new order?

The blood of experience meanders on
In the vast expanse of the valley of time
The new is come and the old is gone
And time abides a changing clime

Recolonize Africa?

ALI A. MAZRUI[5]

Much of contemporary Africa is in the throes of decay and decomposition. Even the degree of dependent modernization achieved under colonial rule is being reversed. The successive collapse of the state in one African country after another during the 1990s suggests a once unthinkable solution: recolonization. To an increasing number of Africans, this is the bitter message that has emerged from the horrifying events in Rwanda.

While Africans have been quite successful in uniting to achieve national freedom, we have utterly failed to unite for economic development and political stability. War, famine and ruin are the post-colonial legacy for too many Africans.

As a result, external recolonization under the banner of humanitarianism is entirely conceivable. Countries like Somalia or Liberia, where central control has entirely disintegrated, invite inevitable intervention to stem the spreading "cancer of chaos," in the phrase of United States Agency for International Development director Brian Atwood.

The colonization impulse that is resurfacing, however, is likely to look different this time around. A trusteeship system—like that of the United Nations over the Congo in 1960 when order fell apart with the Belgian pullout—could be established that is more genuinely international and less Western than under the old guise. Administering powers for the trusteeship territories could come from Africa or Asia as well as from the rest of the UN membership. The "white man's burden" would, in a sense, become humanity's shared burden.

In the 21st century, for example, might Ethiopia (that will by then presumably be more stable than it is today) be called upon to run Somalia on behalf of the UN? After all, Ethiopia was once a black imperial power, annexing its neighboring communities. Why should it not take up that historical role again in a more benign manner that has legitimate international sanction?

Might Egypt re-establish its big brother relationship with the Sudan? Might the UN implore post-apartheid South Africa to intervene to end the Angolan civil war?

Surely it is time for Africans to exert more pressure on each other, including through benevolent intervention, to achieve a kind of Pax Africana based on regional integration or unification of smaller states. Some Afican countries will simply need to be temporarily controlled by others. Inevitably some dysfunctional coun-

---

5. Mazrui, Ali A., "The Message of Rwanda: Recolonize Africa? in *New Perspectives Quarterly*, Fall 1944, (Los Angeles: Institute for National Strategy), pp. 18–20

tries would need to submit to trusteeship and even tutelage for a while, as Zanzibar did when it was annexed by Tanganyika in 1964 to form Tanzania. If Burundi and Rwanda had been similarly united into a larger state where the balance between Tutsi and Hutu would have been part of a more diverse population, the savagery we've witnessed over the past months would very likely not have happened on the scale it has occurred.

If recolonization or self-colonization is the path that lies ahead for Africa, there must be a continental authority to ensure that such an order does not merely mask base aims of exploitation.

What I propose as a longer-term solution to problems exposed by today's crises is the establishment of an African Security Council composed of five pivotal regional states, or potential pivot states, that would oversee the continent. This Council would have a Pan African Emergency Force, an army for intervention and peace-keeping at its disposal. And there would also be an African High Commissioner for Refugees linked to the UN High Commission. While Africa accounts for one-tenth of the world's population, it accounts for one-half of the world's refugees.

The African Security Council that I envision being formed in the coming decades would be anchored in the north by Egypt and in the south by South Africa. Although it is presently experiencing very troubling times, Nigeria would be the pivotal state in West Africa. Its size and resources could give it the weight of India if it can find political stability.

In East Africa, the pivotal country is still in doubt. Ethiopia, among the most fragile of the largest African states today, is the most likely anchor because of its size. Though Kenya is more stable, it is far smaller. In Central Africa, the presumed regional power of the future—Zaire—is today itself in need of trusteeship. If Zaire can avoid the collapse into chaos in the near future. it will be one of the major actors in Africa in the 21st century, taking Burundi and Rwanda under its wing. Zaire has the population and resources to play a major role. In the next century it will even surpass France as the largest French-speaking nation in the world.

As permanent members of an African Security Council, these five states would coordinate among each other and with the UN.

In tandem with the efforts of the UN to establish a peaceful world order, Africans need an African peace enforced by Africans, from Angola to Rwanda and Burundi.

Regional integration is the order of the day in Europe, in North America, in East Asia and even, tentatively of course, in the Middle East. If Africa too does not follow this path, the lack of stability and growth will push the entire continent further into the desperate margins of global society.

These are no doubt frightening ideas for proud peoples who spilled so much blood and spent so much political will freeing themselves from the control of European powers in this century. To be sure, self-colonization, if we can manage it, is better than colonization by outsiders. Better still would be self-conquest. But that implies an African capacity for self-control and self-discipline rarely seen since before colonialism.

The Role of Foreign Intervention in African Reconstruction

IBRAHIM A. GAMBARI[6]

In considenng the role played by external forces, both African and non-African, in reviving collapsed states on the African continent, four main themes emerge. First, although the phenomenon of state collapse is not unique to Africa, its consequences tend to be particularly drastic for the socio-economic fabric of the fragile states and civil societies there. Second, the incidences of state collapse in Africa appear to have increased in the period since the high point of the Cold War, continuing into the aftermath of superpower confrontation. Africa's growing marginalization in the post-Cold War period may, in fact, have accelerated the process of state collapse. Third, the domestic effort essential for putting back together the collapsed states in Africa has to be substantially supplemented by subregional, regional, and international support. Indeed, it may well be that the more complete the collapse of a state, the greater will be the role of foreign intervention in its reconstruction. Finally, foreign interventions are not "neutral," neither in motivation nor in impact; they may be part of the solution to state collapse or part of the problem, or both.

Domestic collapse and foreign intervention are related to the nature of the state. . . . [S]tates have basic characteristics. The state must have a population, territory, governmental apparatus with a monopoly of force for the preservation of peace and order, and "a plenitude of authority, independent of external control except that of international law." . . . Within this spectrum, foreign intervention means that state functions are being performed—whether as assistance or as interference—by another state or groups of states.

The modern African state, though sharing in many of these attributes, is special in several ways. It emerged from the ashes of colonialism, a regime of alien rule that sought to forge political entities out of diverse nations and peoples. African state boundaries, being colonially inherited, are permeable and ill-defined. They contain nations and peoples who straddle the lines—peoples who never really accepted the white man's boundaries, although the independent governments of the new states

5. Gambari, Ibrahim A., "The Role of Foreign Intervention in African Reconstruction," in *Collapsed States: The Disintegration of Legitimate Authority,* I. William Zartman (ed.), (Boulder, CO: Lynne Rienner, 1995): pp. 221-233.

Ibrahim A. Gambari is a permanent representative of Nigeria at the United Nations. He was foreign minister of Nigeria from January 1984 to August 1985.

have tried to enforce them, often with great difficulty. One of the problems faced by states with colonially inherited boundaries, according to Nzongola-Ntalaja, is that "the dogma of the preservation of colonially inherited boundaries" became a license that governments used to oppress minorities and hide their incompetencies and indifference to the suffering of the peoples.

Even in the best of times in Africa, the maintenance of law and order as an attribute of statehood has existed only tenuously, because the instruments of the state, such as the judiciary, the police, and the army, have never really been sufficient to cope with the full demands of governance. As noted by Ekwe-Ekwe, the African state is still essentially the trading post created by European imperialism. Hence, for its peoples, particularly its national minorities, it has no organic essence, and its structure and polity are inherently weak. It is a "non-national state" and it hardly makes any difference whether the prevailing political economy of a given state is capitalist (for example, Nigeria) or postcapitalist (for example, Ethiopia).

International Defined

Intervention in international politics is an old concept. Sometimes it has been defined by international legal publicists to mean "dictatorial or coercive interference by an outside party or parties in the sphere of jurisdiction of an independent political community." However, not all the examples discussed below will be dictatorial, coercive, or interfering. Interventions can take the forms of forcible or non-forcible interference. In the former sense, intervention is open and direct, made often by the use of military force; in the latter, intervention takes the form of coercive economic measures, such as economic embargoes or sanctions; as, for example, U.S. economic sanctions against Cuba or UN economic sanctions against South Africa or Iraq. Intervention can also take the form of proxy interference, through the use of a third party (state or organization). Many wars fought in the Third World during the Cold War were proxy wars, undertaken essentially at the behest of the superpowers, albeit with local collaboration.

Interventions in whatever form they manifest themselves are perceived as directives against the intrinsic sovereign rights of states as political entities. This subversive attribute of intervention reinforces criticism of, and objections to, intervention as a mode of international political behavior. Yet some interventions—as shown in the following cases—take place at the invitation of the state in question, introducing another distinction and ambiguity in the types of intervention.

Foreign interventions in Africa have been both frequent and varied, with both constructive and negative consequences. While on the one hand foreign interventions complicated nation-building processes in Mozambique and Angola soon after these states attained independence from Portugal, intervention also helped to salvage from total collapse Liberia, Chad, and Somalia. . . . The United States-led Operation Restore Hope of December 1992 and the United Nations peacekeeping operation in Somalia have been crucial in helping to restore the collapsed Somali state. The same can be said of the Nigeria-led ECOMOG that (together with UNOMIL, the United Nations Military Observer Mission) is helping to reconstruct war torn Liberia.

The lessons of modern peacekeeping operations in Africa indicate that it is simply not sufficient to pump resources into states to keep the peace in the short-term: Efforts must be extended to include long-term assistance for sustainable political and economic development, to protect against regression and relapse.

Scholars and practitioners debate whether preventive intervention can be separated from reconstructive intervention. For example, can a distinction be drawn between preventive interventions in Shaba (Zaire) and Macedonia and reconstructive interventions in Liberia, Chad, and Somalia? The former are actions whose purpose was seen to have been served as soon as the crisis or threat to the existence or survival of the state was removed; whereas in the latter cases, the purposes of the intervener go beyond restoring peace to include rebuilding political and economic structures, the conducting of elections, and distribution of humanitarian and relief services. These elements may, of course, be preventive as well.

Recently, preventive diplomacy has acquired added importance in efforts to preempt crises from developing out of otherwise minor incidents. There is now some careful deployment of early-warning systems. If further developed, preventive diplomacy can be combined with preventive intervention to achieve peace and development. As donors grow weary of incurring additional financial expenditure for peacekeeping, preventive diplomacy may appear better anal cheaper than reconstructive diplomacy or direct involvement in the restitution of collapsed states.

OBJECTIVES OF FOREIGN INVESTORS

External intervention in Africa's internal affairs did not begin in the post-World War II era of independent states. It was in fact such intervention that led to colonial wars during the European scramble for Africa in the nineteenth century. The Berlin African Conference, held at the behest of European powers in 1884-1885, during which African territories were partitioned, was international intervention par excellence.

Foreign interventions in contemporary African politics for the purpose of assisting collapsed states have definite objectives. In some cases, a foreign power may intervene for the purpose of protecting the life and property of its own citizens in an African country. This was the reason adduced by France and Belgium for intervening in the Congo/Zaire crises in 1964, 1977, 1978, and 1993. In other cases, foreign states intervene primarily to profit from the spoils of the African states—out of what some critics have called "crass opportunism." Some interventions are undertaken in furtherance of specific geostrategic and political interest, as in the Cold War. Unilateral foreign intervention originates in the national interest or foreign policy objectives of the intervening states. The French and Libyan intervention in the protracted conflict in Chad, Cuba's decision to send troops to Angola, and, also in

Angola, covert U.S. support for UNITA were all linked to the national interest of the intervening states.

In cases of multinational interventions, especially those undertaken through multilateral institutions, the objectives, motivations, and interests tend to be diffused and multifaceted. The OAU intervention in Chad from 1981 to 1983 and the ECOWAS intervention in Liberia after 1990 were motivated by a set of objectives that do not readily fit into the standard categories of national interests. In both cases, member-states (of the OAU and ECOWAS respectively) acted collectively in the interests of both regional and subregional political and economic development.

Another form of African intervention that addresses collective interests is intervention within the intervenor's subregion. In this case, subregional and contiguous states intervene unilaterally either to uphold the tenets of extant bilateral agreements or in pursuit of national interests in a subregional context. An example in this case was Tanzanian unilateral action against Uganda in October 1978, resulting in the overthrow of President Idi Amin. In this case, one scholar has aptly argued that "the ultimate determination of which sector of the interventionist forces emerges hegemonic in a given conflict does depend on the complex interplay of the interest and roles of regional powers."

Thus it can be seen that another way of categorizing foreign intervention in African state collapse is into African and extra-African interventions. This will be the focus of the next two sections.

Non-African Intervention

These interventions take place either at the express invitation of the collapsing state or at the invitation of a rebel faction seeking to effect regime change. From the intervenor's side, some actions take place purely to satisfy the intervening state's national interest and some for more collective or humanitarian purposes. The most prominent among such extra-African powers that have intervened in Africa's conflicts are:

- France, mainly on behalf of its former colonial dependencies
- The United States and the former Soviet Union, primarily in pursuit of their strategic global and ideological interests
- To a lesser extent, Belgium and Cuba

Interventions can take many forms. The most visible is military, but other forms of economic and political relations between strong and weak states have interventionist aspects that are hard to separate from normal interactions.

FRANCE'S INTERVENTION IN CHAD AND ZAIRE

The legal basis of France's intervention in the affairs of its former colonies has been the series of bilateral defense agreements entered into with these African states on the eve of their independence, entitling France to deploy troops to the countries when asked to do so. It was on this basis, for examiple, that French troops were deployed to Chad and Zaire when those states felt that their security was imperiled.

France's first intervention in Chad took place in 1969, when several military operations were launched against the National Liberation Front of Chad (Frolinat). France stationed a garrison of troops in Ndjamena. French soldiers halted the advance of Frolinat in 1979.

Between 1980 and 1982, when the state system in Chad was in collapse, the French intervened on behalf of their protege, Hissein Habre. When Libya became involved in Chadian affairs, to the extent of bombing parts of Chad on the side of one of the parties to the Chadian crisis, France protested foreign intervention and canvassed for an OAU intervening force to be sent to Chad. France gave logistic support to the abortive OAU peacekeeping force in Chad when the force was eventually established.

In 1983, France again sent troops to Chad—a third time—to repel Libyan-supported rebel attacks under an operation code named Operation Manta. On this occasion, French troops numbered 2,800 and enforced an "interdiction line" on behalf of the Chad government to prevent the rebel and Libyan forces from pushing south. Though the French did little more than enforce the interdiction line, an uneasy peace prevailed in Chad between Libya, its local allies, and the government. In this way, French intervention helped to sustain Chad from another total collapse.

In Zaire in 1977 and again in 1978, France's support was motivated partly by the desire to protect its growing investment in the country as well as a response to a U.S. appeal for Western intervention to protect the central African state from falling prey to what was perceived to be Cuban and Communist encroachment. French assistance included the airlifting of Moroccan troops and equipment to Shaba, when the rebels had invaded the first time, in 1977. It also included the deployment of paratroops, army engineers, and technicians who directly engaged the insurgents in Shaba and subsequently forced their retreat from Kolwezi into Angola the second time, in 1978.

Military assistance and/or economic assistance from one state to another may not constitute intervention per se. It is what follows such assistance on the part of the giver that determines intervention. What are the motives of the state giving the military and/or economic assistance? What is the reaction of contending groups within the receiving state to such assistance? In the case of Zaire, France's intervention went beyond military assistance: it included urging fellow Western creditors and donors to offer increased financial help to the Mobutu government. France and its Western allies believed that increased Western financial and credit support to Mobutu's Zaire would strengthen the government's hand in dealing with insurgencies and the dangers of Communist encroachment. Accordingly, two conferences were held in May and June of 1978, specifically on ways to restructure the Zairean economy and enhance an African/Zaire security network.

More recently, while French intervention in Zaire continued to take the form of supporting the Zairean government against rebel attack (e.g., the deployment of French troops to suppress the violence of September 2, 1991), changes began to crystallize in France's attitude. France joined the United States and Belgium in pressing for democratic reforms in Zaire, although there are significant differences when it comes to pressing President Mobutu to relinquish power.

BELGIUM INTERVENTION IN ZAIRE

Belgium's King Leopold II entered Europe's race for colonies rather late and the only Belgian colony in Africa was the Congo (Belgium's presence in Rwanda and Burundi was as an international trust: the territory had been put under its administration first under the League of Nations mandate and subsequently under the UN trusteeship system). It is in Zaire that Belgium's influence in postindependent Africa has been most widely felt.

Belgium's intervention in the Congo (now named Zaire) was aimed at protecting investments that, at independence, amounted to about $1 billion, as well as Belgian nationals resident in the country. In all its intervention in Zaire, Belgium consistently supported the African government with troops and equipment to ward off rebel attacks. For instance, in early 1965, Belgian troops assisted in quelling the rebellion against the government in southern Kivu and northern Katanga Provinces. When the second Shaba war erupted in 1978, Belgium sent 1,700 troops, not only for direct combat purposes but specifically to police industrial sites in the troubled region so as to forestall sabotage of production sites.

More recently, Belgium joined pressure groups in Zaire calling for democratization and reform, denouncing Mobutu's authoritarianism. Following the killings of students and university professors in the Lumumbashi riots, Belgium froze all official and bilateral assistance to Zaire, but has been reluctant to press Mobutu to withdraw.

U.S. INTERVENTIONS

U.S. interventions in Africa have ranged from the geostrategic to the humanitarian. In the earlier phase, the United States considered African conflicts from the perspective of the Cold War and felt a need to forestall Soviet expansionism in Africa. The United States adopted counterinsurgency measures to deal with conflicts it perceived as inspired by left-wing, pro-Soviet parties and organizations. Humanitarian intervention increased after the end of the Cold War. The United States sent food and medical supplies to crises spots, aimed at alleviating the hardships of people suffering in collapsed and collapsing states.

In the early 1980s, while the United States recognized France's overarching influence in Chad, it intervened nonetheless to neutralize Libya's expansionist tendencies, beginning with covert support for Habre in 1981. The United States also contributed military and financial support to the post-civil war reconstruction efforts of the OAU peacekeeping force. In 1983, following the collapse of the OAU peacekeeping efforts and the renewal of civil conflicts in Chad, the United States signed a new agreement with the government and delivered military hardware to underscore its support. In 1985, U.S. military supplies were given in support of France's Operation Epervier, aimed at warding off Libya's attack on Chad.

In Zaire, U.S. actions have been two-pronged—aimed at both ensuring the survival of the government and protecting Western capitalist interests in resource-endowed Central Africa. The United States was disposed to supply military hardware to the Zairean government to fight rebel invasions. During Shaba 1 and 2 in 1977 and 1978, the United States supplied C-141 transport aircraft to aid the French and Belgian interventionist force. The United States has also supported economic assistance to Zaire through the Bretton Woods institutions. The United States has consistently contended that Zaire should be kept afloat financially, considering it to be of crucial significance as a Western raw-materials resource enclave.

In late 1992 in Somalia, the United States led a coalition of states in Operation Restore Hope, an unprecedented mission of mercy. The U.S. contingents to Somalia comprised 36,000 servicemen and women—the largest peacekeeping and humanitarian force ever mounted. In the complex war zone of Somalia, they were charged with making the country safe for humanitarian relief. They were also later involved in controlling Somalia's warring factions and maintaining peace until the United Nations could resume its peacekeeping role there.

Subsequently, the United States-led operation was replaced by the United Nations Operations Mission in Somalia (UNOSOM 2), established under UN Security Council Resolution 814 of March 26, 1993. The resolution mandated a UN presence of about 30,000 personnel; the United States agreed in principle to provide a tactical quick reaction force in support of the force commander of UNOSOM 2.

On October 3, 1993, an incident occurred in Somalia when a group of some U.S. soldiers on a mission to capture a number of Somali factional leaders suspected of complicity in the previous attacks on UN personnel and facilities suffered severe casualties. Eighteen U.S. soldiers lost their lives and 75 were wounded. The bodies of the U.S. soldiers were subjected to humiliating treatment.

This event turned out to be a turning point for U.S. involvement in peacekeeping operations in Somalia, with implications for U.S. policy elsewhere. Meanwhile, the United States reinforced its quick reaction force in Somalia and at the same time announced its intention to withdraw its forces from Somalia by March 31, 1994.

African Interventions

Military interventions in Africa by African states have taken place in two forms: intervention by regional or subregional African organizations, such as the Organization of African Unity (OAU) and the Economic Community of West African States (ECOWAS); and intervention by individual, and usually contiguous, states, acting either unilaterally or in conjunction with other African states. In the first category, three cases can be cited; namely, the OAU Inter-African Force in Chad (1981); the ECOWAS Observer Monitoring Group (ECOMOG) intervention in Liberia, since 1990; and the OAU's Neutral Military Observer Group (NMOG) in Rwanda (1992 to 1994) and in Burundi (1994).

OAU INTERVENTION IN CHAD

The OAU intervention in Chad was a novel experience in the history of African peacekeeping operations, for the charter of the organization originally contained no provisions for such action. The only charter reference to conflict management invoked the OAU Conciliation and Mediation Commission and resort to ad hoc institutions in the settlement of disputes.

The decision to establish an OAU force in Chad was taken in Nairobi at the organization's summit in June 1981. The force, commanded by a Nigerian officer, comprised 4,800 troops from Nigeria, Zaire, and Senegal. The OAU force failed to achieve any concrete solution to the Chadian problem and within months was compelled to withdraw. The reasons for the failure—the subject of many scholarly works (Pittman 1984; Zartman and Amoo 1992; Amate 1986)—were inadequate financial and material support combined with logistical, mission, and communication difficulties. A big disappointment was that out of the seventeen states listed to contribute troops, only three mustered the political will and resources to do so. So paltry was the assistance from other African states that Nigeria incurred a debt of $80 million as a result of the exercise, a debt that was never repaid and had to be written off by the Nigerian government. In the end, Habre pushed the inter-African force aside and went to Ndjamena to restore the state himself.

ECOM IN LIBERIA

Though the Economic Community of West African States was established in 1975 to foster economic cooperation and development within the West African subregion, the heads of state of the organization, at their meeting in Banjul, Gambia, in May 1990, felt compelled to intervene in Liberia as mediators, creating a standing committee. In August they intervened militarily to try to halt the country's slide into anarchy via civil war.

From the outset, a number of difficulties impeded the full operation of ECO-

MOG. First, the force lacked universality of membership. Only five countries contributed troops and four of these were Anglophone countries (these four "locals" were joined in 1994 by Uganda and Tanzania). The Francophone states of the subregion accused ECOMOG of being a force with a purpose only to foster the hegemonic interest of particular states, although Guinea, and later Senegal, joined the operation.

Secondly, it was argued by some member-states of ECOWAS that the creation of ECOMOG had no basis in the instrument establishing ECOWAS, notwithstanding ECOWAS protocols on nonaggression and defense.

Thirdly, the mandate of ECOMOG, at least at first, was ambiguous. Neither the diplomats nor the soldiers charged with implementing it knew what to make of it. They did not know whether they were a peacekeeping or a peace-enforcing body; whether they were policing or imposing a ceasefire. Consequently, "complications, dissensions and dissonance" were rife in their interpretation of the ECOMOG mandate.

Finally, ECOMOG faced enormous financial and logistical difficulties. Only a few ECOWAS member-states contributed to the fund for ECOMOG. Nigeria bore the brunt of the financial expenses. In spite of these difficulties, the ECOWAS initiative produced positive results. First, it stopped the carnage and bloodshed that had been rampant in Monrovia prior to the inception of ECOMOG. Secondly, by establishing an interim government in Monrovia, it prevented the continuation of anarchy in the country and averted a disaster that would have equaled that in Somalia. Thirdly, through subsequent diplomatic initiatives, ECOWAS meetings in Côte d'Ivoire produced the Yamoussoukro and Catonou peace accords, which spelled out plans for peace in Liberia, including the encampment and disarmament of the warring factions.

OAU IN RWANDA

The OAU intervened in Rwanda in October 1990 following the outbreak of a civil war in which an estimated force of 10,000 guerrillas, representing the exiled Tutsi-dominated Rwandan Front (FPR), attacked northeastern Rwanda and occupied several towns. Though the Rwandan government succeeded for a while in repelling the attack, civil unrest continued in parts of the country, making the intervention of an OAU force necessary.

The primary objective of the OAU in Rwanda was to monitor a ceasefire brokered in July 1992, in Tanzania, between the Rwandan factions. Unlike the OAU force in Chad, the peacekeeping force had a structured chain of command. The OAU secretary-general was the political boss. Furthermore, it collaborated with a joint political military commission, to which it reported violations of the terms of ceasefire. The commission comprised representatives from Burundi, Tanzania, Uganda, Zaire, Belgium, France, and the United States. The commission's mandate included implementation of both the ceasefire agreement and the peace agreement at the conclusion of the political negotiations. The role of the OAU peacekeeping force was expanded in February 1993 to include not only monitoring of the cease-fire but also ensuring resettlement in demilitarized zones of people displaced as a result of the war. In August a peace agreement was finally concluded at Arusha, under the auspices of the OAU and with Tanzanian mediation, providing for a 2,500-person UN Assistance Mission (UNAMIR) to replace the OAU peace keepers.

Next door, in Burundi, assassination of the elected president in October 1993 and genocidal warfare between the Tutsi army and the Hutus in the population led to the intervention, six months later, of a small OAU force of 50 officers, down from a proposed group of 200 troops from Mali, Burkina Faso, Cameroon, Niger, and Tunisia.

The situation was complicated, however, in April 1994 when an aircraft carrying the presidents of Rwanda and Burundi crashed at the Kigali airport in Rwanda, under circumstances yet to be clarified. Following this incident and the resulting death of the two presidents, the eight-month-old peace in Rwanda was shattered. Ethnic hostilities resulted in up to 500,000 deaths, mainly Tutsis killed by the government soldiers, who were mainly of the Hutu ethnic group.

The OAU has again been active in the efforts of the international community to stabilize and resolve the situation in Rwanda. It is at the forefront of the efforts to raise an envisaged African force of 5,500 to constitute the expanded UNAMIR established by the UN Security Council under Security Council Resolution 918 of May 17, 1994.

However, in Rwanda as in other places, the OAU remains incapacitated by the lack of resources among its member states to carry through their political decisions. This is clearly illustrated by the continuing difficulties it faces in giving concrete expression to its political will to help find a solution to the problems of Rwanda and, to a similar extent, Burundi.

Intervention and Reconstruction: Conclusion

In almost all the cases of foreign interventions in Africa, the evidence suggests that they do not generally provide early or full solutions to the perennial problems of political instability and state cohesion. On the contrary, some unilateral interventions, be it from Africa or elsewhere, have exacerbated and prolonged the crises, introducing extraneous ideological and political dimensions to what were essentially local conflicts. It can be argued that foreign countries intervening in conflict situations in Africa have had little or no interest in the preservation of the state structure as such. Their concerns have almost always been the political complexion of those in control of the state.

Multinational interventions appear to have greater relative merits than unilateral interventions, for two main reasons: First, such interventions diffuse the specific interests that the foreign powers are seeking to project or protect. This may lead to relative impartiality. This has been particularly so with regard to extra-African multinational forces such as (1) the UN peacekeeping forces (ONUC) in Congo that put an end to Katangan secession in the early 1960s; (2) the United Nations Forces (UNAVEM 1 and 2) that monitored elections in Angola in 1992; and (3) the Commonwealth intervention to put down the army mutiny in Tanganyika in 1962. The longer multinational intervention forces stay in a collapsed or collapsing state, the greater the danger of a loss of impartiality and/or effectiveness in carrying out their mandate. Proximity (of countries contributing troops to the intervening force) also contributes to loss of impartiality. Moreover, on the issue of mandate, it is important that the terms be clear and achievable. An imprecise mandate can become a recipe for confusion and worsening of the crisis.

Secondly, few countries are able to intervene in conflict situations entirely on their own. The financial and political costs are prohibitive, unless vital national interests are involved. In the era of superpower rivalries, the risks were considered to be worth taking, but in the post-Cold War era, with socio-economic difficulties facing most states, the prospects for a single power to save a collapsing state have diminished considerably. Even though Liberia had close historical and economic ties with the United States, it was little surprise when that situation was simply ignored by the big powers, at least until the multinational ECOWAS force went to the rescue. And in Somalia the great powers did little for a very long time until the United Nations Secretary-General accused them of having a double standard.

It can be further argued that the multidimensional nature of peacekeeping in collapsed or collapsing states *requires* multilateral intervention. Before actual peacekeeping can begin, the external powers must first try to stop the fighting between the warring factions. They must then try to monitor or impose a ceasefire and this requires considerable experience in peacekeeping and peace-enforcement. Second, efforts must be made to promote political reconciliation among the contending parties and this requires the involvement of countries or multilateral organizations with experience and clout. Third, the countries or organizations involved must be able and willing to provide financial and other resources. It can be seen that the responsibilities involved and the resources needed are too great for unilateral interventions. The topic continues to be the subject of intense discussions and negotiations at the United Nations and the OAU.

UN Secretary-General Boutros Boutros-Ghali (1992) has highlighted aspects of multilateral peacekeeping problems in his report to the organization entitled *An Agenda for Peace*; and Dr. Ahmed Salim has nudged the OAU toward the adoption of new conflict resolution mechanisms. Specifically, Salim's proposals include the setting up of early-warning systems, the training of international peacekeepers anal peacemakers, and the establishment of a pool of international mediators and stand-by national forces for peacekeeping duties in Africa.

Foreign interventions play a strong role in putting together collapsed or collapsing states, but in conclusion it should be stressed that the domestic dimensions of the requirements of state reconstruction are critical. State reconstruction goes beyond the imposition of a foreign-inspired "solution"; rather it involves a complex process of political, social, and economic engineering that must affect positively the internal dynamics of powers and resource distribution in African states. This requires the development of new attitudes by both the political leadership and the citizenry. The adoption of a particular form of democracy is far less important that the practice of political participation from the grassroots up. The institutions underpinning civil society must be carefully rebuilt in collapsed or collapsing states, and the rights of both minority groups and individuals must be protected. The rule of law must gradually prevail.

The issue of prudent resource distribution and management by the state is of fundamental importance in this process and prospect. With Africa these days seemingly marginalized, Africans must realize that the days of passing the buck are over. Africa must mobilize its human, physical, and other resources for the good of all its people. Africans must truly become the masters of their own destiny, no longer objects of international relations.

State Collapse: The Humanitarian Challenge to the United Nations

FRANCIS MADING DENG[7]

In most cases the collapse of the state is associated with humanitarian tragedies resulting from armed conflict, communal violence, and gross violations of human rights that culminate in the massive outflow of refugees and internal displacement of the civilian populations. It is the lack or loss of capacity to cope with the crisis that leads to the collapse of the state and necessitates the intervention of the international community through the United Nations. Yesterday Somalia and Rwanda, and outside of Africa, Bosnia and Haiti, tomorrow Zaire and Sudan come to mind as examples. . . . [S]tates collapse "because they can no longer perform the functions required for them to pass as states." The crisis is particularly acute in Africa where 15 million of the 25 million internally displaced persons worldwide are found. Africa also leads the world in its refugee population.

When the breakdown of civil society or the outbreak of unmanageable civil violence necessitates a humanitarian intervention from the international community, a further crisis situation arises with respect to the precise objectives and conduct of the operations involved. Usually, the immediate purpose of delivering urgently needed relief supplies becomes compelling and overwhelming. Little attention is paid to the conditions leading to the crisis or the longer-term perspective of reconstruction and normalization of a self-sustaining order: in other words, putting the collapsed state back together. Understanding the causes leading to the collapse of the system is critical to developing workable, long-term solutions. But the issue is not only one of managing short-term crises or embarking on the longer-term solutions. The spectrum is even larger: it should begin with the question of whether or not the deterioration of a particular situation merits international intervention, how such intervention is to be conducted, and what precise objectives it should aim at attaining.

The strategy for international response to internal conflicts and communal violence leading to the breakdown of civil order and the actual or potential collapse of

---

7. Deng, Francis Mading, "State Collapse: The Humanitarian Challenge to the United Nations," in *Collapsed States: The Disintegration of Legitimate Authority,* I. William Zartman (ed.), (Boulder, CO: Lynne Rienner, 1995): pp. 207

Francis Deng is a prolific writer on the Dinka of the Sudan and African affairs and is currently a senior fellow of the African Studies Branch of the Foreign Studies Program of the Brookings Institution.

the state should aim at addressing the challenges comprehensively through a three-phase strategy that would involve monitoring the developments to draw early attention to impending crises, interceding in time to avert the crisis through diplomatic initiatives, and mobilizing international action when necessary. A comprehensive strategy of intervention in three phases would require arresting the immediate crisis, appraising the situation with reference to the root causes, and designing a plan of action for the reconstruction of the society and the state, as the case may be.

The quest for a system of international response to conflict and attendant humanitarian tragedies was articulated by Secretary-General Boutros Boutros-Ghali (1992) in *An Agenda for* Peace, referring to the end of the Cold War and the surging demands on the United Nations Security Council as the central instrument for the prevention and resolution of conflicts and the preservation of peace:

Our aims must be:

- To seek to identify at the earliest possible stage situations that could produce conflict, and to try through diplomacy to remove the sources of danger before violence results;

- Where conflict erupts, to engage in peacemaking aimed at resolving the issues that have led to conflict;

- Through peace-keeping, to work to preserve peace, however fragile, where fighting has been halted and to assist in implementing agreements achieved by the peacemakers;

- To stand ready to assist in peace-building in its differing contexts: rebuilding the institutions and infrastructures of nations torn by civil war and strife; and building bonds of peaceful mutual benefit among nations formerly at war;

- And in the largest sense, to address the deepest causes of conflict: economic despair, social injustice and political oppression. It is possible to discern an increasingly common moral perception that spans the world's nations and peoples, and which is finding expression in international laws, many owing their genesis to the work of this Organization.

These aims address "the global law-and-order deficit" that has been described by the former U.S. Assistant Secretary of State for African affairs, Chester Crocker (1992). In an effort, first, to understand why the wave of state collapse in Somalia and elsewhere is flourishing, and its effect on U.S national interests, he wrote:

Historic changes since 1989 have profoundly destabilized the previously existing order without replacing it with any recognizable or legitimate system. New vacuums are setting off new conflicts. Old problems are being solved, begetting new ones. The result of this process is a global law-and-order deficit that is straining the capacity of existing and emerging security institutions.

A new load of demands is now being placed on the United Nations to deploy peacekeepers, cease-fire observers, election monitors, and even civilian administrators. In addition to the requirements of peace accords that create new challenges, these demands stem from the disintegration of governments, states, or empires that no longer enjoy the legitimacy and domestic or external support to survive. Crocker writes:

> We preach to the rest of the world the post-Cold War litany of U.S. goals and hopes: democracy and human rights, free markets and peaceful settlement of disputes. This sermon is fine as far as it goes, but it is a hopelessly inadequate answer to our era of change. Democracy and free markets are not capable of being "exported" by Voice of America broadcasts or "taught" through exchanges of scholars. They cannot be imposed by isolation and sanctions.

Crocker proceeds to outline some principles for meeting the challenges of the law-and-order deficit he diagnoses:

> We do need to address the mounting lack of consensus on basic norms of global political life combined with the shortage of legitimate institutions for handling the resulting security problems. We also need to remedy the scarcity of means for "enforcing" whatever solutions may be agreed upon. Not since the Napoleonic upheavals (if not the Peace of Westphalia in 1648) have the rights of states, people and governments been so unclear.
>
> Under what circumstances are territorial borders to be considered sacrosanct and who shall determine the answer? When do "identity groups" (peoples or ethnic fragments) have the right of secession, autonomy or independence? What "sovereign" rights, if any, do governments have to prevent outsiders from telling them how to treat their people, their economies and their environment? And what about the rights of outsiders to come to the aid of peoples victimized by the actions or inactions of local governments—or to create the functional equivalent of government where, as in Somalia, none exists?
>
> The law-and-order deficit cannot be eliminated by relying solely on ad hoc, unilateral U.S. actions, no matter how forceful the decisions or masterful the execution. We urgently need some internationally agreed-upon rules and criteria as well as dedicated mechanisms for planning and conducting the internationally sanctioned uses of force.

From an institutional or organizational perspective, problems should be addressed and solved within their own framework, with international involvement necessitated only by the failure of the internal efforts. This means that conflict prevention, management, or resolution progressively moves from the domestic domain to the regional and ultimately the global levels of concern and action. Conflicts in which the state is an effective arbiter do not present particular difficulties since they are manageable within the national framework. The problem arises when the existence of the state itself is the subject of the conflict. Under those conditions, external involvement becomes unavoidable.

In the African context, it is generally agreed that the next best level of involvement should be the Organization of African Unity (OAU). There are, however, constraints on the role of the OAU. One has to do with the limitation of resources, both material and human. But perhaps even more debilitating is the lack of political will, since in the intimate context of the region, governments feel vulnerable to the generation of conflicts resulting from the problematic conditions of state formation and nationbuilding and are therefore prone to resist any form of external scrutiny. Since the judge of today may well be the accused of tomorrow, there is a temptation to avoid confronting the problems. The result is evasiveness and neglect.

Beyond the OAU, the United Nations is the next and ultimate level of recourse, representing, as it does, the international community in its global context. But the UN suffers from the same constraints as those that affect the OAU, though to a lesser degree. It has the problem of resources and the reciprocal protectiveness of vulnerable governments.

As recent events have demonstrated, the role of the major Western powers acting unilaterally, multilaterally, or within the framework of the United Nations, though often susceptible to accusations of strategic motivation, has become increasingly pivotal. Indeed, although their motives continue to be questioned, the problem is more one of their unwillingness to become involved or lack of adequate preparedness for such involvement.

Perhaps the most important impetus for the involvement of Western industrial democracies in the breakdown of order abroad is found in the gravity of the humanitarian tragedies involved. While this motive guarantees their involvement in arresting the tragedy, it limits their involvement in its prevention at an earlier stage. This is what brought the United States and the United Nations into Somalia and Rwanda, and also with less fanfare into South Africa, Angola, and Mozambique, and would provide the strongest rationale for intervention into Zaire. Even with respect to humanitarian intervention, however, lack of preparedness for an appropriate timely response is generally acknowledged as a major limitation. Rather than fostering preparation, practices that drive the international system—loose sanctions, military detachment, and uncontrollable arms flows—inadvertently reinforce violent disintegration. Nevertheless, there is a strong presumption that the interests of the Western industrial democracies are powerfully engaged and will eventually be used to uphold and promote humanitarian intervention in crisis conditions of state collapse. Industrial democracies cannot operate without defending standards of human rights and political procedures that are being egregiously violated. Indeed, they cannot themselves prosper in an irreversibly international economy if large contiguous populations descend into endemic violence and economic disorder.

The combination of these compelling reasons and lack of preparedness for well-planned response makes the United States and Western European countries become particularly prone to crisis-induced reactions that are relatively easy to execute and are more symbolic than effective in addressing the major substantive issues involved. Principles are needed to justify effective international intervention, focusing on the objective of establishing basic civil order under conditions where it has fundamentally broken down and is unlikely to be regenerated within a reasonable time or at tolerable cost in human and material terms. As intervention is a major intrusion from outside, and despite the obvious fact that there will always be elements in the country who will welcome such intervention, especially among the disadvantaged groups to whom it promises tangible benefits, resistance on the grounds of national sovereignty or pride is also a predictable certainty, as discussed by Gambari. . . . For that reason, the justification for intervention must be reliably persuasive, if not beyond reproach. "The difference between an intervention that succeeds and one that is destroyed by immune reaction would depend on the degree of spontaneous acceptance or rejection by the local population."

To avoid or minimize this immune reaction, such intervention would have to be broadly international in character. The principles used and the objectives toward which it is targeted must transcend political and cultural boundaries or traditions and concomitant nationalist sentiments. In other words, it must enjoy an effective degree of global legitimacy.

The rationale that could conceivably carry such a burden presumably involves human rights so fundamental that they are not derived from any particular political or economic ideology. . . . Any government that fails to provide the most fundamental rights for major segments of its population can be said to have forfeited sovereignty and the international community can be said to have a duty in those instances to reestablish it. If the absence of functional sovereignty is declared in any situation, assertive measures to recreate it would be allowed.

The three-phase strategy to meet this need would involve monitoring the developments to draw early attention to impending crises, interceding in time to avert the crisis through diplomatic initiatives, and mobilizing international action when necessary. The first step would aim at detecting and identifying the problem through mechanisms for information collection, evaluation, and reporting. The strategy for preventative or corrective involvement in conflict should comprise gathering and analyzing information and otherwise monitoring situations with the view to establishing an early warning system through which the international community could be alerted to act. If sufficient basis for concern is established, the appropriate mechanism should be invoked for the taking of preventive diplomatic measures to avert the crisis. Initially, such initiatives might be taken within the framework of regional arrangements; for example, the OAU, the Conference on Security and

Cooperation in Europe (CSCE), the Organization of American States (OAS). In the context of the United Nations such preventive initiatives would naturally fall on the Secretary-General, acting either personally or through special representatives. If diplomatic initiatives do not succeed, and depending on the level of human suffering involved, the Secretary-General may decide to mobilize an international response, ranging from further diplomatic measures to forced humanitarian intervention, not only to provide emergency relief, but also to facilitate the search for an enduring solution, addressing the causes of the breakdown of internal order. A strategy aimed at this broader objective would require a close understanding of the causal link with the conditions and developments leading to the outbreak of the crisis.

The main objective is that efforts, whether by internal or external actors, should enhance the prospects for providing effective protection and assistance for the needy. Since they fall within domestic jurisdiction, this can best be done through dialogue and cooperation with the government, when one is present. Such cooperation with governments should be predicated on the assumption that sovereignty carries with it responsibility for ensuring protection and assistance for the citizens. Where there is a failure to discharge that responsibility, and masses of people fall victim in consequence, it should be established whether there are objective reasons that may have to do with lack of capacity or resources. In such cases, international cooperation in providing the required protection and assistance can be expected to be invited, or at least welcomed. However, where the need is apparent and masses of the population are affected, and the government is incapable or unwilling to provide protection and assistance, whether by itself or in cooperation with foreign donors, or the state has simply collapsed, then some form of international action becomes imperative.

As Secretary-General Boutros Boutros-Ghali (1992) observed, "The time of absolute and exclusive sovereignty . . . has passed" and it is the task of leaders of states today "to find a balance between the needs of good internal governance and the requirements of an ever more interdependent world." The Secretary-General went even further: "One requirement for solutions to these problems lies in commitment to human rights with a special sensitivity to those of minorities, whether ethnic, religious, social or linguistic."

On the need for balance between the unity of larger entities and respect for sovereignty, autonomy, and diversity of various identities, the Secretary-General noted:

> The healthy globalization of contemporary life requires in the first instance solid identities and fundamental freedoms. The sovereignty, territorial integrity and independence of states within the established international system, and the principle of self-determination for peoples, both of great value and importance, must not be permitted to work against each other in the period ahead. Respect for democratic princi-

ples at all levels of social existence is crucial: in communities, within states and within the community of states. Our constant duty should be to maintain the integrity of each while finding a balanced design for all.

While the Secretary-General underscores respect for the sovereignty and integrity of the state as crucial to the existing international system, the logic of the transcendent importance of human nights as a legitimate area of concern for the international community, especially where order has broken down or the state is incapable or unwilling to act responsibly to protect the masses of citizens, would tend to make international inaction indefensible. Even in less extreme cases of internal conflict, the perspectives of the pivotal actors on such issues as the national or public interest are bound to be sharply divided both internally and in their relationship to the outside world. After all, internal conflicts often entail a contest of the national arena of power and therefore sovereignty. Every political intervention from outside has its internal recipients, hosts, and beneficiaries. Under those circumstances, there can hardly be said to be an indivisible quantum of national sovereignty behind which the nation stands united.

Furthermore, it is not always easy to determine the degree to which the state in a country devastated by civil war can be said to be truly in control; it is often the case that sizable portions of the territory are controlled by rebel or other forces. Often, while a government may exercise effective control of the capital and the main garrisons, its writ over much of the countryside in the war zone will have practically collapsed. How would such partial, but significant, collapse be factored into determining the degree to which civil order in the country has broken down?

A historical perspective on the significance of sovereignty should also reveal that the concept cannot be a value-free property of whomever claims to represent the country. Initially, sovereignty was the prerogative of the crown: the crown was supreme and above the law. The evolution of democratic values and institutions gradually devolved sovereign will and authority to the people. It is through the will of the people, democratically invested in elected leaders or symbolically claimed even by nondemocratic governments, that entitles national authorities to invoke and uphold the sovereignty of the state. Where governments fail to meet their fundamental obligations to the whole or significant parts of the population, the latter are justifiably entitled to withdraw explicitly or implicitly the trust they have placed upon them to be the symbolic custodians of their sovereignty. No government that will allow thousands, or maybe millions, to starve to death when food can be made available to them, to be exposed to deadly elements when they could be provided with shelter, to be indiscriminately tortured, brutalized, and murdered by opposing forces contesting the very sovereignty that is supposed to ensure their security, or otherwise to suffer in a vacuum of moral leadership, can still have a clear face to keep the outside world from stepping in to offer protection and assistance in the name of sovereignty.

As the crises of nation-building that have been building up over an extended period of time, covering significant historical phases, begin to explode into internecine conflicts, creating ethnic or religious cleavages in which large numbers of innocent civilian populations find themselves dispossessed by their own governments and abandoned without protection and assistance, the international community is called upon to step in and fill the vacuum of moral responsibility created by such neglect.

A high-level group convened by the InterAction Council of Former Heads of State and Government (January 21–23, 1993) on the theme, "Bring Africa Back into the Mainstream of the International System," observed:

> During the cold war period, these humanitarian tragedies were not sub-jected to international scrutiny, partly because they were obscured from external observation and partly because the needs involved were rela-tively met through the cooperation of members of the ideological camp concerned. The contemporary scene is now marked by a combination of accessibility of media information about internal conditions and lack of ideologically or strategically based support systems. This has created a situation where the pressures of international public opinion, combined with a growing global consciousness resulting from the removal of cold war barriers, inhibitions and constraints are increasingly prompting the international community to demand humanitarian action. On both moral and political grounds, this pressure can no longer be ignored or resist-ed.

The same questions emerged as the key to the normative framework that the international community is called upon to address: What degree of humanitarian suffering under what conditions should justify what form of international action, by whom, through what operational mechanisms, and with what precise objectives?

This means clarifying the principles, the organizational framework, the opera-tional doctrine, and the precise goals of such intervention. The clarification of the principles would provide guidelines or standards on what would trigger and justify intervention. The organizational framework raises questions as to who would initi-ate the decision-making process for intervention, and once approved, who would conduct the operations. The issue of operations itself raises questions on the mili-tary or civilian forces to be used and their preparedness or training for the task. The issue of objectives raises the question of whether the operations should stop at meet-ing the short-term emergency needs or extend to addressing the causes of the crisis in order to reconstitute a self-sustaining system of public or civil order.

These considerations make it even more important to monitor developments in order to determine the appropriate stage for intervention; how to conduct the process in a particular context; what resources—material, human, and cultural—there are to work with; and what outcome of the intervention should be postulated. In its continued examination of the Secretary-General's *Agenda for Peace,* the Security Council considered the questions of humanitarian assistance, peacemaking, peacekeeping, and peace-building, finding that under certain circumstances "there may be a close relationship between acute needs for humanitarian assistance and threats to international peace and security" (UNSC 1993). The council indeed "[noted] with concern the incidents of humanitarian crises, including mass displacements of population becoming or aggravating threats to international peace and security"; it expressed the belief "that humanitarian assistance should help establish the basis for enhanced stability through rehabilitation and development" and "noted the importance of adequate planning in the provision of humanitarian assistance in order to improve prospects for rapid improvement of the humanitarian situation." This naturally requires planning for the phase beyond the call of emergency.

A dilemma in the international rescue operation lies in the fact that it is often triggered at an advanced stage of deterioration, with law and order broken down, large numbers of people victimized, state authority and legitimacy in collapse, and any protection and assistance by definition only a partial salvation for the survivors. It would be preferable to have in place a preventive strategy to apply before the crisis of collapse: monitoring the developments closely, detecting those trends that threaten disaster, and authorizing timely action to avert the crisis. Even when UN-coordinated intervention can only be mobilized by crisis, a similar strategy for restoring the collapsed state is needed, one that entails keeping basic order in the aftermath of a pacification campaign as an essential aspect of an even broader objective of reconstruction and reconstitution of a functioning and self-regenerating system of legitimacy and authority.

A strategy aimed at this broader objective would require a close understanding of the causal link with the conditions and developments that led to the outbreak of the crisis. It is in this context that the historical evolution of the crisis of governance in the affected countries, and the manner in which the policies and responses of the various actors, from local to global, have interplayed to generate the chain of actions and reactions, becomes a useful guide for designing the action necessary to provide appropriate remedies. An international action triggered by an intolerable degree of deterioration in the situation thus becomes both the end of the three-phase strategy aimed at arresting the crisis and the beginning of a more ambitious process, with the objective of reconstructing and consolidating peace security, and stability.

As the postulated strategy of international response to the crisis of collapse involves three phases, so does the process of restoring and invigorating a self-sustaining system in the country concerned, putting a collapsed state back together. The first phase in this process is one of gathering and processing information about the context to determine how the past explains the present. Then comes the second phase of designing the appropriate measures to be taken in the light of the findings. The third phase would be to put into operation the strategies developed on the basis of a comprehensive analysis of the available information. Just as the three phases of the strategy of response to the crisis are closely intertwined, so would be the phases of the strategy of repair. Indeed, since the pressures of actual involvement are usually considerable, these three phases may have to be conducted in an intense process of simultaneous gathering and processing of information, designing appropriate measures, and applying them with a degree of flexibility that will continue to respond to new information, findings, and policy adjustments as they come.

Much of what is required in this conceptual framework of understanding the various aspects of the problem, in its underlying causes, dimensions of manifestations, and appropriate manner of response, is appropriate policy analysis of conditions and design of strategies. Even with the minimum level of international and operational innovations, the strategies outlined for international response would require the United Nations and the international community to make available resources adequate to the work being effective in providing what it promises. But, at least at the intellectual level, a great deal may depend on the manner in which the potential concern of the international community is tapped and utilized. Since what is needed far exceeds what can be generated through the established state institutions, universities, research institutions, and the NGO community constitute a potential resource that is as vitally important as it is needed.

Among the wide range of tasks that could be independently undertaken would be developing criteria for determining the degree of human rights violations or the scale of human suffering or the degree of breakdown in internal order that would move the international community to intervene. Such a clear setting of standards, even if not formally endorsed by governments and rendered a legally enforceable instrument, if well disseminated, could provide a useful guide and a deterrent to governments and other pertinent actors. Once prepared, its finalization and formal adoption as an official yardstick would in itself be a significant part of diplomatic initiatives in and outside the United Nations system. Such a standard-setting exercise could have a broad policy dimension whose authority would rest more in the moral value-oriented framework than in its legal enforceability. The goal, ultimately, would be for the legal and the moral dimensions to converge in an international instrument setting new standards by which governments would be held accountable. Again, while the final outcome would bear the official seal of governments, the process of preparation could be broad-based, involving individuals and groups, universities and research institutions, lawyers and policy analysts, scholars and activists—a wide network that would benefit from coordination and cooperation.

The prevailing situation in the world today indicates that the international system is going through a significant transformation in two major respects. One is the emergence of human rights as a legitimate area of concern for the international community and a basis for scrutinizing the performance of governments and other domestic actors. Another is the related humanitarian concern of the international community with state collapse and other causes of domestic violence that inflict hardship and suffering on masses of people. Together, these two areas reveal early signs of a new world order in which human dignity for all people at all levels will become a matter of cooperative security for the international community (cf. Zartman and Kremenyuk 1994). This offers a global opportunity that must be seized.

What makes this change particularly significant is that, until fairly recently, the human rights field was considered so sensitive that it was either ignored or treated gingerly as a subject of confidential communications with the governments concerned. Complaints were received by the appropriate United Nations bodies and, if found to be admissible, were transmitted to the governments involved for comments. It was hoped that bringing the complaints to the attention of governments and asking them to respond would raise their level of awareness and motivate them to remedy the situation in question. The actual behavior of the government was not monitored to ensure that the desired result was achieved.

The altered circumstances of the post-Cold War era have now opened doors onto internal conflict and enabled the international community to have a closer and more sympathetic look at the internal conditions and the needs of the large masses of the world population. Along with the increased exposure of internal dynamics to the outside world, a better understanding of these conditions has developed in the international community; and, with it, a concomitant rise in the level of international concern about the conditions of the masses of people trapped and victimized by internal wars and the gross violations of human rights that often follow as a consequence.

Of course, the removal of the centralized controls of the old order has in certain parts of the world resulted in upheavals that have created new problems for both peace and respect for human rights. Conditions in both the former Soviet Union and former Yugoslavia illustrate quite dramatically the consequences of the breakup of the centralized controls of authoritarian regimes and the transformation of the Cold War international order. The "ripple effects" of this breakup have not by any means run their course and it is not yet clear what their consequences might be in terms of alternative arrangements. However, even these upheavals signify a process of liberation from repression. The challenge to the international community is to assist in the reconstruction of durable arrangements based on respect for fundamental rights. With no major strategic or ideological interests creating obstacles to international cooperation, the international community, and more specifically the United Nations, now can play a more assertive and constructive role in promoting peace and respect for human rights.

What all this means is that a new momentum in a global moral imperative is gathering and that world leaders are called upon to transcend national boundaries to meet their moral obligation toward humanity in a world that now claims a higher degree of sensitivity to the ideals of the Universal Declaration of Human Rights than ever before in its history. And if this call is directed to all those who see themselves in an international leadership role because of the global power and authority that they wield, it should obviously be associated with the role of the United Nations. As this role is redefined to meet the emerging global imperatives and challenges, the United Nations itself will need to be reinvigorated structurally and operationally to meet the challenge.

In nearly all the countries where internal conflicts are a major cause of massive human suffering, there is much that the international community, and more specifically the United Nations, can do, not only to provide needed assistance and protection to the affected population, but also to help bring durable peace to the beleaguered countries. It should always be remembered that even an impending collapse of a state is an acute manifestation of a generalized crisis that, unless arrested and resolved at the roots, threatens not only the peace and security of the country, but often also of the neighboring countries, and ultimately international order itself. For that reason, the international community cannot afford to wait too often until conditions have reached the level of a Somalia, Rwanda, Liberia, or Yugoslavia in order to act decisively. Much by way of preventive action could be taken. Such action could make international involvement far more cost-effective than the massive intervention that developed crises require to put a collapsed state back together.

Suggested Readings

For the most part, the recent debate on collapsed states and intervention in Africa has been conducted in the media. Interested students should consult major newspapers (particularly *The International Herald Tribune and The New York Times*) and journals dealing with African and International Affairs. However, two recent books, both edited by I. William Zartman, are recommended:

Collapsed States: The Disintegration of Legitimate Authority (Boulder, CO: Lynne Rienner, 1995).
Ripe for Resolution: Conflict and Intervention in Africa (London: Oxford University Press, 1985).

Acknowledgments

Problems I and II

The editors gratefully acknowledge the following authors and publishers: to Longman, London, for permission to reprint from *Decolonization in Africa* by John D. Hargreaves, pp.2-3, 32, 34, 52-53, 61-62, 113, 180, 187, 191-92; to the Yale University Press for permission to reprint from "The Asian Mirror to Tropical Africa's Independence," by D. A. Low, pp. 1-5, 18, 28-29, and "The United States and the Liquidation of British Empire in Tropical Africa, 1941-51" by William Roger Louis and Ronald Robinson, pp. 31-32, 44-45, 48-49, 54-55, and "From Colonialism to Independence in French Tropical Africa: The Economic Background" by Jean Suret-Canale, pp. 467, 477, 480-81, all three excerpts in Prosser Gifford and Wm. Roger Louis (eds.), *The Transfer of Power in Africa: Decolonization, 1940-1960;* to The Citadel Press for permission to reprint from *Africa: The Roots of Rebellion* by Jack Woddis, pp. 246, 251, 255-56, 260-61, 263, 264-67, 273-76; to the International Institute for the Environment for permission to reprint from *Africa in Crisis: The Causes, the Cures of Environmental Bankruptcy* by Lloyd Timberlake, pp. 7, 9-10, 12; to Lester Crook Publishing for permission to reprint from "Introduction: Ecology and Society in Northeast African History" by David Anderson and Douglas Johnson in Anderson and Johnson (eds.), *The Ecology of Survival: Case Studies from Northeast African History*, pp. 1-2, 4, 12-14, 17-19, 23-24; to the World Bank for permission to reprint from *Reversing the Spiral: The Population, Agriculture and Environment Nexus in Sub-Saharan Africa* by Kevin Cleaver and Gotz Schreiber, pp. 4-8, 10-11; to Lynne Rienner for permission to reprint from "Gender, Resources, Local Institutions: New Identities for Kenya's Rural Women" by Barbara Thomas-Slater and Dianne Rocheleau in Thomas-Slater and Rocheleau (eds.), *Gender, Environment and Development in Kenya*, pp. 11-18; to the Cambridge University Press for permission to reprint from "The Decline of African Agriculture: An Internalist Perspective" by Michael Lofchie, and "Linking and Sinking: Economic Externalities and the Persistence of Destitution and Famine in Africa" by Randall Baker both in Michael Glantz (ed.), *Drought and Hunger in Africa: Denying Famine a Future*, pp. 90-93, 95-100 and 149-157 respectively; to the University of Chicago Press for permission to reprint *The West African Sahel: Human Agency and Environmental Change* by Jeffrey Gritzner, p. 64-66, 72-74, 107-9.

Problems III and IV

Grateful appreciation is also expressed to the Ohio University Center for

International Studies, for permission to reprint from "National Governments and Health Service Policy in Africa" by Robert Stock and Charles Anyinam in Toyin Falola and Dennis Itavyar (eds.), *The Political Economy of Health in Africa*, pp. 217-237, 239; to *Social Science and Medicine*, vol. 39, No. 8 (1994), for permission to reprint from "Primary Health Care in Zimbabwe: Can It Survive?," by Godfrey Woelk, pp. 1031-33; to the *Canadian Journal of African Studies*, Vol. 22, No. 3 (1988), for permission to reprint from "Women, AIDS, and Economic Crisis in Central Africa" by Brooke Schoepf, pp. 626-35; to the Westview Press and University of Natal Press for permission to reprint from *AIDs and STDs in Africa: Bridging the Gap between Traditional Healing and Modern Medicine* by Edward Green, pp. 24-28, 30-37, 39; to *African Affairs*, Vol. 78, July 1979, for permission to reprint from "Medical Expertise and Africa," by Una MacLean, pp. 331-37, and "Ghana's Second Republic," Vol. 72, January 1973, by David Goldsworthy, pp. 8, 15-16, 19, 23, and "Whose Dream Was It Anyway? Twenty-Five Years of African Independence," Vol. 86, January 1987, by Michael Crowder, pp. 7-8, 10, 12-13, 15, 17, 19, and "Developing Democracy When Civil Society Is Weak: The Case of Botswana," Vol. 89, July 1990, by Patrick Molutsi and John Holm, pp. 324-25, 327-29, 331, 333-35, 337-40; to the *Journal of International Affairs*, Vol. 38, No. 2, Winter 1985, for permission to reprint from "Democracy in Tropical Africa: Democracy Versus Autocracy in African Politics" by Robert Jackson and Carl Rosberg, pp. 295-97, 302-5; to the Oxford University Press for permission to reprint from "Women's Politics, the State, and Capitalist Transformation in Africa" by Kathleen Staudt in Irving Markovitz, *Studies in Power and Class in Africa*, pp. 193-97, 202-3, 205-8; to the Africa World Press for permission to reprint from *Recreating Ourselves: African Women and Critical Transformations* by Molara Ogundipe-Leslie, p. 244-49; to Random House for permission to reprint from *The Black Man's Burden: Africa and the Curse of the Nation-State* by Basil Davidson, pp. 8-13, 162-64, 181-85, 262-63, 319-22; to the Princeton University Press for permission to reprint from "South Africa and the Politics of Divided Societies" by Timothy Sisk in his book, *Democratization in South Africa: The Elusive Social Contract*, pp. 284-90, 298-99.

Problems V and VI

We also wish to thank the Yale University Press for permission to reprint from "Bula Matari and the Contemporary African Crisis" by Crawford Young in his book *The African Colonial State in Comparative Perspective*, pp. 1-15, 283-88, 290-92; and from "Arrested Development in Anglophone Black Africa" by David Fieldhouse in Prosser Gifford and Wm. Roger Louis (eds.), *Decolonization and African Independence: The Transfer of Power, 1960-1980*, pp. 135, 145-58; to *The Fletcher Forum of World Affairs* for permission to reprint from "Development in Africa: A Cultural Perspective" by Elliot P. Skinner, pp. 205-15; to the Africa

World Press for permission to reprint from "Consensual Politics and Development Aid in Africa" by Kofi Ermeleh Agori in *Culture and Development in Africa*, pp. 177-86; to Praeger Publishing for permission to reprint from "Alternative Policy Frameworks for African Development in the 1990s" by Robert Browne in Julius Nyang'oro and Timothy Shaw (eds.), *Beyond Structural Adjustment in Africa: The Political Economy of Sustainable and Democratic Development*, pp. 71-82; to the American Academy of Arts and Sciences for permission to reprint from "The Resources of Tropical Africa" by Andrew Kamarck in *Daedalus*, Vol. 111, No. 2, Spring 1982, pp. 149-63; to the Dissent Publishing Corporation for permission to reprint from "The Spectre of Anarchy: African States Verging on Dissolution" by Aristide Zolberg in *Dissent*, Summer 1992, pp. 301-11; to The Council on Foreign Relations for permission to reprint from "A New Colonialism? Europe Must Go Back into Africa" by William Pfaff, in *Foreign Affairs*, January/February 1995, pp. 2-6; to the Institute for National Strategy to reprint its interview, "Hope and Horror in Africa," with Wole Soyinka in *New Perspectives Quarterly*, Summer 1994, pp. 61-62; and "The Message of Rwanda: Recolonize Africa?" by Ali Mazrui in Fall 1994, pp. 18-20; to the World Policy Institute for permission to reprint from "The Blood Experience: The Failed State and Political Collapse in Africa" by Ali Mazrui in *World Policy Journal*, Vol. 12, No. 1, Spring 1995, pp. 28-34; to Lynne Rienner for permission to reprint from "The Role of Foreign Intervention in African Reconstruction" by Ibrahim Gambari, and "State Collapse: The Humanitarian Challenge to the United Nations" by Francis Deng, both excerpts in William Zartman (ed.), *Collapsed States: The Disintegration of Legitimate Authority*, pp. 221-33 and 207-19 respectively.